EVERY DAY GOD

J G DAVIES

Every Day God

Encountering the Holy in
World and Worship

SCM PRESS LTD

334 00412 8

First published 1973
by SCM Press Ltd
56 Bloomsbury Street London

© SCM Press Ltd 1973

Printed in Great Britain by
Western Printing Services Ltd
Bristol

Contents

Preface

Lamentations are frequent nowadays about what is called the elimination of an entire dimension of human experience. The dimension referred to is that of the holy. What these mourners understand by the holy is indicated by the complaint that 'God is no longer conceived as the Numinosum'.[1] There is no need to dispute the fact that experience of the numinous, i.e. of the holy as the awe-inspiring and that which brings dread, is disappearing within technological and urbanized societies but this can only be interpreted as a loss of the sense of the holy if the holy *is* the numinous. To assume this is to beg a fundamental question: what is the holy?

The word 'numinous' was, of course, coined by the German writer Rudolph Otto and was both given currency and analysed in *The Idea of the Holy*, which was published in German in 1917 and has been through countless English editions since then. In a previous work I criticized Otto's understanding, at least as regards its foundation in the New Testament.[2] But that criticism was largely negative, i.e. I argued that from the point of view of Christianity, in so far as that is to be based on the New Testament, the holy is *not* the numinous. I did not, however, provide a positive alternative. It is one thing to say that the holy is not the numinous; it is another to say what the holy is. The present book is an attempt to perform this positive task, so that, while carrying my criticism of Otto further, I am not simply destructive, rejecting one particular understanding without putting forward any alternative to take its place. Only if this attempt – or others – is not successful would it be reasonable to join the ranks of the Jeremiahs.

The starting point of my examination is necessarily the secular universe within which we, in the West, have to do theology today. So I have sought to sketch some of its characteristics which bear on the demise of the numinous in contrast with the sacral universe within which the numinous was entirely at home. To encounter the holy in the world does, however, require some initial concept or model, since, as I argue in the second chapter on the nature of perception, our ability to perceive and what we perceive are determined by our pre-understanding. Next I embark on the quest for a viable model of the holy consistent with the framework of a hominized world and I find this, for the reasons given, in Jesus of Nazareth. There remains the preliminary question of how and where one meets the holy, and the fourth chapter, 'The Place of Encounter', argues that it is in and through, and not apart from, the world, taking world to mean both human relations and the public life of man in history. This is followed by two lengthy excursuses, the one on different modern approaches to the subject of the holy and the other on terminology. Many of the same words are used with entirely different meanings by contributors to the present discussion. Excursus B calls attention to this confusion and provides definitions of the terms as I use them to avoid the possibility of misunderstanding.

On this basis, it is then possible to present certain disclosure situations – derived from novels, films, TV documentaries, etc. – within which the holy may be discerned, from the realms of personal relationships, sex, death, history, politics and work. In the last chapter of this first part I have examined and illustrated the theme of worldly holiness.

Part II relates this thinking to the subject of worship. Beginning with the crisis of worship today, it examines (with the help of insights provided by social anthropologists) worship and ritual and (with the assistance of sociologists) community, fellowship and worship. Further aid is sought from a consideration of some secular rituals, leading finally, after a discussion of mission and worship, to a chapter on rites of modernization which spells out an understanding of worldly worship, i.e. of worship related to the secular universe and to the New Testament model of the holy.

All the notes, which consist in the main of the sources of quotations and references to related works, are printed after the concluding chapter. There they can be safely ignored by the general reader. However, a few that do add something of substance to the text have been marked with an asterisk. For ease of consultation the bibliography has been divided into sections, but of course some books could have been included under more than one heading. The Revised Standard Version has been used for biblical quotations, unless otherwise stated.

In undertaking this study I have trespassed well outside the limits of my own discipline. As mentioned previously, I have ventured into the fields of social anthropology and sociology, and also into that of the philosophy of religion. If to these be added the phenomenology of religion, Old and New Testament exegesis and liturgiology, it will be apparent that I am exposing myself to the possibility of adverse criticism from experts in these several areas. However I am convinced that if it is to communicate, theological understanding – as distinct from the more technical branches of theology – must occasionally attempt such a broad survey, whatever the risk involved. I have sought to supply my inadequacies not only by wide reading but by consulting experts. In particular, I wish to express my thanks to my colleagues John Hick and Daniel Hardy for their reading of the manuscript and their most helpful comments: although they are not responsible for the inadequacies that remain, nor do they necessarily agree with all I have said.

The first draft of this book was completed in May 1971. In July I went on a four months' lecturing tour sponsored by the Association of Theological Schools in South East Asia. I used the substance of what I had written for a series of lectures given in full in St Andrew's Theological Seminary, Manila, and in part at Union Seminary; the Central Philippine University, Iloilo City; Silliman University, Dumaguete; in the Baptist and Lutheran seminaries in Baguio City; and also in Singapore, Hong Kong and Taiwan. I should like to express my appreciation of the generous hospitality and the fellowship I experienced in all these places. In the light of the valuable criticisms I received, I have revised the manuscript and now present it in an improved form.

The University of Birmingham   J. G. Davies

PART ONE

The Holy and the World

I

Exit from the Sacral Universe

The history of Christian thought is the record of theology's constant adaptation to changing circumstances. Because each and every theologian belongs to a certain time and place, his concepts are inevitably related to the situation within which he is working. He cannot detach himself, even if he would, from the sociological, political and economic milieu of his day. The thought-forms he uses, and must use if he is to be intelligible to his contemporaries, spring from the culture to which he belongs.

Augustine's *City of God* would not have been written had the imperial capital not fallen before the onslaught of Alaric in 410. The *Summa Theologica* of Thomas Aquinas is inconceivable without the new-found knowledge of the writings of Aristotle transmitted by Arabic translators and made available through contacts with the adherents of Islam in Spain and also, as a consequence of the Crusades, in the Middle East in the eleventh and twelfth centuries. Or again, many of the works of Martin Luther, such as his *Address to German Nobility* published in 1520, were his response to the contemporary situation. Finally, to come to a more modern example, Walter Rauschenbusch's *A Theology of the Social Gospel* (1917) was nothing if it was not the outcome of the impact of industrial society and scientific thought upon the Protestantism of the United States during the fifty years after the Civil War.

Our present understanding of the holy must similarly be related to and spring out of an awareness of the contemporary world. The contemporary world, however, is in many respects very different from the world within which the concept of the holy was first formulated. Comprehension of this difference is essential if the theologian is to perform his task self-consciously and with a full realization of what he is about. In other words, he has to understand man's exit from a sacral universe and his entry into a secular universe. Unless he is sensitive to the immense transformation which this radical change has produced, both in man's social relations[1]* and in the whole range of his categories of thought, his formulations will scarcely be intelligible and they will be irrelevant to any except the members of a specialized coterie or to those diminishing numbers who unconsciously still live in a sacral universe which, in the West, has passed, or is rapidly passing, away.

What, then, is a sacral – or, as some writers have termed it, a divinized – world? It is one in which the functioning of nature and society is explained in terms of the divine. In the sacral universe, man is at the mercy of nature; not only is he dependent upon it, but he finds himself largely unable to control it. Nature appears to be superior and sovereign, while man is weak and helpless. Nature is the central factor in his life, but, in a pre-technical age, he is powerless to impose his will upon it. Unable to master nature, man then has to seek divine assistance, in order even to live. Nature appears to have almost divine features; it is an epiphany of God himself and the workings of nature are understood as the workings of God.

To man in a sacral universe, nature presents an inscrutable face. Unable to find any explanation for the phenomena to which he is subjected, he attributes their origin to mysterious forces who preside over this external world. Constantly seeking for meaning, he understands natural events in terms of a transcendental reality which alone controls them. Changes in nature, the natural phenomena themselves, are interpreted as due to the irruption of supernatural beings. Observed phenomena are then understood as the manifestations of sacred power.

A vivid illustration of this outlook is provided by the *Chronicle* of Ralph Glaber, who died *c.* 1044 in the monastery of St Benigne at Dijon. Describing the events of the year 993, he writes:

Mount Vesuvius (which is also called Vulcan's Caldron) gaped far more often than his wont and belched forth a multitude of vast stones mingled with sulphurous flames which fell even to a distance of three miles around; and thus by the stench of his breath he began to make all the surrounding province uninhabitable.... It befell meanwhile that almost all the cities of Italy and Gaul were ravaged by flames of fire, and that the greater part even of the city of Rome was devoured by a conflagration. During which fire, the flames caught the beams of St Peter's church, beginning to creep under the bronze tiles and lick the carpenters' work. When this became known to the whole multitude that stood by, then, finding no possible device for averting this disaster, they turned with one accord and, crying with a terrible voice, hastened to the *confessio*[2]* even of the chief of the apostles, crying upon him with curses that, if he watched not over his own, nor showed himself a very present defender of his church, many throughout the world would fall away from their profession of faith. Whereupon the devouring flames straightaway left those beams of pine and died away. . . . At this same time a horrible plague raged among men, namely a hidden fire which, upon whatsoever limb it fastened, consumed it and severed it from the body.[3]* Many were consumed even in the space of a single night by these devouring flames. . . . Moreover, about the same time, a most mighty famine raged for five years throughout the Roman world, so that no region could be heard of which was not hungerstricken for lack of bread, and many of the people starved to death. In those days also, in many regions, the horrible famine compelled men to make their food not only of unclean beasts and creeping things, but even of men's, women's and children's flesh, without regard even of kindred; for so fierce waxed this hunger that grown-up sons devoured their mothers, and mothers, forgetting their maternal love, ate their babes.

Glaber's explanation of this terrible series of natural catastrophes and epidemics is that:

Whensoever religion hath failed among the pontiffs, and strictness of the Rule hath decayed among the abbots, and therewith the vigour of monastic discipline hath grown cold, and by their example the rest of the people are become prevaricators of God's commandments, what then can we think but that the whole human race, root and branch, is sliding willingly down again into the gulf of primeval chaos?[4]

This same attitude – that natural disasters are a punishment inflicted by God for disloyalty and disobedience – may be exemplified from a *Liber Exemplorum* written *c.* 1275. This records a plague in Connaught, and the writer reports how armies of demons had been seen in the countryside.

Such as saw these visions were forthwith smitten with sickness and disease, languishing and taking to their beds with all weakness of body; and many died miserably. 'When I heard this' (quoth the bishop), 'then I called the people together in no small multitude, and preached the word of God, saying among other things: "Ye have now this great plague among you, and it is caused by the demons whom very many of you see oftentimes in these parts. Know ye wherefore the demons have power to bring such evils upon us? This is certainly for no other cause than for your want of faith. For ye fear their power too sore, not believing or thinking or trusting that the Lord will defend you and guard you against all hurt of theirs. Therefore doth the Lord suffer them to have this power of doing you evil which they now work. If ye had stout faith, and if ye believed firmly that the devils have no power but in so far as the Lord suffereth, and if ye would amend your lives, beseeching God instantly to defend you from their wiles, then ye may be sure that they would have no power to hurt you." '5

It would be a mistake to dismiss these, and many other similar reports, as simply evidence of superstition, of popular Christian notions as distinct from the official teaching of the church. While superstitious abuses were castigated by theologians, in the very process of seeking to purify popular belief the same writers reveal the extent to which they themselves were inhabitants of a sacral universe.

A clear example of this is Agobard, who became bishop of Lyons in 816. In his day there apparently existed a number of people known as *tempestarii* or weather-clerks, who claimed that they had the power to control the weather. Agobard attacked them and their practices in his treatise *Against the Absurd Opinion of the Vulgar touching Hail and Thunder*. The bishop asserted that recourse to these people was vain, because weather control belongs not to man but to God. God's relation to nature, he argued, is immediate, and it is not conditioned by the artifices of men.[6] Equally revealing is Agobard's letter to bishop Bartholomew of Narbonne. An epidemic had apparently broken out in a certain district and the terrified populace was crowding into the church of St Firmin, laden with gifts for the saint. Agobard, in true reforming style, berated the people for trusting in the power of a saint to ward off such a visitation, but he rested his case on the thesis that such afflictions were clearly from the hand of God, to whom alone, therefore, offerings should be made.[7]

Within the context of a sacral universe, therefore, nature is a *mysterium* with which one must not tamper. To attempt to unravel its secrets is an impious effort to uncover the hidden workings of God. This does not mean that such attempts were not made in the past, but they were viewed with disfavour. One such experimenter was Giovanni de' Dondi (born in 1318), who was professor first of astronomy at Padua and later of medicine at Florence. One of his comments reveals both the prevailing attitude to nature and the difference that is effected in the understanding of an individual as he seeks to move out of the sacral universe.

There are so many marvellous coherences to be found in every natural object; these are *mirabilia*, not *miracula*, wonderful phenomena accessible to understanding and thought, capable of being investigated, in no sense miracles. . . We are surrounded daily by marvels; when we become familiar with them through use many objects lose their quality of being miraculous and incomprehensible; hence I am no longer filled with wonder and terror as once I was, but have trained myself to look carefully at everything marvellous, to reflect on what I have seen and never allow myself to become unduly astonished.[8]

De' Dondi declares that he is 'no longer filled with wonder and terror', but these words describe accurately the outlook of his contemporaries who inhabited a sacral universe.

The sacral universe itself is nothing if not coherent, i.e. all aspects of what is conceived to be reality are integrated within it. Consequently it is no surprise to find that its view of nature embraces man. Man is believed to belong to the natural order and *therefore* to be related to God in the same way as God is related to nature. This means that God is believed to intervene in human life just as he does in the sphere of nature. In the sacral universe belief in miracles abounds and the lives of the saints are full of amazing events which represent the incursion of the divine. One example will suffice, chosen both because the one who reports the incident is no more, even though no less, credulous than many another, and also because of the incidental charm of the story itself. It is recorded by Caesarius of Heisterbach who wrote his *Dialogus Miraculorum* between 1220 and 1235.

A certain woman kept many bees, which throve not, but died in great numbers; and, as she sought everywhere for a remedy, it was told her that if she placed the Lord's Body among them, this plague would soon cease. She therefore went to church and, making as though she would communicate, took the Lord's Body, which she took from her mouth as soon as the priest had departed, and laid it in one of her hives. Mark the marvellous power of God! These little worms, recognizing the might of their Creator, built for their sweetest Guest, out of their sweetest honeycombs, a tiny chapel of marvellous workmanship, wherein they set up an altar of the same material and laid thereon this most holy Body; and God blessed their labours. In process of time the woman opened this hive, and was aware of the aforesaid chapel; whereupon she hastened and confessed to the priest all that she had done and seen. Then he took with him his parishioners and came to the hive, where they drove away the bees that hovered round and buzzed in praise of their Creator; and, marvelling at the little chapel with its walls and windows, roof and tower, door and altar, they brought back the Lord's Body with praise and glory to the church. For though God be marvellous in his saints, yet these his smallest creatures preached him yet more marvellously.[9]

Precisely the same outlook persists today in many parts of the world. In Ilocos Norte, which is a province of Northern Luzon in the Philippines, it is customary to distribute blessed bread at the mass in honour of St Nicolas of Tolentino. This bread is then taken home and may be used for one of two purposes. It may be worn in the hat to provide protection against lightning. Alternatively, it may be put in the rice fields to safeguard them from being washed away by the torrential rains which accompany the not infrequent typhoons.[10]

Where such is the relationship of Creator and creation, it is normal to find that God can and does intervene in all aspects of daily life. Just as man cannot regulate the incursions of the divine into the realm of nature itself, so the sacred power can break through at any time and in any place. Nothing is too insignificant and trivial to be unrelated to the divine causality. For example, in 1343 a woman went to the market at Pinchbeck, Lincolnshire, to sell two bushels of corn. Finding the price standing at 6d a bushel and wanting at least 7d, she left her grain with a friend until the following week, only to discover that the price had dropped to 5d. Her comment was typical of the sacral outlook: 'O Lord God, this hast thou done to me! The other day I might have had twelve pence, and today no more than ten!'[11]

Or again, there is the case of the wine casks in the monastery of Prum in the archbishopric of Trèves. According to the *Chronicle* of John of Worcester, under the year 1138, the cellarer was constantly finding the bungs drawn and the wine spilt. After discussion with the abbot, it was concluded that this must be the work of evil spirits and so the spigots were duly anointed with holy chrism to counter demonic with sacred power. The result was that a devil was captured and the loss of liquor stopped.[12]

The seeking of justice either by ordeal or combat will serve as a further illustration. In either case it is the divine being who, it is held, determines the issue and so declares the guilt or innocence of those involved. It is true that Agobard, already cited above, objected to both practices, but his main ground for so doing is that, in his view, they make God the servant of man and too lightly presume upon the divine judgment which is unsearchable.[13]

Not only are nature and daily life sacralized, but all elements in human society are, consistently, viewed in the same way. The State is conceived somewhat as a theocracy and the idea of the divine right of kings shows the persistence of this perspective. So in the first of the seventeen canons, passed by Convocation in England in 1640, it was declared that

The most high and sacred order of kings is of divine right, being the ordinance of God himself, founded in the prime laws of nature, and clearly established by express texts both of the Old and New Testaments.[14]

Consequently those who suffer from an evil monarch have to regard this as a punishment for their sins and faithful Christians will make no attempt to have him removed. They will certainly not resort to arms because there is no 'other refuge but fervent prayers unto Almighty God'.[15]*

No matter what element in society we consider, all are understood in the same light. Society as a whole is apprehended as a God-given reality; the *status quo* has therefore to be preserved. Nothing has any autonomy. Politics, philosophy, education – all have to be related to corresponding religious categories, and theology itself is regarded as the Queen of the Sciences, being an explanatory rather than an exploratory science. Sacred learning is the supreme pursuit and 'secular' learning is at a discount. So Jack Cade could address Lord Say in these words:

Thou hast most traitorously corrupted the youth of the realm in erecting a grammar school: and whereas before our forefathers had no other books but the score and the tally, thou hast caused printing to be used; and contrary to the king, his crown and dignity, thou hast built a paper-mill. It will be proved to thy face that thou hast men about thee that usually talk of a noun, and a verb, and such abominable words as no Christian ear can endure to hear.[16]

Within a sacral universe, the function of religion is seen to be threefold. In the first place, referring specifically to Christianity in the West, it was the protector and preserver of society, in so far as it ensured that God was given due veneration. In this way the public well-being and the stability of the state were secured through the granting of the divine favour. The highest good of society was deemed to be the true worship of God, and Christianity fulfilled the supreme end of the state and so had a clearly understood social role. In this respect, it was continuing that of the Roman state religion, being the *cultus publicus*,[17] and the attitude of mind involved is very clearly revealed by the Latin poet Horace in one of his odes.

You will undeservedly suffer for the sins of the fathers, O Rome, until you restore the temples, rebuild the fallen houses of the gods, and clean the images soiled by smoke and grime. It is only because you consider yourself subject to the gods that you rule the world. This is the foundation of everything. Let it remain your goal. Because it scorned them, the gods struck grieving Rome with many blows.[18]

This belief, that every society must have a religion, continued to be held after the Reformation with the thesis that *cujus regio, ejus religio*. It underlay the so-called Elizabethan settlement in England, and at the present day it is represented, for example, by the adoption of Islam by several states as the official religion.

In the second place, religion provided a structure of explanation and legitimation. Man's ignorance was supplied; the inexplicable was resolved in terms of divine activity. Society, state, church, were guaranteed as religious realities to be accepted and supported.

In the third place, religion provided ritual to protect man against a universe which he dominated neither intellectually nor materially.[19] The uncontrollable forces that affect his life can be either favourable to him or not, and so he seeks to protect himself from their injurious acts and to attract their favours. He therefore engages in rituals which negatively safeguard him from them and positively channel the divine assistance in his direction. Hence the development in the Middle Ages of numerous institutionalized devotions, many of them related to saints who were believed to have their special spheres of influence.[20] In this way man's fear of natural catastrophes could be subdued, and a real need of the pre-technical world was met. So the church's prayers were concerned with man's feelings of powerlessness, of fear before the onslaughts of nature, of epidemics, etc. Man besought God to intervene miraculously to control these forces.[21] Since the success of human endeavour depends upon divine help, the hunter must pray before he goes to the chase and the soldier must offer the sacrifice of Christ before going to war. Agriculture itself becomes a ritual: 'The labourer penetrates into and is integrated with a rich and sacred zone. His actions, his work, can have serious consequences.'[22] Hence the blessing of crops and of farm utensils such as ploughs.

To any one familiar with the history of Christian worship, abundant evidence of this relation of ritual to the phenomena of nature will suggest itself. Three illustrations will suffice. First there is the prayer 'for fair weather' included in the 1549 *Book of Common Prayer* at the end of the Communion Service:

O Lord God, which for the sin of man didst once drown all the world, except eight persons, and afterward of thy great mercy, didst promise never to destroy it so again: We humbly beseech thee, that although we for our iniquities have worthily deserved this plague of rain and waters, yet, upon our true repentance, thou wilt send us such weather whereby we may receive the fruits of the earth in due season, and learn both by the punishment to amend our lives, and by the granting of our petition to give thee praise and glory: Through Jesus Christ our Lord.

Cranmer's magnificent litany, printed in the 1552 *Book of Common Prayer*, contains many petitions that belong to the sacral universe, e.g.

From lightnings and tempests, from plague, pestilence, and famine, from battle and murder, and from sudden death.
Good Lord, deliver us.

Finally we turn to the Nile for an example which has had a history of centuries. For millennia Egyptian civilization clung to the narrow span of the river valley. Its very life and survival depended upon the annual rising of the waters to flood level. In the Egypt of the pharaohs, therefore, precise rituals, involving offerings to the gods, were observed to ensure that there was no failure in this natural phenomenon, which would have been so disastrous to society.[23] When Christianity was domiciled in Egypt, it provided a parallel ritual. So in the *Liturgy of St Mark* and in the *Liturgy of the Coptic Jacobites* there are prayers for the rising of the Nile.[24] The prayer book of Serapion of Thmuis (*c.* 350), on the other hand, only contains a petition for rain, but the explanation of this is that Thmuis was in the delta and had a sufficient supply of river water, which was replenished by winter rains blown inland by the prevailing sea breezes.[25]

The ritual also helped man in the face of death and of fear. With infant mortality so high, the average life span being scarcely half of what it is today, with epidemics and famine liable to ravage cities and countryside, death was an ever-present reality in a society subservient to nature. Feelings of terror, dread of evil spirits, a horror of death, the possibility of hell – all this turned man's attention from this world to the next, from the facts of nature to the truths of faith. Masses for the dead, extreme unction, etc. – all these ritual acts gave some assurance of divine protection and alone made life bearable. But the inevitable result of this was a devaluation of both nature and history.

Natural life was regarded as insignificant in comparison with the supernatural. So, for example, divine love was affirmed to be the supreme reality and human love no more than a faint reflection.[26] The world itself was understood to be a shadow-scene of unreality, masking or concealing the eternal, which is the only true reality. This resulted in a sacralization of nature.

Sacralization has both negative and positive aspects. Negatively, it involves the denial of the authentic nature of any person, object or event. It repudiates their immediate ends and primary usefulness and removes them from the secular sphere. Positively, it involves the attribution to any person, object or event of a sacred character. It affirms their final purpose and transfers them into the sphere of the holy. Sacralization is therefore synonymous with divinization. To sacralize is to take something and perceive within it a divine reality which excludes the abiding secular reality. Thus to worship the moon is to sacralize a natural object. In the sphere of ritual, the doctrine of trans-substantiation, as popularly understood, is a sacralization of the bread and the wine, in so far as their substance is believed to be replaced by that of the body and blood of Christ. A modern Roman Catholic writer illustrates this completely when he says of the eucharistic species: 'The consecrated bread is no longer ordinary, common bread, indeed it has ceased to be bread so that it may become the body of Christ . . . In the eucharist, we have only the body of Christ, and we no longer have bread.'[27] He thus denies the worldly reality of the eucharistic loaf, and in so doing sacralizes it and shows himself to be speaking from within the context of a sacral universe.

Sacralization also shelters people from that historical and moral reality where, according to certain parts of the Bible, God is encountered. Hence von Rad says: 'This sacred understanding of the world is essentially non-historical.'[28] Instead of experiencing the world as history, as transition within the continuous flow of events, man in the sacral universe attributes to the world an essentially static nature and understands it as a temporal reflection of an eternal original, the latter being perfect and perfection being understood as unchangeability. This cosmos is then closed and ordered; it is the scene of an eternal drama, in which the chief characters are God and the forces of evil before whom man is powerless. This sacral universe is therefore a God-centred, rather than a man-centred, universe, and man is always dependent upon something outside himself.

What sort of God is the deity of the sacral universe? There is no simple answer to this question. It has to be recognized that from within the perspective of the sacral universe, the divine can be conceived in terms of pantheism or polytheism. Even if one has only monotheism in view, then the sole God can be differently regarded. Indeed writers have distinguished at least two periods in the human experience of religion, the mythical and the metaphysical. The former, adopting the vivid imagery popularized by J. A. T. Robinson, envisages God as being 'up there', and the latter as the one who is 'out there'.[29] In either case he is a transcendent being, standing over against his creation, although liable to make incursions into it from time to time – he is thus very much a *deus ex machina*. Essentially, though, while being the creative ground of all natural features, he exists apart from the world and recourse to him is believed to involve both rejection of and detachment from the world. So, for example, John of the Cross can declare: 'The soul that sets its heart on the good things of the world is supremely evil in the sight of God. And, even as wickedness comprehends not goodness, even so such a soul cannot be united with God, who is supreme goodness.'[30]

This concept of God, and of man's relation to him apart from the world, has a double effect. On the one hand, it results in an acquiescence in the *status quo* – repudiating the world, man does not work to change it. On the other hand, Christian spirituality is based upon an other-worldly 'ready-made model'. Man's task is defined as the carrying out of transcendental concrete laws. His action is thus purely an executive one, in that he is required to behave in accordance with pre-established orders. This reinforces the negation of history, which has been mentioned previously, since the relations of man and man are not direct, each individual being concerned primarily with an eternal divine ideal. Further, it denies man's creative responsibility and posits the existence of an autonomous religious universe, with its own rules of life, distinct from the changes and chances of the everyday world.[31]

While God still presents the aspect of a loving Father, he is also a God of judgment and of wrath, and worship expresses itself physically in the action of kneeling with hands folded, like a serf paying homage to his feudal overlord. The president at the eucharist ceases to face the congregation across the table – representing the accessibility of God – and turns his back upon them, thus symbolizing the unapproachableness of the divine. This last statement points towards the concept of the holy, which like any other aspect of life and thought in a sacral universe is integrated with the understanding of God, man and nature. We do not, however, have to seek far for a definition of the holy in terms of the sacral universe. It has been brilliantly analysed by Rudolf Otto in his classic book *The Idea of the Holy*.[32] This is not to say that Otto consciously set out to evoke the holy from the sacral perspective, but that that is in fact what he has achieved should become clear as his ideas are summarized.

From the outset it is important to appreciate that Otto's concern is to evoke the holy and not to conceptualize it. Indeed, he affirms that 'it completely eludes apprehension in terms of concepts'[33] and that what he is trying to do is to provide 'illustrative substitutes' or 'ideograms'.[34] This has to be borne in mind in reading the following account.

In the first part of his book, Otto is concerned with the numinous – a word he himself coined to refer to non-rational religious apprehension and its object. Since, as he acknowledges, the holy has come to have a moral significance (the holy is the righteous), he concentrates initially upon the numinous, i.e. upon the holy minus the moral factor. Nevertheless, after his preliminary investigation, he declares that the holy is 'not merely the numinous in general, nor even the numinous at its highest development; we must always understand by it the numinous completely permeated and saturated with elements signifying rationality, purpose, personality, morality'.[35] Consequently it is an over-simplification, to which some writers are prone, to identify simpliciter numinous and holy; the latter embraces the former.

According to Otto, the vital element in the experience of the holy is creature-feeling, which is 'the emotion of a creature, abased and overwhelmed by its own nothingness in contrast to that which is supreme above all creatures'.[36] The numinous is that which through its presence gives rise to such a feeling. The appropriate designation of this something is the *mysterium tremendum*. Otto expounds this by considering first the adjective and then the noun. As regards *tremendum*, he distinguishes three facets:

1. *Awefulness*. It is that which produces fear and dread; not, however, ordinary fear, which is only an analogy. The reference is rather to 'a terror fraught with an inward shuddering such as not even the most menacing and overpowering created thing can instil'.[37] It possesses, therefore, the characteristic of 'absolute unapproachability'.

2. *Overpoweringness*. The key ideogram here is 'majesty'. Man experiences this when he recognizes the transcendent as 'the sole and entire reality'.

3. *Energy or Urgency*. This awesome majesty is encountered as active, compelling and alive.

Turning next to the noun – *mysterium* – Otto describes it in two ways:

1. *The Wholly Other*. It is that 'which is beyond the sphere of the usual, the intelligible, and the familiar . . . filling the mind with blank wonder and astonishment'.[38] Its 'kind and character are incommensurable with our own, and before which we therefore recoil in a wonder that strikes us chill and dumb'.[39]

2. *Fascinans*. At the same time as having its aspect of foreboding, the *mysterium* is uniquely fascinating and attractive. It brings bliss, rapture, exaltation – states that are experienced and in part described by the great mystics.

It is not my concern to launch forthwith into a criticism of Otto's evocation of the holy. I have called attention to it at this juncture because it is an all-important element within the sacral universe. Nor is it my intention to ridicule or in any way belittle this perspective; rather it is necessary to understand it.

The sacral universe, as I have suggested above, is a coherent one, in the sense that each aspect is interrelated and each element is more or less integrated with every other. It is a total world view, and, in so far as its various parts lock together, we must expect that what is believed about God will find its complement in what is believed about the holy, and that similarly views of man and nature, etc., will be interdependent. That Otto's understanding of the numinous fits perfectly into this universe is self-evident, if it is compared with the earlier pages of this chapter. But perhaps it would be as well to indicate a few of the more important correspondences.

The holy as the *mysterium tremendum* corresponds both to the mythical God 'up there' and to the metaphysical God 'out there'. As the 'wholly other', he stands apart from creation, brings fear and dread, is the God of the *dies irae*, but by his incursions into the world reveals his energy, for he is active and alive.

Man in the sacral universe feels powerless before the forces of nature; he is dependent upon something outside himself; he experiences creature-feeling. Yet he never ceases to find the divine fascinating, either as a source of help in trouble or as a hope for the life beyond the grave. Some, who live within this general context, enjoy rapture and bliss, but they are few and far between; they are principally the mystics, who in their turn are nearly all monks and nuns, practising extreme asceticism and seeking to detach themselves from the world. Indeed they turn inwards to find the holy and so turn away from nature to which most of their contemporaries are subjected. There is thus something of a split within the laity themselves, attracted to mass but fearful of communion, and between the laity in the world and the religious within their monasteries. Yet the world to all is but the shadow-screen of reality in comparison with the holy who is 'the sole and entire reality'.

Man's confrontation with nature in its merciless fury is an encounter with the holy in all its awesome dread. The wrath of God manifests itself in and through epidemics and other catastrophes. Nature itself is numinous. Man's experience of the holy is set within a framework of natural phenomena which have a divine character. There is a numinous aura about kings and rulers, about popes and bishops. The liturgy itself is celebrated amidst an atmosphere of awe, preserving a tenuous lifeline between this world and the world of heavenly being, where God is resplendent in glory and the angelic choir sings: Holy, holy, holy.

There is, however, a further aspect of the holy, of which Otto has little to say, but, which is nevertheless vital if the concept of the holy integrated into the sacral universe is to be fully understood. This is the aspect of separation or apartness.

It is a commonplace of the phenomonologists of religion, and also of many sociologists of religion, that the holy or sacred and the profane are antithetical realities. So convinced of this was Emile Durkheim that he believed this separation to lie at the very basis of religion.

All known religious beliefs, whether simple or complex, present one common characteristic: they presuppose a classification of all the things, real and ideal, of which one thinks, into two classes or opposed groups, generally designated by two distinct terms which are translated well enough by the words *profane* and *sacred*. This division of the world into two domains, the one containing all that is sacred, the other all that is profane, is the distinctive trait of religious thought. . . In all the history of human thought there exists no other example of two categories of things so profoundly differentiated or so radically opposed to one another. The traditional opposition between good and bad is nothing beside this; for the good and the bad are only two opposed species of the same class, namely morals, just as sickness and health are two different aspects of the same order of facts, life, while the sacred and the profane have always everywhere been conceived by the human mind as two distinct classes, as two worlds between which there is nothing in common. . . This heterogeneity is even so complete that it frequently degenerates into a veritable antagonism. The two worlds are not only conceived of as separate, but even as hostile and jealous rivals of each other.[40]

Consequently the holy is seen to be the quality of that which is set apart, and set apart from the profane; 'it is a transcendental principle which intervenes to effect this setting apart or separation.'[41] There is indeed a general consensus that, in the words of Roger Caillois, 'the only thing that can be validly affirmed in general of the sacred is to be found in the actual definition of the term: it is that which is opposed to the profane.'[42] This opposition can be expressed in a variety of ways.[43] The one is that which is potent, full of power, while the other is powerless; the one is the real, the other the unreal. They cannot, therefore, approach one another without losing their proper nature. Their separation is essential for their integrity, otherwise either the sacred will consume the profane or the profane will contaminate or enfeeble the sacred. The sacred is therefore dangerous. It both attracts and repels man; it attracts him because it is the source of power and it repels him because to encounter it is to be in peril.[44] The sacred – and here we join Otto again – is the 'wholly other'; it is a reality of an entirely different order from 'natural realities', even if it may be encountered through them. In general, therefore, the sacred and the profane must be kept apart because any contact between them could be fatal to both. Their contacts can only be intermittent and must be strictly regulated by rites which can have either a positive or a negative character. Included in the former are rites of consecration whereby someone or something is introduced into the realm of the holy. The negative ones take the form of prohibitions, raising barriers between the two and so isolating them and preventing a catastrophe. These rites allow a certain coming and going between the two spheres, since they provide the conditions within which intercourse is possible. But any attempt, outside the prescribed limits, to unite sacred and profane brings confusion and disaster.

Underlying all this is the concept of two worlds: a sacred world and a secular world – a divine world and the world of men. The holy represents the irruption into the world of men of the power of the divine world. When man encounters the holy, he 'receives a revelation of a reality *other* than that in which he participates through his ordinary daily life'.[45] There are, then, two realms of being, and 'these two worlds, that of the sacred and that of the profane, can only be strictly defined in terms of each other. They exclude each other and they are opposed to each other.'[46]

This apartness of the holy explains the emphasis, within the sacral universe, upon detachment from the world; the quest for perfection is synonymous with separation from secular life. So the ideal of personal holiness is provided by the monks.

They were to be perfect, as Christ Himself was perfect... People outside the monasteries, noblemen, peasants, bishops, church dignitaries, village priests, caught in the toil of secular conflicts and passions, were only too well aware that their lives fell far short of the highest Christian standards. They were convinced – it was the most deeply held conviction of medieval Christianity – that it was impossible to live in the world and be wholly and entirely a Christian. Yet there must be people capable of leading a perfect Christian life, in some place apart, and the monks in their cloister were called on to do this. It is surely significant that the cloister was called 'the gate of Paradise', or simply Paradise itself. All the hopes, prayers and demands the medieval Christian set on the monks and the monasteries were centred in one expectation: that they would achieve the complete sanctity of a perfect Christian life. It was well known that a Christian's highest duty was to become holy, to become a saint. But for most men this could only be achieved vicariously. The world was full of violence, steeped in mortal sin and depravity: amid such confusion only a monk could achieve personal perfection.[47]

In this way the apartness of the holy was vividly demonstrated, as it was in many other ways, too, such as the holy, i.e. separate, character attributed to churches.[48] Once again we see how closely integrated were all the elements of the sacral universe.

Enough has perhaps been said by now to enable the reader to appreciate the main characteristics of that cosmos, but before turning to the world of today and to the transformation in man's categories of thought, it would be as well to let a great medieval scholar have a last word. I select him because although the sacral universe is the normal habitat of *homo religiosus*, whether he be a follower of tribal religion in Africa or Australia or a devotee of Islam in Arabia, the examples adduced to illustrate this thought-world have been largely taken, for convenience, from medieval Christendom. Speaking with sympathy of the Middle Ages in the West, when the sacral universe dominated everything, he says:

Medieval piety has often been reproached for its materialism, its reversion to magic and sorcery, its lack of genuine spirituality, its vulnerability to superstition. Such charges are understandable, coming as they do from people whose experience of life has been quite different, but they do not do justice to the realism and vitality of the faith this piety supported. It was a sober, hard-headed, serious faith, devoid of sentimentality (romanticism of any kind was alien to the medieval temper) but not without joy. Medieval popular religion was militant and it was concerned with justice: these were its two fundamental characteristics, and they enabled it to fulfil an important function in a society dominated by war, when everyone had to fight for his right, and when lawlessness was a daily occurrence. This faith fulfilled another and particularly important function. The whole natural world lay 'in jeopardy', threatened by unknown mysterious powers, full of perils and terrors; in times of famine, pestilence and flood, and in the daily 'accidents' which cost a man his life, such powers came out into the open, revealing that the beauty of outward appearances was only skin deep and that underneath lurked explosive forces always ready to erupt. Experience of this kind could only be matched by a faith imaginative enough to comprehend all terrors and horrors in its image of God. God, the Lord of life and death, was the Lord of dread and equally the Lord of joy; the terrors of the Lord of Sinai, a volcano spitting fire, are felt in the midst of the solemn joy of the Church's celebration of the Mass.

Injustice, war, feuds, the general horror of life – all could be overcome by fighting for justice, for righteous warfare (above all between sinners and the devil), and by observing the solemn ceremonies of God's house and one's own. Call this common medieval piety naive and primitive if you will: in its day it fulfilled vital functions in the life of man and society. To evaluate what was achieved by medieval popular religion, with its mixture of archaic, 'heathen', folk and Christian elements, it is pertinent to ask what functions religion fulfils in the life of a Christian in the industrial society of the twentieth century.[49]

Friedrich Heer's last sentence hints at the problem with which this book is concerned and provides a point of transition from the sacral universe to a consideration of the secular universe.

What, then, is a secular – or, as some writers have termed it, a hominized – universe? It is one in which the functioning of nature and society is explained in terms of themselves. No longer is recourse had to the divine in order to understand either the material world or man. The natural sciences seek out the 'laws' of nature, their interrelationships and their workings: sociology analyses society, while man himself is investigated in terms of biology, psychology, etc.

In the secular universe man is no longer at the mercy of nature, rather he is its master; he does not feel himself a component part of it but its shaper. Through the development of technology, man can control his environment; to a large extent he is therefore liberated from nature, in the sense that he has ceased to be dependent upon its changes and chances. This newly-won domination, precarious though it may be in the face of pollution and the need for conservation, results in a reversal of roles. Whereas previously man was in submission to natural forces, now he can, in considerable measure, bend them to his will. This change in the relationship of man and nature leads to a new concept of man's place in the universe. Man and his power become fundamental values which direct his efforts towards research into development and progress – it is now a hominized world. So man fast becomes lord of nature, discovering its laws and dominating it by scientific and technological means. Indeed, 'with the rise and development of the natural sciences, the world changed from being the environment enfolding man to being the object and material of transformation by man.'[50] Hence the world has become the matter of human, rather than divine, creativity; it is therefore a world without the numinous. To experience the world as nature, which one can subjugate to one's needs, means that it loses its previous dimension as a sacral reality. So far from being inscrutable, its secrets are laid bare.

With the advance of medicine, such illnesses as epilepsy or the plague cease to be envisaged as sacral realities. With increased knowledge of meteorology, storms or droughts are not regarded as divine visitations. A miracle is no more than a natural event which, through ignorance or lack of scientific progress, man has not yet been able to understand. There are in fact no gaps in the web of physical causation through which the divine can manifest its will; there exists no more a kind of porousness in the texture of reality through which an other-worldly power can infiltrate. The workings of nature are not the workings of God; nature can be investigated, put to the question, without any reference to anything outside itself. If, in the early stages of this movement, scientists delighted to praise the Supreme Mathematician as the author of the natural laws uncovered, today they no longer seek to decipher God's intelligibility in the world. In the technological universe, science has largely succeeded in ridding itself of theological postulates and assumptions. It has asserted its autonomy and, so far from recognizing theology as the Queen of Sciences, doubts, when it thinks of theology at all, if it has any role to play.

Society has ceased to be conceived as either a theocracy or a natural phenomenon. The state, according to the Marxist vision, will ultimately wither away. In the thought-world of the Western democracies, the state is a man-made organization to carry out the will of the populace, and if it ceases to perform that function efficiently, it should be changed. From either viewpoint, the state is subservient to man and no longer possesses Godgiven authority which ensures the continuance of the *status quo*.

So far from being static and rigid, society enters into a process of change – change, be it noted, not towards the establishment of a new semi-permanent *status quo*, but change that is constant and never-ending. Society also becomes pluriform with different cultures and sub-cultures existing side by side. The mobility which technology brings cracks open the uniformity of society, so that followers of Islam, Buddhists and Hindus settle, for example, in Great Britain in their thousands. *Cujus regio, ejus religio* no longer makes sense – in relation to religion the state has to be neutral.

The result is that within the secular universe, religion loses the functions it exercised previously in the sacral universe. When change is the key-note, religion can no longer perform the role of protector and preserver of society; if it tries to do so, it will be regarded as a bulwark against progress and as a supporter of social stagnation. When society is pluriform, there can be no *cultus publicus*. Christianity, indeed every religion, becomes instead a *cultus privatus*, with the inevitable abandonment of the public sector of life and with concentration on forms of individual pietism. When science provides structures of explanation, religion is regarded as irrelevant. When man dominates the universe intellectually and materially, he no longer needs rituals to protect himself. If, in former days, it seemed reasonable and eminently practical to sprinkle holy water on an ox that was ill, today few would think of doing this to a farm tractor that had broken down. In medieval agriculture, God was reduced to a secondary cause of the process of production, but at least a link with the divine was preserved; in the modern factory, however, such categories of thought are meaningless – the worker knows that his success will depend upon his own skill, upon the quality of his materials and upon the perfection of his tools. Again, if centuries ago, one observed rituals to ensure the rising of the Nile, such actions seem unnecessary since the construction of the Aswan Dam.

If religion persists in fighting to preserve its former functions, it will soon have to capitulate before the attacks of a technical civilization. Christianity in the West, in particular, having integrated itself, very successfully, with a pre-technical rural civilization, has now to purify itself of the superstitions illustrated above. But this purification will only be real and effective to the extent to which Christianity transforms its theological teaching, its liturgy and its pastoral policy.[51]

This is not to suggest that religion in the sacral universe was the cause of social stagnation. When man is subservient to nature, change is well-nigh impossible and religion can do little more, in such a situation, than confirm an existing state of affairs. It then functions as a kind of emotional container for underdevelopment, providing man in his helplessness with sanctions and support. But once society moves into change, religion becomes incredible or irrelevant unless it, too, is rethought in terms of the change in which it has to be involved.

Just as in the previous section I was not concerned primarily to criticize but to describe the sacral universe, so it is not my intention at this juncture to point out the dangers and difficulties in accepting the secular universe exactly as it is. Nevertheless, it should be recognized that man is not yet completely at home in this new context, and this is especially revealed by his attitude to death, which has been admirably characterized by G. Gorer as involving a 'pornography of death'.[52] In saying this he is drawing a parallel between the Victorian view of sex and the contempory view of death. In the

Victorian era sex was ignored and the fiction was generally accepted that it did not exist; so in the secular universe death is conveniently relegated to a dark, not to say obnoxious, corner. The result, and this is all that I am concerned with here, is that rituals of death lose their meaning, for one does not bring to the forefront of consciousness what one is busily trying to ignore. Consequently there is little general concern about a future life and attention is turned almost exclusively to the present. The world is the supreme reality, and so there is a secularization of the whole of reality.

Secularization is an imprecise term, used in many different ways by different writers.[53] I am using it to describe the process of change, in all its complexity, from a sacral to a secular universe. It involves, therefore, disenchantment, dedivinization or desacralization. It affirms the authentic nature of any person, object or event. It stresses their immediate, rather than their ultimate, ends. It includes the affirmation of the worldly reality of any person, object or event. Secularization also involves the recognition of a certain autonomy, but whereas according to secularism this is absolute, secularization itself does not require more than the recognition of a relative autonomy; i.e., while affirming the essential worldliness of any person, event or object, it does not necessarily require the denial of the possibility of God-relatedness – though this latter is a point to be considered in detail later.

Secularization, therefore, exposes man to history. It enables him to understand himself as an historical being, to experience the world as history, as transition within the continual flow of events. So it is not 'the world above' nor 'the world beyond' which excites modern man, but commitment to a new world which he is concerned to build.[54] The secular universe is therefore centred in man, rather than in God – it is a hominized world. There is a shift from heaven to earth, from God to man. The secular outlook, then, is characterized by a radical immanentism, which rejects 'transcendence' as largely irrelevant and therefore without meaning.[55]*

Man is no longer dependent upon something outside himself; in co-operation with his fellows, he can create the just society, overcome suffering, etc. – or at least so he believes, and this belief determines his understanding of reality and consequently of God.

What sort of God is the deity of this secular universe? At this point in the argument, an answer can be given only in the form of a series of negatives. We can say, from this perspective, what he is not, and my formulation has to consist of a succession of no's to the God of the sacral universe. In the first place, whatever God means today, the name cannot refer to a category of explanation. As such he would simply be a missing link in man's unsuccessful attempt to grasp the meaning of himself and his world. 'The deity becomes just a global hypothesis, a mere cog of an intricate machine.'[56] Every scientific advance would then be a victory against this God and a progressive diminution of the area of his concern. In a pre-technical age, such a God supplied man's ignorance; today he is no longer needed for this purpose.

In the second place, God cannot any longer be conceived as a *deus ex machina*. The supplier of rain, he that was 'a very present help in trouble', the source of assistance – we can manage without such a being. Indeed, technological man will suffer a dichotomy between what he says about God and what he does without reference to such a being, unless he either rejects him or is helped to understand a transposed image of God.[57] After all, the man who minds a machine has ceased to expect a *deus ex machina* to put it right if it goes wrong.

'We do not ask God to do for us what the world is qualified to do. Really to travel along this road means that we trust the world, not God, to be our need-fulfiller and problem-solver, and God, if he is to be for us at all, must come in some other role.'[58] One may in fact say (and here some criticism of the God of the sacral universe is unavoidable):

The false God of religion, the *deus ex machina*, is present when men want him: he comes when he is called. The true God does not: he is the one who did not come to Christ in Gethsemane and on the cross, to get him out of his difficulties. On the other hand the false God is an illusion of religion, and therefore not really present. As an idol, he has no effective existence.[59]

The same point is well made by the late Ronald Gregor Smith in the following passage:

God is not at the end of our enquiries, nor in the stop-gap where our thought fails us. To treat him in this way is to betray a fundamental disbelief both in his work as Creator and his work as Redeemer. The God of Christian belief is not a *deus ex machina* who can be called in, in the name of an other-worldly hope beyond all appearance, a god whose real home is up in the clouds, or in the wings of the theatre where man's little drama is being played out. But he is in the midst of the drama.[60]

His final short sentence raises the whole question with which I am concerned, and it represents an affirmation which many today would reject. It seems to many within the secular universe that God can only be regarded as a *deus ex machina* and that as such he does not exist. This is the theme of *Waiting for Godot*. Samuel Beckett's magnificent play is religious, in the sense that it describes man's spiritual predicament. Man, according to Beckett, is aware of meaninglessness and estrangement, yet he is sustained by hope, i.e. of the possible intervention of Godot. Estragon and Vladimir live in expectation of a *deus ex machina*: 'their attention is always focused on the promise of a coming.'[61] They yearn for some incursion from outside and this is to wait in vain – no one comes or will ever come. To see reality as Beckett does – but not as some of his characters do – is to reject the God of the sacral universe and to put nothing and no one in its place.

By no means all of our contemporaries are prepared to go to these lengths. Surveys show that a large majority still profess belief in a Supreme Being. However when one examines the character ascribed to this Being, he appears to be a distant and nebulous figure. Indeed one can say that in a hominized universe the God of sacrality has become a *deus otiosus*. Such a deity has been acknowledged by numerous primitive tribes. He is believed to have created the world and man, but soon to have abandoned them and withdrawn to the sky. So the Pygmies say: 'God has gone far from us'. The Fang of Equatorial Africa declare:

> God (Nzame) is above, man is below.
> God is God, man is man.
> Each in his own place, each in his house.[62]

It is only in times of calamity that his assistance is sought. So the Hebrews served the local baals in times of prosperity, and only turned from these lesser divinities to Yahweh when beset by dangers and difficulties. In a technical age, these lesser beings – thinly disguised in Western Christendom as saints – are ceasing to have relevance, since fertility, health, etc., are now regarded as dependent upon science. Hence the only God left is the *deus otiosus* who has lost religious actuality and is invoked rarely, in the face of serious disasters.

It is to be expected that, within the context we are considering, the God of the sacral universe will be deemed by many to be an absent being or even dead. In other words, the sacral conception shapes modern man's understanding of the God who is experienced as absent or non-existent. 'We are not talking,' comment two of the adherents of the 'death of God' theology, 'about the absence of the experience of God but about the experience of the absence of God'[63] – but the God whose absence they are experiencing is the God of the sacral universe or, to employ William Blake's telling appellation, 'Nobodaddy'.

With the withdrawal or decease of the God of the sacral universe, there inevitably follows a cessation of the experience of the holy, conceived as the numinous. To think of the holy as the *mysterium tremendum* seems to many to involve the belief, even if that is not intended, that it is essentially uncanny, not to say 'spooky', something entirely outside the range of daily experience. Scholars have pointed out that the feelings of dread and awe that the holy is believed to arouse can equally be induced by an encounter with natural events, persons or things. 'The shudder of numinous horror,' observes S.S. Acquaviva, 'can indeed be related to the world of ghosts, to the fantastic creations on medieval palaces, to the rites of the most terrible Indian deities or to the mystical ecstasy of Meister Eckhart.'[64] The same critic can entitle a book: *L'éclipse du sacré dans la civilization industrielle*, and in this he looks forward to a progressive and ever-accelerating decline in the sense of the sacred which, while critical of Otto, he does understand in terms of the 'wholly other'. Hence he argues that an object reveals the holy whenever it shows itself to be something other than what it was. 'The object becomes an hierophany when it ceases to be what it was and acquires a new character,' which corresponds to 'an ontological transformation of the object.'[65] He is even prepared to say that there must be a 'clear detaching of the hierophanic object from its previous condition and also from the condition of similar non-hierophanic objects'.[66] This is sacralization, pure and unadulterated – it corresponds exactly with the interpretation of the eucharistic species cited above as evidence of this outlook of the sacral universe. Within a secular universe this interpretation of the holy becomes less and less acceptable. Nor can it be separated from previous reference to the absence of God, since 'it is a very short step, but a critical one, to move from the otherness of God to the absence of God.'[67] To similar effect and with equal poignancy is this statement by Sam Keen:

When a wedge is driven between the holy and the quotidian, the concept of God becomes either insignificant or positively repressive and must be rejected if the integrity of human life is to be retained. A God who does not sanctify the everyday is dead, and belief in such a remote God is an intellectual or aesthetic luxury which is of no positive consequence, as it does not lead to the celebration of life. An unemployed God quickly exhausts his capital and becomes a dead God.[68]

Furthermore, the aspect of holiness which is characterized by 'apartness' has lost its credibility. To quote William Hamilton again: 'His holiness and separateness are beginning to look like an indifference.'[69] We can no longer continue to affirm the apartness of the holy and expect man in the secular universe to accept this idea unless we are also prepared to encourage the development of a split mind, i.e. of a mind divided into two compartments which are kept separate from each other without any integration or unification. 'The split mind,' observes Arthur Koestler, 'must evolve two different codes of thought for its two separate compartments: one conforming to theory, the other to cope with facts.'[70] Thus the concept of the two worlds, which is one of the bases of the separation of the holy, leads to a split mind, the one – the spiritual realm of the holy – conforming to theory, while the other – the secular universe – copes with facts. Indeed, 'when a doctrinal system ceases to have any support in the prevailing culture . . . faith can founder because the faithful cannot endure the dichotomy between their faith and their culture based upon concepts entirely foreign to those used in theology: the religious choice then appears as one between two contradictory systems of thought.'[71] Modern man refuses to acquiesce in this dichotomy. The choice before him is, therefore, plain. He can achieve unity by denying the reality of the holy, or he can reconceptualize the holy so that it is seen to exist not in a separated enclave but within the secular universe.

Many of those who still cling to belief, while conscious of the choice before them, are no longer prepared to live out their faith apart from the world and their human earthly relations. They will not accept that 'the holy is a substantative entity, a reality apart'.[72] They refuse to agree that the quest for perfection is synonymous with separation from the world – the way of detachment, which is bound up with this understanding of the holy, and so of holiness, does not present itself as a serious option. Hence, Martin Buber, with a sympathetic appreciation of man's situation in the secular universe, can say:

I lack the mystic negation. I can negative convictions but never the slightest actual thing. The mystic manages, truly or apparently, to annihilate the entire world, or what he so names – all that his senses present to him in perception and in memory – in order, with new disembodied senses or a wholly supersensory power, to press forward to his God. But I am enormously concerned with just this world, this painful and precious fullness of all that I see, hear, taste. I cannot wish away any part of its reality. I can only wish that I might heighten this reality.[73]

No more emphatic rejection of the holy as 'the apart' can be formulated than what is implicit in this statement.

Sufficient has probably been written to furnish an explanation of the title of this first chapter – 'Exit from the Sacral Universe' – and to sketch the background against which the theologian today has to consider the subject of the holy. This background is not, of course, as uniform as may have been suggested, and such figures as 'modern man' or 'our contemporaries' are something of an abstraction. It is incorrect to speak of all societies today as technical ones – even though each and every one desires to become such. Natural disasters still afflict mankind – witness the famines that periodically ravage India or the earthquakes that bring damage to Yugoslavia and Turkey. There does persist an abundance of residual religiosity. Churchmen and some theologians still speak of the 'wholly other'. A high ecclesiastical dignitary can bless bombs for Vietnam, revealing by his action that he continues to live, think and act within the sacral universe. A Roman Catholic priest in California, when a plane crashes on a crowded church without hurting anyone, can say: 'It is God's house. He has protected us.' To suppose that man has come of age, in the sense that he accepts full responsibility for the secular world described above, is to be blind to the complexity of and variety within the contemporary world situation. Nevertheless, a theology which does not take the exit from the sacral universe seriously would itself be less than serious. It would be, in my view, to fail to read the signs of the times and to perpetuate an archaic religion which is already becoming less and less relevant to more and more people.

The problem can be summarized by two quotations. The first comes from Harvey Cox, who is certainly sensitive to the thought categories of the Western world:

The culturally conditioned ways in which people have experienced the holy have become eroded. Religious experience is learned in any culture just as other experience is learned, in the unspoken assumptions and attitudes which children absorb from their parents and from their closest environment. Our forebears learned from their forebears to expect the experience of the holy in socially defined ways, whether in the sunset, in a camp-meeting conversation or in holy communion. This experience was structured by a culture of residual Christendom still bearing traces of what Paul Tillich calls 'theonomy'. But the coming of modern technology and massive urbanization shook the structure of traditional society and thereby dissipated the cultural ethos within which the holy had been experienced.[74]

The second quotation is from an article by J. Watzke and it speaks for itself.

The theoretical problem is whether the experience of the sacred must not be continually redefined, without freezing it into an identification with any one period in man's development (the pictured total awe of primitive man) or any particular form (the rites, practices, beliefs of a particular institution). Among the many *sacreds* of modern society that we are called upon to analyse, the redefinitions of the *religious sacred* would seem to merit our attention, as would secular sources of the sacred.[75]

2

The Nature of Perception

As man creates around himself his hominized universe, some of the main characteristics of which have been described in the previous chapter, his categories of thought and, with them, his perception begin to change. This change of perception, related to the formulation of new concepts, must now be considered, since the encounter with the holy must in some sense involve the perception of the holy. What, then, is the nature of perception?

Although some thoroughgoing empiricists still continue to demur, there is a very wide measure of agreement that perception is determined by concepts. We approach certain things and events with a particular level of expectation, with that psychologists call a 'mental set'. A mental set 'comprises the attitude and expectations which will influence our perceptions and make us ready to see, or hear, one thing rather than another'.[1] There is, then, an interplay between expectation and perception. What we perceive is frequently what we expect. So, according to J. R. Beloff: 'Perception may be regarded as primarily the modification of an anticipation.'[2] Consequently if we do not have what is sometimes called a 'pre-understanding', it is very likely that we shall fail both to perceive what is in front of us and to interpret it.[3] Indeed it can be said that 'direct observation without any conceptual framework is impossible'.[4]

Perception, therefore, is not a matter of passively allowing an organ, e.g. of sight or sound, to receive a ready-made impression from without, like a piece of paper acquiring an ink blot. Human impressions are schematically determined. 'As perceivers we select from all the stimuli falling on our senses only those which interest us, and our interests are governed by a pattern-making tendency, sometimes called *schema*.'⁵

Hence to change one's *schema* will directly affect one's perception. Indeed certain changes can not only alter but actually obliterate certain perceptions. This, I would contend, is precisely what has happened in relation to the holy. Within the setting of the sacral universe the holy was perceived as the numinous, but the result of his exit from that universe and of his entry into the secular world is that modern man, his thought-categories having been transformed, no longer perceives the holy as the numinous. He is therefore tempted to believe that the holy does not exist. His *schema*, his pre-understanding, or whatever one chooses to call it, having been altered, his perception is affected accordingly.

Rather than continuing to discuss the theory of perception in general, let us consider some specific illustrations of the way in which concept and perception are related, selecting them from many diverse fields to demonstrate how universal a phenomenon this is.

My first example is a relatively simple one, in the sense that it is derived from everyday life and can be easily verified by anyone. Many people are familiar with the experience of eating a tasty dish and then, having consumed several mouthfuls, being told what ingredients have gone into its making. Immediately they begin to perceive several tastes that previously they had not noticed. So they may be eating apples baked in white wine. The taste of the wine is not pronounced, being masked by the sauce, but to be informed that the apples have indeed been cooked in wine is to be enabled to detect the underlying flavour of alcohol. So perception is in part determined by knowledge or rather, in this case, by belief. Let me expand this. Suppose it is my wife who tells me that apples have been baked in wine. My past experience has led me to believe that my wife is trustworthy, that her statements are usually true and are never deliberately misleading. Hence on this occasion I believe my wife's statement about the wine, i.e. I accept that the apples have indeed been baked in wine. This means, further, that I now believe that there *is* wine in the recipe, and it is by this belief that I am enabled to perceive the wine. In so far as I also trust my perception, this perception confirms my previous belief.

For some slightly more complex examples, we turn to the field of the visual arts, and in particular to sculpture and painting. To many people the iconoclasm of Cromwell and the Puritans is unforgivable

As we read the accounts of the visitation of churches by William
Dowsing and of the wholesale destruction of many works of
medieval art, we tend to shrink at the barbarity, to moan at the
Philistinism, to deplore the lack of appreciation of beauty, and we
are tempted to condemn Dowsing and those like him as uncultured
savages. This judgmental attitude, however, completely misses the
point. Our judgment is being determined by our perception, whereas
theirs was totally different. We can only persevere in condemnation
if we remain ignorant of the way in which man's perception of art
has changed since the seventeenth century. This process of change
has been very clearly analysed by André Malraux. There is no need
to reproduce his fascinating exposé here in full, but one passage may
serve to illuminate the transformation that has taken place.

What our African explorers discovered was not Negro art but fetishes,
and what the conquistadors discovered was not Mexican art but Aztec
idols. Similarly all the objects collected by Europeans on their island
voyages passed for 'curios'... Idols became works of art only when
they were given a new frame of reference and could enter into an art
world unknown to any civilization anterior to ours. Europe discovered
Negro art when it could see African carvings in the context of Cézanne
and Picasso – not as fetishes in an ambience of coconuts and croco-
diles. . . To begin with the metamorphosis of the past was a metamorphosis of our way of seeing. . . Modern art is not enough to account for
these rediscoveries: but by subordinating appearance to creative vision,
it has given access to a world in which a Mexican god becomes a statue,
not a mere fetish.[6]

In the light of this, we can now understand the Puritan behaviour.
The holy objects they delighted to smash were to them *not* works of
art but idols, even fetishes. In so far as any of their contemporaries
resisted them, it was not on the grounds that this was not the way to
treat art treasures, but that this was a blasphemous attack upon
legitimate objects of devotion. Our changed perspective enables us
to see them differently; our concepts, within a new frame, provide
us with an entirely fresh way of perceiving these cult objects – in
the words of the title of the book by Malraux, from which I have
just quoted, there has been *A Metamorphosis of the Gods*.
A seventeenth-century architectural drawing provides another
example. Matthäus Merian produced a careful illustration of what
he believed to be a faithful copy of Notre Dame in Paris. 'As a child
of the seventeenth century,' comments E. H. Gombrich, 'his notion
of a church is that of a lofty symmetrical building with large,

rounded windows, and that is how he designs Notre Dame. He places the transept in the centre with four large, rounded windows on either side, while the actual view shows seven narrow, pointed gothic windows to the west and six in the choir.'[7]

Ironically we can contrast Merian's design with a lithograph of the cathedral of Chartres by Robert Garland. By 1836, when he made this, Gothic was beginning to fascinate architects and designers. So when Merian, against a different background of ideas, turned a Gothic building into a Romanesque, Garland achieved the opposite, i.e. he represented the western façade of Chartres with pointed arches, whereas in fact there are rounded Romanesque windows.[8] In either case, the artist did not begin with a neutral visual impression, but with his own idea or concept, for, as Gombrich comments, he 'will tend to see what he paints rather than to paint what he sees',[9] and he quotes elsewhere James Barry to the effect that 'nothing is seen even in the spectacle before us, until it be in some measure otherwise previously sought for.'[10]

Finally, from the field of art, there is the amusing experience of T. E. Lawrence showing to some Arabs the portraits of themselves which Kennington had painted for *The Seven Pillars of Wisdom*. They completely failed to recognize them as pictures of men, let alone as their likenesses. They turned them upside down and sideways up and then suggested that they represented a camel, because the lines of the jaw were shaped like a hump. Since a picture is an abstraction of lines and colours and since this was something entirely new to them, they were unable to interpret them as men or sunsets.[11]

Two other illustrations can be adduced from social anthropology. First there is the case of H. A. Junod, who wrote about the Tsonga of Mozambique. His first account was published in 1898 and his second fifteen years later. In between these two he read *Les rites de passage* by van Gennep. This pioneering study gave a completely new insight into the question of ritual. Junod adopted this *schema* and was then able to observe much in Tsongan life which he had previously failed to notice. 'Van Gennep,' says M. Gluckman, 'helped to raise Junod's work from run-of-the-mill reporting of customs, till it ranked, and still ranks, among the great monographs.'[12] In other words, change the concept and perception is also altered.

A similar experience is recorded by V. W. Turner, who tells how those initially studying African tribal life neglected completely their ritual practices. He continues:

> With eyes just opened to the importance of ritual in the lives of the Ndembu, my wife and I began to perceive many aspects of Ndembu culture that had previously been invisible to us because of our theoretical blinkers. As Nadel has said, facts change with theories and new facts make new theories.[13]

In making such an affirmation, Turner is not in opposition to the scientific outlook prevailing at the present day. That this is so is evident from the conclusions of K. R. Popper:

> Theory dominates the experimental work from its initial planning up to the finishing touches in the laboratory. . . Even the careful and sober testing of our ideas by experiment is in its turn inspired by ideas: experiment is planned action in which every step is guided by theory. We do not stumble upon our experiences, nor do we let them flow over us like a stream. Rather, we have to be active: we have to '*make*' our experience.[14]

An excellent illustration of this is Louis Pasteur's discovery of the distinction between tartaric and paratartaric acids. Eilhardt Mitscherlich, a celebrated German crystallographer and chemist, had affirmed that their salts are identical in all particulars, except that they behave differently towards polarized light. The two, he stated, have the same chemical composition and the same crystalline shape. Pasteur, however, had a different concept as his point of departure. He believed that different optical activity must be associated with irregularities in shape, and he undertook a systematic observation of the tartaric and paratartaric acid crystals. He at once saw small facets on them similar to those on quartz, which had escaped the notice of Mitscherlich. According to R. J. Dubos, this was 'a telling example of the part played by a working hypothesis in the process of discovery ... preconceived ideas influence our perception'.[15] Pasteur's pre-understanding resulted in an advance in knowledge, while Mitscherlich's acted as an impediment. In this connection one may note the dry remark of Bertrand Russell to the effect that observers of animal behaviour often record that animals display the national characteristics of the observers, with those studied by Americans rushing about in an energetic fashion while those observed by Germans sit still and think![16]

This structuring of perception by one's mental set is exemplified in all fields of human endeavour, even within the somewhat bizarre field of visions induced by drugs. There is in fact evidence that a person's experience in such cases is affected by the beliefs he already has. For example, the Mexican Peyote tribes consume the 'buttons' of a species of cactus known as peyote, which contains mescalin. These tribes have been much influenced by Roman Catholicism and it is therefore not surprising to discover that in their visions they frequently see the Virgin Mary. Similarly, it is reasonable to suppose that the pantheistic experiences of Aldous Huxley, while under the influence of the same drug, were given their particular form by his profound knowledge of Eastern thought.[17]

Two concluding examples may be selected, one from New Testament scholarship and one from the New Testament itself. The nineteenth century saw the publication of a great number of lives of Jesus. In effect, these all represented him as a nineteenth-century liberal. The authors themselves failed to appreciate what they were doing; their perception of Jesus was dominated by their concept of him and their lives simply embodied that concept. It took an Albert Schweitzer, with his *Quest of the Historical Jesus*, to make clear the limitations of their perspective.

Or again, we may turn to the story of the meeting of the risen Jesus with Mary Magdalen in the garden. Mary is in no doubt that Jesus is dead and that someone has removed his corpse. 'They have taken away my Lord, and I do not know where they have laid him.' When, therefore, she meets a person near the empty tomb, it does not occur to her for a single moment that this could be Jesus. 'She turned round and saw Jesus standing, but she did not know that it was Jesus. Jesus said to her, "Woman, why are you weeping? Whom do you seek?" Supposing him to be the gardener, she said to him, "Sir, if you have carried him away, tell me where you have laid him, and I will take him away." ' Mary's concept thus prevents any recognition of Jesus; indeed she only perceives who he is when he discloses himself to her. 'Jesus said to her, "Mary." She turned and said to him in Hebrew, "Rabboni!" '[18]

The intimate relationship of mental set and perception undoubtedly involves a continual risk of what is known as 'projection'. There is always the possibility that a *schema* will lead us to project a mental image on to an object or event with which we are confronted. Thus, we may look at blots of ink, cloud-formations or coals of fire and think we see therein faces or weird beings. What is before us then becomes no more that a screen on to which we project our own ideas. In the act of perception there are always two possibilities. There is the possibility of projection, so that we see something that is not there but is simply the reading into it of a preconceived idea. But there is also the possibility of discernment, so that we see what *is* there precisely because a preconceived idea enables us to recognize it.

Obviously, in writing of the encounter with the holy it is with the second of these possibilities that I am concerned. But how can the fallacy of projection be avoided so that one can, with some confidence, speak of the possibility of discernment? It has to be recognized that the function and meaning of anything is determined by its context. Hence whether or not a perception corresponds to reality depends upon its meaningfulness within its context. To see faces in the fire is obviously a projection which does not correspond to reality, since in the context of fire it is meaningless to suppose the presence of faces. Similarly, to see phantoms or insects in ink-blots is a projection which does not correspond with reality, because it is absurd to suppose that an ink-blot should be intended to be anything. When, however, later in this study, I attempt to point to the presence of the holy in, for example, a personal relationship, this will only be discernment, and not projection, if it is indeed a recognition of what is there and of what is meaningful within its context. In other words, any event should be capable of a consistent interpretation. If we recognize the holy within an event, we can only say that this is neither a projection nor an illusion, if its presence is consistent with an interpretation of the event as a whole. A *deus ex machina* interpretation is not consistent, because it involves something extraneous to the situation. But the possibility exists of discerning the holy within a human situation, as long as this perception neither denies the reality of the situation as human nor drags in the holy from outside the observed event. Indeed, from the point of view of man that can be detected as a projection which amounts to an estrangement from or an alienation of that which is human.[19]

However, while firm expectation may result in hallucination, preunderstanding, if correctly related to a situation, may facilitate perception. So, for example, I may be listening to an indistinct conversation, and if I have already some inkling of what the topic under discussion might be, then I can indeed 'hear' much of what is said, in the sense that my mental set supplies the *lacunae* in my receptivity. This means that my perception is also structured by what I deem to be relevant factors. I will ignore, and therefore also fail to perceive, what I consider to be irrelevant to my understanding of the conversation.

This question of relevance is of the utmost importance in the encounter with the holy. If I do not consider the holy to be relevant to a particular situation, it is very probable that I will not perceive the holy in that situation. This does not mean that the holy is absent; it simply means that my perspective can obscure the observation of its presence. One ignores what one regards as irrelevant aspects of reality. So according to Arthur Koestler:

> Every drawing on the blackboard – whether it is meant to represent the wiring diagram of a radio set or the circulation of the blood, the structure of a molecule or the weather over the Atlantic – is based on the same method as the cartoonist's: selective emphasis on the relevant factors and omission of the rest. A map bears the same relation to a landscape as a character-sketch to a face; every chart, diagram or model, every schematic or symbolic representation of physical or mental processes, is an unemotional caricature of reality.[20]

Thus perception depends upon the appreciation of relevance, and if the holy is regarded as irrelevant, it will simply not be perceived.

Nevertheless, it may be objected that in the end of the day the result will be no more than a series of non-cognitive statements. That is to say, I may not be saying anything about reality as such but only about a certain way of looking at reality. My formulations may be no more than non-cognitive affirmations which express my particular attitude and viewpoint and do not disclose the reality *per se*. I cannot accept this sharp opposition between cognitive and non-cognitive statements, nor can I agree that so-called non-cognitive statements tell us nothing about reality and only about one's way of looking at reality. As T. W. Ogletree expresses it:

> On the one hand even cognitive statements cannot be wholly separated from the subject who utters them. They always presuppose the adoption of some viewpoint or stance towards reality. . . On the other hand, non-cognitive statements, the ones concerned with a perspective in terms of which life can be significantly lived, need not be totally emptied of all cognitive claims. To be sure, our deepest commitments cannot be tested by objective techniques of verification. Still, we take them seriously because we believe they help us to perceive something of the way things really are.[21]

The relevance of this to the present study is as follows. To describe a mental set, or to put forward an image of the holy, is to present a way of looking at reality, but this itself can help us to perceive reality. It breaks through the sharp opposition between the cognitive and the non-cognitive.

I am not claiming that there is no such thing as what F. I. Dretske has called 'non-epistemic seeing',[22] but I am claiming that some things cannot be observed without a proto-belief or proto-knowledge, and that, in the terms of my main concern, the holy belongs to such a category. Moreover, it is important to recognize that it is possible to see things in what Dretske calls a 'secondary epistemic way'.[23] So I may see a blanket covering a chair. The blanket is so arranged that no part of the chair is visible, but because of my knowledge of both I can know that beneath the one is the other. I then perceive the chair indirectly or mediately, because of my proto-knowledge. A Red Indian, on the other hand, who knows what a blanket is but has never seen a chair, could not be aware that the blanket was on a chair; he could only infer it from his knowledge of blankets, their texture, lack of rigidity, etc. Whereas a Hottentot, completely ignorant of blankets and chairs, would be entirely unaware of the chair's existence. He could only perceive it mediately, if he were given the necessary proto-knowledge.

This secondary epistemic way of perceiving leads us on to the subject of experience, although a fuller analysis of this subject will have to wait to a later point in this book.

Experience is obviously very closely related to perception, in that not only do we have to perceive in order to experience, but also concepts affect experience as much as they do perception. Indeed, concepts can determine experience even to the extent, for example, of limiting biological activity or affecting bodily functions. So an orthodox Jew may become physically ill if compelled to eat pork. A Methodist may experience nausea if required to drink wine at the eucharist instead of unfermented grape juice, and a Catholic layman may vomit at the prospect of receiving the chalice. If, however, the concepts are changed, the experience will vary accordingly. A Jew who ceases to believe that pigs are to be classified as unclean, a Methodist who accepts that alcohol is permissible, a Catholic layman who convinces himself that he should follow the example of the apostles at the Last Supper in not only eating the host but drinking from the cup – each of these will cease to experience discomfort.

Examples can, of course, be multiplied. A man who believes that his self-identity is essentially based upon his 'virility' will consider it right to have intercourse with as many women as possible and may indeed force himself to perform sexually, even in circumstances of physical satiety, in order to protect his identity as an embodiment of virility. Conversely, another man who believes that his love and devotion commit him to sexual relations with his wife alone may find himself quite impotent if he tries to have intercourse with someone else.

Perhaps more striking are the symptoms of possession and of neurosis which may be induced by one's own *schema*. According to P. L. Berger and T. Luckmann:

> The rural Haitian who internalizes Voudun psychology will become possessed as soon as he discovers certain well-defined signs. Similarly the New York intellectual who internalizes Freudian psychology will become neurotic as soon as he diagnoses certain well-known symptoms. Indeed, it is possible that, given a certain biographical context, signs or symptoms will be produced by the individual himself. The Haitian will, in that case, produce not symptoms of neurosis but signs of possession, while the New Yorker will construct his neurosis in conformity with the recognized symptomatology.[24]

Thus concept, perception and experience are all fused together in one whole, each element affecting and, in part, determining the other and having a profound influence on personal relations and conduct. We may turn to Shakespeare's great tragedy *Othello, the Moor of Venice* for further light on the matter. The plot is so familiar that only its main features need be recalled. It is the story of how Iago brings about the ruin of his master. Iago's hatred of Othello is a compound of envy at the Moor's pre-eminence, of disappointment at Cassio's being made lieutenant in his stead and of bitterness at the rumour that Othello has bedded Emilia, his wife. The method adopted by Iago to destroy Othello is suggested to him by Brabantio, the father of Desdemona. Furious at finding that she has married Othello without his knowledge or consent, Brabantio declares:

> Look to her, Moor, if thou has eyes to see;
> She has deceiv'd her father and may thee.

So Iago sets out to convince Othello that Desdemona is an unfaithful wife. His first step is to involve Cassio in a brawl which incurs him the disfavour of Othello. Next he induces Cassio to seek for pardon through the good offices of Desdemona. In a soliloquy, at the end of the second act, Iago reveals his plan.

> whiles this honest fool
> Plies Desdemona to repair his fortunes,
> And she for him pleads strongly to the Moor,
> I'll pour this pestilence into his ear –
> That she repeals him for her body's lust;
> And by how much she strives to do him good
> She shall undo her credit with the Moor.
> So will I turn her virtue into pitch;
> And out of her own goodness make the net
> That shall enmesh them all.

With superb, if perfidious artistry, Iago drops a number of hints and allusions which soon begin to have their effect upon Othello's attitude.

> Trifles light as air
> Are to the jealous confirmations strong
> As proofs of holy writ.

Othello now suspects Desdemona of adultery with Cassio, and once he has adopted this mental set he interprets every innocent word and action as evidence of her unfaithfulness. Her importunity on behalf of Cassio becomes a demonstration of guilty lust. Her failure to produce a handkerchief, which was his first gift to her and which she has mislaid, is taken as proof that she has presented it to Cassio as a love-token. When Othello sees at a distance the lustful leers of Cassio in conversation with Iago about his paramour Bianca, he immediately assumes that Desdemona is the subject of their talk. When Cassio laughs at the suggestion that he should actually marry Bianca, Othello perceives this as a triumphant cackle at his success with Desdemona. When Bianca then enters carrying the handkerchief which Desdemona has failed to produce and which Iago has himself obtained and given to Cassio, Othello is convinced that his wife has herself given it away. Driven all but mad with jealousy, Othello eventually kills the offending Desdemona and, upon discovering that he has been entirely misled, he takes his own life.

The bearing of this story upon our present concern will be obvious, but it may be emphasized by a poignant comment on the subject of jealousy in general by the psychologist R. Mucchielli.

Jealousy is not a simple feeling... It is, as far as the jealous person is concerned, a structure which organizes perception and gives a meaning to all the facts perceived. A structure of this kind creates a pattern, i.e. it actively arranges, fashions or gives form to data by 'taking them in a certain way' which is characteristic of the jealous person.[25]

So by approaching the subject of perception from this point of view the previous conclusion is confirmed, viz, that concepts affect perception and hence personal relations. If *Othello* illuminates this with a brilliant light, other less extreme, everyday experiences can also be called in evidence.

Take the case of a mother and her son who has recently become engaged to be married. The son's attitude to his fiancée will differ considerably from that of his mother, especially if the latter is possessive. The son, in the first flush of romantic love, is liable to perceive only the good qualities of his fiancée and, even if some faults are discerned, he will perversely declare that these only make her more lovable. The mother, probably quite unaware of the un-conscious fear that she is about to lose her son to another, will rationalize her latent antagonism by cataloguing the faults the young lady possesses. Possibly astute enough to avoid a direct attack and assert that she is quite unworthy of her son, she will seek to 'open his eyes' by oblique remarks and sceptical hints. The fiancée is differently perceived by each one and the relationships between each pair differ accordingly.

From the educational field another example can be chosen. Recent studies of children at school have demonstrated that their progress in work is affected by the attitude of their teachers. Those who are believed to be lacking in intelligence and are treated as such do not reach the same level of attainment as those who are regarded as clever. When, however, the so-called less-advanced pupils are sub-jected to a different approach, in that the teachers convey to them a confidence in their own abilities, their performance is improved. In other words, the mental set of the teacher can actually determine, or at least profoundly affect, what any child can accomplish.

The extent to which mental set influences perception in personal relations can also be shown by an examination of the story of Jesus and the woman with the cruse of ointment, as it is recorded in Luke's gospel.[26] The Pharisee, who is Jesus' host at the dinner, clearly regards sinners as outcasts whom a 'good' person will avoid. Con-sequently, if a person associates with a sinner, considerable doubts are raised as to whether or not he or she is 'good'. Hence when the woman washes Jesus' feet with her tears and anoints him with per-fume, the Pharisee says: 'If he was a prophet, he would know what sort of woman this is who is touching him; for she is a sinner.' His mental set has affected his relationship both to the woman and to

Jesus. As regards the former, his position is one of alienation and condemnation; as regards Jesus his position is moving towards one of rejection.

Jesus, on the other hand, does not begin with the pre-understanding that sinners are outcasts with whom one mixes at the risk of contamination. He sees this particular sinner as a fellow human being in need of acceptance and love. His mental set, therefore, issues in a different relationship. He perceives in the woman's action a spontaneous expression of the sense of honour due to him and he objects to a criticism that would shame her for performing a deed of loving service. The Pharisee, dominated by a fear of the uncleanness of sin, only sees the sin in the woman; Jesus, dominated by a human graciousness towards others, perceives the sin but does not allow it to affect his perception of the woman as a human being in need of loving acceptance. This analysis both illustrates and confirms J. Piaget's conclusion about any observer that 'what he perceives is always related to his perspective'.[27]

This brief excursion into the theory of perception has been necessary in part because, except for a limited number of books concerned with the philosophy of religion,[28] it is a subject which is not commonly discussed in theological treatises. It is also necessary because it has a direct bearing upon my main concern, viz. the encounter with the holy, and in the concluding paragraphs of this chapter I must indicate how this is so.

As a consequence of his exit from the sacral universe man has changed his concepts. But he has also changed something else; he has altered his whole conceptual framework. The result is that the concept of the holy formulated in past centuries has no longer any meaning within the new matrix of the hominized universe. As Dretske says, if we alter our background belief 'the world stays the same, but what we see of it is changed'.[29] Because of the relationship of concept and perception, analysed above, until such time as the understanding of the holy is changed to correspond with this new framework – if that is possible – man's perception of the holy must progressively decline. As he becomes more and more at home in his new world and as his thinking is progressively integrated with the discarding of disparate and outmoded categories, the encounter with the holy, if it is still presented as the numinous, will no longer fall within the field of his experience. The encounter with the holy as the numinous will only be possible for that dwindling number of the human race whose thought-world remains that of bygone days. In other words, since our perception is governed by selective codes that lend coherence to our vision, they can at the same time restrict its scope. Our thought-patterns affect our perception, and so they can raise an obstacle in the way of our seeing something outside the pattern.[30]

In this situation the task of the theologian is clear. He has to present a new understanding of the holy that is consistent with the new framework. In making this attempt, he has to be on his guard against indulging in mere projection and he has to show the relevance of what he says to concrete situations. Moreover, he has to put forward a model of a mental set or provide a convincing proto-knowledge that will render possible the recognition of the holy. The reverse of this positive approach was castigated long ago by William Blake. He was quite ready to admit that 'the true method of knowledge is experiment',[31] but he insisted that everything depends upon the mental attitude of the experimenter. If, for example, you begin with doubt you will end only with doubt. Blake emphasized this with keen irony when he suggested what should happen if an object assumed the point of view of a doubting subject:

> He who Doubts from what he sees
> Will ne'er Believe, do what you Please.
> If the Sun & Moon should doubt,
> They'd immediately Go out.[32]

Perception, for Blake, is a mental act; consequently he declared:

> This Life's dim Windows of the Soul
> Distorts the Heavens from Pole to Pole
> And leads you to Believe a Lie
> When you see with, not thro', the Eye.[33]

When you see, or perceive, through the eye, then it becomes possible for you to enlarge your vision. 'If the doors of perception were cleansed, everything would appear to man as it is, infinite.'[34]

Following this line of thought, my next task, to which I turn in the following chapter, is clear, viz. to delineate a proto-understanding of the holy. Only when this has been done will it be possible to go on to describe the incidents, etc., in and through which the holy may be recognized within the conceptual framework required by the secular or hominized universe.

However, there is one further matter requiring brief consideration before we pass on. It is conceivable that an objection from the side of a certain orthodoxy may be brought against what I have just written. It could be contended that my approach necessarily involves the view that it is man who finds the holy rather than that the holy finds man. So Ignazio Silone, in an essay about his novel *Bread and Wine*, asserts that his hero Spina is not seeking God; rather, God is pursuing him, after the manner of Francis Thompson's 'Hound of Heaven'.[35] This is in accordance with one strand of biblical teaching which presents the encounter with the holy as a divine self-disclosure. So, what is all this talk about a mental set to assist man to perceive the holy? Yet there is another strand in both the Old and New Testaments which shows that the finding and disclosure can be two aspects of the same event. Elijah makes his long and exhausting journey to the desert of Sinai to meet Yahweh and there Yahweh reveals himself to him. Here the disclosure cannot be separated from the search. Again, not only does Jesus call men to him but men seek him out.[36] Therefore to delineate a model of the holy and to suggest ways in which the holy may be perceived does not deny that the ensuing encounter is an act of revelation. The two aspects of the experience cannot be divided. Any meeting is at the same time a recognition and a disclosure. At the very moment when I meet the holy, the holy meets me.

3

The Model of the Holy

My immediate task, as defined at the end of the last chapter, is to describe a model of the holy which is consistent with the new frame of reference provided by the hominized universe and which will enable us to perceive and so to encounter the holy within that universe. In other words, I have to delineate a model which may function as a referent and so create a mental set or proto-understanding to assist perception. But where is such a model to be found? It is *a priori* likely that the religious literature of the world will not provide such a model, for it was produced from within the sacral universe. Indeed even a cursory reading, by one who is neither an Islamist nor an expert in Hinduism, of either the *Koran* or the *Upanishads* indicates that in general the concept of the numinous dominates these texts. Nevertheless as a Christian theologian I naturally turn to the Bible, although I do so in the knowledge that this, too, may prove of no assistance. Indeed such an examination can result either in the recognition that any model or models to be derived from the scriptures are irrelevant to the modern world or, which would be rather surprising, in the demonstration that a viable model can be discovered. Only in the latter case, if the Bible does provide a model consistent with the frame of the secular universe, can it be said that we have found what we require.

To approach the Bible in this way has the advantage that, since it consists of both Old and New Testaments, we shall be considering two religions – the Hebrew and the Christian. Nevertheless, it will be necessary to be on one's guard constantly against the risk of reading in rather than out the proto-understanding of which we are in search. Since this is not a work of apologetics, further justification for beginning with the Bible in this way is not necessary, and the reader will judge for himself how far the exegesis is accurate and how far the model adduced serves the purpose for which it is intended. This is to say that the validity of a model derived from the Bible will rest, not upon an appeal to authority, but upon a demonstration of what I. T. Ramsey has called its 'empirical fit'. By this he means that its validity depends upon the extent to which it is able to match a wide range of phenomena and upon its overall success in meeting a variety of needs.[1]

The Old Testament Model

The Old Testament, being not a book but a library to which many different writers have contributed over many centuries, does not present an understanding of the holy entirely free from contradiction. Nevertheless the several authors are at one in conceiving the holy to be synonymous with the divine. The holy is the essentially divine; it is that which is distinctive of God, that which constitutes his nature.[2] To declare that God is holy is not, in the first instance, to assert anything about his character but to affirm his supreme Godhead. As an epithet, therefore, 'holy' stresses the uniqueness of Yahweh, who is not to be confused with the deities worshipped by other nations – 'There is none holy like the Lord.'[3] Holiness refers to the inner essence of the divine being. So the statement that 'the Lord God has sworn by his holiness' means exactly the same as 'the Lord God has sworn by himself'.[4] Holiness is not, then, an attribute of God; it is not one divine quality among others; rather, it expresses what is characteristic of God and corresponds to his deity.[5]

Frequently Yahweh is defined as the holy one, the term holy being synonymous with the divine;[6] in other instances the terms God and holy are put in parallel.[7] So holiness and deity are identical, and to say that God is holy is not to describe him but to emphasize that he is the one he is.

It follows from this that 'holy' and 'holiness' can only be applied to persons or objects in a derivative sense. Since God alone is holy, nothing and no one can be holy in themselves; they are only holy when placed in relation to the divine being.[8] Holy and holiness in this connection do not denote a quality but a relationship or, in other words, people and objects will only be called holy or have holiness ascribed to them in virtue of their relation to the divine. This can be illuminated by the analogy of 'a healthy seaside resort'. Obviously such a place is not healthy in itself, nor is healthiness a quality which can be ascribed to it. We can only use the phrase with any meaning if it relates to the people who go there. Healthy can be applied to a place when it refers to a relation between the place and the health of those who stay or live there. Similarly, holy can be applied to a place when it refers to a relation between that place and God.[9] The holy man is thus the God-related man, and holy objects or events are similarly those that are related to the divine.

Negatively, then, the word holy expresses the difference between God and man: 'I am God and not man, the Holy One in your midst.'[10] So the first effect of holiness is to keep man at a distance.[11] The holy is therefore that which is separate[12] and it is also that which induces awe and dread. Abraham, pleading with the Lord for the righteous remnant in Sodom, is aware that he is 'but dust and ashes'.[13] Jacob, waking from his dream of the ladder, declares: 'Surely the Lord is in this place; and I did not know it.' And he is afraid, and says, 'How awesome is this place!'[14] Moses at the burning bush hides his face, 'for he was afraid to look at God'.[15] Isaiah, as he hears the 'holy, holy, holy' of the seraphim, cries out: 'Woe is me! For I am lost!'[16] He declares: 'The Lord of hosts, him you shall regard as holy; let him be your fear, and let him be your dread.'[17] According to the Psalmist: 'Holy and terrible is his name!'[18]

The inevitable outcome of this note of separation and terror is that the holy is also regarded as separate from ordinary living. 'Holiness,' summarizes Pedersen, 'is not consistent with the claims of everyday life; normal souls are given it for a time after which they again discard it.'[19] So a dividing line is drawn between the holy and the common, and the Lord informs Aaron: 'You are to distinguish between the holy and the common, and between the unclean and the clean.'[20] In similar vein the temple area is measured out in Ezekiel's vision so as to 'make a separation between the holy and the common'.[21]

The opposite of the holy is thus the unclean, and here other aspects of our subject come to the fore. In the Old Testament holiness includes the idea of wholeness or completeness. This may refer to completeness in a social context, so that those who have not fulfilled some project they have undertaken, such as building a house or planting a vineyard, are disqualified from the sacred activity of warfare.[22] Holiness is further related to the idea of conformity to the class to which one belongs. So incest and adultery are against holiness in the sense of right order.[23] Theft and lying are wrong, not because they conflict with a moral law, but because they are contrary to holiness. Holiness in this connection has also a physical aspect, and hence the sacrificial victims prescribed in Leviticus have to be unblemished. Certain animals are classified as unclean, because they are either dissimilar from the Hebrew's own livestock and therefore outside the established order[24] or are in themselves 'disordered', e.g. mice which use 'hands' for walking and insects that crawl, as distinct from the locust that hops.[25]

In the light of this it is comprehensible why the holiness, i.e. the divinity, of God is so little associated with morality or ethics. H. Ringgren can indeed conclude that 'the ethical aspect of holiness plays a very subordinate part in prophetic preaching.'[26] Ethical ideas are seldom actually combined with the word 'holy', with the possible exception of Leviticus 19.2b: 'You shall be holy; for I the Lord your God am holy.' It is the idea of God in general, rather than holiness in particular, that gradually becomes more ethical.

If the unclean is the opposite of the holy, not so much on ethical grounds but, as indicated above, because it is a falling short of wholeness, there is some ambiguity and indeed contradiction about the identification of the common and the profane. The profane is equivalent to that which is normal, that which belongs to everyday life. In itself it need not be antagonistic to the holy.[27] Nevertheless there is a tendency to accept a developed series of contrasts. This begins with the antithesis between the holy and the unclean, then between the holy and the profane or common. So there is an inclination, more pronounced in some Old Testament books than in others, to regard the everyday as common, profane and unclean, and entirely apart from the holy. As these contrasts developed, there was a movement of thought and practice towards making holiness subject to certain well-defined limitations. The holy was centred in the temple at Jerusalem and protected within the central shrine, the holy of holies, and it was regarded as operating in less and less intensified forms as one withdrew further and further from the temple.[28] Holiness then became bound up, almost exclusively, with the cult, which was regarded as the normal way of achieving contact with the holy or divine. The result of this was the elaboration of religious institutions and the sheltering of the people, through myth and ritual, from that historical and moral reality where, according to many of the prophets, God is to be encountered.[29]

This schematic presentation of the Old Testament understanding of the holy has unavoidably obscured two points. First, that there was a development, and second, that there were features which are scarcely reconcilable with the account already given.

The development aspect need not concern us for long; all that is important to notice is contained in this brief summary by E. Jacob:

> There reappears the character of tabu which had been supplanted by that of relationship, and the distinction between the sacred world and the secular world is found among all those in Judaism who are the heirs of the thought of Ezekiel. Within the sphere of the sacred itself there are various degrees of holiness, there is a distinction between what is holy and what is very holy, which would possess no meaning when holiness was regarded solely as a relationship. . . In addition, the materialization of holiness led to its being regarded less as an attribute than as a state.[30]

The aspects of Old Testament teaching which conflict with the general picture are three in number. First, in opposition to the frequent emphasis upon the awesomeness of the holy and its unapproachability, there are some passages which speak of the nearness of the divine to man. 'What great nation is there that has a god so near to it as the Lord our God is to us, whenever we call upon him?'[31] Second, it has been stated previously that holiness is the innermost essence of God. Here we have to note that this essence is identified by Hosea with love. In 11.8f., Yahweh agonizes over the prospect of having to condemn and destroy Israel and concludes that he will not do this.

> My heart recoils within me,
>   my compassion grows warm and tender.
> I will not execute my fierce anger,
>   I will not again destroy Ephraim:
> for I am God and not man,
>   the Holy One in your midst,
>   and I will not come to destroy.

It is therefore the incomprehensible creative power of love that marks Yawheh as holy. So when God says: 'I will love them no more,'[32] this is tantamount to God ceasing to be God.

The third and final feature to be noticed is expressed in two forward-looking passages, which have an eschatological character. The first is Numbers 14.21, where Yahweh says to Moses that the day is coming when 'all the earth shall be filled with the glory of the Lord'. So the existing limitation of Yahweh's holiness to a special cultic sphere is regarded as something temporary, that is to be followed by an ultimate universalizing of it. The second passage is Zechariah 14.20f., which affirms that household pots and even the bells on the horses' harnesses are to become as holy as the vessels in the temple. 'This means,' comments von Rad, 'that then the whole realm of the secular will be taken up into Yahweh's holiness.'[33]

While noting these aspects for completeness and because they will concern us later, we must now look at the Old Testament understanding of the holy as previously described and face the question as to whether or not it provides a model consistent with the frame of the secular universe.

The first thing to note is that Rudolf Otto had no difficulty whatsoever in finding his concept of the numinous in the Old Testament,[34] and there is no reason to doubt his accuracy. Both von Rad and Eichrodt [35] have no hesitation in affirming that the Old Testament holy is the 'wholly other', thus agreeing with and endorsing, from their own academic expertise, the findings of Otto. The Holy One of Israel is the awesome *mysterium tremendum* who brings terror and dread but is also *fascinans*. If to this be added the characteristic of separation between the holy and man and between the holy and the common, the progressive virtual identification of common, profane and unclean, and the limitation of the holy to the cult, we have a model which in no way corresponds to the matrix of the secular universe. It fits fair and square into the centre of the sacral universe, and so can be of little assistance at the present day.[36]*

This conclusion does not mean that this exercise has been fruitless. Quite apart from the three disparate aspects, consideration of which has been postponed, there are certain insights which may be of help and do not necessarily conflict with the secular universe frame. There is the identification of the holy with the divine and there is the interpretation of holiness as involving a relationship. Moreover a clear grasp of the Old Testament model enables us to perceive it when it is reproduced again and again in the writings of the Fathers and their successors, from the middle of the fourth century onwards, and by their remote heirs at the present day. In particular we have to remember that as we move on to the New Testament model this exposition of the Old Testament background is an indispensable preliminary to understanding what the apostles and their associates have to say on this very subject.

The New Testament Model

In seeking to discover a model of the holy in the New Testament, a simple beginning may be made by an examination of the frequency with which the term is used in relation to particular subjects. Holy or *hagios* is employed some two hundred and twenty-seven times. On ninety-three occasions it is joined to the word *pneuma* in the title 'Holy Spirit'. In eight or nine instances, depending upon one's interpretation, it is applied to Christ and in only seven or eight to God. Sixty-one times, where the English versions usually translate it as 'saints', it denotes Christians. This leaves only some fifty-seven other examples. This distribution immediately suggests three questions: Why is holy so repeatedly conjoined with Spirit? What does the term mean as applied to Christ? Why is it used so seldom with reference to God?

The answer to the first question is relatively simple and it also provides us with a preliminary understanding of the term. The word 'spirit' unqualified is obviously ambiguous. It may refer to the spirit of man;[37] it may represent one of the spiritual forces believed to be in rebellion against God, and hence the need for the gift of 'discernings of spirits'[38] in order to distinguish spurious from genuine prophecy. It may be used of angels[39] and also of unclean spirits.[40] To qualify the Spirit of God as holy was therefore to distinguish him from all other spirits with whom Gentile Christians were in danger not of confusing but of comparing him. Hence, while in itself the adjective adds nothing to the noun, its conjunction with Spirit emphasizes the Spirit's divine origin and authority.[41] Consequently, the holy, as in the Old Testament, is here synonymous with the divine.

If we next examine the few instances in which it is applied to Christ, we find that it is used with the same meaning. In the Lucan infancy narrative, Jesus is designated as holy because of his divine origin through the operation of the Holy Spirit.[42] In the Marcan account of the ministry, he is recognized as 'the Holy One of God' by the unclean spirits.[43] This implies more than that he is the popular Messiah; rather, he is the divine envoy who is to destroy the forces of evil. In John, Jesus is similarly called 'the Holy One of God',[44] and this is equivalent to saying that he is the Son of God, in the sense of ascribing deity to him. Likewise in Revelation, Christ as 'the holy and the true' has the same predicates as God himself.[45]

God, too, is hymned by the four living creatures in the book of Revelation as holy.[46] He is referred to by Jesus, according to the Fourth Gospel, as 'holy Father',[47] while in I Peter 1.15 we read: 'he who called you is holy'. This sparsity of references to the holiness of God is not to be explained on the grounds that the entire Old Testament understanding of the holy is presupposed, but by the recognition that the New Testament writers, as P. Bonnard expresses it, 'are interested in the holiness of God only in so far as that holiness has just been revealed in the person of Jesus'.[48] In other words, if you ask what is the New Testament perception of the holy, the answer is not given by its authors in a series of concepts; it is given by the telling of a story, the story of Jesus. To them the holy is not an idea but a personal reality external to their consciousnesses, whom they have encountered.

For the apostles and their associates, the model of the holy is provided, not by the Old Testament, but by the figure of a man – Jesus of Nazareth, who was the contemporary of most of them. Indeed one of them can say: 'That which was from the beginning, which we have heard, which we have seen with our eyes, which we have looked upon and touched with our hands, concerning the word of life – the life was made manifest, and we saw it, and testify to it.'[49] Hence whatever the New Testament tells us about the holy, 'it does so in the human terms provided by the human figure of Jesus Christ'.[50] To take Christ as the model, therefore, does not mean that we have to 'translate' the holy into human terms; this has already been done. As Paul says to the Colossians, Christ is 'the portrait' of the invisible God.[51] This immediately calls in question – and indeed involves the rejection of – certain Old Testament ideas.

According to the Old Testament, as we have seen, to speak of the holy is to affirm a separation between the divine and the human; it is to declare a distance between the two. The New Testament knows of no such gulf. The man Jesus is designated as Emmanuel, i.e. God with us,[52] which is not primarily a name but a description of his person and work; it refers not so much to the idea of the divine presence as such but to his activity in and through Jesus. Similarly,

Paul on the Areopagus can say: 'he is not far from each one of us,'[53] while the reaction of the crowds to Jesus is to proclaim that 'God has visited his people'.[54] The holy is no longer the unapproachable but that which has drawn near. He is no longer a stranger, separate from man, but accessible in the midst of human life, for the aloofness of the holy has given place to the nearness of Jesus, with whom the Old Testament concept of the holy passes away. Indeed to recognize Jesus as the Holy One and then to interpret this, because of the Old Testament pre-understanding, in the sense of separateness is to make nonsense of the whole of his story. 'The holy God ceased to be shrouded in awesome mystery and could now be loved through the intermediacy of Jesus.'[55] Trust replaces obeisance; adoration becomes communion; the Father replaces the God of the Burning Bush, and while there is a sense of wonder and an ecstasy of self-surrender to the divine beneficence, there is no longer shuddering awe before the *mysterium tremendum*. The story of Jesus renders impossible the identification of the New Testament model of the holy with the 'wholly other'.

Nevertheless there are some New Testament passages which have been interpreted as evidence for a continuation of the concept of the numinous. In the main these are those that refer to people's fear in the presence of Jesus, and there is also one incident which appears to represent Jesus' own fear before his Father.

Before examining these in a little detail, there is one general consideration to be borne in mind. The nature of the holy as it may be perceived in the gospels is not to be defined simply by considering reactions to Jesus. *A fortiori* it is conceivable that these reactions were conditioned by the mental set of those who met him. Their pre-understanding, especially as Jews, would inevitably involve the model of the holy to be discerned in the Old Testament. So to encounter Jesus in the belief that in him the holy was active would necessarily have included an interpretation in terms of the numinous. One passage will suffice as a possible illustration of this, viz. Mark 16.8. In the preceding seven verses the evangelist recounts the visit of the women to the tomb, their discovery that the stone enclosing it has been rolled back and their encounter with a young man who tells them that Jesus has risen. The narrative then continues: 'They went out and fled from the tomb; for trembling and astonishment had come upon them; and they said nothing to any one, for they were afraid.' The interpretation of this verse depends upon whether or not it was intended to be the conclusion of the gospel – it being recalled that neither the so-called 'longer ending' (vv. 9–20 in the RSV notes) nor the 'shorter ending' (added after v. 8 in the RSV notes) is part of the original text. If verse 8 were not the end of the gospel, then the fear and trembling would not be greatly emphasized and presumably the missing conclusion explained how they were overcome. If, however, Mark did deliberately finish with v. 8 then, following D. E. Nineham, one would have to understand the statement to the effect that 'the women's profound emotion is described in order to bring out the overwhelming and sheerly supernatural character of that to which it was the response ... and perhaps to suggest to the reader that if he has even begun to understand the full significance of what had occurred, he too will be bound to respond with amazement and godly fear'.[56] In this latter case, I would suggest that we have an example of an interpretation of an unusual event in terms of the numinous, such an understanding being determined by the mental set. The reaction, however, could well have been a mistaken one, and indeed, as we shall see, such seems to have been the view of Jesus himself who, time and again, sets out to correct the outlook of his followers which was conditioned by a pre-understanding in terms of the numinous.

In the account of the miraculous draught of fishes, we read how Peter falls down at Jesus' knees, saying, 'Depart from me, for I am a sinful man, O Lord.'[57] His experience was therefore structured similarly to that of Isaiah in the temple, overcome by the awesome majesty of the holy and conscious of his own unworthiness to be in such a presence. But Jesus does not depart and instead admonishes Peter with the words: 'Do not be afraid.' This is a frequent feature of the gospel records: as often as fear is mentioned, so often does Jesus assure his followers that this is misplaced. When he stills the storm, he asks: 'Why are you afraid? Have you no faith?'[58] He comforts his disciples, terrified at seeing him walk on the water and believing that he is a ghost, with the words: 'Take heart, it is I; have no fear.'[59] Again, according to the Lucan resurrection narrative, the disciples are startled and frightened, believing the risen Jesus to be a spirit. 'And he said to them, "Why are you troubled?"'[60] In every case the grounds for fears are not unreasonable, but in every case the disciples are gently taught that this is a wrong reaction. Indeed, in what may be termed the appendix of the Fourth Gospel we are presented with a pattern of behaviour significantly different from that which had previously characterized the disciples. Whereas, as we have just seen, Peter was overawed by the first miraculous draught of fish and asked Jesus to go away from him, in John 21, which records a second superabundant catch, Peter is so eager to join Jesus that he does not wait for the boat to reach the shore, but jumps into the water. No longer is there fear – though there is a certain respect and reserve – but an earnest desire to be with the Lord.

This constant affirmation not to fear cannot be explained as a re-production of an Old Testament convention. It is true that there are some passages[61] where God or his messenger tells those addressed not to fear, but these are too few in number to support the views either that they represent a regular Old Testament feature or that the gospel writers have been influenced by them.

The accounts of the Transfiguration, which itself is often adduced as an experience of the numinous, are more complex. In the first place, while fear is ascribed to the three apostles by each of the synoptic writers, they each disagree as to its cause and occasion. According to Mark, they are afraid at the appearance of Moses and Elijah;[62] according to Luke, fear only wells up when the cloud overshadows them,[63] while in Matthew they become scared when they hear the heavenly voice.[64] In none of the accounts, therefore, is the disciples' fear directly and immediately concerned with the transfiguration of Jesus himself. Moreover, all the accounts are agreed in ascribing to Peter the words: 'It is well that we are here.' Fearful or not, Peter is glad of the opportunity to be a witness. Finally in Matthew, Jesus is recorded as saying: 'Rise, and have no fear.' It is difficult to maintain in the light of this evidence that the Transfiguration itself is a revelation of the numinous which induces dread. Undoubtedly this can be read into it, and has been read into it, but I cannot myself read out of it 'awe . . . before the shuddering secret of the numen',[65] for that is to go beyond the evidence.

The Agony in the Garden is an incident of which I have previously made an analysis,[66] but since it is closely related to this stage of our discussion, I must reproduce the main features here. Rudolf Otto makes much of this event but, in my view, this is another example of his finding what he wants to find. It is true that, according to Mark, Jesus 'began to be greatly distressed and troubled',[67] and the Greek words used in this passage may suggest shuddering awe, but this must be taken to refer to an intense degree of horror and suffering at the prospect of the torture and death that lie before him.[68] In this connection it is helpful to appreciate the difference between the death of Socrates and the death of Jesus.

Socrates died without any fear. His belief in the immortality of the soul made death nothing but a door through which the magnificent soul could leave the prison of our body. But Jesus did not know about the immortality of his soul. He knew that death is the last enemy of man and also the great enemy of God. He is the annihilator, the one who throws us into nothingness, into the pit of ultimate loneliness. Therefore the Gospels, in the unbearable story of the Garden, tell us that Jesus was in anguish of spirit, his sweat falling to the ground like drops of blood, his heart breaking with grief. Jesus knew, as we do, that death is the end.[69]

So the incident depicts a natural human experience in the face of man's inhumanity to man and at the prospect of death; there is no need whatsoever to interpret it as an experience of the *mysterium tremendum*. Moreover, there is one feature of the account that suggests the exact opposite of Otto's exegesis. Jesus is represented as addressing God not in the formal and ceremonial phrases regularly adopted in Jewish prayers, but as *'abbā*, which is the more familiar term used by children to address a human father. Such amazing familiarity is the very antithesis of shuddering dread before the numinous.

I would, however, be less than honest about the New Testament evidence as a whole were I not to draw attention to two other passages: one in the book of Revelation and the other in the epistle to the Hebrews.

In Revelation 4 the seer describes his vision of heaven. The scene is one of worship. Dominating it all is the Lord God Almightly upon his throne, from which 'issue flashes of lightening, and voices and peals of thunder'. Round the royal seat are four living creatures who sing: 'holy, holy, holy'.

And whenever the living creatures give glory and honour and thanks to him who is seated on the throne, who lives for ever and ever, the twenty-four elders fall down before him who is seated on the throne and worship him who lives for ever and ever; they cast their crowns before the throne, singing,

> 'Worthy art thou, our Lord and God,
> to receive the glory and honour and power,

for thou didst create all things,
and by thy will they exist and were created.'

It is difficult not to see in this description an evocation of the
numinous. What has to be recognized is that the whole passage is a
mosaic of Old Testament quotations and allusions. The lightning
and thunder recall the theophany on Mount Sinai;[70] the four creatures are those in the apocalytic vision of Ezekiel 1; the song repro-
duces that of the seraphim in Isaiah 6, the second half of which
supplies the substance of the elders' response. So far, then, from
the author transforming his images in the light of the advent of
Christ, in this passage he has merely reproduced those that existed
previously. Adoration – the falling down of the elders – has certainly
not been replaced by communion. In other words, this passage is
pure Old Testament and, as such, it does suggest the numinous,
and as such, if I may use the phrase, it has not been Christianized.
Apart from the verses from Hebrews, to be considered next, it stands
out like a sore thumb in contrast to the whole New Testament
understanding of the holy.

In Hebrews 12 recourse is had to the same theophany on Mount
Sinai. The passage reads:

For you have not come to what may be touched, a blazing fire, and
darkness, and gloom, and a tempest, and the sound of a trumpet, and a
voice whose words made the hearers entreat that no further messages
be spoken to them. For they could not endure the order that was given,
'If even a beast touches the mountain, it shall be stoned.' Indeed, so
terrifying was the sight that Moses said, 'I tremble with fear.' But you
have come to Mount Zion and to the city of the living God, the
heavenly Jerusalem, and to innumerable angels in festal gathering, and
to the assembly of the first-born who are enrolled in heaven, and to a
judge who is God of all, and to the spirits of just men made perfect, and
to Jesus, the mediator of a new covenant, and to the sprinkled blood
that speaks more graciously than the blood of Abel. See that you do not
refuse him who is speaking. For if they did not escape when they refused him who warned them on earth, much less shall we escape if we
reject him who warns from heaven. His voice then shook the earth; but
now he has promised, 'Yet once more will I shake not only the earth
but also the heaven.' This phrase, 'Yet once more', indicates the removal
of what is shaken, as of what has been made, in order that what cannot
be shaken may remain. Therefore let us be grateful for receiving a
kingdom that cannot be shaken, and thus let us offer to God acceptable
worship, with reverence and awe; for our God is a consuming fire.

Here again, whatever one's mental set, I do not see how one can avoid reading this as an evocation of the numinous, and commentators on this epistle are at one in saying that both the scene on Mount Sinai and the heavenly Jerusalem are charged with the presence of the *mysterium tremendum*.[71] It is true that the author is drawing a contrast between the old and new covenants, but this is in terms of the shadow to the reality, of the inferiority of Moses to the superiority of Jesus, and the numinous aspect is ascribed to both. But at what cost is this ascription made? It is made at the cost of completely ignoring the holy as love. So Hugh Montefiore observes that there is nothing throughout this whole section about 'the intimacy of love nor the tenderness of human affection. God is conceived as transcendent and austere. . . Our author's final word to his readers here is not about the attraction of divine love but about the fearfulness of holy wrath.'[72] The writer is indeed affirming the numinous at the expense of the gospel of love. His last sentence is very revealing: 'Our God is a consuming fire.' I know of no better, and at the same time of no more pithy comment on this than the words that William Blake once wrote on the reverse of one of his paintings: 'God out of Christ is a consuming fire.' With this aphorism Blake demonstrates the extent to which, in the passage under review, the author of Hebrews is reproducing a pre-Christian model of the holy.

This brief examination of these two passages leads to five conclusions. First, they do evoke the numinous. Second, they do so because they do not go beyond the Old Testament, which they largely reproduce. Third, they must be regarded as a left-over or throwback to that which, from the standpoint of other New Testament writers, belongs to a bygone era. Fourth, they conflict, therefore, with the general New Testament understanding of the holy. Finally, they must be considered insufficient in themselves to provide an acceptable alternative and are inadequate evidence to support the thesis that shuddering dread before the numinous is an essential part of the New Testament conception of the holy. Like the three disparate elements we found in the Old Testament, these constitute a disparate element within the New.

There are, however, some New Testament passages which refer to 'fear' as an attitude appropriate to Christians. Paul speaks of 'knowing the fear of the Lord'.[73] He exhorts the Philippians to 'work out your own salvation with fear and trembling'.[74] This fear, however, is not a response to the encounter with the holy; rather, it is a correlative of faith. It is to be understood in relation to that self-sufficiency which makes man look to himself instead of to the holy. Fear, in this context, is the knowledge of man's powerlessness and his dependence upon God's grace. Without this fear, faith itself can provide a false security, therefore: 'Do not become proud, but stand in awe.'[75]

Fear in the sense of dread before the numinous is widely ruled out by the New Testament writers. According to Paul, 'You did not receive the spirit of slavery to fall back into fear, but you have received the spirit of sonship.'[76] Hence, as the author of I John makes clear, 'There is no fear in love, but perfect love casts out fear.'[77] The ideas and sequence of thought are obvious, but they are so important for the argument that they must be spelled out in full.

In effect, what Paul is saying is that through the action of Jesus man's relation to the holy has been transformed. Prior to his advent that relationship was analogous to the association of a master and slave, with fear as the predominant and appropriate attitude of the latter. Now, however, the analogy has been changed to become that of a father and son, with mutual love as the dominating factor in their intercourse. Within this bond of love, there is no place for fear, in the sense of dread or terror. So holiness, which is the innermost essence of God, is now identified, as it was by Hosea himself, with love: 'God is love, and he who abides in love abides in God, and God abides in him.'[78] This love is exercised and known in identification and self-giving, and so Jesus can be described as the one who 'gave himself for us'.[79] But identification and self-giving are the antitheses of apartness which, in the Old Testament, is a necessary aspect of holiness. Moreover, this self-giving is interpreted in terms of service: 'I am among you as one who serves.'[80] So with the coming of Jesus there is a smashing of images. Previously God had been conceived as king and therefore envisaged as an Eastern potentate, majestic, fearsome and terrible. This imagery is entirely done away with through Jesus, whose key category is 'Father'. With this new minting of the imagery of deity, holiness, too, which is its synonym, is radically transformed. The Holy One is the servant; holiness is love in active service of others. So the law of love profoundly modifies the Old Testament law of the holy,[81] and the New Testament model is correspondingly very different from that of the Old Testament one in general.

This contrast is especially evident when we consider the relationship of the sacred and the profane. In the Old Testament there is a certain dichotomy between the two, but the New Testament consistently affirms that this has been overcome through Christ. Indeed the 'profane' is a category which is foreign to New Testament thought and is ultimately meaningless for Christians. There is Paul's unambiguous statement that 'I know and am persuaded in the Lord Jesus that nothing is unclean (*lit.* common) in itself; but it is unclean for any one who thinks it unclean'.[82] This text alone disposes of the sacred/profane polarity, as well as showing Paul's own appreciation of the extent to which a mental set affects perception, but it is by no means an isolated statement. According to Luke, Jesus said, 'Everything is clean for you,'[83] and Mark records a conversation with his disciples to the same effect and makes the editorial comment: 'Thus he declared all foods clean.'[84] The same thesis is endorsed by Peter's vision at Joppa, when in answer to his protest that 'I have never eaten anything that is common or unclean', he is told: 'What God has cleansed, you must not call common.'[85] Peter rightly concludes that this is not just a question of food, 'but God has shown me that I should not call any man common or unclean.'[86] Indeed every aspect of life can now be taken up into holiness. There is an attack upon the observance of special 'holy' days[87] and upon submission to regulations such as 'Do not handle, Do not taste, Do not touch'.[88] This act of cleansing has been effected once and for all through Jesus who 'made purification (*lit.* cleansing)'.[89] He it was who 'gave himself for us, that he might . . . purify (*lit.* cleanse) unto himself a people for his own possession'.[90] The division between the holy and the profane has thus been brought to an end, for the holy has come down to the level of the profane so that what is common may be elevated to the level of the holy.

The very etymology of the word profane demonstrates that it is an unacceptable category for Christians to use. Profane derives from the Latin *pro fano*, i.e. before or outside the temple. But according to Paul: 'We are the temple of the living God.'[91] The Greek word translated temple is *naos*, i.e. the sanctuary or holy of holies. To Paul this shrine is not an isolated and insulated space; it is the community living in the world. Any idea of profane, therefore, as the sum total of common life outside the sphere of the holy, is foreign to his thought. In this particular the New Testament understanding of the holy embraces one of the isolated aspects of the

Old Testament teaching and proclaims its fulfilment, viz. the prophecy of Zechariah, considered above, which looks forward to the day when the whole realm of the secular will be taken up into holiness.[92] Nor, to refer to another of the Old Testament disparate notes,[93] can holiness any longer be limited to the cultic sphere; it has been universalized and at the same time worship has been desacralized.

One important consequence follows from this rejection of the category of the profane; it means that recourse to the phenomenologists of religion to discover a viable model of the holy is fruitless. Mircea Eliade speaks for all when he states: 'Religious experience presupposes a bipartition of the world into the *sacred* and the *profane*.'[94] To refuse to follow him is not to call in question the accuracy of his observation. Undoubtedly his perceptive interpretation of religion and religions reveals the wide extent to which the sacred/profane division is basic. Without question, too, this dichotomy became part of Christianity from at least the fourth century onwards. I would agree, therefore, with Martin Buber when he says:

This separation has formed part of the foundation of every religion. Everywhere the sacred is removed and set apart from the fulness of the things, properties, and actions belonging to the universal, and the sacred now forms in its totality a self-contained holiness outside of which the diffused profane must pitch its tents. The consequence of this separation in the history of man is a twofold one. Religion is thereby assured a firm province whose untouchableness is ever again guaranteed it by the representatives of the state and of society, not, for the most part, without compensation. But at the same time the adherents of religion are thereby enabled to allow the essential application of their relation of faith to fulfill itself within this province alone without the sacred being given a corresponding power in the rest of life, and particularly in its public sphere.[95]

My one point of disagreement arises from the fact that I cannot find this separation in the New Testament, and in so far as that work is authoritative for Christianity *its* foundations cannot be said to have this division as a necessary part. Indeed, I would endorse the statement of Teilhard de Chardin, that 'by virtue of the Creation and, still more, of the Incarnation, *nothing* here below is profane for those who know how to see it'.[96]

The conclusions to be drawn from this discussion of the sacred/profane question, in the light of the previous rejection of the numinous, are four in number. First, although, according to the phenomenologists of religion, the sacred and the profane are opposites, so that the holy is always to be defined negatively as the non-profane, the New Testament requires us to acknowledge that the common is no longer unclean nor profane, in the sense of having no relation to God or being outside his concern, and it may be both the sphere and vehicle of the holy. The second conclusion follows from this, viz. that contemporary studies which begin from phenomenology are unlikely to give us much help in our task – but more of this below.[97] The third conclusion is that, since according to the phenomenological approach holy and profane are to be interpreted in terms of each other, the profane being the not-holy, then we can give the latter some content by observing religious practices and so affirming that everyday life, including sexual relations, etc., is outside the sphere of the holy, which is thus narrowed down. But once the negative approach is rejected, it becomes possible to seek a positive content for the holy and to investigate the relation of the holy to everyday life. But since the New Testament has little place for the numinous, R. Otto's attempt to provide a positive content is not acceptable. Finally, I conclude that, in seeking a viable model of the holy, we should not start from phenomenology, and I endorse the views of A.-M. Roguet that one should not take one's departure from R. Otto, M. Eliade or R. Caillios,[98] and that just as in seeking to define Christian priesthood one must begin with the priesthood of Christ and not from priesthood in general, so holiness must be understood in relation to him and not in terms of a general concept.

However, before continuing an examination of Christ as the model, some attention must be given to the New Testament understanding of holy and holiness as applied to other individuals. In the Old Testament we have seen that this is possible only in a derivative sense and that the terms are best understood to mean 'God-related' and 'God-relatedness'. Is this so in the New Testament? The answer involves surveying a number of passages in which are to be found not only 'holy' and 'holiness', but also 'to sanctify' and 'sanctification'. In English the close connection of these is obscured; in Greek they all derive from the same root which can only be represented by saying, for example, that 'to sanctify' is the same as 'to holify'.

To sanctify is to consecrate or devote someone to a holy being in order to fulfill his purpose or purposes. It is to designate someone to carry out a particular task. Hence to say that God has sanctified his people is to declare that they have been elected by him, and so one may speak of the church as a holy people in the sense that they are God's chosen agents. To be holy is to be claimed by God for himself. Holiness then does mean, as in the Old Testament, God-relatedness, but with a specific end in view. It is therefore not something acquired but bestowed. To accept this vocation is also to acknowledge an obligation to active holiness;[99] those who respond have a responsibility for 'holy conduct'.[100] This demand for sanctification can be understood in either of two ways.

First, it may be understood in a negative sense to involve asceticism and so to result, according to Bultmann, 'in the ideal of individualistic holiness of the *homo religiosus*'.[101] In this respect holiness is concerned with the salvation of the individual. Second, it may be understood in a positive sense as pointing the individual into fellowship with others, so that he may perform the good in selflessness. This latter view ultimately stands under the commandment of love.

When the stress is on the first, holiness is conceived as a personal quality; it ceases to be a relationship with God, involving being for others, and is envisaged instead as a goal to be sought or a perfection to be obtained. It thus stands in sharp opposition to the second. 'Then the waiver of self demanded by the commandment of love is no longer motivated by interest in one's neighbour and interest in fellowship with others but by interest in one's own salvation.'[102] 'Holy conduct', in this first sense, is based on a concept of holiness as a quality to be won or acquired by renunciation of the world. In the second sense, however, 'holy conduct' is a demand for God-relatedness lived out in love of one's fellow men in the service of the world. It is this latter that predominates in the New Testament – the striving after holiness in terms of individual perfection requiring asceticism did indeed enter Christian thought at an early date, but not until the end of the apostolic age. Within the canon itself there is even to be found some admonition against forms of asceticism; I Tim. 4.3 is directed against those who 'forbid marriage and enjoin abstinence from foods'. 'Holiness rather is love in action, but a love which is guided not by looking towards some "work" to be accomplished but by asking what needs and troubles of my neighbour or of society encounter me in any particular here and now.'[103] To speak of holiness as a moral quality is, therefore, despite the strong ethical note sounded in the New Testament, incorrect; it is rather a life-style, characterized by a relation to the holy which is actualized by loving self-giving.

In reaching such a conclusion our argument has come full circle. By this I mean that this understanding of holiness is entirely at one with the preliminary understanding of Jesus as the model of the holy. In each case holy and holiness relate to the divine; in each case there is an identification of the divine with love and, in each case, this is regarded as involving self-giving and service. This was to be expected if the New Testament is consistent, but it could not be assumed without investigation; the fact that it has proved to be the case endorses the validity of the previous analysis of Jesus as the model of the holy.

In speaking of Jesus in this way, as the model and even as the embodiment of holiness, I am well on the way to identifying holiness with Christlikeness. This is a legitimate step to take, as long as one is conscious of what one is doing. 'It is rather as though one had coined the word "socratiness" to refer to the essential character of the man Socrates,' observes O. R. Jones, 'and in such circumstances Socrates would of course provide the paradigm case of socratiness. The only way to explain what was meant by "socratiness" would be by reference to the word "Socrates" from which it was derived.'[104] So, as I have previously stressed, if, with the New Testament writers, we take Jesus as the 'paradigm case' of holiness, it is his story that provides the model. But to retell that story here should be something of an unnecessary exercise; rather, I wish to draw attention to and comment upon a limited number of aspects to fill out the picture of the model I have so far drawn.

These aspects – it is as well to recognize from the outset – are likely to be very varied. If the holy is indeed translated into human terms in Jesus, then every facet of life – his actions, teaching, personal relations – may disclose the holy. We are therefore not looking for a single distinctive characteristic of holiness, which makes it something *sui generis* and separate from everything human. To consider Jesus as the model is to accept the possibility of the rich character of the holy and to reject a stereotype. This, incidentally, reveals a further weakness of exclusive concentration on the numinous, for if this be presented as the specific element in the holy it prevents those who do not experience it from recognizing the holy. Once, however, the diversified nature of the holy is understood, the way is once again open for man to perceive and encounter it.

The first aspect to be noted is really a renewed emphasis upon what has already been said above. The holy reveals itself in outgoing concern. So Jesus, seeing the sorrowing mother of the dead young man at Nain, 'had compassion on her and said to her, "Do not weep" '.[105] Even in the agony of torture at the crucifixion, he says, 'Father, forgive them; for they know not what they do.'[106] This love is actualized in service, of which the supreme acted parable is the *pedilavium*. At the Last Supper, according to John, Jesus removes his clothes, dresses himself in the garb of a slave and performs the menial task of washing his disciples' feet. An apt and sufficient comment on this is provided by the remark of Daniel Jenkins that 'the holiness of Christ is always found on earth in the form of a servant'.[107]

This serving love extends to and embraces even the unlovable. Jesus has no hesitation in touching lepers – the outcasts and pariahs of society – nor in consorting with publicans and sinners.

The second aspect may best be described as the 'ordinariness' of the holy. To a certain extent the holy is *incognito*; it is unrecognized because it is not something extraordinary. When Jesus visits his native town, the people say: 'Is not this the carpenter, the son of Mary and brother of James and Joses and Judas and Simon, and are not his sisters here with us?'[108] The Nazarenes could not believe that an ordinary artisan was the Messiah; if he came from a humble family in their midst, he could not come from God. Indeed man finds it difficult to accept that the holy should trivialize itself, but if the *man* Jesus is the Holy One, this is precisely what has happened. Hence the author to the Hebrews does not hesitate to declare that 'he had to be made like his brethren in every respect'.[109] So when those concerned about the demise of the numinous complain that 'once the Mystery is brought down to the level of the market-place, it soon evaporates',[110] they reveal a lack of understanding of what is involved in incarnation. In part, Christian belief in the Incarnate One can be expressed as the mystery bringing itself down to the level of the market-place. This ordinariness is also to be associated with lowliness, light being shed on this by a story which C. G. Jung has recorded. A student came to a rabbi and said, 'In the olden days there were men who saw the face of God. Why don't they any more?' The rabbi replied, 'Because nowadays no one can stoop so low.'[111] Here, of course, the holy as serving love and as ordinariness touch one another, and the pedilavium is an illustration of both. No wonder that Jesus says, according to Matthew, 'I am gentle and lowly in heart',[112] and that Paul can speak of his humbling of himself.[113]

Yet there is another side to the coin. The holy as encountered in Jesus is also the unexpected, the surprising, the disconcerting. Repeatedly the evangelists say of those who met him that 'they were astonished beyond measure'.[114] There is nothing conventional about the holy, and at the same time there is a certain sublimity about it which leads, not to awe, but to wonder and respect. This wonder is similar to the attitude one may adopt towards great paintings; we marvel at man's capacity to create, by means of forms, lines and colours, these remarkable appearances of visual realities. It is the same wonder experienced by a man in love who wonders that one so beautiful and so gracious can reciprocate his devotion. It is the same wonder as that of the brain surgeon who marvels at the intricacy and economy of the organ with which he has to deal. 'Can this really be?' is the question that typifies this response. Can this love, this service and this ordinariness be, at the same time, a glimpse of sublimity? The New Testament writers have no doubt that it can be such, although they acknowledge that this sublimity is both veiled (the *incognito*) and still discernible, even in the face of a crucified man on a cross.[115]

The holy is also that which is devoted to the humanization of man. This means that it does not abase him but raises him to dignity. We have not, according to Paul, received the spirit of slavery but of sonship.[116] This dignity may have been lost by poverty, exploitation, racial discrimination or social ostracism. Take the story of Zacchaeus, a rich man but a chief tax collector and therefore hated by his fellow-countrymen. When Jesus comes to Jericho, Zacchaeus is eager to see him, but being a short man and standing at the back of the crowd, he is only able to do so by climbing up a sycamore tree. 'And when Jesus came to the place, he looked up and said to him, "Zacchaeus, make haste and come down, for I must stay at your house today." So he made haste and came down, and received him joyfully. And when they saw it they all murmured, "He has gone in to be the guest of a man who is a sinner." '[117] The effect upon the despised Zacchaeus of this public salutation and acceptance of his hospitality is to ennoble him with a new feeling of happiness and self-respect -- he 'received him joyfully'. So he who encounters the holy is given a sense of his own dignity. Alternatively one may express it thus:

the holy is that which is life-enhancing; that which brings enrichment to human living; that which therefore brings joy. Joy indeed
is a frequent feature of the gospel records. We have just had an
example with Zacchaeus and we may add to this the joy of the
Seventy coming back to Jesus after their mission and his own joy
in their return.[118] It is this that underlies the saying in the Fourth
Gospel: 'I came that they may have life, and have it abundantly.'[119]
The holy is therefore that which brings wholeness. Here we touch
on the centre of an interconnected series of ideas expressed in the
New Testament in terms of healing, cleansing, salvation, restoration[120] and perfection. This last word comprehends the concept of
completeness, whole-heartedness, that which lacks an inner division,[121] and it points towards maturity and adulthood.[122] But this
should not be understood in a narrowly individualistic sense. All
these aspects of humanization have to be worked out in social relations. This becomes apparent when we turn to a further effect of the
encounter with the holy, viz. the establishment of *shālōm*.

The Hebrew word *shālōm*, like its Greek equivalent *eirēnē*, is
usually translated by 'peace', but it is too rich in content for a
single equivalent to be sufficient. Its fundamental meaning[123] is that
of 'totality', and this includes the idea of harmonious community,
since man can only develop and mature in conjunction with others.
'There is "totality" in a community when there is harmony, and
the blessing flows freely among its members, everyone giving and
taking whatever he is able to.'[124] *Shālōm* therefore denotes not a
state but a relationship,[125] a personal relationship, and this includes
unity, solidarity, the exercise of mutual responsibility and confidence,
a present fulfilling of obligations and a community of will. Indeed
'it expresses every form of happiness and free expansion, but the
kernel in it is the community with others, the foundation of life.'[126]
Shālōm also embraces salvation, in the sense not of deliverance
from the miseries of this world into another, but of wholeness and
well-being and growth. So it involves neighbourliness, responsible
freedom and hope. Indeed *shālōm* refers to all aspects of human
life in its full and God-given maturity: righteousness, trust, fellowship, peace, etc. *Shālōm* is not something that can be objectified and
set apart; it is not the plus which the haves can distribute to the
have-nots, nor is it an internal condition (peace of mind) that can
be enjoyed in isolation. *Shālōm* is a social happening, an event in
interpersonal relations. It can therefore never be reduced to a simple

formula; it has to be found and worked out in actual situations within which the holy is to be encountered.

This social context also relates to the dialogical nature of the holy. By 'dialogical' I mean two things: (i) that the holy is that which overcomes separation, *without eliminating otherness*; (ii) that the holy is characterized by openness. Both of these may be illustrated by the story of the woman of Samaria at Jacob's well.[127] Jesus arrives at Sychar in Samaria, tired after a gruelling journey in the hot sun. He is alone because his disciples have gone into town to buy food. He sits down close to the well. A Samaritan woman approaches to draw water and Jesus opens the dialogue with a request for a drink. The woman's reply reveals her surprise at his openness and freedom, at his complete ignoring of convention, because, on the one hand, there was a bitter prejudice of the Jews against the Samaritans, and, on the other, it was a precept of contemporary moralists that 'a man should not salute a woman in a public place, not even his own wife'. She expresses her astonishment and this enables Jesus to go further. It is true that he is a Jew, but if she knew more and appreciated the opportunity offered to her by his presence, she would be asking for a greater gift – the living waters of life. The woman is further puzzled, but does not break off the dialogue; she seeks to understand. Jacob gave this well, and in the ordinary sense it contains living, that is running, water; is Jesus then claiming to be greater than the Patriarch? Jesus' answer is that his gift is greater because it is inexhaustible; it is the eternal water of eternal life. The situation is now reversed and the woman makes her request. She asks Jesus to give her this water, not because she appreciates his meaning, but to save her from her daily toil. With one crisp command Jesus cuts through the narrow limits of her thought: 'Go, call your husband.' The woman, who has shown a certain readiness to enter into dialogue, now manifests a reserve and is shy of exposing herself completely. She denies that she has a husband, and this denial could lead to a termination of the dialogue. Her statement, however, is a half-truth, because she does indeed belong to no one, having been married to five different men. Jesus then tells her that her denial is true, and the woman perceives that he must be a prophet, for this is the only explanation of his insight that occurs to her. She acknowledges him as such and then raises a further question about the place of worship. Jesus has laid bare her sin and she wants to know at what altar she must make her sacrifice. At what sacred place is she to pray for forgiveness? Shall she go to Gerizim, which is the Samaritans' holy place, or to Jerusalem where the temple is the centre of the Jewish cult? Jesus does not directly answer the question but leads her on to ground where the question does not arise at all. God is not to be sought in a local habitation; now, with the advent of the last times, he is to be worshipped in Spirit and in truth. The woman is puzzled once more and says that she will have to wait until the Messiah comes to clear up this and other difficulties. The dialogue is in danger of coming to an end, but Jesus, in order to assist the woman to a responsible decision, makes a declaration which impels her to go further; he asserts that he is in fact the Messiah.

In this account the positive features of dialogue are revealed. Jesus enters into a truly personal relationship with the woman; there is a reciprocal communication; there is a quest for real understanding; there is a steady perseverance in the search for truth. There is openness on Jesus' part and a growing trust on the part of the woman. The relationship, therefore, is one of love, for love never seeks to destroy nor to absorb; it always recognizes and preserves otherness. The holy as dialogical represents freedom and manifests otherness by not encroaching upon the otherness of those it encounters. Hence the 'otherness' of the holy is a function of the divine servanthood, and as such it is a constantly new factor within the world of man's pride.

Openness as related to the dialogical nature of the holy is concerned with candour, sincerity, lack of dissimulation, and directness. Reference to it has already been made in analysing the story of the woman at the well, but further examination is needed. Let us begin with human openness. According to John Macquarrie:

What makes us, as human beings, different from rocks and stars and even animals, is just the astonishing multiplicity of ways in which we stand open. We are open to the past through memory and open to the future through anticipation, and so we are open to the possibility of becoming responsible selves. Again, we are open to our world, so that we can understand it and, within limits, transform it and become creative within it. We are open to other human beings (themselves having this kind of openness) so that we can enter into personal relations with them and push outward the horizons of genuine community.[128]

Through Jesus the holy is revealed as correspondingly open, not closed in on itself. This means that the holy takes the risk that is inseparable from all openness, because to come into the open is to be exposed. Indeed in Jesus 'the full openness of God and the potential openness of man have converged'.[129] All human existence possesses this potentiality of openness, although it is often inhibited and obscured in everyday life; but in Christ, as the model of the holy, it is fulfilled and manifested.

This affirmation of the openness of the holy stands in the way of a too facile definition. If the holy were self-enclosed and apart, it would be easier to conceptualize, but being open it cannot be pinned down and so limited by our definitions. Here the openness of the holy joins its other aspects of unexpectedness and spontaneity.

This exposure of the holy is an essential part of the active fight against evil in which it is engaged. That this is a central feature in the ministry of Jesus scarcely needs emphasis. The evangelists represent him as in continual conflict, whether with evil spirits, with man's pride, as exemplified even by the apostles, or with the Jewish authorities, who failed to recognize the holy in him. Consequently the holy is that which frequently gives offence. So his attack upon the idea of uncleanness, by declaring that it is not that which goes into a man's mouth but that which comes out that defiles him, prompts the disciples to ask: 'Do you know that the Pharisees were offended when they heard this saying?[130] Jesus himself takes the view that 'blessed is he who takes no offence at me'.[131]

Because the holy gives offence, it provokes opposition, and if it persists in openness, rather than escaping by withdrawal from the world, its way may be that of suffering. From this aspect the holy is to be understood in terms of self-denial, culminating in the bearing of the hatred that it may elicit. Jesus on the cross shows the lengths to which the holy is prepared to go in self-surrender and love to absorb into itself the evil of mankind.

To stand before the crucified one is either to be drawn to the holy or to be repelled by it. In either case, the encounter with the holy involves judgment. To say this is to point to an aspect of the holy which is unlikely to be popular at the present day. There seems to be abroad what may perhaps be described as a certain moral flabbiness. On all sides one witnesses the adoption of judgmental – 'holier-than-thou' – attitudes towards others, coupled with a refusal to let any one judge us. Of course, some would be prepared to concede that we may judge ourselves, but this frequently means no more than that we accomplish this by reference to what we are and what we do and so simply find our own level; hence we acknowledge nothing and no one over against us by which or by whom we are judged. Such a view does not correspond to the New Testament model of the holy. Jesus is unmistakably regarded as the judge,[132] but if this is to have a meaning we have to enquire what judgment is.

In the New Testament, judgment is employed in two different ways. First, it can refer to condemnation and second, to separation. The first is not applicable to Jesus' activity, and so the Fourth Gospel states that 'God sent the Son into the world, not to condemn (RV judge) the world, but that the world might be saved through him'.[133] Nevertheless, the same author can ascribe to Jesus the words: 'For judgment I came into this world.'[134] The contradiction is apparent only, for in this second quotation it is separation and not condemnation that is intended. This separation is not a theoretical concept but may be observed; it is a phenomenon that is a factor of everyday life and so a present process. Constantly men and women are either responding to the holy or reacting away from it. Neither response nor reaction are necessarily conscious according to the teaching of Jesus. This is evident from the parable of the sheep and the goats. Using the language of myth, Jesus looks forward to a Last Judgment when mankind will be finally separated. This division, however, is the recognition of a separation that already exists and is operative in ordinary life. It is determined by one's encounter with the holy, even if the holy has not been recognized as such. The Son of man, in the parable, invites one group into his kingdom on the grounds that they have fed him when he was hungry, given him to drink when he was thirsty, and visited him when he was sick or in prison. They ask in turn when they have in fact performed these acts of service towards him, and they receive the reply: 'As you did it to one of the least of these my brethren, you did it to me.' The second group is dismissed precisely because 'as you did it not to one of the least of these, you did it not to me'.[135] Hence in J. A. T. Robinson's succinct phrase, 'mankind is ultimately to be judged by its own humanity, by what it really means to be man'.[136] For the holy embodied in Jesus 'confronts us with nothing alien to ourselves. He confronts us with our own humanity.'[137] Once understand this and we can say that we judge ourselves; but now the standard of judgment is not just self-created, it is the standard of love expressed in the service of others, which is why forgiveness is inseparably connected to the granting of forgiveness to one's brother.[138] The unforgiving man, who does not minister to the needs of his fellows, is lacking in holiness, as defined above, i.e. he is not God-related by loving service, and is therefore under judgment. He is separated from the fellowship of love in which mankind should be knit together. He falls short of the model of the holy as disclosed in Jesus, and therefore the holy judges him. This understanding of judgment is not far removed from that to be found in the Old Testament. There judgment is not primarily condemnation; rather, 'when the judge is the source and defender of justice, he is the saviour and the deliverer. . . In the oldest conceptions of God judgment is an attribute of salvation.'[139]

Because judgment is in this way a present reality and related to the encounter with the holy, we have also to note the historical character of that meeting. Indeed 'unless the holy takes historical form and becomes related to life in the world it may be dissipated in aesthetic enjoyment or contemplation that leaves life unaffected.'[140] This is to recover one of the primary emphases of the prophets, which has been obscured by the Old Testament model of the holy, viz. that the holy is to be encountered in and through history.[141]

However, to speak of history is to call attention to a new tension in human living that has replaced the former polarity between the clean and the unclean, the sacred and profane. This new tension may be described as that which exists between the 'already' and the 'not yet', i.e. it is an eschatological tension. This may be expressed in less technical jargon by saying that the encounter with the holy refers not only to the *now* in itself but to the *now* in to which the future is breaking. The reality of the present lies in its possibilities for the future. The encounter with the holy in the present therefore brings hope.

The meaning of these somewhat cryptic remarks may be illuminated by reference to the distinction drawn by Jürgen Moltmann between an epiphany-based religion and a promise-centred faith. The former understands the encounter with the holy as the manifestation of the immutable; it is a meeting with the eternal presence in the now. The purpose of this disclosure of the holy is to be found in the event itself, in the epiphany; it may, for example, be to hallow a place or an individual. It serves to sanctify and protect life and, by this communion with the eternal, to ensure the stability of society. The result can be an opting out of history in favour of contemplating the absolute. The encounter is thus a completed, self-contained event, resulting in a religious sanctioning of the present. In contrast to all this, a promise-centred faith understands the encounter with the holy as a meeting with him who brings an anticipation of the future. The purpose of the disclosure is to point to the future which is thereby opened up. So, for example, the confrontation with the holy which Paul experienced on the Damascus road was not a self-contained incident wherein he contemplated the eternal, but a commissioning to service in the world. The disclosure is thus open-ended, forward-looking. The promise points away from the encounter 'in which it is uttered, into the as yet unrealized future which it announces'.[142] The purpose of the disclosure therefore lies not in itself; instead it leads to a break-away from the present towards the future. The encounter neither endorses nor supports the *status quo*, but creates a dissatisfaction with the present and promotes 'continued new impulses towards the realization of righteousness, freedom and humanity here through the promised future that is to come'.[143] So, to give another example from the New Testament, the narratives of the resurrection appearances never suggest that these were concerned with a blissful experience of union with the eternal, but, instead, they involved a commission to service and mission in the world.[144]

The way of holiness, therefore, is not one of resignation; it is not the acceptance of the present, without taking into account the effect of the promise and so of the future. Nor is it an endorsement of the *status quo*, rendered supportable by moments of bliss through encounter with the eternal. Rather is it a pilgrimage in hope which wrestles with the present in the light of the promises and of the future. In this way freedom becomes a possibility, since it consists, in part, in openness to the future, which is why I stated above that encounter with the holy in the present brings hope.

It follows from this sequence of thought that the holy cannot be conceived as that which dwells beyond history; the holy is not 'up there' or 'out there' but 'before us'. Inaugurated eschatology, of the kind I have been describing, does not deny the 'already', but it does allow for hope in the 'not yet' and therefore for action, in union with the holy, to bring about the 'not yet'. But the future is 'not erected out of the potentialities of our human freedom and human action. Rather, this future calls forth our potentialities to unfold themselves in history.'[145]

It may help the reader if, before proceeding further, I were to note briefly the principal aspects of the holy which have emerged from this short study of the New Testament model. My list is not, of course, exhaustive. As I stated above, if the holy is translated into human terms in Jesus, then every facet of his life may disclose the holy. I have been selective without intending to be exclusive, and the summary is as follows. Negatively, the holy is not the numinous nor is it the opposite of the profane – a term that has ceased to have meaning for Christians. Positively, the holy is the divine, and this means that it is to be identified as love expressed in the service of others. The holy is both ordinary and sublime; it is unexpected and disconcerting; it may induce wonder but not fearful awe; it is concerned with humanization, restoring dignity, wholeness and establishing *shālōm*. The holy is dialogical, overcoming separation without eliminating otherness and being entirely open and exposed. Its exposure is most evident in its conflict with evil, which causes offence and may involve suffering. The holy carries judgment, not in the sense of condemnation, but of separation between those who, consciously or not, serve the holy in terms of ministering to human need. It has, therefore, an historical character, which is best understood in terms of the tension between the 'already' and the 'not yet'. The encounter with the holy is, however, not a meeting with the eternal outside time, as if it could be situationless, but with that which opens the way to and points towards the future.

The quest upon which we embarked at the beginning of this chapter was for a model of the holy consistent with the secular universe. Although a final verdict on the extent to which Jesus may be accepted as such a model must await further investigation – as, in succeeding chapters, I attempt to show how this model matches a wide range of phenomena – a tentative preliminary assessment is feasible.

We have seen that, according to the New Testament, the model of the holy is provided by the figure of a man: this very fact indicates that such a model may be presumed to fit within the framework of a hominized world. Moreover, the New Testament writers make it clear that the holy is not separate from the human, that there is no gulf between the divine and man, and that the holy indeed confronts us with nothing alien to ourselves but with our own humanity. The holy, too – so the message runs – is accessible in the midst of life in the secular world. These several points strongly support the conclusion that we have found what is required.

Without such a model, we could not expect to encounter the holy, for as I argued in the chapter on the nature of perception, our perception is determined by our models or concepts. We can, then, only perceive the holy in the secular world if we possess a proto-understanding of the holy – a model which is consistent with the hominized frame of reference. Only then is recognition of the holy within that context possible.

This point is so vital that I hope I may be excused if I reformulate it from a slightly different perspective. In his study of the *Biblical Encounter with Japanese Culture*,[146] Charles Corwin argues that in every language and culture there is to be discerned a dominant concept that colours all others. He designates this dominant concept 'a concept-clearing-centre': i.e., all other concepts are affected by it. So in Japanese thinking he maintains that *man-in-the-cosmos*, or *man-in-nature*, is the dominant concept. In Christian thought, on the other hand, it is God's revelation in Christ that constitutes the concept-clearing-centre. Using this terminology, it may be said that to take Jesus as the model of the holy is to accept him as the concept-clearing-centre; i.e., in seeking to specify the dominant concept of the holy that should affect and make possible our experience, I am pointing to the figure of Jesus. The function of this dominant concept should be to enable us to perceive the holy in all walks of life. Because concepts influence our perception, the acceptance of a dominant concept determines what we perceive around us. So it is Jesus who provides the objective reference in the quest for the holy. As the model of the holy he enables us to confront the holy in the world, and this meeting is only possible when we have a *schema* related to the world which enables such a perception to be had.

However, we must now give some thought to the place of encounter – to the how and where of the meeting with the holy – before proceeding to examine further the model's empirical fit with the secular or hominized universe.

4

The Place of Encounter

In discussing the how and where of the encounter with the holy, we must take up again the subject of experience, which was touched upon briefly in the second chapter.[1] There we saw how perception and experience are connected and how the one affects the other. Now we have to analyse human experience in greater detail.

Granted that experience involves a series of acts of perception which are meaningfully related, we must also acknowledge that it is an objective product of the intersection of reality on the one hand and a self-conscious being, capable of receiving that reality, on the other. Experience is therefore not something that is private and mental; it is basically encounter and so embraces both the one who experiences and that which is experienced. This is not to say that experience cannot mislead us, but this is not because it is constituted of nothing but subjective ideas and feelings. Experience could not lead into error if it were not an actual encounter with and participation in the real world. At the same time, if we fail to notice what is there, i.e. if we do not perceive it, we may remain ignorant of its presence and so have no experience of it.

Experience also involves 'frameworks of meaning within which what we encounter is interpreted and evaluated'.[2] This does not mean that experience is simply a matter of inference. We do not start with a datum from which we infer the existence of something or somebody else; we start with an experience which contains in itself the presence of a reality not immediately known as such.[3] It follows that whereas experience can be direct, *it is always mediated*. When we meet other people, as long as we are open towards one another and free from dissimulation, our encounters are direct ones, but at the same time they are not immediate. This is so because, in the first instance, experience does not constitute reality but is itself the medium through which reality is disclosed. It is also so because my experience of another person is mediated to me through his words, his bodily actions, etc. Experience defined in this way may be said to correspond to the 'secondary epistemic way' of seeing referred to in chapter 2.

Human experience can be, and indeed frequently is, multi-dimensional. This is not another way of describing its potential richness, rather it is an emphasizing of its various levels. For example, a table can be experienced as a collection of data, or as a superb example of craftmanship, or as an object of historical interest. Related to these levels of experience are also layers of interpretation which interlock. So I may see a small white cube on a saucer. When I observe it more closely I realize that it is a lump of sugar. My first interpretation still remains valid – the object *is* a small white cube – but now I have made a new interpretation which both includes and goes beyond the first. For another example I will reproduce that advanced by John Hick.[4] Here the object is a piece of paper covered with writing. An illiterate savage may interpret this as something made by man. A literate person, unfamiliar with the language in which it is written, can interpret it as a document. Another, who knows the language, can read the writing and define exactly what kind of document it is, e.g. a recipe for omelettes or a love letter. Each person is answering the question 'What?' Each answer is at a different level; yet each successive level includes that which precedes it.

With the several aspects of this analysis in mind, let us now turn to the encounter with the holy. If human experience arises out of the intersection of reality and a self-conscious being, the encounter with the holy has to be seen, not as a tissue of subjectivity, but as a meeting with the real world, i.e. the encounter is something objective and that which is encountered transcends the subjectivity of the individual.[5] Further, we must eschew an inferential approach, because this would not result in an experience of the holy but would rather be an account of the experience of something else from which the conclusion would be drawn that the holy is real. In other words, we cannot read the holy off the face of events; events can only be occasions for encounter if they are interpreted through some standard or normative disclosure – this is precisely the function of the

model of the holy embodied in Christ. This disclosure is not something apart from human experience, because experience is the only
medium through which anything can be apprehended by man. So,
as we have seen, the New Testament record is the narrative of
human experience, interpreted as a disclosure of the holy.

Consequently, the experience of the holy, although direct, is
always mediated. The encounter with the holy is *always and at the
same time* the experience of something else. It is true that the
mystical approach seeks to rise above all that separates us from the
holy; it envisages a union without anything in between; but in contrast to this, if we take the New Testament seriously, we have to
affirm that every disclosure of the holy is a concurrent disclosure of
something else.[6] The difference between those who perceive and
those who do not is that the former experience the 'something else'
as having a dimension of the holy, whereas the latter only experience
the 'something else'. Alternatively expressed, one may say that the
encounter with the holy takes place through a mediated and interpreted experience in which both experience and interpretation are
interwoven. In this case the multi-dimensional aspect of experience
comes to the fore and, with it, the interlocking layers of interpretation. The parable of the Good Samaritan may serve as an illustration.

As he travels along the road to Jericho, the Samaritan reaches a
certain point on the route where he notices a random configuration
of flesh, earth and stones. He interprets this to be an injured man
prostrate on the ground. If he does not ignore him, like the priest,
but considers the situation further, he will become aware of a moral
compulsion to go to the aid of the stranger. So he interprets the
situation further as one that requires him to give assistance. He may
also, and this is in part the theme of the parable, recognize the unknown man as his neighbour and so he may encounter the holy. The
ethical and spiritual significance of the scene are lost on the priest,
but not so on the Samaritan. Nevertheless he is not forced to
acknowledge this significance; his is a voluntary act. Nor is he compelled to be aware that he is encountering the holy; but if he perceives it, then his recognition is not something apart from either the
natural or the moral sphere. In John Hick's phrase, there is an
'apprehension of the divine presence within the believer's human
experience'.[7]

This exegesis of the parable of the Good Samaritan enables us to go further in our analysis. It helps us to see that the encounter with the holy is not a matter of inference for the believer, but of fact. Moreover, it requires us to re-emphasize that the encounter is not divorced from all other objects of experience. The holy meets us in and through our material and social environment. We experience the holy not apart from the course of everyday life, but in and through it. Human experience has as its necessary basis the material world, within which there is the possibility of personal relationships. The latter do not call in question the reality of the former and indeed would be impossible without it; rather, the latter rest upon and include the former. The view I am propounding is that there is a further level of experience, as we penetrate into its depths. This layer is the experience of the holy. Nevertheless, this encounter is not separate from the material world nor from the world of human relations; rather, it is involved in them and is impossible apart from them.

This dual thesis – that the encounter with the holy is always a mediated one and that the instruments of this mediation consist of the material world and the world of human relations – cannot be too strongly asserted. The rest of this study will carry little conviction if it is not accepted. Nevertheless many Christian readers are likely to find some difficulty in endorsing such a view. For centuries they have had commended to them the dictum that their task is the 'flight of the alone to the Alone'. They have had held up to them the contemplatives, with unmediated union as their goal, as the example of perfection. They have been told that asceticism and world denial constitute *the* Christian way. They have been provided with a mental set which, in my view, is called into question by the New Testament and which has at certain periods, when the church has been closest to its inheritance, been itself opposed by leaders of Christian thought.

Throughout the first centuries of its history the church waged an unremitting war upon the adherents of docetism. Docetism, which is a term derived from a Greek verb meaning 'to seem', teaches that the humanity of Christ was only a semblance; he seemed, he appeared to be a man, but in fact he was not. He was a divine being whose humanity was entirely unreal. The encounter with the holy, therefore, is not only direct but unmediated; it is certainly not mediated through the manhood, which is no more than an appearance. In opposition to this, the church consistently asserted the full humanity of Jesus. Whatever else he was, he was a real man. Indeed some of the New Testament accounts go out of their way to stress the sheer physicality of Jesus, for example the Lucan resurrection narrative, in a consciously anti-docetic vein. But once the humanity of Jesus is taken with absolute seriousness, and at the same time it is believed that he is the Holy One, then his role as mediator necessarily follows. According to H. R. Niebuhr, 'Jesus Christ is not a median figure, half God, half man; he is a single person wholly directed as man towards God and wholly directed in his unity with the Father towards man. He is mediatorial, not median.'[8] To recognize this mediatorial function is to affirm that, from the Christian standpoint, the experience of the holy is always a mediated one. Moreover, since 'wherever the divine is manifest, it is manifest in "flesh", that is, in a concrete, physical and historical reality',[9] then the experience of the holy cannot be something isolated and encapsulated, something apart from everyday life, which itself is rather the locus of encounter. One perceives the holy, if at all, 'inlaid in the folds of life', to use a vivid phrase of Martin Buber.[10] This is yet another reason for rejecting the approach of Rudolf Otto, for he 'emphasized so much the irreducible originality of the religious experience that he removed it out of its human, historical and socio-cultural context'.[11] But when Jesus is taken as the model, then the holy does not belong to a special sphere of life but to all spheres of life. It is, however, as man that Christ is the mediator; he is mediator in his humanity according to the ways of humanity. Human encounter requires mutual availability, and this, in its turn, is possible only through man's 'bodiliness' and not apart from it.[12] So to encounter Christ and thus to meet the holy is only possible through his humanity, and this demonstrates the mediatorial basis of experience. The encounter with the holy − I repeat − is *always* and *at the same time* an encounter with something else. To think otherwise is to be a docetist; it is to deny the reality of Christ's manhood and, ultimately, of our own. But the encounter with the holy arises not out of detached subjectivity but out of life. Because of this, it is misleading to speak of 'religious' experience as something distinct from ordinary experience; the meeting with the holy arises out of the whole life of man in real intercourse with the divine in and through the world. Hence the proper contribution of an analysis of experience to our understanding of the holy will be obscured if that contribution is sought only in the special realm of 'religious' experience. This was precisely the mistake of Rudolf

Otto. Rather we have to understand the holy in relation to the whole of human experience conceived as possessing a dimension of holiness.

If Christians persist in believing that the encounter can be unmediated, they are not taking seriously Paul's dictum that 'now we see in a mirror dimly, but then face to face'.[13] The last phrase appears four times in the English versions of the New Testament, twice translating *stoma* and twice *prosōpon*. In three of these instances it is used of a meeting between fellow human beings, once referring to the right of an accused person to confront his opponents[14] and twice to an impending visit and the joy of personal encounter.[15] In the fourth passage from I Corinthians, it is evident that according to Paul an unmediated experience of the holy in this life is not possible – 'now we see in a mirror dimly'. It is only 'then', i.e. at the final consummation, that there will be an unmediated meeting – 'face to face'. So the presence of the holy is not an epiphany of the unchanging absolute before whom we mutely adore, wrapt in contemplation. Such a reaction would deny the tension between the 'already' and the 'not yet'; it could lead man to abandon history for the bliss of the eternal now; it could induce him to be socially irrelevant because, content with contemplation, he would see no need to change society. There are in fact two forms of eschatology which are fraught with danger. There is a futuristic eschatology which promotes a lack of concern for the present because only the future is real and brings that perfection for which we crave. There is also a realized eschatology which produces the same result because we no longer live out of the future in hope with the intention of recreating the world, and instead seek to pass from moment to moment of eternal contemplation.

The experience of the holy does not allow us to escape from the tensions of existing situations, as if, having become aware of the holy, we concentrate only upon that and discard the human reality through which it is mediated. On the contrary, 'a direct relation to God that includes no direct relation to the world is, if not deception, self-deception; if you turn away from the world in order to turn to God, you have not turned towards the reality of God but only towards your concept of God.'[16]

In the last quotation, from Martin Buber, 'world' is used in a very specific way. It refers mainly to the world of human relationships. Here it is apposite to recall that the context of our thinking is the secular universe, within which nature has been desacralized and has lost its numinous character. This does not necessarily mean that any experience of the holy is now impossible; rather there appears a new, or better, a newly rediscovered locus of that encounter, i.e. human relations. It is through the other that we meet the holy; the holy seeks to encounter us in the openness and freedom of encounter between men. So, according to Dietrich Bonhoeffer, the holy 'addresses us through every man; the other human being, that puzzling inscrutable thou, is God's call to us, God himself who comes to meet us[17] .... Christ will wander on earth as long as men exist, as your neighbour, as he through whom God calls you, speaks to you, makes demands on you.'[18] In other words, man mediates the holy to man. This conclusion is the logical outcome of accepting Jesus as the model of the holy. But before attempting to examine the meaning of this, let us consider a story.

Manolios, one of the principal characters in *Christ Recrucified* by Nikos Kazantzakis, tells his companions of a certain monk who after years of effort gathered together the sum of thirty pounds to enable him to go on a visit to the Holy Sepulchre in Jerusalem. As he left the gate of his monastery to set out on his pilgrimage, he met a poor man in rags, to whom eventually he gave all his savings, and then returned to his cell, surrendering all hope of ever visiting the holy city. Manolios continues:

'This evening, after so many years, I understand who the poor man was whom he met as he left the monastery.'
Manolios fell silent. His voice was beginning to tremble. His friends drew nearer to him on the bench. 'Who was it?' they asked anxiously.
Manolios hesitated a moment. At last calmly, like a ripe fruit falling at night in a garden, his word fell:
'Christ.'
The three comrades jumped. As though suddenly there had appeared among them in the darkness, sad, poorly dressed, persecuted by men, with his feet bleeding from walking, a fugitive, Christ.[19]

At a later stage in the novel, Manolios says to Father Fotis:

'I look for God in the great difficult moments; you show him to me in each moment that passes. I seek him in violent death; you make me see him in the humble struggle of every day.'

The priest replies:

'We shall find God where we are going. And we shall find him not as he is represented by those who have never seen him – a rosy-cheeked old man, sitting blissfully on woolly clouds – but in the form of a voice sprung from our inmost being to declare war' – war on all forms of injustice, and oppression, whether moral, economic or political.[20]

I have reproduced these two passages quite deliberately as representing a necessary element in my methodology. This statement, too, can be illuminated by another incident. The grandson of a disciple of the Baal-Shem was asked to tell a story.

'A story,' he said, 'must be told in such a way that it constitutes help in itself.'[21]

This is to say that a story has an immediate effect; it conveys a meaning and a perception of truth. It is, of course, possible to abstract from the story and, in the light of reflection, to conceptualize. The result is the objectification of an intersubjective reality, known in personal relations. Such a procedure is not without value, for concepts, too, can be evocative, but it can never be a complete substitute for a story. This is why the gospel, as we have seen, is mainly the telling of a story; i.e., in the New Testament the holy is presented through narrative form. The theologian, however, cannot avoid conceptualization, but this means that his formulations are by way of being abstractions, and to that extent are not to be identified with the reality to which they are intended to point. With this caution in mind, some further examination of the thesis that man mediates the holy to man – as shown by the extracts from the novel by Kazantzakis – is in order. This will involve the consideration of three subjects, to two of which reference has been made previously: the parable of the Sheep and the Goats and that of the Good Samaritan, in conjunction with Jesus' summary of the commandments.

According to the parable of the Sheep and the Goats,[22] those who are accepted into the kingdom are the ones who have served their brothers in distress. It is further asserted categorically that in so doing they have ministered to Christ. It is true that some exegetes have suggested that this story is not one of Jesus' own compositions and, further, that 'the least of these my brothers' refers to Christians only. As far as the present argument is concerned, this first point is irrelevant; the parable is there in the New Testament and that is what we are considering. The second point is almost certainly ruled out by the universalism of the setting – it involves a gathering of 'all the nations'.[23] If we ask, in the light of this parable, what are the human experiences in which man encounters the holy, the answer appears quite clear that it is through the meeting with one's fellow-men and especially with those in distress. In other words, human encounter involves a real meeting with the holy, which therefore takes place on the horizontal plane of our human relations.[24]

According to this parable, then, the person in distress is a mediating reality, mediating, that is, the holy. It has to be noted in this connection that it is always possible to say of any mediating reality that it both 'is' and 'is not' that same reality in relation to which it performs the function of a mediator. Hence to speak of serving Christ in the person of a neighbour is to refer to an action which in one sense is not to and for Christ, although in another sense it is. The brother is a mediating reality who mediates Christ; he both is and is not Christ. 'The cup of water given to the poor man is in fact given to Christ. This does not mean that the poor man is Christ, but that he is for us, whether we know it or not, the veil through which we meet Christ, in such a way that the act towards the poor man is, in reality, an act that has Christ for its term.'[25]

If this statement were to be left as it stands, it could be open to the criticism, often advanced by Marxists and some atheist existentialists, that it actually destroys the love of one's fellow-men, because they are loved only as the representatives of the holy, i.e., it is not the men but the holy in the men that we serve. If this is so, then the men fade away; they are no more than pegs on which to hang the only interesting reality – the holy. Moreover, if this were so, all that would have happened would be the substitution of sacralized human relations in the place of desacralized nature. Indeed there are those who reject the holy precisely because they believe that to accept it is to threaten man's very nature. To them the choice is between either the holy, with a supposed inevitable compromise of humanity, or its denial, so that man may be man.[26] To answer this I must supplement the consideration of the first item by the second, viz. by the summary of the commandments: 'You shall love the Lord your God. . . . You shall love your neighbour as yourself.'[27]

According to this summary Jesus enjoins love of God and love of neighbour together. He thus indicates that there is no short cut to the holy without passing through the love of the neighbour. So the author of I John declares: 'If any one says, "I love God", and hates his brother, he is a liar; he who does not love his brother whom he has seen, cannot love God whom he has not seen. And this commandment we have from him, that he who loves God should love his brother also.'[28] I cannot improve upon John Baillie's comment upon this: 'We can reach God only through our neighbour. We cannot love him except in loving our neighbour. Nor does God reach us or manifest his love to us save through our neighbour – that is, save in togetherness with him.'[29]

Jesus' own comment is provided by the parable of the Good Samaritan. This story is not to be understood in terms of general philanthropy. Jesus does not answer the question about the identity of the neighbour by listing all possible categories of human beings, but what he does do is reverse the question: 'Who is nearest to the one in need?' So he shatters the 'old concentric grouping in which the I is at the centre, but maintains the organizing concept of the neighbour, and by means of this concept sets up a new grouping in which the Thou is at the centre. This order, however, is not a suggestion that applies schematically to all men and places. It consists only in absolute concreteness. It is built up from case to case round a man in need. Whoever stands closest to the man in need . . . the same has a neighbourly duty towards him.'[30] In other words, Jesus does not provide a theological or philosophical or scientific definition of a neighbour. He says to his hearers: *you* decide who your neighbour is. In reaching this decision conventional religion is of no help – the priest and levite pass by on the other side. The Samaritan was simply moved by something human – compassion, pity, love – arising out of the situation and he acted upon it. By acting as a human being, he affirmed his common humanity with the victim. When it is recalled that this parable is an explanation of what 'neighbour' means in Jesus' summary of the commandments, we can readily appreciate how the love of God and the love of neighbour and the serving of both are inseparable.

If we relate these various ideas, then, we reach the conclusion that the brother in distress, in the parables of both the Sheep and the Goats and the Good Samaritan, is a sacrament of the meeting with the holy. Hence it would be in vain to look for divine epiphanies; there is an end to theophanies. Instead, 'I am directed to the simple truth of my human relationships and of my human tasks; it is there, by the grace of the Spirit, that I must live out in Christ my relationship as a son to the Father.'[31] In so far as any theophany can be envisaged in Christian thought, then it must be eschatologically conceived. The parable of the Sheep and the Goats looks to the Last Judgment; only *then* will the holy be manifested as he is; only then will there be a face-to-face encounter; only then will the full meaning of our actions be disclosed, viz. that in all our human relationships the holy was present.

The same approach was adumbrated in the Old Testament by Jeremiah and is further emphasized by Jesus in an isolated saying. According to Jeremiah 7.1, the prophet is ordered to stand at the temple gate and proclaim to all who come to worship that they must first amend their ways in relation to their neighbours. They can only worship if they 'truly execute justice one with another'. Similarly Jesus requires one who has actually reached the altar and is offering his gift to leave it there, should he remember that his brother has something against him. He has first to be reconciled with his brother, before he can complete his offering.[32] These two passages are agreed in affirming that the holy is found through one's neighbour and not one's neighbour through the holy. 'The neighbour is considered as something with a prior existence of his own and worthy of being valued for himself.'[33] I therefore agree with another of John Baillie's statements: 'All this mediation is part of God's gracious purpose in refusing to unite me to himself without at the same time uniting me to my fellow men – in making it impossible for me to obey either of the two great commandments without at the same time obeying the other.'[34]

So in the encounter with the holy through and in the neighbour, we do not by-pass the latter; we do not sacralize the experience so that the natural human reality ceases to exist. What we do is to discover that experience is multi-dimensional; each layer interlocks, so that we find the Holy One through humble and loving service to others. Hence we may reaffirm the conclusion that the realities within human experience through which we encounter the holy are our relations with our brother men. In other words, through the Incarnation the holy has inserted himself historically into the heart of the network of human intercourse, or we may say that the *primary* lesson to be learned from the Incarnation is, not that it proclaims that God has become man, but that it demonstrates that God is to be met through man. Hence the saying 'I am the way'[35] means that the way to God is through man. This conclusion may also be expressed in the form that the holy is now met in and through the secular and by means of world involvement. If we now examine this slightly different formulation, the subject may be further clarified.

I am contending that the holy is not an *a priori* category; it is not something that can be apprehended apart from other experiences; it is not something separate – an entity that can be detached and described *per se*. It is always encountered in, with and under ordinary human experience. One may perhaps speak of it as the depth of that experience – although this is only one possible image among many. Consequently the holy cannot be known apart from the secular. According to Paul Tillich, 'The holy needs to be expressed and can be expressed only through the secular, for it is through the finite alone that the infinite can express itself. . . . The holy cannot appear except through that which in another respect is secular. In its essential nature the holy does not constitute a special realm in addition to the secular.'[36] Holiness, therefore, is not withdrawal from the world; Jesus consents to abide in the world and to allow the world to have its way with him.[37] So the path of holiness is the way of world-involvement. This conclusion could also have been reached – in terms of Christian theology – not by beginning with a model of the holy but with the doctrine of creation, since to acknowledge the world as a divine creation is to repudiate any notion of the holy demanding separation from the world. Contemporary man therefore does not have to retain two modes of experience side by side, if he is to encounter the holy. He does not have to divide 'religious' experience from everyday experience: the two interpenetrate.[38] The choice before him, if he is to be an integrated being, is neither to dismiss the Christian faith in the face of everyday experience nor to withdraw from everyday living in order to retain his faith. Rather, it is to recognize or to reject the essential unity of the sacred and the secular.

To achieve this integration, it is not necessary to assume that the holy and the secular are identical. Separation is one thing; distinction is another. Rather, I am saying that every natural reality has at least two dimensions: the first (secular) is its own existence and its immediate end, while the second (the sacred) is its relation to the holy. Everyday experience has within it the dimension of the holy, if we can but perceive it. Everyday experience is the place of encounter, but in such manner that our ordinary human experience is not devalued but enhanced.

This dual nature of experience cannot be acknowledged if we persist in thinking in terms of the sacred/profane dialectic, for this would be to fall foul of the so-called law of contradiction in logic – that a thing is either A or B but cannot be both. So, for example, a

stone cannot be hot and cold at the same time. Obviously nothing
and no one can be sacred and profane at the same time, since the
one is the antithesis of the other, each being defined as the negative
of the other. We have, however, previously seen that 'profane'
is not a category acceptable to Christian thought. Sacred and secular
are not opposites but twin aspects of reality. So just as a stone can
be both heavy and grey at the same time, because greyness and
heaviness are not antitheses, so human secular experience can also
include an encounter with the holy.

Illustrations of this duality are not difficult to find and indeed
two such – the white cube of sugar and the wounded traveller
succoured by the Good Samaritan – have already been adduced.
Let us consider some further examples.

A painting of a horse is evidently two things at once. It is the
representation of an animal and it is also a conglomeration of
areas of paint on canvas. Similarly there are drawings of reversible
cubes, which at one moment appear to stand out and at another
to recede. We cannot see them standing out and receding at the
same time, but we know that they are both. Accordingly we can
know that sacred and secular are two aspects of one reality. Perhaps more to the point is the associative character of language. When
I read a poem, many of the words have a richness and a depth of
meaning precisely because of the manifold associations they suggest
to me. Without such associations the words would have a minimal
effect. A single word, which consciously can only have one meaning
at a time for me, takes on a complexity and an evocativeness which
makes the poem appeal to me. So Paul, writing to the Romans, can
speak of the money that he collected for the Gentile Christians to
give to the Jewish nucleus of the church in Jerusalem as the 'fellowship'.[39] He does so because the collection is to be the medium for
cementing the one fellowship of Christians together, which was in
danger of splitting up into two groups – respectively Jewish and
Gentile. I, of course, can only think of the money as money and of
the fellowship as fellowship, but the use of the word *koinōnia* for
the contribution introduces me into a world of meaning far more
complex than that constituted by a one-to-one correspondence of
word and meaning. Similarly, when I encounter the holy through
the secular, this richness is also present, and unless I appreciate the
duality I lack awareness of the totality of the experience. It is true
that we respond to a meeting as a whole, while our analysis pro-

ceeds in linear form, i.e. we consider first one aspect and then another. But in life, it is the totality that we experience. The analysis may deepen our experience, just as the foreknowledge of the ingredients of a dish enables us to appreciate the various flavours, even in their unity. So the analysis of the sacred-secular unity can help us to appreciate the complexity and depths of an everyday experience. The mediated experience of the holy through the secular is therefore unitary.

Just as the previous thesis – that man mediates the holy to man – was illuminated by reference to the gospels, so our present concern – that the holy is to be encountered in and through the secular – can be similarly clarified. The first thing to note in this respect is that the gospel story is about a secular event, about an event within this world. If we cut through the pietistic devotion that surrounds the figure of Jesus, we become aware that it is accurate to style him, as does J. J. Vincent in the title of a valuable study, *Secular Christ*.[40] The record is of Jesus walking, talking, eating, drinking, arguing, teaching, healing. He spends little time in what is normally considered to be 'religious' activity. Nevertheless it is also the evangelists' conviction that this secular figure is the Holy One of **God.**

The secularity of Jesus becomes evident from even a cursory glance at his actions and teaching. That healing is a secular event, no one can doubt, but notice the story of the paralytic.

'Which is easier, to say to the paralytic, "Your sins are forgiven", or to say, "Rise, take up your pallet and walk?" But that you may know that the Son of man has authority on earth to forgive sins' – he said to the paralytic – 'I say to you, rise, take up your pallet and go home.'[41]

By these words Jesus demonstrates the unity of the holy and the secular. J. J. Vincent comments: 'The earthly, mundane act of healing the body is the act whereby the divine forgiveness now available in Jesus is communicated.'[42]

Or again, let us return to the story of Zacchaeus. This shows how the holy is confronted in everyday decisions. When Jesus hears Zacchaeus' response to his visit, he says: 'Today has salvation come to this house.'[43] But, asks Vincent,

How had the salvation come? By a man seeing in Jesus eating with him at his home, the present possibility of acceptance and forgiveness, represented by the prophet [or] righteous man who has come to the house. How did salvation come? By Zacchaeus seeing in the presence of

Jesus the demand for self-sacrifice to the poor and repayment four times over to those defrauded. This is salvation – secular self-sacrifice, secular reinstatement, secular compensation. The only way in which man may know salvation is in his secular discipleship.[44]

Turning next to Jesus' parables and drawing once more on J. J. Vincent, we need to notice that their purpose is 'to direct people into their own experience to see the true significance even of the secular events themselves, now that the open possibility of the kingdom stands before them'.[45] The parable of the Rich Man and his Goods is a perfect example of this. The farmer has prospered to such an extent that he has more harvest than space to store it. So he decides to pull down his barns and build larger ones, and says to himself: 'Soul, you have ample goods laid up for many years, take your ease, eat, drink and be merry.' But God said to him, 'Fool! This night your soul is required of you, and the things you have prepared, whose shall they be?'[46] This raises the question, which Jesus' hearers are expected to put to themselves, whether or not man may not be blind to the real issues in secular living, as was the rich man when he thought he had only himself and his barns to consider.

Jesus' teaching is all of a piece in this respect. Even the Beatitudes, in their more original unspiritualized Lucan form, depend entirely on worldly conditions: 'Blessed are you poor. . . . Blessed are you that hunger now. . . .'[47] Even such a saying as 'You cannot serve god and mammon'[48] – even this does not point away from the secular universe. If a man decides to serve God, 'his service will not be in an area or in terms different from that in which he would have served mammon'.[49] I endorse entirely J. J. Vincent's summary that Christ, or the Holy One, is already present in the secular deed, perhaps in every secular deed, when a man's only thought is to respond authentically and generously to what is asked of him in the confronting situation.[50]

From this follow three negative conclusions:

1. The holy and the secular are not identical but distinct, despite their essential unity.
2. Their unity does not violate the secular, but allows it to be truly itself.
3. The holy is not an extra added to, or brought in from the outside into, the human experience.

    1. In speaking of the distinction within the unity of the holy

and the secular, I am pointing to the concept of 'otherness'. In every human situation a relation is observable, whether it be between a tool and its user and or between one person and another. In the latter case, the relation is only possible because there is a difference between them. In personal encounter, it is the otherness of the other that rises before us. We are constantly confronted by a reality that transcends our own individual experience. This 'otherness' characterizes the holy just as much as it does the secular; hence they are distinct.

2. 'Holiness,' according to Martin Buber, 'penetrates nature without violating it.'[51] Indeed it is only when something possesses an authentic existence than one can speak of a positive relation to the holy, for the holy is not concerned with the inauthentic. In other words, the holy does not seek to make something what it is not, but rather to liberate something to be what it is called to be. Indeed the acknowledgement of the holy involves the consistent secularization of all those objects that have been sacralized. This means that to perceive the holy is at the same time to appreciate the truly secular nature of all created things.

> No special places, times, persons or communities are more representative of the One than any others are. No sacred graves or temples, no hallowed kings or priests, no festival days, no chosen communities are particularly representative of him in whom all things live and move and have their being. . . . The counterpart of this secularization, however, is the sanctification of all things. Now every day is the day that the Lord has made; every nation is a holy people called by him into existence in its place and time and to his glory; every person is sacred, made in his image and likeness.[52]

It is only if the holy is the numinous, and therefore alien to the secular, and wholly other, that the secular will be violated by its presence.

3. To discover the holy within human experience is not to add to that experience something that was not there before, as if our consciousness of the holy had caused its presence, drawing in from outside the situation some *deus ex machina*. To perceive the holy is to make explicit what is in the experience itself; it is to illuminate the experience from within. In other words, my argument is that our secular experience contains elements that inwardly refer to the holy. Its presence is neither an ornament nor an embellishment. One is simply recognizing another layer and so the multi-dimensional

nature of human experience. The holy, then, is not something extra to the secular from above or outside it; it is within the secular and mediated by it. Its discernment does not involve the addition of either a super- or a sub-structure divorced from the experience itself; rather, it is to understand the experience as itself disclosing its own experiential content more clearly.[53]

To a number of readers, several of the statements that have been made so far in this chapter will have suggested parallels both with the teaching of the Hasidim and with the I-Thou philosophy of Martin Buber. A brief account of each of these in turn will serve to advance and clarify further my argument.

Hasidism was a movement within Judaism founded by Rabbi Israel ben Eliezer. He was known as the Baal-Shem, i.e. the Master of God's Name, and lived from *c*. 1700–1760 in Podolia and Wolhynia. Knowledge of the teaching in the English-speaking world today is largely due to the efforts of Martin Buber, who has written critical studies on the subject, published translations of the sayings and stories of the Hasidim, and has embodied their outlook in a novel entitled *For the Sake of Heaven*. It is not my intention to attempt a full critical study of this body of teaching, but simply to point out the areas of correspondence between Hasidic ideas and my own, making a liberal use of quotations from Buber's works.

It has been my concern to emphasize above that the encounter with the holy is always a mediated experience in and through the material world and the world of human relations, and that this requires not world-denial but world-involvement. This is precisely the view of the Hasidim. Martin Buber summarizes their position as follows, contrasting it with the attitude of world-rejection:

Some religions do not regard our sojourn on earth as true life. They either teach that everything appearing to us here is mere appearance, behind which we should penetrate, or that it is only a forecourt of the true world, a forecourt which we should cross without paying much attention to it... In some systems of belief the believer considers that he can achieve a perfect relationship to God by renouncing the world of the senses and overcoming his own natural being. Not so the hasid. Certainly, 'cleaving' to God is to him the highest aim of the human person, but to achieve it he is not required to abandon the external and internal reality of earthly being, but to affirm it in its true God-oriented essence and thus so to transform it that he can offer it up to God.[54]

So Buber can say that 'the world in which you live, just as it is and not otherwise, affords you that association with God, which will redeem you'.[55] This is a faithful reproduction of Hasidic ideas, as demonstrated by the following sayings:

The Rabbi of Ger said: 'I often hear men say: "I want to throw up the world." But I ask you: "Is the world yours to throw up?" '[56]

According to the Rabbi Hayyim Meir Yehiel of Mogielnica: 'I do not want the rungs of the spirit without the garment of the flesh.'[57]

Consequently, to the Hasidim the holy is to be encountered in all spheres of life.

Rabbi Moshe of Kobryn affirmed that 'God says to man, as he said to Moses: "Put off thy shoes from thy feet" – put off the habitual which encloses your feet, and you will know that the place on which you are now standing is holy ground. For there is no rung of human life on which we cannot find the holiness of God everywhere and at all times.'[58]

Buber himself expresses the same idea when he says: 'At each place, in each hour, in each act, in each speech the holy can blossom forth.'[59]

This encounter is to be sought especially in human relationships and through love of the neighbour. Here Hasidic teaching comes remarkably close to that of the New Testament.

According to Buber: 'Creation is not a hurdle on the road to God, it is the road itself. We are created along with one another and directed to a life with one another. Creatures are placed in my way so that I, their fellow creature, by means of them and with them find the way to God.'[60] A further statement from his pen is virtually a summary of what we have already found in the gospels and in I John: 'You cannot really love God if you do not love men, and you cannot really love men if you do not love God. . . . One cannot have to do essentially with God if one does not have to do essentially with men.'[61] An even closer parallel is provided by the saying of a *zaddik* that 'If someone says to you that he has love for God but has no love for the living, he speaks falsely and pretends that which is impossible.'[62] Buber also maintains that 'whatever we do to our fellow men is bound up with what we do to God'.[63] That this is faithful to Hasidism is clear from the following sayings:

According to a *zaddik*: 'The real love of God should begin with the love of men. And if someone should tell you that he has love of God but has no love of men, then know that he is lying.'[64]

On one occasion a merchant complained to the Rabbi Meir Shalom of a competitor who had opened a shop next to his own. The Rabbi replied: 'You seem to think that it is your shop that supports you and you are setting your heart upon it instead of on God who is your support. But perhaps you do not know where God lives? It is written: "Love thy neighbour as thyself: I am the Lord." This means: "You shall want for your neighbour what he needs just as you do for yourself – and therein you will find the Lord." '65

This mediation of the holy through fellow human beings is particularly exemplified, according to certain of the Hasidim, within the marriage relationship. So Rabbi Mendel of Rymanov says: 'Where there is peace between husband and wife the Divine Presence rests in their minds.'66 The experience of the holy is also connected with the coitus whereby a man and his wife consummate their union. So Rabbi Yehiel Mikhal of Zlotchov, commenting on the verse 'Be fruitful and multiply', says: 'Be fruitful, but not like the animals, be more than they, grow upright and cleave to God as the sprig clings to the root, and dedicate your copulation to him.'67

This approach does not involve either a violation of the secular or a by-passing of the human reality. So the Shekinah, i.e. the divine presence, in Buber's novel declares that 'one cannot love me and abandon the created being'.68 Buber himself asserts that 'man cannot approach the divine by reaching beyond the human; he can approach him through becoming human'.69

The Hasidim also see the holy as involved in suffering. This is evident from a statement by the Yehudi, the chief character in *For the Sake of Heaven*:

He has apportioned to the world his *Shekinah*, his "indwelling", and has permitted his *Shekinah* to enter into the process of history and to share the contradictions and sufferings of the world... The *Shekinah* is not inviolable by stripes and wounds; it has identified itself wholly with our fate, our misery, our very guilt. When we sin, it experiences our sinfulness as something that happens to it. It shares not only our shame but also the disgraces which we would not acknowledge as such; these it tastes in all their shamefulness.70

In effect, the way of holiness for the Hasidim may be described as that of consecration of the world. They neither accept the world as it is nor seek to by-pass it in the direction of a supernatural realm, but consecrate it in the sense of seeing the holy in everything.71 Indeed one can say that the Hasid way is in accordance with the logic of the Incarnation. That logic can be formulated in five steps.

1. In Christ the holy is embodied in man in all his human perfection.

2. As each man realizes his potentialities and approaches nearer to his own human perfection, he is approaching the condition of Christ.

3. Hence, since the Incarnation, man, in order to find the holy, needs to do nothing else than become a fully mature human being.

4. This movement towards perfection is centred in the service of one's neighbour.

5. Hence by finding the way to one's neighbour, man achieves his full humanity and at the same time encounters the holy.[72]

This is but to repeat, in a slightly different form, the substance of the earlier pages of this chapter.

Of the various strands that form the Hasidic teaching, one in particular stands out as in need of further elaboration in order to define more precisely the how of the encounter with the holy in the secular world. This strand is the one of suffering, which Hasidism shares with the New Testament model.

If we consider the secular world, we cannot fail to notice how time and again it displays the operation of a 'law' that life is secured through death. Scientific advance, for example, is only possible through the giving up of old certainties and the confession of ignorance in order to discover new truths. Political and economic progress cannot be achieved unless people overcome their desire to retain what they have, to conserve the past rather than to allow it to die. Human maturity cannot be attained unless childhood passes away. Time itself illustrates the same structure, for tomorrow only comes into being through the ending of today. Human happiness is realized largely through the death of self-love. Artistic creation, too, involves the same process. So the modern Filippino poet Ricaredo Demetillo meditates upon what he calls '*Ars Poetica*'.

> The line of course and rhythm too.
> But one begins not with those two
> But with the nothingness,
> That awful emptiness
> Which glares before the eyes,
> Where talent gasps and dies.
>
> On that blank, one must gaze
> Until it spurts a blaze
> Of knowing miracle
> And Adam starts to call

> Creation, each by name
> That is as pure as flame.
>
> Then forge the poem word by word
> Until it cuts strict like a sword
> To that hard core which is the truth.
> All else reject, false or uncouth.

In the following poem, 'The Way of Art', he returns to the same theme.

> To solve the problem of one's art
> Solves, too, that of one's life and death. . . .
>
> One masters too the paradox
> Known to all martyrs to be true:
> Who loses life gains it anew –
> A strange saw to the frugal flocks.[73]

This 'law' of life through death applies to the whole of human existence, according to R. Roqueplo, 'when it is in comformity with the truth: whether it is a matter of personal opening out in the bosom of the social community, whether it is a matter of responsibilities, of love, of progress, of research . . . this sacrificial rhythm of action in conformity with the truth will be found. . . . Does this not suggest that the salvation brought by Christ consists essentially in replacing man in the truth of his own natural condition?'[74] Roqueplo, legitimately it seems to me, finds the prototype of this sacrificial way in the paschal event – in the suffering, death and resurrection of Jesus. He therefore finds meaning in the earthly realities as constituting the road to the holy.

To live according to this paschal pattern is to face suffering, through which we may encounter the holy. The conflict with evil, too, may lead to suffering, as it did for the New Testament model of the holy. Indeed the fact of evil raises acutely the question of meaning, and its accompanying suffering confronts us with the question of the holy. This does not require us to grapple with the problem of causality, nor to engage in theodicies; we are not faced with a theoretical situation requiring a theoretical answer. Suffering and evil demand an effective response, so that they may be overcome. But such a response, putting into action the intention to remove evil and establish good, is a response to the holy. This does not lead to a denial of the reality of evil and suffering, nor to a turning away from the situation, but to a serious endeavour to grapple with what confronts us. Those who do this are serving the holy and, even if unconsciously, are at the place of meeting – 'inasmuch as . . .'

Although the influence of Hasidism on the thought of Martin Buber was considerable, this in no way detracts from the originality of his own I-Thou philosophy. He first formulated this in a seminal study entitled *I and Thou*, which was published in Germany in 1923 and in an English translation by Ronald Gregor Smith in 1937. In subsequent writings Buber clarified and refined his ideas.

The basis of his position is to be found in the acknowledgement of a distinction – which once understood, appears to be undeniable – between the world of I-Thou and the world of I-It. In the former the subject is in relation with other subjects, while in the latter he is faced with objects. There is, therefore, a twofold attitude which man adopts, depending upon whether he is confronted by persons or is connected with things.

The world of I-It is one of separation, for it raises a barrier between subject and object and renders mutual relations impossible. The world of I-Thou is one of unity, for its characteristic situation is that of meeting, and in the reality of this meeting there is no reduction of either the I or the Thou. The world of I-It involves a functional outlook, i.e. the subject considers things as objects to be used. The world of I-Thou involves a recognition of the boundlessness of the other; it respects the freedom of the Thou, encounters with whom require complete openness, a surrender of becoming for being, of dissimulation for frankness, and a refusal to dominate. So there is an affirmation of simultaneous existence, without which the individual would be living, as it were, in a fog where each existence is self-contained and isolated.

This summary should not be interpreted to mean that Buber's distinction rests on the facile one between people and things. Persons, too, can be treated as objects, and so the world of I-It can and does embrace other human beings. Indeed, Buber is emphatic that one cannot sustain an I-Thou relationship indefinitely. Once the relational event has run its course, the Thou is bound to become an It, i.e. to be objectified, but the relation can be restored so that the other again ceases to be an It and becomes a Thou.

As far as the relation itself is concerned, Buber lays great stress on what he calls the 'in-between'. The I-Thou mutuality is not grounded in the sphere of individual subjectivity but in that *between* persons.[75] This is to say that the relation between two people is not to be located within them as individuals but between them. 'On the far side of the subjective, on this side of the objective, on the narrow ridge, where *I* and *Thou* meet, there is the realm of "Between".'[76] What is essential in personal encounter, therefore, does not take place in each individual separately, but between them, 'in a dimension which is available only to them both'.[77] This 'between' can only be known in lived relations. Love may serve as an example. According to Buber, love is not a feeling, although it may be accompanied by feelings. 'Feelings dwell in a man; but man dwells in his love.' In other words, 'love is *between I* and *Thou*'[78] – it is a relation: it designates an in-between which could not exist without the relation through which the two have access to it. Hence the need to understand that a prerequisite of relation is 'distance'; one can only enter into a relation when the other has been perceived as independent.[79]

Buber then goes a stage further in his thinking. He declares that 'Spirit is not in the *I*, but between *I* and *Thou*.'[80] This is to say that 'the extended lines of relations meet in the eternal *Thou*. Every particular *Thou* is a glimpse through to the eternal *Thou*.'[81] So man's relation to the eternal Thou does not take place in an altogether different dimension from his relation with the human Thou; on the contrary, the I-Thou meeting is at the same time an encounter with the divine. 'In each *Thou* we address the eternal Thou.'[82]

The basis for this understanding may be found in another of Buber's theses, viz. that in order to enter into a personal relation with the absolute, it is first necessary to be a person again.[83] But how do we become persons? Buber has no doubt about the answer to this, and few would disagree with him. Human beings achieve personal existence through dialogue with others. 'A person makes an appearance in relation with other persons.'[84] Hence the very process whereby we become persons enables us to enter into a personal relationship with the divine. R. L. Howe expresses this with admirable clarity in words that are in principle an exposition of the thought of Martin Buber.

Dialogue brings us face to face with truth in a relationship of love. As each person speaks and responds honestly to the other, each moves towards the other and includes him. This kind of meeting between man and man cannot occur without an implicit meeting between man and God. To really see another is to see the Other, and to really love another is to love the Other. When we are truly known by another we are known by God, and to be truly loved by another is to know the love of God. Dialogue, as we have been thinking of it, is more than communication. It is communion in which we are mutually informed, purified, illumined, and reunited to ourselves, to one another, and to God.[85]

But when I speak of man achieving personal existence, I am also implying that that existence should be characterized by wholeness. However, 'man can become whole not in virtue of a relation to himself but only in virtue of a relation to another self. This other self may be just as limited and conditioned as he is; in being together the unlimited and the unconditional is experienced.'[86] So through the concept of wholeness we arrive again at the encounter with the eternal Thou.

Buber is very hesitant to say much of the eternal Thou because, in Kierkegaardian vein, he maintains that 'if to believe in God means to be able to talk about him in the third person, then I do not believe in God. If to believe in him means to be able to talk to him, then I believe in God.'[87] This follows logically from certain of his premisses. In the first place, he understands the function of philosophical thinking to consist in *Deixis* (the pointer), the striking example, and not in *Apodeixis* (the demonstration).[88] Secondly, to speak of the divine in the third person would be, for Buber, an objectification; it would be to transfer the eternal Thou to the realm of I-It. Thirdly, Buber is convinced that 'the living God is not only a self-revealing but also a self-concealing God'.[89] This hiddenness has a dual character. On the one hand, it means that the divine is not readily identifiable and so not easily objectifiable. On the other hand, this self-concealment is an aspect of the dimension of faith; this is the necessary *incognito* that allows the possibility of faith while respecting human freedom. Yet at the same time this remoteness is also man's fault; it is not God that abandons man but man who fails to perceive him. As Buber says, 'often enough we think there is nothing to hear, but long before we have ourselves put wax in our ears'.[90] Particularly in adversity it may seem that the divine has withdrawn and that his countenance is hidden, but as one of the Hasidim – Rabbi Pinhas – remarked: 'It ceases to be a hiding, if you know it is hiding.'[91]

It should be apparent by now that the position formulated by Buber on a philosophical basis is all but identical with that I have outlined on a New Testament basis. There is a difference of terminology but not of substance. Buber understands the I-Thou relation as the locus of encounter with the eternal Thou; I understand personal relations as the locus of encounter with the holy. Buber sees mutuality as essentially dialogical; I have argued that one aspect of the New Testament model of the holy is precisely its dialogical nature. Buber sees wholeness arising out of the encounter with the eternal Thou in the I-Thou relation; similarly I have discussed wholeness as an effect of the meeting with the holy. Buber speaks of the hiddenness of the eternal Thou, while I have called attention to the *incognito* of the holy. Finally, Buber insists upon the necessity for distance, which is another way of describing that otherness which I have suggested is just as much a characteristic of the holy as it is of the secular. Nevertheless, despite these agreements, there appear to be differences in our two positions which should not pass unexamined.

Buber has little time for 'experience'. As he understands it, experience is something within a man and not between him and the world; it therefore lacks mutuality and belongs to the realm of I-It. 'The world has no part in the experience. It permits itself to be experienced, but has no concern with the matter. For it does nothing to the experience, and the experience does nothing to it.'[92] Indeed, 'I do not experience the man to whom I say Thou. But I take my stand in relation to him.'[93] Consequently the meeting with the eternal Thou does not arise out of experience, and therefore not out of detached subjectivity, but out of life.[94] By contrast, I have frequently alluded to experience in the previous pages, but this difference is no more than a matter of semantics. Whether experience is a legitimate category or not depends upon how it is understood. I have argued above that experience is not something that is private and mental but is basically encounter, and this means, therefore, that I, too, understand experience in terms of, and not in antithesis to, relation.

There is, however, another contrast between our two positions which cannot be resolved so easily. Buber lays great stress on the 'in-between', whereas I have suggested that the presence of the holy is not only to be located there but also in the other person. To serve the brother in distress is to minister to Christ in the person of the other, and not simply to meet him in the in-between. The christological model of the holy does not fit Buber's philosophy, because, according to Christian belief, Christ himself is the in-between; he himself is the relation, the holy in human form. Moreover, Christians see Christ as the image of God – a belief that Buber cannot accept – and all human beings as created in that image, which can therefore be met in the other through personal encounter. So where Buber accepts only one locus, the in-between, I perceive two, the in-between and the person of the other. Hence, in my view, the holy is present in the other, but this recognition is possible because of the existence of the in-between. It is the dialogical relation that enables me to have glimpses of the holy. To illustrate the difference between these two positions, we have only to recall the incident reproduced above from Kazantzakis' novel *Christ Recrucified*. Manolios affirms that the beggar at the monastery gate was Christ – Buber, concentrating exclusively on the in-between, could make no such identification. The practical effect of this difference is that the paradigm or disclosure situations which I shall present later in this work are not always ones which, in strict accordance with Buber's philosophy, would be accepted by him as such.

Buber's philosophy, although immensely influential, has not escaped some adverse criticism. In particular, it has been objected that to build a philosophy exclusively upon the I-Thou relation is to leave man unmanned before many other relations which form the major part of his life, e.g. his work, his connection with things and with impersonal forces.[95] The result can be the fostering of a privatizing tendency, i.e. of a tendency to concentrate upon the private person rather than upon society. So a Christian theology, based solely on the I-Thou relation, would lose any societal dimension; it would be apolitical and irrelevant to much of human living.[96] But personal existence cannot be limited to a series of I-Thou meetings, because it then becomes a personalism that withdraws before the industrial world. On the contrary, 'man is destined to be a person in all areas of social life, wherever he joins forces with others, either temporarily or more permanently, in groups and projects that are either necessitated by the common situation or freely chosen'.[97]

This objection may be pin-pointed by means of an example, viz. that of charity. From an exclusive I-Thou standpoint, charity becomes a private virtue, related to interpersonal meetings or the neighbourhood, possibly extended through some national organization, such as Oxfam, which itself is really no more than an organ for increasing the realm of private charity. But the result is the confining of love to the closed-circuit of the I-Thou relations. Hence J. B. Metz objects that 'it is not possible to restrict love to the interpersonal sphere of the I-Thou. We must interpret love, and make it effective, in its societal dimension. This means that love should be the unconditional determination to bring justice, liberty and peace *to the others*.'[98]

R. Roqueplo describes a situation which bears directly on this matter. He tells of a certain woman who established a group to visit the old, the sick and the poor in a depressed neighbourhood. So successful was this venture that the civic authorities accepted responsibility for the work and placed the woman in charge of their newly-formed organization. The result was that she spent her time in a central office as an administrator and ceased to have direct contact with her fellow human beings in distress. Her reaction to this different form of service was to fear that she was no longer being faithful to Christ, and she wished to give up her office duties and return to her visiting. Roqueplo comments:

> The Christian today would commit a grave sin if he paralysed the working of social welfare structures on the false pretext that these collective structures involve the rejection of interpersonal relations. Whether we like it or not, we are no longer in the days of St Vincent de Paul and of the distribution of bread to the poor. The modern method of washing the feet of the poor is to struggle for a world in which the poor have a better deal. The modern method of visiting the sick is to do everything to suppress sickness. The modern method of feeding the hungry is to create a viable economy. The modern method of welcoming strangers is to establish an effective political universalism. In our socialized universe, my brother man is only truly and effectively served by the mediation of economic structures and political and ethical ideas, and many today devote themselves to the service of man by devoting themselves to the working of these structures and to the promotion of these ideals.[99]

Monsignor Joseph Gremillion is making the same point when he rephrases the words of the Son of Man to those whom he welcomes into the Kingdom: 'I was hungry and you discovered a non-polluting pesticide – on credit terms peasants can afford.'[100] Hence engagement in these secular activities is to be understood as the secular form of man's devotion to the holy. Nevertheless Roqueplo goes on to emphasize that it is essential to preserve some direct relations, otherwise devotion to the large concerns can easily become an opportunity for individual glory and power. Moreover, the poor need not only a cup of water but direct confrontation with the love that the cup of water expresses. Yet these political and economic struggles, to the extent to which they are truly motivated by the desire to improve the lot of less fortunate brothers, 'constitute a privileged experience that mediates and involves our relationship to God. It follows that every human activity, to the extent to which it is a service of men, participates in this experience'.[101]

However, in fairness to Buber, it should not be forgotten that he does attempt to include things within the I-Thou relationship. He takes a tree as an example. He points out that this can be considered on many different levels – as a beautiful object or picture, as movement, as a living entity, as a species, as an expression of law.

It can, however, come about, if I have both will and grace, that in considering the tree I become bound up in relation to it. The tree is now no longer *It*. I have been seized by the power of exclusiveness.

To effect this it is not necessary for me to give up any of the ways in which I consider the tree. There is nothing from which I would have to turn my eyes away in order to see, and no knowledge that I would have to forget. Rather is everything, picture and movement, species and type, law and number, indivisibly united in this event.

Everything belonging to the tree is in this: its form and structure, its colours and chemical composition, its intercourse with the elements and with the stars, are all present in a single whole.

The tree is no impression, no play of my imagination, no value depending upon my mood; but is bodied over against me and has to do with me, as I with it – only in a different way.

Let no attempt be made to sap the strength from the meaning of the relation: relation is mutual.

The tree will have a consciousness, then, similar to our own? Of that I have no experience. But do you wish, through seeming to succeed in it with yourself, once again to disintegrate that which cannot be disintegrated? I encounter no soul or dryad of the tree, but the tree itself.[102]

I have to admit that, as far as I understand this account, I remain unconvinced. Buber maintains that a relation necessarily involves mutuality, i.e. both *I* and *Thou* are affected by it, but he is unable to explain how a tree itself is involved in this mutuality. It is one thing to recognize the otherness of the tree, as something that stands over against me, confronts me and refuses to become a mere object for use, but it is another to see the tree's part in the in-between. Nor do I find any more enlightening a further example that Buber gives in his 'Replies to my Critics', specifically to face this objection.

I choose, as always, an example which has powerful memories for some people: this time the Doric pillar, wherever it appears to a man who is ready and able to return to it. Out of a church wall in Syracuse, in which it has once been immured, it first came to encounter me: mysterious primal mass represented in such simple form that there was nothing individual to look at, nothing individual to enjoy. All that could be done was what I did: I took my stand, stood fast, in face of this structure of spirit, this mass penetrated and given body by the mind and hand of man. Does the concept of mutuality vanish here? It only plunges back into the dark, or it is transformed into a concrete content which coldly declines to assume conceptual form, but is bright and reliable.[103]

This seems to me more an 'experience', as Buber understands the term, than a relation, and if this is so then he has not found his way out of an individualistic personalism. Yet, while agreeing with this general criticism of Buber, I would not wish to dispute that the I-Thou relation is *one* of the loci of the encounter with the holy – this only becomes misleading when it is considered to be the exclusive place of encounter. We may leave to a later stage a fuller examination of the extent to which the world of I-It can also be such a locus.[104]

The way is now almost clear to consider paradigms of the encounter with the holy. The material available appears to be limitless, for if the holy is mediated in and through the secular, then the whole of secular life should be capable of providing examples of disclosure situations. One can turn to real-life situations, to plays, television documentaries, films, novels, etc.

However, there is an important limitation to be noted, especially when the material is in written form. In his sensitive study of *Tolstoy and the Novel*,[105] J. Bayley differentiates between two types of fiction: those works which enable the reader to share in the lives of the characters and those which require him to contemplate them. Bayley entitles the latter genre 'pastoral', which he defines as 'the process of making everything in a world of literature characteristic'.[106] The author of a pastoral novel provides a frame within which the individual is determined. Where there is a conscious 'pastoral' ideal, this frame may take the form of an ideology – the characters then conform to this ideological framework and express ideas and engage in actions in agreement with the ideology. The reader can then only contemplate the character (unless he shares the ideology); he cannot participate in their lives. So we can share in *War and Peace*; we can only observe Balzac's *Comédie Humaine* –

the difference between observation and participation being obvious when we recall that to participate in a kiss is by no means the same as to observe one.

In the pastoral novel or play, because the author pulls the wires, as it were, and the characters are simply his puppets, having no life of their own, the reader or spectator cannot become involved. One can only contemplate the characters through the eyes of the author. It then becomes difficult, if not impossible, when the author's own conscious beliefs rule out any chance of an encounter with the holy, to draw on this type of literature for disclosure situations. If the author himself cannot perceive the holy, neither will his characters, and the events he describes will be set within a framework which precludes that experience.

The novels of Jean-Paul Sartre belong to this 'pastoral' type. Sartre writes to exemplify and embody in narrated action his own atheist existentialism. Hence, comments David Anderson, 'one wonders whether the characters he invents are more like exemplars of a theory than possible individuals'.[107] Indeed he is prepared to say that the novels are 'rather depressing and inhuman', that participation is a dimension entirely lacking, that there is no sharing in the being of others and hence no love.[108] If this is accurate, then Sartre does not provide any models of the I-Thou relation and thereby excludes any paradigm of the holy. I doubt if even Camus presents a figure of genuine humanity, because he himself cannot believe in the possibility of authentic existence, without which the holy can only be discerned dimly.

The same applies to what Martin Esslin has called the 'Theatre of the Absurd'. The plays that he brings together, perhaps not always correctly, certainly have a number of characteristics in common. Each one is basically 'religious' in the sense that it gives a vivid picture of man's spiritual predicament. This predicament combines a declaration of the meaninglessness of life with the explanation that this arises from the absence of the holy. The world of the absurd exists because of the loss of the sense of the sacred. In this situation some of the characters, e.g. Estragon and Vladimir in *Waiting for Godot*, hope for a *deus ex machina* – while the playwright himself is convinced that such an intervention from outside is impossible. The characters all experience estrangement and alienation. Indeed in Brecht's *In the Jungle of Cities*, one of them says: 'If you crammed a ship full of human bodies till it burst, the loneli-

ness inside it would be so great that they would turn to ice.'[109]
Homes in No by Manuel de Pedrolo and *One Way Pendulum* by
N. F. Simpson[110] are two further brilliant examples of the demise
of the inter-human.

One of the playwrights, Adamov, explicitly attributes this separation to the absence of the holy. 'I am separated. What I am
separated from – I cannot name it. But I am separated.' In a foot-
note, he adds: 'Formerly it was called God. Today it no longer has
any name.' Elsewhere he says:

> The name of God should no longer come from the mouth of man.
> This word that has so long been degraded by usage no longer means
> anything. To use the word God is more than sloth, it is a refusal to
> think, a kind of short cut, a hideous shorthand.[111]

The logical outcome of this thought-sequence is taken by Samuel
Beckett, who finally dispenses both with characters and plot, e.g.
in both *Waiting for Godot* and *Endgame*. According to Esslin:
'Characters presuppose that human nature, and diversity of personality and individuality, is real and matters; plot can exist only on
the assumption that events in time are significant. These are precisely the assumptions that the two plays put in question.'[112]

If we take this generalized picture as a whole, then we are presented with a moving account of man's plight in the secular universe. We are not, however, provided with any solution; there is no
way of escape, because this very perspective precludes the perception of the holy according to the New Testament model – indeed
awareness of the model is entirely lacking to these writers. Nevertheless there is much in this analysis with which I am in entire
agreement. No more than Beckett can I accept a solution in terms
of a *deus ex machina*. With Simpson and others I am bound to
acknowledge the fact of alienation, and with Adamov I understand
this as arising from a loss of the sense of the holy. But my disagreement is just as great. Against Beckett I must affirm that persons are
real and so matter, and that events in time are significant. I cannot
accept the general hopelessness, because my hope is not based where
Vladimir and Estragon rest theirs, on some visitor, as it were, from
outer space. Indeed the resolution of their plight would not, cannot
be achieved by the entrance of Godot, but only by the recognition
that God was there all the time; such a way of perceiving the situation is not shared by Beckett nor by his characters, and so *Waiting*

for Godot cannot serve as a paradigm of the holy. Moreover, I consider that because of this perspective these writers do not present man's *total* situation, whereas it is only within the total situation that the holy can be discerned. I would assert that the possibility of overcoming alienation lies within each human situation, precisely because it is there, from within, that it can be illuminated by the recognition of the holy. Perhaps it may be said that they present the world of secularism rather than the secular or fully hominized world.

If the authors of the Theatre of the Absurd sound the death-knell of the numinous – which is to be welcomed – they do not help anyone to perceive the relevance to man's situation of the New Testament model of the holy. Indeed, as long as we can see the hominized world through their confined field of vision, we are prevented from acknowledging disclosure-situations. It is to be hoped that the theatre will not rest at this point, for it can enable the spectator to transcend the confines of his personal identity and to participate in other forms of existence – when this is achieved the theatre may once again assist a meeting with the holy.

Nor do many so-called Christian writers give much assistance. It is true that T. S. Eliot has described man's plight in unforgettable poetry, both in *The Waste Land* and *The Hollow Men*:

> Our dried voices, when
> We whisper together
> Are quiet and meaningless
> As wind in dry grass
> Or rats' feet over broken glass
> In our dry cellar . . .
>
> In this last of meeting places
> We grope together
> And avoid speech
> Gathered on this beach of the tumid river [113]

But Eliot's proposed solution is a return to the sacral universe. His *Four Quartets* are an embodiment of the mystic vision, of that situationless, ahistorical, unmediated union that turns away from the world.

> At the still point of the turning world. Neither flesh nor
> fleshless;
> Neither from nor towards; at the still point, there the
> dance is,

But neither arrest nor movement. And do not call it fixity.
Where past and future are gathered. Neither movement
    from nor towards,
Neither ascent nor decline. Except for the point, the
    still point,
There would be no dance, and there is only the dance.
I can only say, *there* we have been: but I cannot say
    where.
And I cannot say, how long, for that is to place it in
    time. . . .

Descend lower, descend only
Into the world of perpetual solitude,
World not world, but that which is not world,
Internal darkness, deprivation
And destitution of all property,
Desiccation of the world of sense,
Evacuation of the world of fancy,
Inoperancy of the world of spirit;
This is the one way, and the other
Is the same, not in movement
But abstention from movement; while the world moves
In appetency, on its metalled ways
Of time past and time future.[114]

Sublime though this is, I venture to suggest that it is a far cry
from the New Testament model of the holy. But Eliot is certainly
consistent when he quotes with approval from John of the Cross,
using this sentence as an epigraph to 'Sweeney Agonistes': 'Hence
the soul cannot be possessed of the divine union until it has divested
itself of the love of created beings.'[115] This is certainly to turn away
from the secular situation in which 'what can be directly experienced
empirically discloses and evokes something deeper than that which is
immediately experienced, something that reveals precisely the deeper
basis and condition of possibility of the secular event'.[116]

There are some Christian novelists who operate within a framework of naive supernaturalism. The novels of Charles Williams are
supreme examples of this pastoral genre, used in the service of a certain ideology of the holy. In each and every one of them Williams
seeks to find a place for the holy to enter the human scene from outside. In *Many Dimensions*, for example, it is a stone from the crown
of Suleiman ben Daood that operates as the locus of the numinous
presence. Charles Williams certainly points to the holy, but it is the
holy in terms of the *deus ex machina* – it has aspects of the spooky

and the uncanny. It is not discerned from within the human situation but represents an irruption from elsewhere. Novels of this type – however enjoyable to read – are of little assistance. Other 'religious' novelists fail to provide glimpses of the holy in the sense I have outlined previously; their only concern with the holy is in terms of the other-worldly. Both Evelyn Waugh and Graham Greene paint this world as evil; only the world beyond death is the sublime reality. So Colin Wilson remarks, not unfairly, that they share an identical technique of conversion in that 'their world is meant to depress the reader into feeling the need for religion'.[117] Perhaps the suitable material available is not as extensive as once seemed likely.

There is, however, a non-Christian author who is of considerable interest in relation to my concern, the American Norman Mailer. Few contemporary writers are as concerned as he is with the question of meaning. In his fascinating books, which are a challenging blend of reporting, comment and autobiography, he is consistently raising the question: what do these human events mean? So he has written about the mass demonstration in Washington against the Vietnam war (*Armies of the Night*), about the first lunar landing (*A Fire on the Moon*) and about Women's Liberation (*The Prisoner of Sex*). Mailer hopes to grasp meaning by relating these events or movements to the ultimate and he quotes several passages from the Bible. He himself admits that he is something of a medievalist and indeed he does operate, paradoxically enough, since he is very modern in many respects, within the sacral framework. This is revealed by his frequent use of such terms as mystery, fear, terror, dread, awe and apocalyptic – the reader cannot but notice the number of times these words occur and the quest for the numinous that is implicit in them. Yet, in so far as these accounts are reasonably full descriptions of the human reality, within which the holy is to be met, I shall be drawing on his work later in this study.

However, if we also avoid the naively supernatural, we do not have to deny that in reading a novel or seeing a play we can frequently enter into a relation. Our own stance (which need not always be identical with that of the author) *vis-à-vis* a novel or play may provide the possibility of an 'in-between', and therefore enable us to interpret them from a perspective which allows for the holy. In so far as novelists and playwrights succeed in involving us in their scenes, those scenes can be disclosure situations. In effect this means approaching them in an attitude that Tillich has described as 'belief-ful realism'. 'Realism' indicates that we are not concerned with some special reality, but with the reality around us, secular reality. 'Belief-ful' describes the proper attitude to the reality, viz. that we must not remain on the surface, but penetrate into its depths and apprehend or be apprehended by the holy. Such an approach is not cavalier; it does not seek to dominate; it does not require standing back from reality but participating in it, so that the whole may be apprehended, and within that totality the holy itself.[118]

EXCURSUS A

The Holy in a Cul-de-sac

Throughout this study my chief concern is to present a positive understanding of the holy, and consequently I have attempted to keep negative criticism to a minimum within the body of the text. Nevertheless concepts of the holy other than the one I am putting forward are current at the present day, and these cannot be simply ignored.

The most widespread concept, and the only one to which I have referred in the previous chapters, is that which derives from Rudolf Otto and interprets the holy as the numinous. No matter where one turns, one is faced with affirmations about the *mysterium tremendum* and the Wholly Other. In innumerable theological works the concept of the numinous is endorsed without any questions being asked. For example, in the introduction to *Man's Concern with Holiness*, G. Curtis asserts the validity of Otto's analysis,[1] and, later in the same volume, P. Eudokimov can declare that 'holiness above all else is the reverse of everything worldly; it represents the eruption of something utterly different from the world'.[2] R. Jones, in what is otherwise a very helpful study, perhaps more philosophical than theological, *The Concept of Holiness* (1961), devotes much attention to a further elaboration of Otto's position.

But not only theologians perpetuate this outlook. It is to be noted amongst sociologists of religion. The very title of P. L. Berger's most recent work reveals his mental set; he has called it *A Rumour of Angels* (1969). It would be presumptive to dismiss this book out of hand on these grounds alone, and indeed Berger's two principal theses have a direct bearing on my main concern, so it will not be too much of a digression, in an *excursus,* to direct attention to them here.

Thesis I is a continuation of an argument which Berger had already formulated in a book which he wrote with T. Luckmann, *The Social Construction of Reality.* There they had argued that 'subjective reality is always dependent upon specific plausibility structures, that is, the specific social base and social processess required for its maintenance'[3] Applying this to the church, Berger contends that Christians are to be characterized as a 'cognitive minority', i.e. they are 'a group of people whose view of the world differs significantly from the one generally taken for granted in their society'.[4] In his view it is their assertion of the 'supernatural' that marks this cognitive deviance. To him it is essential to preserve this, because otherwise 'the whole edifice of traditional piety takes on the character of a museum of religious history. People may like museums, but they are reluctant to live in them.'[5] Hence the need to cling to the supernatural, which he identifies with the numinous, and to belong to a community – even if a minority group – that can provide the necessary plausibility structure.

Now no one can deny there are degrees of cognitive deviation between various groups and the pluralistic society in which we live today, but one does not have to accept unnecessary deviations. One should not subject people to the tension of adopting a certain standpoint, in opposition to society in general, unless the particular view is an essential element in what is apprehended as true. My principal argument is that the supernatural/numinous outlook is not one to which Christians are committed by the New Testament, and that to insist upon it creates an unnecessary deviation. In other words, I accept the reality of the holy, but my understanding of it is, I believe, in accordance and not in conflict with contemporary modes of experience.

Berger's 'Thesis II' is more a programme recommended to theologians. 'I would suggest,' he says, 'that theological thought seek out what might be called signals of transcendence within the empirically given human situation. . . . By signals of transcendence I mean phenomena that are to be found within the domain of "natural" reality but that appear to point beyond that reality.'[6] Elsewhere he writes: 'The discovery of Christ implies the discovery of the redeeming presence of God within the anguish of human experience. Now God is perceived not only in terrible confrontation with the world

of man, but present within it as suffering love.'[7] With some altera-
tions this is precisely the programme I am pursuing – but the altera-
tions are all important. For 'symbols of transcendence' I substitute
'paradigms of the New Testament model of the holy'; I replace
'pointing beyond the "natural" reality' by 'a mediated experience
in and through and not apart from the natural reality'; instead of
'terrible confrontation' I read 'the ordinariness of the holy'. These
three points of difference emphasize the extent to which Berger still
operates within the ambit of the numinous.

If anyone thinks that this is an unfair representation of Berger's
thought, let him consult another work by the same author, viz.
The Sacred Canopy. In this Berger emphatically states: 'I have tried
to operate here with a substantive definition of religion in terms of
the positing of a sacred cosmos. . . . The differentiation in this definition, of course, is the category of the sacred, which I have taken
essentially in the sense understood by *Religionswissenschaft* since
Rudolf Otto.'[8]

The numinous finds its place also in the philosophy of religion. So
I. T. Ramsey, in his *Religious Language*, describes 'a characteristi-
cally religious situation' as 'one of worship, wonder, awe'[9] and says
that it is nothing if not odd.[10] To Ramsey I am much indebted for
his analysis of disclosure situations, and this has determined the form
of my next chapter. The examples he adduces are most illuminating.
So he points to Nathan's confrontation with David, after the king
has arranged for the murder of Uriah in order to take Bathsheba.
The prophet tells the story of two men, one rich and one poor, and
how the former takes the latter's only possession – one little ewe
lamb. When David condemns the rich man, Nathan retorts: 'You
are the man.' Ramsey shows how this incident is a disclosure. David
recognizes that the story is about himself, and that in judging the
rich man he is judging himself, and so he shares in the story and
thus is enabled to recognize the judgment of God.[11] Again Ramsey
clarifies one's understanding of the fulfilment of prophecy. Commenting on the ministry of Jesus as an example of fulfilment, he
says: 'What happens now is that this language is brought alongside
other facts which are plainly quite different from the original facts
in relation to which there was the *original* disclosure, and the claim
is made that there is now a *further* disclosure.'[12] This I have adopted
as the basis of my own approach, viz. to take the New Testament
model of the holy, where the story of Jesus is a disclosure event, and

to bring this into relation to present-day happenings in order to seek
a further disclosure. But while acknowledging my indebtedness to
these valuable insights provided by Ramsey, I have to state my disagreement with his implicit acceptance of the numinous and with
his assumption that a paradigm of the holy must be odd – it is
only odd if the holy be the wholly other, whereas I am contending
that it is through the ordinary that we encounter the holy.

The numinous also finds its way into literary criticism,[13] and the
quest for it, as a literary theme, has been comprehensively described
by Colin Wilson, first in his two critical studies, *The Outsider*
(1956) and *Religion and the Rebel* (1957), and then embodied in
Gerard Sorme, the chief character in his novel *Man without a
Shadow* (1965).

The Outsider is a Nietzchean figure who has little time for the
common run of humanity – 'other people are the trouble' and
'society is a hall of distorting mirrors',[14] i.e. hindrances in perceiving the infinite. The Outsider is further characterized by a
'nagging dissatisfaction with the range of his everyday experience'[15]
and 'is haunted by a sense of the futility of life'.[16] To him the
world is a cheat and a deception; it is a wretched place, peopled
with mediocre, dull and boring individuals. He has to isolate himself from society, because as long as he remains an obedient member
of it he cannot achieve a vision of the world that is radically different
from that of his fellows. Therefore 'salvation lies in extremes'.[17]
Gerard Sorme clings to the belief that 'the human spirit is not confined to the flat earth of consciousness'[18] and seeks in sexual activity
an outlet into eternity.

I know that this power exists in me for other purposes than sex.
Sometimes it can be evoked by music or literature or ideas. Something
like it flows in me now as I write this because I am writing with excite-
ment, enjoying being able to put down these ideas into words. I feel like
a detective cross-examining the world, trying to trap it into admissions of
purpose. I know bloody well it exists – an immense power and purpose.
So why am I usually left out? This damned lying cheat of a world. I
don't know yet why I exist. I feel superfluous, like a gramophone in the
middle of the Sahara Desert. And yet there are times when I *almost* get
plugged in, when some of my plugs find their sockets, and there's a
whisper of power in my nerves.[19]

Sorme finds a common characteristic in these experiences, viz. that
there is 'a kind of conquest of time', which 'is a movement toward
the godhead I speak of'.[20] He recognizes that what he is doing is

'trying to break into reality with his crowbar of reason',[21] whereas, as Wilson himself believes, 'that everything is infinite is an *existential* truth not accessible to reason'.[22] Clearly Wilson is in pursuit of the numinous, conceived also as the non-rational, and while he, and his principal character, make a violent effort, I do not see this as a viable road for man in the secular universe. Not only is it too individualistic and cut off from personal relations, but it presupposes that the goal can be obtained apart from one's fellow men. Wilson thus misconceives the locus of encounter. Basically he seeks the holy apart from and by rejecting the human world. The Outsider does not grasp the possibility of meeting the holy in the common: indeed, the common nauseates him, so that he repudiates it. Moreover, he fails to grasp the historical character of the meeting and is still subject to outmoded concepts of eternity and non-temporality, while at the same time yearning for an unmediated encounter. Wilson's continued interest in the numinous is shown by his most recent book *The Occult* (1971), which reaffirms the non-rational and the importance of mystical apprehension.

There are affinities between Gerard Sorme and those who hope for the numinous by the taking of drugs. There is the same scepticism of reason and the same understanding of the experience they seek as ahistorical. To read Tom Wolfe's *The Electric Kool-Aid Acid Test* (1969) is to recognize that LSD-takers are looking for an enlargement of consciousness. Their experiences exactly correspond to Otto's analysis of the holy – the experiences can be either fearful, inducing dread and horror, or blissful, thus pointing to the *fascinans* aspect of the numinous. Aldous Huxley's *Doors of Perception* (1954) is acknowledged as one of the 'sacred' texts of the movement. Huxley argued that the brain functions as a kind of reducing valve. The mind receives a flood of information from the outside world, which the brain filters into a trickle in order to cope with it. But, so the argument goes, man has become so rationalized that the trickle is very tiny indeed and in effect has eliminated too much and possibly most of man's potential experience. Hence Huxley sought liberation through mescalin, as do the puppet-characters in his last novel *Island* (1962), who are addicted to *moksha*-medicine, and those today who resort to LSD. The result is an opting out of society; it involves a rejection of the world and a corresponding reluctance to engage in activity to change it. Certainly the enlargement of consciousness which it is claimed to promote is no spur to social action. Wrapt contemplation of the *mysterium tremendum* is the summit of life's endeavour.

The taking of drugs may be regarded as a temporary release from burdensome reality, but the primary question is whether or not the experience itself is of any value. To answer this one has to have in mind some criteria that would enable an experience to be classified as valuable. I would suggest two: an experience may be regarded as valuable if it assists the person undergoing it to live an integrated life and, following from this, if it has a positive effect on life as a whole. The available evidence indicates that experiences under drugs are not particularly enlightening about life, do not lead to wholeness and cannot be retained long enough to be subjected afterwards to rational analysis by the clear mind. They are isolated moments, discontinuous with normal life. Huxley himself was bitterly disappointed that his feelings vanished in his waking state, so that he could not examine them properly. In other words, the so-called 'enlightenment' is lost once the trip is over, so that there is no continuity between it and everyday life. The 'cleansing of perception' is momentary and results in no permanent illumination.

It is, then, reasonable to conclude that resort to drugs is a flight from responsibility and Timothy Leary symbolizes this way of life perfectly with his slogan: 'Turn on, tune in and drop out'.[23] So far from an enlargement of consciousness, what is achieved is the shutting out of awareness of the real world for a period. This is a form of escapism that ultimately results in the practice ceasing to be even a diversion. Mind-adjusting chemicals are a short cut to the kind of satisfaction to be derived from successful mental or physical effort. But man cannot hide from himself perpetually that he is trying to secure the result without the effort, and this frequently produces a sense of guilt. Consequently it may be said that drug addicts are attempting to reconcile the impossible, viz. in the words of Stuart Hall, 'to achieve the primitive state of contemplation via the medium of the most modern chemical aids'.[24] Moreover, man is also deeply convinced that visions in one's cups are unreliable and that a trip is a deviation from reality, and so to endorse drug-taking as an element in a way of life is to argue against one's inner knowledge. In sum, this ahistorical experience stands in sharp contrast to the encounter with the holy, when that is understood in terms of the New Testament model.[25]

Huxley's thesis has been subjected to considerable criticism, e.g.

by R. C. Zaehner in his *Mysticism, Sacred and Profane* (1957), but then so have Otto's views, without their inadequacy being generally recognized and alternatives sought. R. W. Hepburn has pointed out that the feeling of numinous awe does not of itself require to be interpreted as a cognitive experience of any being at all. It could be the result of contemplating the beauty of nature and need have nothing to do with the holy.[26] As John Baillie states: 'All those occurrences which to the eye of faith reveal the divine presence are capable of being explained without apparent remainder in purely naturalistic terms'[27] – which is what we would have expected in the light of the previous discussion of layers of interpretation. S.S. Acquaviva criticizes Otto along the same lines. He points out that the different feelings which Otto believes the holy to produce: dependence, submission, fear, etc., may be aspects not of the holy but of the experience itself. So he asks: 'Does the experience express itself in the feeling of dependence, or does the feeling develop because we have had previously an experience of the holy?'[28] That is, the feeling may be an effect of the encounter with the holy, but, if so, it tells us nothing definite about the holy in itself. This feeling may then be simply the derivative of the meeting, a *posterius*, which does not take us into the heart of the reality encountered. Indeed, whatever aspects of the holy as defined by Otto we consider, whether it be that which fascinates or that which repels, we can find similar feelings produced by entirely non-sacred events, persons or things.

Nevertheless, Acquaviva does accept Otto's category of the Wholly Other. He reaches this position by the following steps:

1. Man's principal characteristic is his self-consciousness.
2. Man's knowledge in general is obtained by comparison, confrontation and relationships.
3. His self-consciousness is obtained in the same way.
4. But this very capacity enables him to know that which is not himself and so to encounter the Wholly Other.[29]

The final stage in this sequence is, however, a *non-sequitur*. Man's self-consciousness does indeed allow him to know that which is not himself and so to encounter the 'other' – but nothing in the logic requires the insertion of the adverb 'wholly'. Moreover, following J. Watzke, I would contend that Acquaviva has not really identified the heart of the problem he has set himself. The so-called decline of

the sacred is in fact an institutional crisis. It arises out of 'an institutional failure to communicate with the individual and the
general culture in terms of a meaningful and relevant set of symbols'.[30] In other words, since 'religious' experience is related to the
socio-psychological culture of persons and groups, because the experience of the holy preserved in the church, largely in terms of the
numinous, relates to the past socio-psychological culture of the
sacral universe, it is inevitably regarded as irrelevant by the man
who inhabits the secular universe.

Other critics of Otto, who may be mentioned briefly, include John
Oman, who, writing long ago, admitted Otto's fervour but took the
view that it often 'produces more heat than light'.[31] Oman was prepared to advocate reverence before the holy, but he would have nothing to do with abject cringing before the wholly other, and in a
magnificent passage he distinguished between these two attitudes:

As reverence, the sense of the holy is the humility which is the foun-
tain-head of all right and courageous independence in seeking truth, and
truth only: as awe, it is trivial and even a shuddering fear of all enlightenment. As reverence, it is the graciousness, the sincerity, the high
responsiveness which gives us deliverance both from the mere pleasing
of the senses and the artificial taste of our time, and makes it both small
and great before the austere sublimity of true beauty of form and
character: as awe, it is as a cloud of blackness upon the earth and of
horror upon our souls, leaving us nothing in which to rejoice, and no
spontaneity of feeling by which to appreciate. As reverence, it is regard
for our neighbour and our souls which gives us independence of the
canons of respectability and what we may call traditional divine juris-
prudence, enabling us to exercise freely our own judgment of good in face
of our situation: as awe, it imprisons us in traditional rules and formal
respectabilities.[32]

John Baillie returned again and again to a critique of Otto,
characterizing his sense of awe as a feeling of eeriness, evoked by
the presence of that which is 'shuddersome' or even 'spooky'.[33] He
repudiated the concept of the holy as the wholly other, as something
alien, because in yielding to the demand that the holy makes upon
us we are finding our highest good.[34]

Yet the unquestioned acceptance of the numinous goes on, despite
the fact that, apart from the Outsider and the drug-takers, secular
man finds it largely meaningless. Hence the constant laments, e.g.
by Gavin Reid in *The Gagging of God*, that 'secularity is removing
the numinous aspects of life from our experience'.[35] But to bemoan

the passing of the numinous is, in my view, to desire the continued enclosure of the holy within a cul-de-sac. For this concept presupposes the pre-technical era; it belongs to a sacralized universe with all its supernaturalist trappings.

Of course, many modern theologians are perfectly well aware of the existence of a cul-de-sac, and perhaps those who have made the most strenuous efforts to find a way out are the ones whose names are associated with the slogan 'the death of God'. Both William Hamilton and Thomas J. J. Altizer have little time for the numinous, and they question the whole basis of Otto's position in the religious *a priori*. Otto had argued that while man has certain initially-given natural forces, he also possesses an innate religious consciousness that lies in the mind independently of sense experience.[36] So man has, as it were, an autonomous faculty which enables him to recognize the numinous-holy. This has enabled Otto and some of his followers to present an apology for religion on the grounds of the so-called universality of the numinous. Such a claim does not fit the facts. There have been societies which worshipped beetles and turtles that 'neither exude nor inspire a numinous force'.[37] The gods of ancient Egypt were rather dull, with little numinous aura. Otto therefore failed to distinguish between religious knowledge and its subject-matter, so that he sought a specifically religious factor such as the *numinosum* in the subject-matter itself. Moreover, the claim that religion is an original constituent of human nature is not one that either Hamilton or Altizer will allow. They are convinced that God will not force himself on man, not even by building into him an inescapable need for religion.[38] Hence they declare:

> The breakdown of the religious *a priori* means that there is no way, ontological, cultural or psychological, to locate a part of the self or a part of human experience that needs God. There is no God-shaped blank within man. Man's heart may or may not be restless until it rests in God. It is not necessarily so. God is not in the realm of the necessary at all; he is not necessary being, he is not necessary to avoid despair or self-righteousness. He is one of the possibles in a radically pluralistic spiritual and intellectual milieu.[39]

This means that one cannot say with Otto that the holy is a unique datum of experience – the wholly other – but it does not preclude the possibility of understanding the holy as mediated through all experience or a recognition of the unity of the sacred and the secular.[40]

However, the main point of departure adopted by Hamilton and Altizer is elsewhere than in the numinous, as indicated by the title of one of Altizer's first books, *Mircea Eliade and the Dialectic of the Sacred* (1963). Altizer's basis is essentially the phenomenology of religion, which leads him to understand the sacred as the antithesis of the profane. So he asserts that 'the meaning of the sacred is reached by inverting the reality created by modern man's profane choice'.[41] In a joint work we find the following supporting statements:

> Critical definitions of religion in all their variety show that the sacred and the religious life is the *opposite* of the profane and secular life.
>
> All religions proclaim or celebrate a way *to* the sacred *from* the profane.[42]

Altizer is also convinced that modern man has chosen the profane,[43] and he identifies himself with that choice, interpreting this to mean that man can only know the sacred as the Nothing.[44] Moreover, he recognizes that man today regards himself as purely historical being, i.e. he has 'immersed himself in the immediate temporal moment'.[45] Consequently the realm of the sacred is closed and one cannot but proclaim the death of God. Now granted the premiss, the conclusion follows with inexorable logic – it cannot be faulted. However, it is precisely the premiss that I cannot accept.

I have argued above that 'profane' is not a category acceptable to and usable within Christian theology. As a consequence of the Christ-event, the common or secular has ceased to be the profane – that which is not related to the divine – and has therefore become the potential medium of encounter with the holy. To suggest that man has to choose between the sacred (the non-profane) and the profane is to present an illusionary choice, if the profane no longer exists. But Altizer is so bound up within his own dialectic that he can declare: 'Once an awareness of the profane is banished, therewith will vanish an awareness of the sacred: for if the sacred is the opposite of the profane it can no longer be manifest when the profane has disappeared.'[46] He never pauses to consider whether, if the profane is abolished by Christ, the secular can mediate the holy. Nor does he appreciate that the encounter with the holy can be and indeed, in the light of Christ, must be essentially historical. To reject sacralization, to live in a secular universe, to opt for history, is not to deny the holy, since it is in and through the secular within time that the meeting takes place. Altizer, in particular, ties himself up in the logic of his own definitions, and consequently, though he may lead us out of one cul-de-sac, it is only to enclose us in another.

My critique can be expressed in a slightly different form. Once we accept that the profane has no meaning for Christians, we can no longer interpret the holy negatively as that which is not the profane. If the holy has any meaning today, it must be understood on some basis other than that of the phenomenology of religion. But this new understanding is thrust upon us by the New Testament, with its insistence that the profane is no longer a category of life and that the model of the holy is the secular Christ. Altizer is, of course, correct in detecting in historic Christianity more than traces of the dichotomy of the sacred and the profane, and this form of Christianity does belong to what he calls 'archaic religion'. But this, if my analysis of the New Testament model is correct, is a misunderstanding of the Christ-event and a falling away from the New Testament interpretation. Unless we can rediscover the holy within the secular universe, we shall only experience the death of God. But such a rediscovery cannot refer either to the numinous or the non-profane of religious phenomenology.

P. Antoine seeks an escape from the cul-de-sac by maintaining that the holy is not a category of Christian theology at all, but belongs essentially to religious phenomenology, where it generally means both the numinous and the non-profane. He contends that this understanding is meaningless within a technological society and, further, he accepts the division between the sacred and the profane, but believes that it can only be overcome by removing the concept of the holy.[47] I cannot accept these points as they stand. While the holy is a category of religious phenomenology, it has a long history in Christian thought and is undeniably present in the New Testament – one simply cannot cut the Gordian knot in this cavalier way. We have to understand the holy, not from the basis of phenomenology, but in the light of Christ, and we cannot just dispense with the term. Further, while the holy as the numinous or the non-profane is without meaning in a technological society, Antoine does not consider the possibility of a new interpretation that would render it understandable. Finally, his acceptance of the sacred/profane dichotomy, while reasonable on the basis of the phenomenology he rejects, will not do, since the second term – profane – is without content from the Christian perspective. I am at one with Antoine in his assertion that through Christ there is a rupture with the past, but I see that rupture, not as a negation of the holy, but as issuing in a totally new understanding of it.

I have now completed my brief survey of a select number of modern approaches to the holy. Such a negative criticism has been necessary because of what Paul Tillich describes as 'the destruction of the religious experience through false interpretations of it'.[48] If the approaches of such writers as Otto and Altizer are invalid, they necessarily result in destroying the perception of the holy. Whether or not my approach is any more helpful and avoids yet another cul-de-sac, I must leave my readers to judge.

An Attempt to Clarify the Terminology used in Discussions of the Subject of the Holy

Many authors preface their books or articles with a series of definitions so that the readers may have no doubt about the meaning of the terms used. I have so far not attempted this because it has seemed to me that, for example, a definition of the holy could only emerge as the result or end-product of the investigation. Nevertheless much confusion is introduced into the discussion of the holy because of ambiguous terms and because there is no general agreement about their meaning. Some writers regard 'holy' and 'sacred' as synonyms – which is what I have done in the previous chapters – whereas others distinguish between them. Some employ 'profane' where I think 'secular' more suitable. Others speak of 'sacralization' where I would understand 'consecration'. Because of this ambiguity and because my argument is now reasonably well advanced, I propose to attempt some clarification of the main terms relating to our subject.

The most difficult aspect of the terminological confusion to be sorted out is that which concerns the relationship of the words 'holy' and 'sacred'. No clear distinction can be drawn between these two either on the basis of etymology or on that of usage. 'Holy' has been employed as the English equivalent of the Latin *sacer* and *sanctus* and of the French *sacré* and *saint*. *Sacer* carries with it the connotation 'consecrated to a god', and is the opposite of *profanus*, while *sanctus* sometimes means 'divine'. *Sacré* is employed in relation to religion and worship, but since one can speak of *un saint temple*, there is no clear differentiation, although *saint* has overtones of 'perfect', as in *un saint homme*, i.e. one who lives according to the divine law. The English word 'holy' may refer to that which pertains to a god or is set apart for religious use, and 'sacred' implies consecration to a deity. One might reasonably conclude from this that holy and sacred are interchangeable and that any slight difference of nuance between them would have to be detected in the light of their context.

Nevertheless, some contemporary theologians do seek to draw an absolute distinction between holy and sacred.[1] In effect they use the first to mean 'divine', while they regard the second as referring to a relation. Hence they contend that God is not sacred but holy, and that Christ, in so far as he is divine, is holy but not sacred. So 'the sacred is subordinated and relative to the holy, because the holy is divine'.[2]

The difference becomes clearer if it is examined in the light of the classical doctrine of the person of Christ. 'In Christ we find a perfect conjunction of the sacred and the holy. He is sacred as man-God, mediator, sign of the relation with the divine. But he is at the same time holy: he is God, because he is the Holy One of God.'[3] That which is sacred, therefore, is that which mediates a relationship with God, and so one can speak of the sacred elements at the eucharist. The bread and wine are the means whereby the worshipper is related to the holy. It would therefore be incorrect, according to this view, to speak of the elements as holy.

The sacred, then, is that which brings us close and enables us to attain to the holy. To this there are two corollaries.

First, this understanding of the sacred has nothing to do with the sacred of magic, because its purpose is not to put the holy at our disposal; instead it respects the otherness of the holy.

Yet, second, while maintaining this necessary appropriate distance in terms of otherness, it does not allow that separation which is produced by 'the sacred of prohibition, tabu and the *tremendum*'.[4]

So the sacred is to be interpreted as a relation of meaning, and it expresses itself in signs and symbols which permit an encounter with the holy without compromising its otherness.

Unless the relational character of the sacred is constantly borne in mind – so the argument continues – there is the temptation, to which many often succumb, to think that the signs themselves possess holiness, i.e. the relation becomes confused with the object and the sacred with the holy. This is precisely the danger to which Paul Tillich drew attention when he said that 'if the holiness comes to be considered inherent, it becomes demonic. This happens continually in the actual life of most religions. The representations of man's ultimate concern – holy objects – tend to become his ultimate concern. They are transformed into idols.'[5] Moreover, once sacredness is attributed to objects or persons in this way and regarded as a characteristic or quality permanently within them, then the way is open to regarding other objects and other persons as profane, and the whole sacred/profane dichotomy re-emerges. Then the result is sacralization, because with the replacement of a mediating and relational role by an inherent holiness the secular reality is eclipsed, and indeed, when the profane is regarded as that which is unrelated to the divine, it *has* to be eclipsed, if creation is to be brought into final union with God.

The distinction which I have just been describing is very important and, in my view, is undeniably valid. But, after all, it is not the words we use which establish distinctions but the meaning we give to the words. Now there can be no questioning that holy and sacred have been used interchangeably for centuries by writer after writer. The time is almost certainly past when one could introduce a clear and unambiguous differentiation, using each term to correspond with a single and different concept. To be consistent one would have to talk about 'sacred communion' and not 'holy communion', about the 'sacred city' and not the 'holy city', etc. The result might be greater clarity of thought, but I doubt if such a reversal of usage could be achieved, and it certainly could not be secured without much confusion. It has therefore seemed to me that I should continue to use holy and sacred as synonyms, while trying to make clear from the context what particular aspect I have in mind when using either one or the other.

In the light of this discussion and of the foregoing chapters I would now like to propose the following working definitions:

1. The holy (noun) = the divine.
2. Holiness (as applied to God) = the otherness and nearness of the divine.
3. Holy (adjective) and sacred (adjective) = God-related.
4. Holiness and sacredness (as applied to man) = God-relatedness.
5. Holy worldliness or worldly holiness = relatedness to God in and through the world.
6. Sanctification = a process of developing God-relatedness, the

final goal of which is not identification but union. It refers, therefore, to a progressive opening out to the holy without ceasing to
be human.

7. Consecration = the explicit affirmation of God-relatedness or the
   making explicit of that relation.
8. Secular = that which belongs to the world; that which is natural
   in relation to the reality of nature, and that which is human in
   relation to mankind.
9. Secularization = the process of change from a sacral to a secular
   or hominized universe, involving disenchantment and dedivinization. It affirms the authentic worldly nature of persons, objects or
   events.
10. Sacralization = the attributing to something or someone of an
    inherent holiness, which is believed to subsume and replace their
    authentic secular nature.
11. Secularism = the belief that the secular is absolutely autonomous
    and that nothing is related to God.
12. Profane = that which is not God-related.

Most of these terms are dialectically related; change one and many
of the others will have to be changed; understand one and this will
comprehend several of the rest. The definition of consecration, for
example, is inseparable from that of secularization, since the one is
impossible without the other; while sacralization is the antithesis of
both. An example will help to make this clear. If we sacralize the
eucharistic bread we cannot speak of its consecration, i.e. of the
explicit declaration of its God-relatedness, because, once it has
ceased to be bread and has become divinized, there is no longer any
possibility of a relationship. For a relation to exist there have to be
two parties or one party and an object – in this instance: bread and
God. But if the bread is no longer bread, there can be no relation
between it and God. Consecration therefore demands secularization
as its necessary basis.[6]

Nor is consecration possible if secularism is the mental set adopted.
Secularism refuses to acknowledge the possibility of God-relatedness
and, therefore, consecration as the affirmation of God-relatedness is
meaningless. Secularization itself does require the recognition of a
certain autonomy on the part of the secular reality, but whereas
according to secularism that is absolute, there is no need to assert
more than a relative autonomy. That is, the consecration does not

deny the reality of the object in itself; it simply affirms the God-relatedness of that reality and confirms it in its relative autonomy. Secularism and sacralization are, therefore, opposites and each in isolation becomes demonic. The affirmation of the secular at the expense of the holy or of the holy against the secular results in a loss of authenticity on both sides. Human beings can be degraded by those who look through the spectacles of sacralization, like the Spanish Inquisitors, just as much as by those whose vision is determined by secularism, like the agents of suppression in the Stalin era.

Indeed everything worldly is the creation of God. The Incarnation reaffirms the creaturely and autonomous reality of the world and so desacralizes the secular that it may be truly itself. The Incarnation stands against all forms of sacralization because it reveals God in action in and through the secular, neither apart from it nor divinizing it and transforming it into something other than itself. This understanding is safeguarded by the orthodox belief that Jesus is both God and man and that, even after the Ascension, the manhood persists unimpaired by the union. Jesus was the holy one because his life was the living out in flesh and blood of a relationship to God. Secular realities and the realities of faith have their origin in one and the same God who, according to Christian belief, is both Creator and Redeemer. To set these in opposition to one another is to assent to a form of Gnosticism, and sacralization is an implicit fostering of this opposition. All secular realities have an immediate end; to encounter the holy in and through them is not to deny these finite ends but to comprehend them in an ultimate end. So the secular can be both affirmed and consecrated.

Secularism and the profane go together, but Christians in repudiating the first cannot consistently admit the second, since to do so would be to deny the relationship of a part or aspect of reality to God. So, for example, a Christian can never say that dancing in a church building is a profane act, unless he regards all dancing as sinful, for his very declaration would itself be a profanation, i.e. an assertion that some human activity – other than sin – is not God-related.

It is, of course, much easier to divide the sacred from the secular, to reject the latter and seek to follow the path of world denial. It is easier in the sense that the position may be more readily defined. It is less easy to accept the relative autonomy of the secular and then seek through the secular the way to the holy. This involves seeking the holy amidst the ambiguities of life, and to this task we turn in the next chapter.

5

The Holy and Personal Relations

In this and the following chapters I shall be recording, either by direct quotation from novels or in my own words, a series of disclosure-situations, i.e. situations in and through which we may recognize the holy. These situations, if we follow the conclusions of the previous chapter about the place of encounter, are to be sought in personal relations and everyday events. It is when these are approached with the model provided by Jesus as the referent that we may be able to perceive the holy. Armed, as it were, with this pre-understanding of the holy – or this mental set, *schema*, etc. – we should be able to discover if it permits us to identify the holy within the situations described. If such perception is possible, then the empirical fit of this model within the framework of the hominized universe will have been further demonstrated. My intention is, then, to tell a number of stories in and through which I consider that encounters with the holy may be discerned. The importance of the recounting of tales as a method for evoking the holy has been mentioned previously, but it is worth re-emphasizing.

Zorba the Greek, the principal character in Nikos Kazantzakis' novel of that name, once asked his employer about the meaning of life. When questioned in this direct way, he found it difficult to produce immediately an intelligible answer. 'If only I could never open my mouth, I thought, until the abstract idea had reached its highest point – and had become a story.'[1] This is the method of the Hasidim, and also of the writers of the New Testament who convey their understanding of the holy by telling the story of Jesus.[2]

Nevertheless, if the reader is to find anything of interest in the subsequent stories and is not to be disappointed by them, it is important that he realize both what they are not intended to achieve and how their function is to be defined positively. This is not a book of Christian apologetics. I am not, in this chapter for example, arguing from personal relations to the holy. The facts that constitute the incidents described are not the bare facts of the kind a thorough-going empiricist would admit, because 'they are already interpreted as meaningful within a universe understood as the realm where the divine becomes evident in the human'.[3] I am simply saying, therefore, that if you adopt the mental set I have outlined previously, then in some I-Thou relationships you may encounter the holy; i.e., by reference to the model, which is Christ, we are enabled to see how a situation may be evocative of the holy. The notes that follow each description are an application of the model and indicate what the holy means for me. My hope is that these will assist others to perceive the holy, possibly in situations where they have not previously looked for it. All this means that I am not concerned with the *existence* of the holy but with its *reality*. The difference is this. I take 'to exist' to mean 'to be part of a system'. Now to view the holy in this way is to make it one finite existent besides others *within* a system, whereas I consider the holy to be the ground and goal of the entire cosmic system. The 'real' I take to mean that which 'possesses definite characteristics permitting distinction and discrimination; it is not the exclusive possession of a single individual and it reveals itself as having a status beyond the self which experiences or thinks it'.[4] The problem of the holy therefore, is, not that of its existence but of its reality.

However, the meaning I discern in certain incidents, in which I perceive the holy, is not something solely subjective, in the sense that it originates in my emotions or cerebration and is then projected into an objective happening. On the contrary, with Martin Buber this meaning is the one 'I perceive, experience, and hear in reality'.[5] This does not require the investing of an event with a meaning from outside it. Rather, I am saying that the event becomes meaningful because the perception of the holy within it affects my relation to the event. In other words, to say that something has meaning, when understood in the light of the presence of the holy, is not to attribute to the something an extraneous quality, but to show how I stand in relation to it, that relation being affected by the discernment of the holy. The holy is that which gives meaning to events in that its presence affects our interpretation of the events and so the meaning we perceive within them.

I am, of course, working not with scientific but with personal disclosure models – the terminology is that of I. T. Ramsey.[6] Scientific models generate deductive verification, while personal disclosure models work in terms of empirical fit. That is to say, I am seeking to demonstrate their internal consistency, their agreement with the New Testament model of the holy, and the extent to which the recognition of the holy enables one to perceive an incident in its total context and with its total content.

> In each event which comes into your life you are invited, or if you like, you are challenged, to respond to this event as one in which simultaneously with its everyday meaning you recognize and acknowledge that God is here at work. This does not mean that you replace the ordinary meaning of the event with a divine meaning. But it means that in this event, within it, not destroying it, you acknowledge that God is present.[7]

Hence the ambiguity to which I have referred previously; hence the acknowledgment of interlocking layers of meaning, none of which invalidates the others. The signs of the holy are not, of course, simply objective phenomena; they constitute something that addresses us, and to become aware of this we have to be open, ready to respond. The point of departure for this is not in some remote transcendence, but in human relations where the interiority of the creative presence may be discerned.

The stories themselves all indicate that the encounter with the holy is mediated; they show, too, that the holy is to be found in the ordinary. 'The signs of address,' says Martin Buber, 'are not something extraordinary, something that steps out of the order of things, they are just what goes on time and again.'[8] In a sense, therefore, they are about the obvious, remembering Arthur Koestler's amusing remark that the 'Lord Almighty seems to be fond of the trick which Poe's character employed when he let the secret document lie open on his desk – where it was too obvious to be seen'.[9] Indeed, scarcely any of these stories is overtly religious, for to identify the holy with the religious is fallacious. We are not, therefore, looking for isolated moments of 'religious' ecstasy or bliss, since the holy is related to all of life and is to be encountered in the whole of life. This is not to suggest that every moment mediates equally the presence of the holy, although potentially every moment can and may. Rather, there is a consciousness of the divine will as the background of life and as 'a reality which may at any time emerge to confront us in absolute and inescapable demand'.[10]

It will be evident from what has just been said that these tales are intended to be aids to the recognition of the holy. My purpose is, therefore, at one with that of Teilhard de Chardin in his *Le Milieu Divin*, where he wrote that 'these pages put forward no more than a practical attitude – or, more exactly perhaps, a way of teaching how to see'.[11] The hints provided are inevitably partial, because the encounters, though direct, are mediated – 'now we see in a mirror dimly'. Nor will the tales function properly if they fail to engage the reader, i.e. unless the reader himself participates in the incidents recorded. This involves being aware of the dual aspect of each event, in that each one describes the relations of the persons in the story to one another, while there is, further, the relation of the reader himself to the incident described. By means of this latter relation – this in-between – it may be possible to perceive the holy even where, e.g. because of alienation, the characters in the story are not themselves aware of it. One cannot discern the holy from *outside* a situation, but only from within. Hence recognition requires our involvement as persons. Only then will the integrity of the secular be preserved, instead of being denatured by sacralization. It is not a matter of adding to an experience a dimension that was previously lacking; it is, rather, a consideration of an experience from a particular perspective that enables discernment of the holy, without the nature of the secular *per se* being changed.

The holy then is 'not an extra to those day-to-day events, but appears in and through them. It is truer to say that God is met through the world than over and above it. He comes not "plump down from above", but is to be glimpsed in every event, in every needy hand upraised, every conflict of will, every utterance of hope or love.'[12] Consequently the holy is not a mystery to be discerned only by an élite or by the theologically sophisticated. Yet there is no compulsion to recognize it. 'The word does not enforce its own hearing. Whoever does not wish to respond to the Thou addressed to him can apparently go about his business unimpeded.'[13]

The notes that follow each description are aids to perception; if they are not read in this light they could possibly be misconceived as an objectification of the holy. As we move from the concrete situations to a discussion of them, there is a risk of abstraction, so that the holy becomes an object of thought freed from the limitation of the actual. It becomes an idea, an object, an It, instead of a directly perceived reality within a mediating event. The notes are no more than indicators to help those who allow themselves to become involved in the situations described to perceive the holy as a Thou within lived reality, instead of as a precise concept on a page of theological writing.

Disclosure Situation I – The Convict

Silvano Ceccherini's prize-winning Italian novel *The Transfer* has as its chief character a convict named Olgi who has already spent twenty years of a life sentence for murder. He is being transferred from one prison to another, and the narrative simply describes the journey, the stops on the way and the people he meets. He is suffering from a heart disease which eventually kills him and, at the time of the incident I am about to reproduce, he is undergoing a bout of intense pain and is in despair. Then he notices one of his fellow prisoners.

> He looked at the fair boy, who had taken off the raincoat that made him look wretched. He wore a short-sleeved shirt open on the chest. His skin, through sunburn and the warm flow of his blood, gleamed golden.
> Olgi couldn't take his eyes off him. Through that handsome youth, all his unquenchable love of life rose again and stood triumphantly on the ashes of his misery. Nothing really died on earth: youth was immortal, beauty indestructible.
> This certainty – of the perennial flow and renewal of life – made him suddenly forget his own life, his own trouble.
> ... the fair boy went out and vanished, unaware that he had illumined anyone.[14]

Notes

It is not difficult to discern within Olgi's experience several of the aspects of the New Testament model of the holy. First, there is wonder: 'Olgi couldn't take his eyes off him.' He marvels at the handsomeness of the youth. Second, the experience is life-enhancing, leading to wholeness and well-being, so that Olgi attains self-forgetfulness and a deep love for living and for other people. Thirdly, the encounter is one of promise bringing hope: this is the eschatological aspect of the holy. Because the way of holiness is not one of resignation nor the acceptance of the present without taking into account the effect of the promise and so of the future, Olgi suddenly forgets 'his own ills, his own troubles'. Indeed his 'unquenchable love of life rose again and stood triumphantly on the ashes of his misery', despite his disease and despite the long years of imprisonment that still lie ahead.

This incident is a perfect illustration of Franz Kafka's conviction that 'it is entirely conceivable that life's splendour forever lies in wait about each of us in all its fulness, but veiled from view, deep down, invisible, far off. It *is* there, though, not hostile, not reluctant, not deaf.'[15] The meeting illustrates, too, the reverse truth of Paul Tillich's statement that 'religion has very often been nothing more than the superfluous consecration of some situation or action which was neither judged nor transformed by this consecration'.[16] Olgi's experience, on the contrary, is one of illumination – although the boy was 'unaware that he had illumined anyone' – whereby he is himself transformed through his encounter with the holy in and through the young man.

One new thing we do learn from this scene. While one cannot deny that Olgi's relationship to the youth belongs to the world of the I-Thou, his experience does not derive from any direct personal knowledge of his fellow-prisoner; in fact he has never seen him before, does not know his name and never sees him again. One may conclude, therefore, that while the I-Thou is facilitated by familiarity with the other, it does not require this as an exclusive *sine qua non* for its existence.

Disclosure Situation II – Belle de Jour

Belle de Jour is the title of an imaginative French film, directed by Louis Bunuel, and based upon a not very inspiring novel of the same name by Joseph Kessel.[17] The film is a sensitive study of sexual frigidity.

It opens with a dream sequence showing the husband, Pierre, with his wife, Séverine, in a carriage. Pierre makes affectionate advances to Séverine who resists them and is dragged from the conveyance, strung up on a rope, lashed and finally abandoned by her husband to the lust of an ugly oaf of a lackey. As the story unfolds, the meaning of Séverine's dream becomes apparent. A flashback reveals that she had been caressed and sexually stimulated as a little girl by a brutal servant, and this has rendered her incapable of sexual pleasure except under circumstances of degradation. She is thus not able to respond to her husband's love and consequently feels guilt and the need for punishment. The opening dream, therefore, combines the rejection of Pierre with punishment, the lashing, and with a carnal relationship under humiliating circumstances. Here is a vivid presentation of a broken relationship: the husband is shut up within his own hurt at the apparent spurning of his love, while the wife is incarcerated within the icy walls reared by her own frigidity. Neither the husband's tenderness nor his self-restraint can break through to the wife in her imprisonment.

Yearning for the wholeness she does not possess, the wife enters a brothel, adopting the pseudonym of Belle de Jour, and makes herself available there every afternoon. In this situation, which she regards as both distasteful and degrading, she finds herself capable of sexual pleasure. Her guilt, however, is only further increased, as revealed by another dream in which she is tied to a tree and plastered with filthy ordure. Séverine is eventually discovered by a friend of her husband's who comes to the brothel as a client. The subsequent dream shows husband and friend duelling, for they are now in a sense rivals for her favours, but the sole bullet fired hits her, the victim of the frigidity which has driven her to assume the role of a prostitute.

Séverine at last decides to give up her dual life but is traced to her home by a gangster client who has become infatuated with her. Believing that her refusal to continue to see him is due to the existence of her husband, he shoots him and is himself killed by the police while attempting to escape. Pierre does not die but is left both blind and paralysed.

In the final scene Séverine and Pierre are together in their living room. Séverine says that she has ceased to have her terrifying dreams. Because the husband is no longer capable of sexual relations, she has no guilt towards him; she no longer has to reject him because he can no longer make advances. The friend now pays a visit and, in order to relieve Pierre of his guilt at being a physical wreck and so unable to show his love for his wife, tells him of Séverine's infidelity, considering it better for Pierre to seethe in resentment than to suffer in hopelessness. Séverine dreams once more. The husband appears well again, so the carriage is driven in, but now it is empty – for husband and wife have virtually ceased to exist; there is no longer relationship nor any chance of a relationship, and without such an I-Thou encounter they are no longer persons.

Notes

Throughout, this is a story of alienation and estrangement. The characters have almost no rapport. The husband and wife cannot make any real contact; the clients in the brothel treat the women as mere objects to gratify their physical appetites. Because there is no relation, no in-between, there is no awareness of the holy. The alienation proclaims the absence of the holy and the consequent dehumanization of all concerned. Only if Séverine had become whole and had entered into normal sexual relations with Pierre could there have been an in-between and so a discernment of the holy.

Yet there is another side to this. While the characters lack any in-between, the film itself is not of the pastoral type, but involves the spectators so that they participate in it. Through this relation, an in-between – embracing spectators and husband and wife – becomes possible. So paradoxically the film demonstrates both the absence of the holy and at the same time its presence, in that the holy is also that which hides itself, and it does so in this sequence of events by mutely sharing in the suffering of both husband and wife. Because there is no I-Thou relation, the activity of the holy to bring wholeness is not known, but because of our own involvement in the film we can discern the holy as that which hides itself in suffering and is present through compassionate identification in human distress. Here it is possible to appreciate the aspects of *incognito* and of lowliness and of identification through suffering love which have emerged from our examination of the New Testament model.

The hiddenness of the holy preserves the freedom of the characters whose wholeness lies in its pursuit through the restoration of relationship; they are not compelled to follow this way by the holy, for the holy is not a *deus ex machina*, although it could absorb the guilt and sin of the two concerned, if they were awakened to its reality. Let us recall the Hasidic saying: 'It ceases to be a hiding, if you know it is hiding.' The tragedy of *Belle de Jour* is that, whereas we may know this, there is no one in the story itself to help either Séverine or Pierre to reach such a level of consciousness.

Disclosure Situation III – In the Ladies' Room

In *Rites of Passage* by Jean Rikhoff, there is an account of a New Year's Eve party of local residents in an hotel. Carolyn Tryson has been having an affair as a consequence of which she is at odds with her husband. She retires to the ladies' room where she meets her lover's wife, who is herself ignorant that Carolyn is one of the many women with whom he has been philandering. She unburdens herself of her grief and concludes by thanking Carolyn for listening to her so sympathetically, with the words: 'I always think of you as a good person.' This sentence profoundly affects Carolyn, who is already upset because her lover has indicated that he is tired of her. She now realizes her hypocrisy and her own responsibility for the situation in which she finds herself. The narrative continues:

For the first time Carolyn was conscious of Christ as a real figure, someone who had suffered, who had actually hung, suspended from nails, hour after hour, a man in torment, deserted, despairing, dying under an uncaring sky. He had suffered. It was the first time these words had meant anything to her. Like the rest of them He had suffered, and because of that she was able to feel close to Him, to understand, however little, what the pageant meant – the life and death of a man with a tongue that could make them have meaning. It was an individual to whom she paid tribute now, someone who, from fragmented episodes and meaningless phenomena, had fashioned a whole history, a purposeful pattern, an end for all of them, and lifted it from simple suffering and sacrifice to an act that meant more than its component parts, who had given to the suffering meaning.

Ultimately, Carolyn thought, it was not man that should ask *why*? But life that should ask that question of each individual. Each man on his own should respond as best he could, so that in the end it was not man who questioned life but life that questioned man.

And what would you answer, what would you say when life asked, *To what purpose*? Something inside said, To be responsible, that is the essence of what we should all be, responsible.

It seemed to her that to be responsible you had to confront your fears and name them – love, alcohol, unworthiness – what ever they were, and they were legion, ask anyone. But only after you labelled them were you able to live with them, to act against them.[18]

Notes

In this extract the author has almost done my work for me; she has shown how in the meeting of two unhappy women, in the unglamorous surroundings of a hotel rest room, it is possible to encounter the holy. Little remains to be added, beyond relating the incident more directly to those aspects of the New Testament model which I have previously spelled out.

There is, first, as in *Belle de Jour*, the identification in suffering, now recognized by the chief character herself. Alternatively this may be defined as the acknowledgment of the paschal pattern. Natural life itself, in order to be truly itself, must be sacrificial. So there is no spiritual life, characterized by a spirit of sacrifice, over and above the natural sacrificial life; the two are conjoined. In her suffering and in that of her confidante, Carolyn recognizes this pattern and perceives, too, that this, which is inherent in the situation, gives meaning and purpose. This enables her, through her encounter with the holy, secondly, to accept responsibility, which is an element in the process of humanization. Carolyn advances further in self-awareness by meeting the other, and, whereas previously crushed by her lover's rejection and full of self-pity, she rediscovers her dignity as a human being. Now she can go forward, amidst all the trivia of life, in responsible freedom and hope. Certainly this encounter does not result in an acquiescence in her *status quo* nor in passive contemplation. Carolyn's life has been deeply affected.

The meeting with the holy, therefore, does not refer simply to the 'now' in itself – to the few minutes spent in the rest-room – but to the 'now' into which the future is breaking. Carolyn's experience, mediated through her conversation with the wife of her lover, results in a break away from the present into the future. Hence the event is not a manifestation of the immutable, as it would be according to an epiphany-based religion. Rather, it is a confrontation with him who brings an anticipation of the future, and so it illuminates what it is to have a promise-centred faith.

Disclosure Situation IV – The Vigil in the Hospital

I am in a hospital room. There is a smell of disinfectant. The shaded light barely enables me to see the figure of my friend prone on the bed. It is midnight – two hours since he had a severe stroke. He is suffering acutely, not only physically but mentally, as incoherent phrases that he utters from time to time reveal an inner anguish. I kneel by the bedside in the company of his wife. Hour after hour passes – one o'clock, two o'clock, three.... Occasionally I am conscious of my knees, for the oblong of carpet is neither thick nor comfortable. Occasionally we speak together – the wife and I.

'He does not seem to be getting worse.'

'Poor dear.'

A nurse comes in and feels his pulse. We scarcely notice her.

'Do you think he is holding his own?'

'He is putting up a great fight.'

Four o'clock. The consultant examines him again. He shakes his head. He has already told me that he is unlikely to live out the night.

The wife speaks to her husband, quietly and urgently, willing him to live, calling him by name. We both feel utterly hopeless. She can only express her love by her endearing words or by stroking his forehead and wiping off the phlegm that sticks to his lips.

Five o'clock. It seems the daylight has been permanently shut out – but what difference can it make?

I ask the wife if she would like me to say a prayer. She is grateful. I speak hesitatingly about our bewilderment in the face of such suffering, and our hope that, if he dies, we will be strong enough to bear the loss.

Six o'clock. A grey light edges through the curtains. The seemingly interminable night is over. He is still alive.

Notes

I cannot tell how far this description has enabled the reader to be a participant in the scene. What I do know is that this account is no more than a skating over the surface of what was taking place. It does not contain any clear indication of what he, she and I were experiencing. Yet it is precisely there and in the unspoken, but very real, in-between that one may glimpse the holy.

I was conscious not only of my friend's suffering and distress but of the presence of the holy, not as some fourth entity silently observing what was happening, but as personally present in the suffering itself, identifying itself with the anguish, bearing it in and with us. My recognition of this self-giving love, which knows no barriers and no limits, makes me wonder at this selfless outpouring in limitless concern. How do I know this is an encounter with the holy? Because having accepted the New Testament model, I am aware that the holy is infinite love that reveals itself in suffering. In seeking to support my friend's wife and in being there for my friend, I am serving Christ. I am not Christ to my friends – they are Christs for me. I do not devalue the persons of my friends by this understanding; indeed my love for them is actually intensified, and gratitude wells up that this love is being deepened so that I am embraced with them in love of Christ. The depths of our ordinary human love extend to and are included within the holy, whose very nature is love.

Disclosure Situation V – The Widower and his Son

A widower is sitting in his living room with his son. The latter is a
first-generation university student in his third year, but now on
vacation. The result of his higher education is that, both intellectually and culturally, a large gap has opened up between him and
his father. He is reading a textbook, his father the sporting news in
the local paper. Neither speaks to the other. The son does not do so
because he knows that what interests him does not mean much to
his father and is indeed largely outside his comprehension; the
father does not do so because he feels his son is growing away from
him and has little interest in his hopes and fears. To speak is likely to
invite a curt rejoinder. From time to time each thinks about the other.

'I can manage very well without him,' thinks the father.

'He really is becoming impossible,' thinks the son.

'He's all stuck-up . . . hasn't got his feet on the ground . . . when I
was his age . . .'

'He's so limited in his interests as to be absolutely boring.'

Although each one regrets the lack of communication in his heart of
hearts, and each has a certain feeling of guilt, neither is able to
bridge the gap.

'Things weren't like this in the old days. . . . Surely, it's not my
fault; I haven't changed at all. . . . I wonder what his mother would
have said?' – so the father.

'How I ever looked up to him, I don't know – and yet he is my
father. But he's such a stick-in-the-mud . . . always the same . . .
and he won't do anything about it.'

Eventually they go their separate ways to bed.

Notes

In analysing this situation, it will be convenient to begin with the
concepts of guilt and wilfulness. Both father and son are experiencing guilt, in the sense defined by the Swedish psychiatrist Hans
Trüb. It is a consequence of one's refusal to respond to the legitimate
claims and address of the other. Both are indulging in wilfulness, as
explained by another psychiatrist, Leslie H. Farber.[19] He maintains
that human wholeness is achieved in and through dialogue. When
there is only monologue, as in the situation before us, the individuals
grasp at an illusion of wholeness to reassure themselves. This is wilfulness, i.e. the attempt of the will to make up for the absence of
dialogue by handling both sides of a no longer mutual situation.

Not being in communion with one another, both the widower and his son fill the emptiness with their own selves, which are only partial because their wholeness is lost through their failure to meet. So both father and son engage in an interior dual monologue – represented by their various thoughts – and justify to themselves their failure to establish contact; this justification, in turn, reassures them of their supposed wholeness.

Since the holy is dialogical and is known in relationship, these two persons are unaware of any encounter. The reassurance of themselves by interior monologue is an illusion which precludes the recognition of the holy, while the only true liberation from their guilt is through the re-establishment of a dialogical relation of which they have become incapable.

Our participation in the scene as readers enables us to recognize, first, the *incognito* of the holy, hidden by the broken dialogue. The holy thus surrenders itself to the human condition to the point of self-abnegation. Only if one or other of the pair, possibly with the assistance of a third party, is prepared to accept for himself such self-abnegation and so to become identified with the holy from this aspect, and both accept and live out the paschal pattern – only then could the I-Thou relation be restored and full recognition of the holy be made possible. Only then could the father and son become aware of the non-compulsive pressure of the holy, from within their situation, towards that action that would re-establish the in-between and remove the burden of guilt.

Further, our involvement in the scene carries with it the acknowledgment that the lack of relationship between the two is a crucifixion of the holy. But in this very fact lies the possibility of reconciliation and therefore of 'newness'. The situation could be transformed – from within – if either the father or the son could hear the summons addressed to them by the holy broken upon their alienation. The address can be ignored; it is nevertheless there to be heard. According to Paul Tillich:

> The depth, the dynamic structure of a historical situation, cannot be understood by a detached description of as many facts as possible. It must be experienced in life and action. The depth of every present is its power to transform the past into the future. It is, therefore, a matter of venture and decision.[20]

If this is applied to the present disclosure-situation, it follows that should the father and son allow their broken relationship to persist, there would be no transformation of the past into the future – the past will simply continue. If they could recognize the holy in their situation, then they would become conscious both of judgment and of the possibility of newness. Without this encounter, there can be no hope for them and they remain closed to the future that the holy places before them, with no venturing forward because of no decision. We, the readers, can acknowledge the eschatological tension between the 'already' and the 'not yet', but precisely because father and son do not perceive this they are unaware of the reality of the present which lies in its possibilities for the future.

Disclosure Situation VI – The Mother and the Naughty Child

A child of four has been naughty; she is sent to her room. Feeling alienated from her mother because of what she has done, for which she feels guilty, she stands, angry and hostile, inwardly seething with resentment. Then she notices a corner of wallpaper, just above the skirting-board, that is loose. She kneels down and takes the edge; she pulls it; it comes away from the wall. Deliberately and systematically she shreds as much as she can. In this way she symbolically inflicts an injury upon her mother.

Eventually her mother comes upstairs and discovers what her daughter has done. Her natural human reaction is to mete out further punishment to her, possibly to slap her. If she gives way to this – and what is more normal, even if it be prompted by vindictiveness? – she will only increase the existing alienation, intensifying the separation and so perpetuate the broken relationship, adding her own wrong-doing to the child's.

The child, enclosed in her own self-justifying rage, can do nothing of herself. She cannot create forgiveness; this can only come from the injured mother. The mother takes her daughter in her arms, despite the initial struggles of resistance. She strokes her hair, kisses her forehead. The sobs gradually subside. They discuss together how to repair the damage to the wallpaper. Reconciliation has been achieved.

Notes

Where is the holy in this situation? The mother's action is both a witness to and an instrument of the mediation of forgiveness by the holy. The restored relation of parent and child is both an analogy of the restored relation of the holy and mankind through Christ and a means whereby the holy acts now within the human situation, since in and through the mother's forgiveness the holy conveys forgiveness. The holy is here encountered as that which brings *shālōm*, i.e. trust, peace, interpersonal harmony, community of will, solidarity and confidence.

However, if the mother acts as the holy, not recognizing the forgiveness mediated by it and therefore substituting her forgiveness for its, the holy will not be evident either to her or her child. But if the mother explicitly, for her daughter's benefit and her own, relates her forgiveness to the divine forgiveness, if she shows how her own act of reconciliation is patterned upon and makes actual the divine act of reconciliation, then both child and mother will become aware of an encounter with the holy. While the holy is present through the act of forgiveness, the meeting will be unconscious unless the mother is able to make it explicit. If she succeeds, then we meet no *deus ex machina*, but the holy in the heart of the situation.[21]

Disclosure Situation VII – Old People

April 1968. A television programme entitled 'Put Out More Candles', photographed and directed by Lord Snowdon.

This is a sensitive study of old people. We are taken into geriatric wards, where they lie helpless, waiting to die. We are taken into Old Folks' Homes and see them sitting around in their common room, sometimes talking, more often silently isolated. We visit one-room flats, where we meet an old lady whose sole companion is a budgerigar and where an old man stares continuously down from his window at the distant streets below.

The theme of this documentary could appropriately be described as 'the generation of the lost'. Rows upon rows of the unwanted, the uncared-for. People dying alone, their mouldering corpses only discovered a week or more later. People whose relatives now live too far away to visit them. People who have no relatives left and no friends.

Notes

To watch and to become involved in this programme is to become aware that one's reaction includes two elements. There is a sense of guilt at one's own failings towards the aged, both relatives and others, coupled with a sense of love outgoing towards these frequently unattractive and unlovable derelicts. This is an encounter

with the holy in judgment and in the mediation of love. One judges
oneself by one's failure to fulfil the standard of love in the service
of others. One recognizes one's separation from the fellowship of
love in which mankind should be knit together. One falls short of
the model of the holy disclosed in Jesus and therefore the holy
judges one.

The encounter is not situationless; it is in the here and now. But
this 'now' is not a self-contained event. The purpose of the disclosure is to point to a future which is thereby opened up. For us, the
spectators who become participants in the scenes, this recognition of
the eschatological tension carries with it responsibility for action, in
order that through service we may be agents of the holy, bringing
hope and wrestling with the situation in the light of the future.

Disclosure Situation VIII – The Mediator

On Thursday, 4 April 1968, Martin Luther King was assassinated
as he stood on the balcony outside his hotel room in Memphis. The
news was conveyed to Britain on the following day in the form of a
television biography of the civil rights' leader. There were passages
from his speeches in which he vehemently declared his belief in
justice, in the need for equality of opportunity for all men, and in
the brotherhood of white and black. There was an extract from his
final speech, the day before he was murdered by the bullet in his
throat, in which he stated that death was always a present possibility
but that he was not afraid.

I've been to the mountain top. And I've looked over, and I've seen the
promised land. I may not get there with you, but I want you to know
tonight that we as a people will get to the promised land. So I'm happy
tonight. I'm not worried about anything. I'm not fearing any man. Mine
eyes have seen the glory of the company of the Lord.

There were interviews in which he repudiated violence and
asserted that the way to be followed in the black quest for freedom
was that of 'non-violent resistance, that combines toughmindedness
and tenderheartedness and avoids the complacency and do-nothing-
ness of the softminded and the violence and bitterness of the hard-
hearted'. He opposed segregation on the grounds that 'it is a blatant
denial of the unity which we have in Christ. It substitutes an "I-It"
relationship for the "I-Thou" relationship, and relegates persons to
the status of things.'

Different scenes demonstrated the extent of the hostility which built up against him – the curses of many of his own colour who did not regard his peaceful campaigns as sufficiently militant and the odium of many whites who regarded him as an agitator disturbing the even tenor of their ways. Eventually that hostility expressed itself through a bullet.

Notes

It is not necessary to have been a viewer of television to be conscious of the impact of Martin Luther King as a man – his story is well known. This particular programme simply served to concentrate those various aspects of his life that revealed him as a mediator. His consistent endeavour was to achieve reconciliation between two bitterly opposed forces and his actions were performed in the full consciousness that he could be destroyed in the process. This eventually took place. Like Jesus crucified, he absorbed into himself the hatred of both sides and was thus both a witness and a mediator of the forgiveness of the holy.

Martin Luther King, then, is to be seen as an image or embodiment of the holy, i.e. he himself, in his own person, was an in-between. His death was the consummation of his whole lived-out forgiveness. In the words of William Blake, 'he who will not comingle in Love, must be adjoin'd by Hate',[22] hence:

> Mutual Forgiveness of each Vice
> Such are the Gates of Paradise.[23]

King's death was another death in the divine image, of which the prototype is the crucifixion of Christ. To be compassionate, as was Martin Luther King, is to suffer with and on behalf of others. Such a death can be either a reconciling or a divisive act. Just as Christ on the cross can attract or repel, so that those at the foot are under judgment, so to be confronted with the death of the black leader is to encounter the holy, either as that which reconciles and pays the price or as that which separates and puts asunder those who refuse fellowship and openness in love.

Disclosure Situation IX – The Innocent who achieves Maturity

Verdi's *Rigoletto* presented by the Rome Opera in the Baths of Caracalla. This is not just a performance with spectators, but a powerful drama in which the audience cannot but be involved.

It is the story of a man whose public and private life are entirely separate. In public, as the Duke of Mantua's jester, Rigoletto the hunchback is a sycophant and lickspittle, willing to aid his master in his lustful adventures and providing him with the wives and daughters of the courtiers to be instruments of his sensual gratification. He is ready, too, to taunt those who suffer as a result of his pandering. In private, he is a loving father, anxious to safeguard his beautiful daughter Gilda from the pitfalls of life, and so he shuts her away in an inconspicuous house, cutting her off from contact with the real world.

Rigoletto's very anxiety proves his own undoing. He it is who, unwittingly, lets the Duke into the house – the Duke having been attracted to Gilda whom he has seen in church. Rigoletto it is who draws attention to Gilda by his furtiveness and so attracts the notice of the courtiers, who finally kidnap her and surrender her to the Duke's passion.

Rigoletto, his daughter now thrown back at him by his satiated master, can think of nothing but revenge. He arranges with a cutthroat named Sparafucile to have the Duke killed at an inn whither he goes from time to time to enjoy the favours of Sparafucile's own sister, Maddelena.

On the night of the killing, Rigoletto takes Gilda to the inn to witness the Duke's assignation and further unfaithfulness, and then he bids her dress as a youth and fly to Verona. After she has left, he gives his final instructions to Sparafucile to stab the Duke, put the body in a sack, and pass it to him to throw into the river Mincio.

Throughout the evening the unsuspecting Duke amuses himself with Maddelena, who herself begins to pity him and finally persuades her brother to spare him should anyone call at the inn before midnight who can be a substitute. Gilda, who has changed her clothes but has been drawn back to the inn by her love of the Duke, overhears this conversation and decides to sacrifice herself for him.

She knocks at the door, is admitted and killed. Sparafucile places her body in a sack and carries it to the waiting Rigoletto. Then the Duke's voice is heard from within the inn. The hunchback tears open the sack to find his own daughter, who dies in his arms, declaring that she has willingly given her life that the Duke might live.

Notes

The chief character in this opera is without question Rigoletto, whose tragedy it is, but his daughter is no less central to the action. Upon her first appearance, it is clear that her being shut away from the world and cossetted has made her into a naive, not to say insipid, innocent, with little self-awareness and no maturity. Her experience with the Duke and its aftermath radically transform her. She shows unsuspected depths of character. Eventually Gilda reveals herself as an embodiment of true holiness, in that she demonstrates a capacity to continue to love even when the object of her devotion is exposed as unlovable. She accepts him without judging him; she is prepared to die and does die for one who affronts her.

Here the holy is to be discerned as selfless love which assists personalization, i.e. from a shadowy existence Gilda advances to one that is authentic. In effect this is a story of what psychologists call the process of individuation, which she achieves by involvement with the world. Gilda could have escaped her fate, but instead consciously chose the path of suffering. Here is wholeness and an enhancement of life even, paradoxically, in death. There is a sense of ennoblement conveyed, as well as the recognition on Gilda's part of the challenge to responsible action.

Disclosure Situation X – The 'Demo'

In *The Poisoned Stream* by Hans Habe, Francesco Vanetti is the son of an Italian newspaper proprietor. He is in his early twenties, but has been dominated by his father to such an extent that he has so far failed to realize his identity. Then he and some of his friends become involved in a demonstration against the US Embassy in Rome.

I get scared in case Sofia takes another car, but Sofia goes straight over to my Alfa and I roar off before anyone can squeeze in between us. You drive like the devil, says Sofia, I drive like two devils, I love you, I say, I love you too, she says, if I go to bed with anyone I'll go to bed with you, she says, you don't need to go to bed with me, I say, I love you.

The sky has put on a grey beard, the street is jet-pitch-black. We've lost the other cars, we get stuck in a hellish traffic jam, everyone toots like a madman, I toot like ten madmen, I look in the rear mirror, the other cars aren't ours, Sofia says they aren't coming, they're chicken, I say no, they aren't chicken, they can't drive, that's all. A traffic policeman plants himself in front of me, I see the red light anyway, I'm not colour-blind, ME says: I'll flatten the man, ME would like to flatten law and order, authority has to be flattened, but the light turns green, I don't need to flatten authority. I park the car outside the Hotel Palazzo degli Ambasciatori, right under the No Parking sign, they ought to paint fasces on the signs, red, white and green, the colours ought to be on prescription, we mustn't get caught *in flagrante*, I say, Sofia laughs, let's run before a policeman comes, I say, Sofia gives me her hand, I squeeze her hand, we run.

We're not too late, the street is crammed with people, hundreds of heads are a single head, the Hydra only had nine heads, the Hydra has nine hundred heads, WE have one body and nine hundred heads, the police only have bodies, no head. We storm the Embassy, we can't storm the Embassy, the Embassy is a marble-smooth monster, a stone Moloch with glass eyes, they defend it, the defenders defend the aggressor, I don't think of the aggressor, I think of the defenders, I think of the slave-drivers who are slaves themselves, I think of the bridges. Sofia links arms with me, she has hard little breasts, ivory-yellow, I link arms with a friend, he looks like me except that his beard is longer, I put my head down like a bull taking a toreador on its horns, I shall take the policeman on my horns, I am ME. It starts to rain, a razor-blade rain, it's cold, I don't care, *Ten Days that Shook the World*, by John Reed, Vladimir Ulyanov and Rykov and Krylenko and Dzhugashvili alias Stalin, one doesn't have to be a Stalinist, Stalin was a hippie himself, today could be the first of the ten days, November 6th, the rain douses the flames, the American flag stops burning. The walls give way, the cotton-wool walls of the aggressor-defenders give way, a steel helmet tumbles to the ground and rolls, steel helmets should be banned, steel helmets should be put on prescription, the steel helmet won't fit me, my friend puts the steel helmet on, laughter frisks about like a billy-goat, the glass eyes of the marble monsters are quite close, Sofia lets go of me, take this, she says, someone distributes stones, someone distributes stones like Easter eggs, I get a handful of stones, I throw my stones, I aim at the steel helmets, I aim at the glass eyes. A policeman grabs at me, I'll be arrested, I tell myself, my name is ME, that isn't a name, what's your real name, my name is Francesco Vanetti but I'm ME nevertheless, my father is Carlo Vanetti, call my father, he'll have a heart attack. I taste blood in my mouth, I feel nothing, I lick blood, my tongue tastes of blood, you're bleeding says Sofia and throws a stone, she holds the steel helmet in her hand, the steel helmet is full of stones, the Easter-egg basket is full of stones, I put my hand to my temple, my hand is full of blood, my hand isn't bleeding but my hand is full of blood, I can only see through one eye, you need a doctor says Sofia. She takes me by the arm, she clears a path for me, if she sleeps with anyone she'll sleep with me but she sleeps with no one. I see an ambulance on the corner of the Via Bissolati, no ambulance I say, we're back at the car already, I haven't got a ticket, no ticket today, the first day, *Ten Days that Shook the World*. You can't drive says Sofia, I can drive, I say, you're needed here, I say. I climb behind the wheel, my head swims. MY head doesn't swim, ME sees crystal-clear, ME starts the car, ME switches on the windscreen-wipers, the windscreen is cloudy, my brain is cloudy, ME gets under way, I see Sofia in the rear-view mirror, Sofia is waving, she has a stone in her hand.[24]

Notes

The way in which the account of this incident has been set up in type by the publishers of the novel draws attention to one of its most important features. Each time Francesco uses his own personal pronoun, it appears in capitals – ME, ME, ME. In effect, his participation in this demonstration progressively brings self-awareness. By sharing in this joint action with others, Francesco begins to realize his own identity. His name ceases to be a meaningless label and refers to a self-conscious human being – 'my name is ME, that isn't a name, what's your real name, my name is Francesco Vanetti, but I'm ME nevertheless'.

Francesco is involved in collective, rather than community action, i.e. he is included in an impersonal aggregate rather than in a group knit together by interlocking I-Thou relationships. Nevertheless, this experience mediates an encounter with the holy. Now, for the first time in the novel, I and ME have content. Francesco, like Zacchaeus in the gospel, is no longer abased, no longer subject to the spirit of slavery. His meeting with the holy, though unconscious, raises him to dignity and sonship. Here is humanization and an enrichment of human living. Joy is experienced at this liberation from immaturity.

Francesco, however fleetingly, overcomes his inner division and achieves adulthood by interaction with others through whom the confrontation with the holy takes place. There is *shālōm*, even in the midst of violence, between him and his fellow demonstrators: solidarity, confidence, a community of will, responsible freedom and hope. There is openness and candour, without dissimulation, so that Francesco can declare his love for Sofia. There is exposure, resulting in injury, because of a readiness to engage in conflict with what is believed to be evil. Francesco finds the experience unexpected and disconcerting – *Ten Days that Shook the World*. There is no endorsement of the *status quo* nor an ecstatic union with the absolute, but the beginning of a pilgrimage in hope which wrestles with the present in the light of the future – the eschatological tension between the 'already' and the 'not yet' is clearly evident.

Disclosure Situation XI – The Strike

On 3 April 1970 a strike began in the Flat Drawn department of the Sheet Works, one of the Pilkington glass plants in St Helens, near Liverpool. It spread with great rapidity, involved over 11,000 men and lasted for seven weeks. It was, however, an unofficial strike and the General and Municipal Workers Union, to which the men belonged, refused to support it. There therefore emerged what became known as the Rank and File Strike Committee, consisting of the men's leaders as distinct from the union officials. After a few initial moves, the Pilkington directors more or less occupied the side line, while the union and the committee struggled over the questions of power and authority.

Tony Lane and Kenneth Roberts, two Liverpool sociologists, decided forthwith to investigate the strike. They carried out a survey to discover the attitudes and opinions of a sample of 187 rank-and-file workers, and they observed, at close quarters, the activities of the committee during the latter half of the stay-out, attending meetings, joining delegations, talking to the people at street corners, in public houses and on the picket lines. They followed this with a series of interviews. Their report *Strike at Pilkingtons* describes the effect of this total experience upon a number of the men.

They quote the reaction of a participant in the walk-out on the first Friday:

There was a feeling of elation, a feeling of liberation about the place, even though everyone did seem to be confused about what was going on. The way some of the men were talking it was as though they had done something big for the first time in their lives. And it was the long-service men who were doing all the shouting – the blokes who got up and spoke in the canteen were all long-service men of about forty to fifty years of age.

Lane and Roberts comment:

To go on strike is to deny the existing distribution of power and authority. The striker ceases to respond to a managerial command; he refuses to do his 'work'. A new dimension of living can thus be revealed to the striker; an existence in which 'ordinary' people are able to control events and command the attention of 'them'. The experience of this new reality can transform the striker's perception of normal life. What was 'normal' can no longer be regarded as 'natural'. Attitudes towards work and authority become critical as opposed to acquiescent. The sudden acquisition of these insights hits the striker with a blinding clarity; hence his feelings of liberation and elation.

From these initial revolutionary sensations the development of the strike, for some individuals, offered an interesting and even exciting education. Those who supported the strike and were actively involved in its organization found themselves administering affairs and attracting public attention on a scale that they had never previously experienced. Some individuals enjoyed the strike; it was much better than being at work.

As one striker told us, 'I enjoyed it without a doubt. I enjoyed the freedom it gave me to express myself which was something entirely new to me after working in factories. It gave me a little bit of scope to use the abilities that I have. Educationally it was great. I liked the companionship of the pickets; I liked the feeling of being involved in a struggle; there was a great feeling of "oneness" that I really enjoyed.'

This experience of the strike, however, could not have been shared by more than 900 of the strikers.

Later, they add:

The strike for most of the Rank and File Strike Committee was then a liberating experience, because for the first time in their lives they had cast aside the bonds that constrain most people in their everyday lives. They were their own masters, for instead of having their actions largely dictated by a system of authority in which they were subordinates, they were now in a position to decide for *themselves*. From being in a world where their actions were mainly dictated by other people, they were now in a world which was more evidently of their own making.... There was a freedom to *do* something: 'People have become free to fight a system that they know is wrong. People have got it off their chests, they've felt free,' said a man who has worked at Pilkingtons for thirty years....

Little wonder then that wildcat strikers sometimes talk as if they have 'done something big for the first time in their lives'. Such people are proclaiming their humanity and protesting that their work situation denies it.[25]

Notes

The most remarkable thing about the comments of these sociologists and of the workers themselves is the identity of vocabulary used by them in this report and by me in describing previously encounters with the holy. Such words, phrases and sentences as the following are part of a common terminology: 'liberation', 'freedom', 'a new dimension of living', 'elation', 'enjoyment', 'proclaiming their humanity', 'a world which was more evidently of their own making', 'the experience of this new reality can transform the striker's perception of normal life'. Adopting the mental set I have specified above, the experience of these workers can be seen clearly to mediate the holy. Even when our terms are not precisely the same, there is a shared meaning; e.g., the statement that 'these insights hit the striker with a blinding clarity' recalls the unexpectedness of the holy. The entire process was one of humanization, restoring the dignity of human life and bringing authenticity into the world of work. There was *shālōm* – 'a great feeling of "oneness"'. There is an overlap here with the experience of Francesco at the demo, and in both cases there is hope wrestling with the present in the light of the future.

To say this is not to sacralize the human experience itself nor to deny the explanations of the sociologists. It is only because the experience is both real and valid that it can mediate the holy. Of course, it has to be acknowledged that this was an extraordinary event, in the sense that it was totally unexpected, that industrial relations were believed to be good and that no such action had been taken for many years. But, in stressing that the holy is not the 'wholly other' and is to be met in and through the ordinary, I am not discounting the possibility of peak experiences also mediating an encounter. Moreover, however unexpected, the stuff of the strike was made up of what man does in the world – certainly no aura of the numinous surrounds the action at Pilkingtons.

Disclosure Situation XII – The Hijackers and the Minister

During the night of Monday, 30 March 1970, a Boeing 707, on a routine flight from Tokyo to Fukuoka, was seized at sword-point by nine left-wing Japanese students. The hijackers ordered the pilot to fly to North Korea. Captain Ishida informed them that he had insufficient fuel and that they must land at Itazuka air base. There twenty-three of the hundred and twenty passengers were allowed to leave the aircraft which, after five hours' delay, took off for Pyongyang. The pilot, however, landed the plane at Kimpo in South Korea, which had been camouflaged to give the impression that it was in fact Pyongyang. The hijackers discovered the truth and for seventy-nine hours they kept the passengers confined. Finally, after prolonged negotiations, it was agreed to allow the travellers and the stewardesses to evacuate the aircraft in exchange for Mr Shinjiro Yamamura, the Japanese deputy Minister of Transport who offered himself as hostage. The plane then flew on to North Korea and Mr Yamamura was eventually released.

Comments

The Birmingham Post on Saturday, 4 April, carried a leader about this incident. It was headed 'A Redemptive Act', and in itself this editorial comment in a secular newspaper contains all that is required by way of analysis. It reads as follows:

What men are capable of at their best and at their near-worst has been demonstrated before the whole world in connection with one and the same incident – the hi-jacking of the Japanese airliner, with the holding of its passengers to ransom in circumstances of utterly cruel mental and physical stress, and the means by which the release of the majority of them was eventually secured.

The nine Japanese students, dedicated to violent revolution, had been de-humanised, inhumanised by a political ideology in which the end justifies any means. They behaved with complete callousness and selfishness to other human beings whom they held captive in the confined quarters of the aeroplane for three days, often in intense heat.

One of the stewardesses said of the passengers: 'They had to sit in their seats all the time. They could not move. Your bones started aching, adding to the sense of tension. We missed meals and the hunger intensified the feeling of terror. We were haunted by hunger and terror. The hi-jackers constantly swung their swords around. We could not even stand up. It was just like in hell.' When the hi-jackers' blackmail succeeded they refused to allow the pilot to be replaced and forced him, after his ordeal of exhaustion and stress, to fly them and their new captive from Seoul in South Korea to Pyongyang in Communist North Korea.

Nothing can justify such behaviour. It is a crime against humanity as much as any of the crimes which its perpetrators may think they are repudiating; the solidarity of the human race comes first. Yet, these men, ideologically blinded to the true character of what they are doing, must themselves be the subject of genuine concern, even though they would repudiate that concern with anger. They have become stuffed bodies of dogma, from which common humanity has leached away. That is why, when the process has gone its full course, they and their actions have the machine-like quality that is so disturbing to others.

If the story of the hi-jacked Japanese aircraft had to be left there, or at the later stage with its suggestion of a possible, and certainly dishonourable, repudiation by the Communist North Korean Government of its guarantee to return the arliner and its occupants to Japan, it would be depressing indeed. It would be yet another modern instance of mankind seen in the worst light. But there is a redeeming element that counter-balances any tendency to a feeling of hopelessness. It is to be found in the courage and the deliberate self-sacrifice of Mr Shinjiro Yamamura, the Japanese Vice-Minister of Transport who offered himself as a hostage for the 100 or so passengers and crew.

This was, literally, a redemptive act that transformed the immediate situation and transforms the whole scene for us. Against the hatred and violence of thought and action of the Japanese students who plotted and carried through this terrorism has to be set the calm, self-sacrificing and basically loving regard for his fellow men of the Japanese statesman. Human nature is capable of both types of action. Mankind's future depends on redemptive goodness overcoming evil.

Disclosure Situation XIII – The Drunkard

George Caldwell, the chief character in *The Centaur* by John Updike, is walking through the country snow. He recalls an incident
from his childhood when he was out with his father, who was a
minister of religion.

The intervals between the hedgerow trunks passed him like ragged
doorways and he remembered walking on some church errand with his
father down a dangerous street in Passaic; it was a Saturday and the
men from the sulphur works were getting drunk. From within the
double doors of a saloon there welled a poisonous laughter that seemed
to distill all the cruelty and blasphemy in the world and he wondered
how such a noise could have place under the sky of his father's God. In
those days he customarily kept silent about what troubled him, but his
worry must have made itself felt, for he remembered his father turning
and listening in his backwards collar to the laugh from the saloon and
then smiling down to his son, "All joy belongs to the Lord".
It was half a joke but the boy took it to heart. *All joy belongs to the
Lord.* Wherever in the filth and confusion and misery a soul felt joy,
there the Lord came and claimed it as his own; into bathrooms and
brothels and classrooms and alleys slippery with spittle, no matter how
dark and scrabbed and remote, in China or Africa or Brazil, wherever
a moment of joy was felt, there the Lord stole and added to his enduring domain. And all the rest, all that was not joy, fell away, precipitated
dross that had never been. He thought of his wife's joy in the land and
Pop Kramer's joy in the newspaper and his son's joy in the future and
was glad, grateful that he was able to sustain these for yet a space
more . . . he discovered then in giving his life to others he entered a total
freedom.[26]

Notes

Analysis of this incident is virtually superfluous, since the author has
himself interwoven it with an interpretation that indicates an encounter with the holy. The holy is that which brings joy, and this
joy can be mediated even through a drunkard's laugh and a father's
understanding. Coupled with this is George Caldwell's realization
that the meeting also brings liberation. The self-giving of Jesus
mediated through the self-offering of one human being to another
enables man to enter 'a total freedom'.

Disclosure Situation XIV – A Theological Conference

In September 1969 a consultation was held in Geneva under the
auspices of the Faith and Order Department of the World Council
of Churches. The subject for discussion was 'The Worship of God

in a Secular Age'. The participants divided into groups. One of these sections contained an apparently ill-assorted collection of people. There was an Orthodox bishop, somewhat traditional in his approach; an American theologian who doubted if the name 'God' had any meaning and was sceptical about the possibility of worship at all. There was a Methodist bishop full of goodwill and an Anglican priest who had strong reservations about the whole consultation.

The first session was quite remarkable in that from the very outset it was fully dialogical. Truly personal relationships were immediately established; there was reciprocal communication; there was a quest for real understanding; there was a steady perseverance in the quest for truth. Complete openness and frankness characterized the entire proceedings. The relationship became one of love, no one seeking to destroy the intellectual standpoint of another nor to dominate in any way. There was sincerity and directness. Each participant exposed himself, keeping nothing back. There was spontaneity and unexpectedness.

At the end of the first long dialogue together, the American theologian said: 'Now I have some understanding of what worship is. We have been doing it together.'

Notes

Here again extended analysis is probably unnecessary, especially if the above description be set side by side with this statement by Dietrich Bonhoeffer:

Is it not precisely the significance of these conferences that where someone approaches us appearing so utterly strange and incomprehensible in his concerns and yet demands a hearing of us, we perceive in the voice of our brother the voice of Christ himself, and do not evade this voice, but take it quite seriously and listen and love the other precisely in his strangeness? That brother encounters brother in all openness and truthfulness and need, and claims the attention of others, is the sole way in which Christ encounters us at such a conference.[27]

Bonhoeffer's words express with absolute clarity the point that to engage in dialogue is to encounter the holy.

It will be appreciated that this chapter could be extended indefinitely by the piling of disclosure situation upon disclosure situation. But further instances are scarcely necessary and would not add to my argument. The fourteen examples adduced should be sufficient to demonstrate the validity of my opening remarks in this chapter. They show how the encounter with the holy is mediated through human relationships. They make clear that this meeting is not extraneous to the situation and that the integrity of the secular is preserved without sacralization. Consequently it is evident that this understanding in no way conflicts with the internal consistency of the incidents described. We have seen, too, that there may be several layers of meaning and that therefore the reader's freedom to respond or not to respond is preserved and the essential ambiguity of the human situation is not glossed over. The examples show further, through their variety, that every moment potentially can and may mediate the holy.

Finally, the various aspects of the holy that have been evoked are in complete agreement with the New Testament model. Indeed, if these aspects are summarized, it will be seen that they are identical with those analysed previously in relation to that model. In Chapter III, we saw that the holy induces wonder, brings wholeness and opens up the future. It is hidden and identified with suffering. It brings meaning, purpose and hope. It is dialogical and establishes *shālōm*. It mediates forgiveness and reconciliation, as well as judgment. It leads to humanization, to self-awareness, to dignity, to the enhancement of life and to joy. Similarly, in this chapter, we recognize wonder, wholeness and openness to the future ('The Convict'); *incognito* and identification in suffering ('Belle de Jour'); sacrifice, meaning, hope ('In the Ladies Room'; 'The Hijackers'); suffering ('The Vigil in the Hospital'); dialogue ('The Widower and his Son'); reconciliation and *shālōm* ('The Mother and the Naughty Child'); judgment, guilt and outgoing in concern ('Old People'; 'The Hijackers'); mediation and reconciliation again ('Martin Luther King'); humanization and enhancement of life ('Rigoletto'; 'The Strike'); self-awareness, dignity, exposure and *shālōm* ('The Demo'; 'The Strike'); joy and liberation ('The Drunkard'; 'The Strike'); and dialogue once more ('A Theological Conference').

Because the model of the holy, i.e. Jesus, is not divorced from human life, it is reasonable to conclude that it does fit the secular or hominized universe.

Perhaps this summary will help us to appreciate the substantial rightness of the view expressed by Harry Gibbon in *The Wind Shifts*, a novel by Alan Sharp.

All my folk were religious in one way or another. I was brought up to be religious only there isn't any religion that I can have. Sometimes when I think the most religious things in my life were just lying in bed when I was little on Sunday mornings and my mother and father having breakfast and me knowing they were just next door and feeling all safe or when my mother would wash her hair and dry it at the fire and she'd let me comb it for her, all hanging down and we'd roast apples on the hob and the smell of the apples and the sugar and my mother's hair drying, or when I used to take my father's tea up to the yard where he was working late and the smell of wood in the saw-mill. That's what's really most religious, not God or Jesus or anything and how can you believe in that, it's all in the past, just a memory.[28]

Although I would disagree with the final sentence and suggest that Harry Gibbon had possibly been misled in his understanding about both God and Jesus, I would endorse his perception of every-day events as, in his terminology, 'religious', or, in my terminology, 'encounters with the holy'.

There is, however, one aspect of human relations, indeed its most intimate form, that is missing from this series of disclosure situations and that is the sexual act. It is to this that we turn in the next chapter.

6

The Holy and Sexual Relations

Never before, since the invention of printing, have so many books been published containing detailed descriptions of human beings copulating. Scarcely a single novel is issued nowadays without it containing at least one and probably several accounts. This 'frankness' in relation to the sex act has also extended to films and to the stage, where a brief period of simulation has been succeeded by public performances of coitus. It might appear therefore that, since the subject is so extensively treated, there exists a great richness of material upon which to draw in order to examine the subject of the holy in connection with this most intimate of human relationships. Unfortunately this is not so.

The erotic literature of the twentieth century is almost exclusively concerned with one individual's sensual enjoyment by means of another. It looks at the sexual reality in terms of the world of I-It. It conceives sex largely as a physical activity and therefore, since man is more than his physical organism, fails to present it as a fully human act. Scene after scene simply shows the exploitation of one individual by another, but, as Leslie Paul says, 'to exploit another sexually is to devalue the other, and sexual exploitation runs counter therefore to all that Christianity seeks to establish for man'.[1]

The understanding of sex in terms of the world of I-It is powerfully conveyed in this description:

A young woman is walking down a city street. She is excruciatingly aware of her appearance and of the reactions to it (imagined or real) of every person she meets. She walks through a group of construction workers who are eating lunch in a line along the pavement. Her stomach tightens with terror and revulsion; her face becomes contorted into a grimace of self-control and fake awareness; her walk and carriage become stiff and dehumanized. No matter what they say to her, it will be unbearable. She knows that they will not physically assault her or hurt her. They will only do so metaphorically. What they will do is *impinge* on her. They will demand that her thoughts be focussed on them. They will use her body with their eyes. They will evaluate her market price. They will comment on her defects, or compare them to those of other passers-by. They will make her a participant in their fantasies without asking if she is willing. They will make her feel ridiculous, or grotesquely sexual, or hideously ugly. Above all they will make her feel like a *thing*.[2]

When we read the accounts of sexual activities or are spectators at the scenes, we are not learning about humanization but about dehumanization. Indeed some representations are only to be defined as bestialization, e.g. the 'blue' film called 'Leda and the Swan', which consists of nothing more than the sexual penetration of a woman by a dog.

Many writers perpetrate the supreme crime of making sex boring. Henry Miller's *Tropic of Capricorn* and *Tropic of Cancer* belong to this category. Moreover, his descriptions would appear to be masturbation fantasies tricked out with pseudo-philosophical musings which are an insult to the intelligence. Miller, and many others like him, fail completely to understand sex as a *relation* within the context of the I-Thou; coitus is not displayed as an in-between, but simply as a series of isolated acts of egocentric physical indulgence.[3]

Acknowledgement of the relational nature of coitus is essential to a perception of it in its depths and not simply at the level of the animal. We have to remind ourselves in this connection that a person only comes into being in relation to other persons.

The permanent resistance of every personality against any attempt to make it a thing, to appropriate it and deprive it of its self-determination, is the presupposition for the rise of personality as such. Without this resistance of the 'thou' to the 'ego', without the unconditional demand embodied in every person to be acknowledged as a person in theory and practice, no personal life would be possible. A person becomes aware of his own character as a person only when he is confronted by another person. Only in the community of the I and Thou can personality arise.[4]

The validity of this statement is made clear by Alexander Solzhenitsyn's novel *The First Circle*.[5] This is the story of three days in the lives of some inmates in a special prison at the height of Stalin's post-war terror in 1949. There is a constant contrast between the freedom of exchange among the prisoners, all occupied in a common enterprise of technological research, who can expect nothing worse than death, having experienced most other forms of suffering, and the life of fear and suspicion that dominates both the world outside and the behaviour of the prison officers. The prisoners are persons. But the others, under the shadow of arrest, dare not speak their minds; they have little or no self-determination and cannot be open to one another, and so the presupposition of personality is lacking. Outside the prison, individuals do not share their thoughts, lest they be regarded as suspect or an informer be present. There is a curious inversion, so that the prison appears to allow a reasonably full life, while the exterior society is really a prison. Outside, individuals are made into things and appropriated; inside, because of the top priority of the task committed to the prisoners, there is free exchange and discussion and the development of personality. Solzhenitsyn's novel thus demonstrates the truth of what Tillich has expressed in concepts in the quotation given above. The majority of contemporary erotic literature, however, signally fails at this very point and does not insert coitus within the nexus of I-Thou relations.

It also fails to embody any fundamental understanding of personal integrity. 'Integrity here is not a general term for moral goodness: it means specifically a way of life which is integrated.'[6] If a man is alienated from his body, physical acts appear to him to be distasteful and he is incapable of any adequate understanding of sex. Conversely, if a man regards himself as a body only, his physical acts cannot be other than on the same level as those of the animals. Neither of these two is integrated. It is only when sex is recognized as both physical (secular) and spiritual (sacred) that it can be invested with a human meaning. So the author who considers sex as nothing more than a physical exercise, distinct from the mental, moral and spiritual aspects of human life, gives us cardboard or one-dimensional figures lacking integrity. To say this is not, of course, to deny the obvious, viz. that coitus has a physical basis; it is, however, to affirm that this is not all and that to be content with this is to be less than mature.

If these accounts are dismissed, the extent of the available material is drastically reduced. The remainder is of two kinds. There are, first, those descriptions that do not deny that there is more to sex than just the physical but show how often sexual relations can be hollow and without meaning. There are also those – and there are not many – that give a sensitive account of coitus as a fully human act between two persons in relation, in and through which we may obtain glimpses of the holy. If we begin with an example of the first of these, then the illustration of the second will stand out more prominently by contrast.

John Updike's *Couples* (1968) will serve as an excellent example of inauthentic sex relations, but a more condensed account is to be found in Hermann Brock's trilogy *The Sleepwalkers*. The second part of this is the story of August Esch and includes a study of his relationship with Frau Hentjen, the proprietress of a drinking house, mainly frequented by sailors. Frau Hentjen is self-contained, cold and withdrawn, to such an extent that Esch's sexual advances, to which she submits, do not succeed in penetrating her isolation; indeed he is simply enveloped within it. This is Brock's account:

Esch should really have admitted that his mistress stood on the same plane as himself: for if he kept love in a subordinate place Mother Hentjen ignored it. In that she was his match, although moved by other considerations than his. She regarded love as something so profoundly secret that she scarcely ventured to pronounce the word. She forgot again and again the existence of this lover who was now established and whom she could not prevent from stealing in upon her of an afternoon when she was taking her nap or at night when her last customers had departed, and again and again at his approach she was overwhelmed with petrified astonishment, a state of petrification that only began gradually to wear away when the dim parlour and the alcove had received them both: then it dissolved into a feeling of detached isolation, and the dark alcove in which she lay looking up at the ceiling began to float away till soon it seemed no longer a part of her familiar house, but was like a soaring chariot hanging somewhere in infinite space and darkness.

Only then did she realize that somebody else was there beside her, occupied with her, and it was no longer Esch, it was no longer even a man she knew, it was a Someone who had strangely and violently thrust himself into her isolation, and yet could not be reproached for his violence since he was a part of that isolation and could be found only within it, a Someone, quiet and yet threatening, demanding assuagement for his violence, and therefore one had to play the game with him that he demanded, and though the game was compulsory it was yet strangely guiltless, since it was engulfed in isolation and even God shut His eyes to it. But he with whom she shared the bed was little likely to suspect the nature of that isolation, and she was sternly on her guard to keep him from impinging upon it. A profound muteness enveloped him, and she would not let that disconcerting silence be assailed, even should he mistake it for insensibility or stupidity. Silence abolished shame, for shame was born only in speech. What she felt was not bodily lust but release from shame: she was so isolated that, as if alone for all eternity, she could no longer be ashamed of a single fibre in her body. He could not understand her muteness, and yet was disheartened by the shameless silence that invited and submitted to him in brutish immobility. She gave him barely a sigh, and he was all agonized expectation and hope that she would finally let her voice go in a cry of satisfied animal lust. Too often he waited in vain, and then he hated the solicitous crook of the arm with which she invited him to lay down his head and sleep on her plump, unmoved shoulder. But when she sent her lover away it was with hard abruptness, as if she suddenly wanted to annihilate both him and the knowledge he shared with her: she pushed him out through the door, and as he stole down the stairs he could feel her hatred at his back. That gave him an inkling that it was a strange, strange land he had been in, and in spite of himself the knowledge always impelled him back to her again with torment and increasing desire. For even in the bliss of losing himself, of sinking tranced and nameless in the shamelessness of sex, the desire to overcome the woman kept stubborn vigil, the desire to force her to acknowledge him, to make the present moment flame up in her like a torch that burned up all else, so that in its glare she should be aware of her mate, and out of the silence of night that enveloped everything should let her voice ring out passionately, and say 'du' to him and to him alone, as if he were her child. He no longer knew what she looked like, she was beyond beauty and ugliness, beyond youth and age, she was only a silent problem that he was set to master and to resolve.

Although in many respects Esch could not have wished for a better, and even had to admit that it was a lofty kind of love, surpassing ordinary standards, that had laid its spell upon him, yet it always annoyed him, time and again, that whenever he came into the restaurant Mother Hentjen, anxious lest the other customers should suspect something, was so markedly cold to him that against her will she made him conspicuous. Had it not been that he wanted to avoid further notice and even scandal, and had not the cheap and bountiful dinner been in question, he would simply have stayed away. As it was, he made an effort to be compliant and to strike the happy mean in his visits; but he could not manage it, he could not please Mother Hentjen whatever he did: if he appeared in the restaurant she put on a sulky face and obviously wished him gone, and if he stayed away she asked him spitefully if he had perhaps been off with a negress.[7]

Brock recognizes the extent to which this relationship denies the true nature of coitus. Esch kept 'his love in a subordinate place', while Frau Hentjen 'ignored it'. He, despite the satisfaction of his physical desire, is far from satisfied with what takes place because of her muteness and immobility and apparent lack of involvement. He wished 'to force her to acknowledge him', to address him in terms of familiarity and endearment, but, at this stage of their relationship, this was all in vain. The author appreciates the extent to which the in-between is missing, and so the full meaning of the sex act remains unrevealed. He comments that 'it was engulfed in isolation and even God shut his eyes to it'. So the holy is only present in the suffering that is inseparable from this monological relationship and is therefore hidden from both August Esch and Frau Hentjen. Unlike John Donne there is no true love and therefore no true desire to seek the holy.

> Here the admiring her my mind did whet
> To seek Thee God; so streams do show their head.[8]

As far as Esch and his mistress are concerned there is no communion, i.e. union with one another, and therefore there is lacking what is most characteristic of persons in relation.

Brock's account may be contrasted with the sexual reality described by D. H. Lawrence, and as we pass now to *The Rainbow* we shall discover how through an intimate I-Thou relationship consummated in coitus the holy is to be encountered.

This is the story of Tom Brangwen, the slow thinking, entirely non-intellectual farmer who 'loved anyone who could convey enlightenment to him through feeling'.[9] He eventually marries the widow of a Polish doctor, Lydia Lensky. The opening chapters tell of their courtship, wedding and the birth of their first child. Their love for one another is strong, but they have not as yet attained a real union. Lydia is isolated and unsure, while Tom finds her cold and unresponsive. 'His wife was obliterated from him, she was in her own world, quiet, secure, unnoticed, unnoticing.'[10] Their relationship is somewhat similar to that of August Esch and Frau Hentjen. One night they are sitting by the fire in the living room, when Lydia makes a move to break through the barrier between them.

'Come here,' she said, unsure.
For some moments he did not move. Then he rose slowly and went across the hearth. It required an almost deathly effort of volition, or of acquiescence. He stood before her and looked down at her. Her face was shining again, her eyes were shining again like terrible laughter. It was to him terrible, how she could be transfigured. He could not look at her, it burnt his heart.
'My love!' she said.
And she put her arms round him as he stood before her, round his thighs, pressing him against her breast. And her hands on him seemed

to reveal to him the mould of his own nakedness, he was passionately lovely to himself. He could not bear to look at her.

'My dear!' she said. He knew she spoke a foreign language. The fear was like bliss in his heart. He looked down. Her face was shining, her eyes were full of light, she was awful. He suffered from the compulsion to her. She was the awful unknown. He bent down to her, suffering, unable to let go, unable to let himself go, yet drawn, driven. She was now the transfigured, she was wonderful, beyond him. He wanted to go. But he could not as yet kiss her. He was himself apart. Easiest he could kiss her feet. But he was too ashamed for the actual deed, which was like an affront. She waited for him to meet her, not to bow before her and serve her. She wanted his active participation, not his submission. She put her fingers on him. And it was torture to him, that he must give himself to her actively, participate in her, that he must meet and embrace and know her, who was other than himself. There was that in him which shrank from yielding to her, resisted the relaxing towards her, opposed the mingling with her, even while he most desired it. He was afraid, he wanted to save himself.

There were a few moments of stillness. Then gradually the tension, the withholding relaxed in him, and he began to flow towards her. She was beyond him, the unattainable. But he let go his hold on himself, he relinquished himself and knew the subterranean force of his desire to come to her, to be with her, to mingle with her, losing himself to find her, to find himself in her. He began to approach her, to draw near.

His blood beat up in waves of desire. He wanted to come to her, to meet her. She was there, if he could reach her. The reality of her who was just beyond him absorbed him. Blind and destroyed, he pressed forward, nearer, nearer, to receive the consummation of himself, he received within the darkness which should swallow him and yield him up to himself. If he could come really within the blazing kernel of darkness, if really he could be destroyed, burnt away till he lit with her in one consummation, that were supreme, supreme.

Their coming together now, after two years of married life, was much more wonderful to them than it had been before. It was the entry into another circle of existence, it was the baptism to another life, it was the complete confirmation. Their feet trod strange ground of knowledge, their footsteps were lit-up with discovery. Wherever they walked, it was well, the world re-echoed round them in discovery. They went gladly and forgetful. Everything was lost, and everything was found. The new world was discovered, it remained only to be explored.

They had passed through the doorway into the further space, where movement was so big, that it contained bonds and constraints and labours, and still was complete liberty. She was the doorway to him, he to her. At last they had thrown open the doors, each to the other, and had stood in the doorways facing each other, whilst the light flooded out from behind on to each of their faces, it was the transfiguration, glorification, the admission.

And always the light of the transfiguration burned on in their hearts.

He went his way, as before, she went her way, to the rest of the world there seemed no change. But to the two of them, there was the perpetual wonder of the transfiguration.

He did not know her any better, any more precisely, now that he knew her altogether. Poland, her husband, the war – he understood no more of this in her. He did not understand her foreign nature, half German, half Polish, nor her foreign speech. But he knew her, he knew her meaning, without understanding. What she said, what she spoke, this was a blind gesture on her part. In herself she walked strong and clear, he knew her, he saluted her, was with her. What was memory after all, but the recording of a number of possibilities which had never been fulfilled? What was Paul Lensky to her, but an unfulfilled possibiliy to which he, Brangwen, was the reality and the fulfilment? What did it matter, that Anna Lensky was born of Lydia and Paul? God was her father and her mother. He had passed through the married pair without fully making Himself known to them.

Now He was declared to Brangwen and to Lydia Brangwen, as they stood together. When at last they had joined hands, the house was finished, and the Lord took up his abode. And they were glad.[11]

As in the previous chapter, I now propose to comment upon this account and, by reference to the model of the holy, to draw out the mediating encounter with the holy which is involved, and is indeed made quite explicit by Lawrence himself in his final sentence.

Lawrence's intention in this passage is identical with that which lay behind his more widely known but, from a literary point of view, less successful *Lady Chatterley's Lover*. The publication of the latter by Penguin Books in 1960 led to a court case, and several of the comments made by experts during the trial are pertinent to my analysis. Dr J. A. T. Robinson, at that time Bishop of Woolwich, declared that Lawrence was attempting to portray coitus 'as in a real sense an act of holy communion'.[12] Professor Richard Hoggart, in similar vein, testified that according to Lawrence 'the physical act is meaningless unless it relates to one's whole being: in other words, back to God'.[13] Dilys Powell contended that 'in Lawrence's book, which has great elements of sacredness, sex is taken as being something to be taken seriously, and as a basis for a holy life.'[14]

What is it, within the experience, that allows such statements to be made? First, there is the recognition of 'otherness'. Tom and Lydia 'had stood in the doorways facing each other', yet 'he went his way, as before, she went her way', and 'he did not know her any better, any more precisely, now that he knew her altogether'. This otherness is brought out most explicitly by Lawrence in a comment he included in *Women in Love*. Summing up the sexual experience of Birkin and Ursula, he says: 'She had her desire fulfilled. He had his desire fulfilled. For she was to him what he was to her, the immemorial magnificence of mystic, palpable, real otherness.' Their joint experience was 'never to be seen with the eye, or known with the mind, only known as a palpable revelation of living otherness'.[15] Each is then encountering a reality that transcends their experience as individuals; each is able to recognize an aspect of their relationship that refers inwardly to the holy. Love indeed is an overpowering of separateness without the elimination of otherness, and this is precisely the effect of a meeting with the holy.

The life of two such people now becomes, as human life should be, a shared life. So Sebastian, the hero of *Incognito* by Petru Dumitriu, declares:

A man and a woman alone is not a whole being. Truly to love our sexual partner is the most sweet and exquisite of all sensual delights. The sexual act may be an occasion of conquest and exaltation of self, particularly in the man, or of self-abnegation, particularly in the woman; it may be the triumph of the technician, perhaps of the artist; it may be altruistic in some men, egotistical in many women. But to know oneself half of a true pair, certain of its purity and integrity, and the whole encompassed by warmth and tenderness, compassion, pity and gratitude; this is the only way of overcoming our loneliness.[16]

Alienation, which witnesses to the crucifixion of the holy, is now replaced, for Tom and Lydia, by the recognition, however dimly, of the reality of the holy, precisely because within the I-Thou they have encountered the eternal Thou. Their mutual love is not some abstract principle which can be defined, more or less accurately, in words – it is a pattern of life, within which coitus is included, which embodies the holy as love itself. Love is then not just a feeling nor a universal benevolence; it is a relation to persons, a form of behaviour in the presence of others, to and for them – it is the very nature of the holy offering itself to others.

Gerard Sorme, the principal character in Colin Wilson's *Man without a Shadow*, at which we have already glanced, is on somewhat the same lines as Lawrence when he writes in his diary:

This is my theory: when a man and a woman get into bed together, they imagine they are going to titillate one another; there is no one else, just the two of them. But this isn't true. *There is a third.* In the very act of sex, they are performing an incantation that arouses the sex-god, whose business it is to drive the world in the direction of evolution. . . .

Yes, I remember it now, the sensation I experienced after that first night with Caroline. I remember lying beside her, staring at the light in the opposite wall, and feeling an immense exaltation, *as if I were a magician who had just succeeded in raising elemental spirits.* It was a feeling that there are other forces in the world besides the ones of which we are fully aware, forces that hide below the surface, but are fully cognisant of everything that goes on. These forces inject meaning into the world. The world is meaningless without them, like the scenery stored in an empty theatre.[17]

I cannot myself accept the accuracy of some of this phraseology and have already had occasion to criticize Sorme's quest for the numinous. His view of 'injection' certainly suggests the *deus ex machina*; but if allowance is made for this, then he is saying, with Lawrence, that in and through coitus we do meet the holy.

To Lawrence, as his ideas are expressed in *The Rainbow*, the experience is one of transfiguration. The encounter with the holy is transforming. The American novelist, Saul Bellow, prefers resurrection as a suitable description of the experience. Hertzog, in the novel of that name, is reflecting upon his relationship with Ramona, with whom he is having an affair.

Here was a man, Hertzog, who knew what it was to rise from the dead. And she, Ramona, she knew the bitterness of death and nullity, too. Yes, she too! But with him she experienced a real Easter. She knew what Resurrection was. He might look down his conscious nose at sensual delights, but with her, when her clothes were off, he knew what it was. No amount of sublimation would replace that erotic happiness, that knowledge.[18]

Whether we use the image of transfiguration or of resurrection, the important fact to appreciate is that coitus is not an incident isolated from life. As Richard Schribel expresses it: 'The true drama of sexual encounter often occurs not in the act of love itself but in the life that surrounds it, conditioning and creating its quality.'[19] It carries with it a promise for the future and opens the way to the future. The promise is of union in freedom, of wholeness – Tom and Lydia can now enter the future of their living together in hope. Yet there is always an incongruity between the present reality and the fulfilment – it is 'already' but 'not yet'. There is always an overspill, so that the holy which is recognized in the promise remains superior to the partial fulfilment.[20]

But the contextual aspect of coitus becomes clearer if we relate it to times of crisis in married life, and this serves to emphasize the self-giving nature of the sex act. We may take as an example a couple who have suffered a tragic bereavement in the death of a small son. The natural grief that is consequent upon such an event often tends to turn each of the partners in on themselves. Almost like a wounded animal, that will curl up in isolation and wants to be left alone, the man and his wife will hug, as it were, their grief to themselves. In these circumstances the very idea of sexual intercourse may be repugnant. Associated as it is with pleasure and joy, it almost seems sacrilegious to engage in coitus when mourning the loss of a child. Sex act and grief appear to be opposed, indeed antithetical to one another. Let us, however, analyse this a little further. When grief turns an individual in on himself or herself and therefore creates a barrier between the partners, that grief cannot be regarded as good. As long as it reinforces isolation and concern for the self, for that is what it does, it is a hindrance to the mutuality which is the basis and goal of marriage. If, in this situation and realizing the self-enclosing nature of this sorrow, the partners recognize that they must unite with each other to comfort one another, then this involves the self-giving of one to the other. The supreme means of this human self-giving is sex. So coitus is a right and proper action even in tragic circumstances. It only becomes repugnant if it is regarded as nothing but a pleasurable, entirely physical act. But seen in depth as essentially a coming together, with pleasure as the by-product, it can be a source of consolation, of sharing the situation, of strength to face it together. It is then a sacramental means of meeting the holy. I use 'sacramental' here in accordance with Tillich's definition, viz. it is 'nothing else than some reality becoming the bearer of the holy in a special way and under special circumstances'.[21] Coitus can and does establish *shālōm*. It is a mutual ministering, in times of stress, of the cup of cold water, a sacrament of love and support even in the depths of misery. It does not remove the cause of the sorrow, nor indeed, after the orgasm, will the feeling of loss disappear, but now it can be borne because it has been openly shared by the two people. From this perspective, so far from being distasteful in these circumstances, coitus may be seen as the *right* way to establish *shālōm*.

It should scarcely need stating that this understanding of coitus involves the rejection of any idea of using other people as objects for self-gratification. Moreover, it also involves acknowledgement of the reality of the other person, who does not then become a mere instrument mediating the holy. There is no thought that the relation to the holy is *the* essential one and that to one's sexual partner secondary. While it is in and through this relation that we encounter the holy, if it is less than genuine or if it is debased, one would simply not perceive the holy. This may be clarified by resorting to the concept of happiness. If we seek happiness *per se*, we shall never find it. Happiness is a by-product of our service to and relations with others. Similarly, if we seek the holy *per se*, we shall never find it. The encounter with the holy is a by-product of our relations with others. It is the depth within the relation, and the encounter with it is inseparable from the relation. Coitus, then, is not to be comprehended as a means to an end, viz. the encounter with the holy. Only in so far as the human communion is understood as being valuable in itself, shall we obtain glimpses of the holy. There is indeed a great deal of truth in Dietrich Bonhoeffer's remark:

To put it plainly, for a man in his wife's arms to be hankering after the other world is, in mild terms, a piece of bad taste, and not God's will. We ought to find and love God in what he actually gives us; if it pleases him to allow us to enjoy some overwhelming earthly happiness, we mustn't try to be more pious than God himself.[22]

In no sense then is coitus, as a mediation of the holy, a devaluation of persons or of the secular reality. It is an enhancement of life and a way to personal identity. There is no sacralization involved in this approach. Just as Lady Chatterley's sexual ecstasy altered her vision of the world,[23] without falsifying it, so coitus transforms, transfigures, resurrects personal relations and advances union without transmuting the basic human reality into something other than itself. Coitus is neither to be repudiated nor risen above, but is to be made the very stuff of an extension of experience, by perceiving the holy in and through it.

At the risk of some objectification, I propose to conclude this chapter by some extended conceptualization.[24] This is all the more necessary because the theological understanding of coitus is only slowly emerging in the present century. Nicolas Berdyaev once said, with accuracy, that the majority of works on sex and marriage produced by Christian theologians 'strongly remind one of treatises on cattle breeding'.[25] With little or no basis in the Bible, the church for centuries adopted a negative attitude to sex and has been slow to formulate any positive understanding of it. It has constantly maintained that the primary purpose of coitus is procreation and that consequently intercourse for any other reason is to be deprecated and may in fact be sinful. Such a concept, which fails to take account of the significance of sex in the sphere of personal relations, debases the act and leads to the attitude which was crudely but clearly expressed by the medieval mystic Margery Kempe, and which unfortunately has been typical of much Christian teaching on the subject in the past: 'The debt of matrimony was so abominable to her that she would rather, she thought, have eaten or drunk the ooze and the muck in the gutter than consent to any fleshly communion.'[26] While not denying that procreation is one of the purposes of intercourse, I would deny that it is its primary purpose, as a brief consideration of some of the psychological and biological factors involved will make evident.

From the psychological aspect it is to be noted that the love of a man for his wife is more lasting and less easily dissolved than the love of either of them for their offspring. Such a condition is scarcely compatible with the view that the *raison d'être* of marriage and intercourse is the production of children, for the children are born to parents already united in the bond of love. 'If procreation and not community of life were the first thing, we should have to maintain that this experience of love is a deep deception and an evil because, in this case, it prevents man from seeing what is most essential.'[27] Romantic love, from which the married state stems, is truly realized in bodily act. Sexual intercourse is the means of renewing and perpetuating that love.

From the biological aspect it is to be noted that coitus is possible when procreation is impossible, viz. during pregnancy and after the menopause. Further, the generative act is distinct from the production of semen, which takes place independently of any willed act, nor is intercourse primarily concerned with the mingling of the seed, which once deposited in the female organism is independent and may or may not unite. The possible resultant conjunction of sperm and ovum is a result of the union of persons, but coitus will often have to be repeated before it can in fact become an act of generation. Hence even its immediate biological object may be said to be union.

That the meaning of the sex act is to be found in what Doms calls 'community of life' or union is also evident from the nature of the act as a whole and from the nature of man in particular. Human beings express themselves by means of personal acts that produce effects; it is these effects, e.g. words, and not the personal acts themselves, that are communicated to other persons. But in coitus there is a direct meeting of the personal acts, not merely of their effects. Moreover, since coitus is impossible in isolation but is a common act in which both share, it involves a most intimate personal relationship which finds its meaning not in the possible remote consequences of child-bearing but in the immediate unity established thereby between the man and his wife.[28] Again, as man is more than a physical organism, unlike the animals he cannot perform any function that is solely physical without connection with his mental, moral and spiritual life. The sex act is never the mere activity of a few organs but includes the whole personality. To assume otherwise is to fall into the error of the Nicolaitans who, regarding the body as worthless and its acts as having no spiritual significance, indulged, quite rightly on their false premises, in a bestial licentiousness.[29] The Christian view of man requires one to find a significance in coitus, and its meaning is that it both builds up and consolidates the union between a man and his wife that they may be 'one flesh'. It builds up and realizes the union because it is a means of self-giving. The marriage act is not intended for the satisfaction of selfish desires nor for any so-called self-fulfilment, but for self-offering. This giving of each to the other wholly is a common personal act of unity which both expresses and realizes that state to which they are called, viz. that of being 'one flesh'. The effect of this progressive advance in unity is the overcoming of separateness and a meeting with the holy.

The curse of egotism is the exclusive acknowledgement of absolute significance for oneself alone and denial of it to others. Though reason shows this to be unjust, it is only by love and not by abstract thought that one is led to recognize the absolute importance of another. This recognition is itself a means of deliverance from egocentricity. Coitus, too, continues this overcoming of separateness and it also involves union between the partners and the holy. That which separates a man from a woman, viz., their egocentricity, is that which separates them from the holy, and in so far as they overcome it and are made one they are united, too, with the holy. Within marriage the path of holiness cannot be other than through sexual relations.

There could be no more clear example of my overall thesis that the holy is a mediated reality than coitus. In itself coitus is a form of *human* mediation. There is a legitimate duality, which is not a dualism, that is comprehended in unity. To caress a woman is to feel the contact both with the hand and with her skin. The experience of the holy is not only similar to the sex act, displaying the same structure, it is also mediated by it.

In conclusion I should perhaps assert that this chapter does not constitute a plea to turn Christianity into a fertility or orgiastic cult. It is, rather, a challenge to recognize coitus within the married state as one means of encounter with the holy. Nevertheless, it should not be forgotten that while, as I have stressed, coitus can overcome separation, it may lead to the replacement of egocentricity by a duocentricity. Romantic love cannot be a path to the holy if, in overcoming selfishness, it merely establishes a double selfishness, whereby husband and wife, possibly together with their children, become no more than an extension of selfhood. So William Blake could ask:

> Is this thy soft Family-Love
> Thy cruel Patriarchal pride,
> Planting thy Family alone,
> Destroying all the World beside?[30]

Only when a married pair live a life for others, sustained by their mutual relations, will their sexual communion continue to mediate the encounter with the holy. This conclusion may help us to appreciate the aptness of the remark addressed to Christ near Cana by an old woman in *The Last Temptation* by Nikos Kazantzakis: 'Wherever you find husband and wife, that's where you find God; wherever children and petty cares and cooking and arguments and reconciliations, that's where God is too.'[31] It also illuminates the Hasidic saying, previously quoted: 'Be fruitful, but not like the animals, be more than they, grow upright and cleave to God as the sprig clings to the root, and dedicate your copulation to him.'[32]

In effect, what I have attempted to achieve in this chapter is to give substance to Sam Keen's dictum; 'The sacred must be rediscovered in what moves and touches us, in what makes us tremble, in what is proximate rather than remote, ordinary rather than extraordinary, native rather than imported.'[33]

7

The Holy and Death

While I was reading Bonhoeffer's *Letters and Papers from Prison*, after completing the previous chapter and before beginning this one, I came across some words which are often quoted. 'I should like to speak of God not on the boundaries of life but at the centre, not in weaknesses but in strength; and therefore not in death and guilt but in man's life and goodness.'[1] Although I was not conscious of it, all the previous chapters could be regarded as an attempt to execute this programme, for the principal tenor of my argument has been that the holy is encountered at the centre of life, in ordinary everyday human situations. Nevertheless, while this remains my chief and necessary emphasis, especially in view of the tendency in Christian thought to treat God 'as a stop-gap for the incompleteness of our knowledge',[2] it is not to be denied that the holy can and may be encountered in border situations also. To illustrate this, I take as the subject for this chapter death and dying.

To some modern philosophers of religion and to some theologians times of crisis are so many openings into the depths of life, into its ground and purpose. Hence they maintain that those who fail to meet the holy in the everyday may be 'shocked' into a realization by entering upon a border-situation. J. E. Smith, for example, finds three pointers or occasions in our experience where we can perceive the holy, and these are usually associated with crises and, in particular, with death. They are:

1. The awareness of the contingent and derivative character of human life, involving the question of its ground or origin.

2. The awareness of the limit of human life, involving the question of the destiny of the self.

3. The awareness of freedom and responsibility, involving the basis and content of obligation or the direction which human life ought to take.

So he concludes that 'when man encounters these three points at which his life is related to something unconditional, he encounters the signs or marks of God. The Absolutely Exalted is present in these experiences and the task of rational reflection is the recovery of that presence through the discovery that these marks are indeed the genuine marks of God.'[3] This follows in part from a previous statement which, with a slight change of terminology, I would endorse, viz., 'The holy provides the final purpose giving point and poignancy to all the details of profane [*sic., sc.* secular] existence, while the profane [*sic., sc.* secular] is the body of life and the medium through which the holy is made fully actual.'[4]

I would not deny that there is truth in these three points, nor that it is possible to discern them in situations of death and dying and so to understand this border-situation as an encounter with the holy. Hence Henderson, one of Saul Bellow's characters, remarks: 'It's too bad, but suffering is about the only reliable burster of the spirit's sleep. There is a rumour of long standing that love also does it.'[5] Yet I must frankly confess to sharing a certain distaste, in laying emphasis upon this in relation to death, with Zorba the Greek when he attended the dying courtesan Madame Hortense. He discovered her fumbling under her pillow.

As soon as she thought she was in danger she had taken out of her trunk a crucifix in gleaming white bone and thrust it under her pillow. For years she had entirely forgotten it and it had lain among her tattered chemises and bits of velvet and rags at the bottom of the trunk. As if Christ were a medicine to be taken only when gravely ill, and of no use so long as you can have a good time, eat, drink and make love.[6]

To behave like Madame Hortense, however natural, is to betray something of a craven and indeed superstitious spirit; it is to attempt to use the holy in a manner little short of magic. Conversely, to thunder 'Prepare to meet thy God' at Madame Hortense is to attack her in her helplessness and weakness and raises doubts about the genuineness of any reaction.

It is, moreover, apposite to recall that the Christian attitude to death does not envisage it – any more than it does coitus, examined previously – as an isolated event. To be present at the bedside of the dying is not to be the spectator of a self-contained 'end-game'. The process of dying and the death itself are the outcome of how the person concerned has coped with his life.[7] Indeed 'our confrontation with nothingness no longer waits upon the moment of death. Meaninglessness, vacancy, non-being has to be dealt with here and now'.[8] In other words, death embraces the whole of life,[9] and if death in life has had no meaning for the dying person, neither will his death as a terminal event. So, according to Gerhard Ebeling, 'The talk about God which is really understandable and relevant is that which sees life itself as the place of encounter with him, and not death or some artificially-induced funeral mood. God enters into real relation with death for us only when he is understood as the one who encounters us in the midst of life.'[10] Similarly, C. G. Jung asserts that 'only he remains vitally alive who is ready *to die with life*'.[11] The likelihood is that if one has failed to observe the paschal pattern in previous years and thereby has not encountered the holy, one will not suddenly – although it is not impossible – meet the holy on one's death bed. Of course it is possible to adopt the outlook of a Sartre and declare that death reveals the absurdity of life; alternatively, one can affirm the meaningfulness of life and so of death. The point of departure is all-important. Indeed it is only by giving meaning to life that one can give meaning to death, and this suggests that, after all, death is not to be regarded as the isolated border-situation that many believe it to be. 'Those whose lives have no meaning cannot give meaning to their death.'[12] Hence, instead of regarding death as a crisis which marks the end of life, we should rather see it as the last act, which can fulfil the previous temporal existence. One could then apply to it Buber's phrase that 'our human way to the infinite leads only through fulfilled finitude'.[13] Dag Hammarskjöld noted in his diary: 'Seek the road which makes death a fulfilment.'[14] He believed that death from the dominion of self-centredness should be continuous and that life itself should be a perpetual sacrifice of self for the sake of others. It is from this perspective that one can regard death at the end of life as a fulfilment.[15]

Unfortunately many people today are not afforded the opportunity to do precisely this, viz. to make their death their own and the consummation of their life. The reasons for this are various. Modern society deprives man of his own death by keeping him in ignorance of it or by representing it simply as a regrettable fact that has to be accepted with Stoic resignation.[16] The secrecy that surrounds death at the present day, the refusal to tell patients the facts (as far as they are known), the lies even that are purveyed – all this deprives the dying person of his dignity and humanity and both falsifies and distorts the relationship between him and his partner or close relatives.[17] Animals live in worlds more or less determined by their own instinctual structure; they are programmed, as it were, by their inner drives, and so their worlds are closed in terms of possibilities. Not so the world of man, which is imperfectly programmed by his own constitution. It is an open world.[18] But, as Arnold Toynbee puts it:

If man stumbles into death in the animal's blind way, he is actually degrading himself to a lower spiritual level than theirs, since – possessing, as he does possess, the power of meeting and facing death with his eyes open – he will in this case have refused to make use of his distinctively human faculties.[19]

In his short poem entitled 'Death', which W. B. Yeats wrote on the political assassination of his friend Kevin O'Higgins, precisely the same point is made.

> Nor dread nor hope attend
> A dying animal;
> A man awaits his end
> Dreading and hoping all;
> Many times he died,
> Many times rose again.
> A great man in his pride
> Confronting murderous men
> Casts derision upon
> Supersession of breath;
> He knows death to the bone –
> Man has created death.[20]

Without this realization, man's freedom to act is prevented, whereas 'we should actively consent to death rather than merely resigning ourselves to it. Only in this will we be able to transfigure what in the material order is a biological necessity into a free, i.e. human, act.'[21] So Herman Feifel says: 'We are mistaken to consider death as a purely biological event.'[22] Bonhoeffer's distinction is helpful in this context, that is, his differentiation between 'the death from within' and 'the death from without' – death as freely accepted and death as a biological event only. 'We may pray that death from without does not come to us till we have been made ready for it through this inherent death; then our death is really only the gateway to the perfect love of God.'[23]

This may be expressed in a slightly different way. Since death is the death of a person, it must be understood as a human act. It is, therefore, not only a biological fate but a personal act in so far as it is accepted. Death can then become the highest act by which man completely disposes of himself in the absolute surrender of self. It is not just to be suffered passively, but to be consented to. At this point the argument comes back to the previous emphasis upon death as not an isolated incident.

> Obviously it could not be an act of man, if it is conceived as an isolated point at the end of life. Death has to be understood as an act of consummation . . . which is achieved through the acts of the whole life in such manner that death is axiologically present all through human life. Man is enacting his death, as his own consummation, through the deeds of his life. Thus, death is present in his deeds, that is, in each and every one of his free acts, the acts by which he freely disposes of his whole person.[24]

Hence John Hinton can report that 'many speak quite positively of this feeling of consenting to life's ending, often they use the word *accept*'.[25]

It will be evident from the above that I am not attempting to treat of death in all its complexity. There are many kinds of death, some of which preclude the kind of knowledge and awareness of which I have been writing. It does not apply to murder victims, to the casualty in a car crash, to anyone who meets with a sudden death and had no knowledge that he was about to die. It does not apply to those whose diseases affect the functioning of the brain so that they are completely out of character, nor to the vegetables kept alive only by drugs. What the relationship is between these latter categories of persons and the holy, I cannot know. But while I am not able to specify it, and I would not wish to go beyond the evidence, I cannot adopt a judgmental attitude and declare that it is impossible. In such cases it is as well to heed the warning of William Blake:

> But go! merciless man! enter into the infinite labyrinth of another's brain
> Ere thou measure the circle that he shall run.[26]

Nor am I concerned with involuntary death on behalf of others, as when a man rescues a child from drowning at the expense of his own life. The encounter with the holy here is too evident to require dwelling on the subject. Jesus' own death was a revelation of serving love, and those who sacrifice themselves, as he did, mediate the holy accordingly. Nor again need we delay with martyrdom, i.e. death accepted for a cause, since this can readily be understood as meaningful, even if it is not the consummation of a life devoted to that for which one is prepared to die. There is, moreover, a martyrdom of anguish and weakness 'whereby man is, as it were, killed before he dies, through devilish modern techniques that murder the person, taking man completely from himself before the life of his body is extinguished'.[27] Rather, I am concerned with those who undergo a normal terminal illness, remembering that this still applies to most people and that according to 1967 figures there is a proportion of about one chance in eight of experiencing pain in the final stages.[28]

We must now turn to the heart of our subject and see how death, understood as a human act, involves an encounter with the holy. This involves the consideration not only of the patient but of those who minister to him and of wife or husband, relatives and friends. As will become apparent, these three cannot always be held apart.

If we begin with the dying person, it may seem that nothing can be said. Only another Lazarus, back from the dead, could tell us what the experience of dying and death involves. But this is not entirely true. In so far as anyone has lived according to the paschal pattern, death is by no means unfamiliar to him. Moreover, the death of a loved one can and does constitute an authentic experience of death for us. A most moving account of this is provided by Augustine in his *Confessions*, where he tells of the passing of a boyhood friend.

During those years, when I first began to teach in Thagaste, my native town, I had found a very dear friend. We were both the same age, both together in the heyday of youth, and both absorbed in the same interests. We had grown up together as boys, gone to school together, and played together. . . . There was a sweetness on our friendship, mellowed by the interests we shared.

The friend then had a fever, fell into a coma, was baptized, recovered consciousness for a few days, after which the fever returned and he died.

My heart grew sombre with grief, and wherever I looked I saw only death. My own country became a torment and my own home a grotesque abode of misery. All that we had done together was now a grim ordeal without him. My eyes searched everywhere for him, but he was not there to be seen. I hated all the places we had known together because he was not in them and they could no longer whisper to me 'Here he comes!' as they would have done had he been alive but absent for a while. I had become a puzzle to myself, asking my soul again and again, 'Why are you downcast? Why do you distress me?' But my soul had no answer to give. If I said, 'Wait for God's help', she did not obey. And in this she was right because, to her, the well-loved man whom she had lost was better and more real than the shadowy being in whom I would have her trust. Tears alone were sweet to me, for in my heart's desire they had taken the place of my friend.[29]

Through Augustine we appreciate that to experience death is to be faced with loneliness and a sense of abandonment and loss. So there is a personal involvement in the suffering and hopelessness that Christ underwent as he hung on the cross. For the dying person this identification can be an encounter with the holy, if death can be accepted. John Hinton has observed that 'in the fatally ill, acceptance and resignation to death seem appropriate, permitting peace of mind'.[30] This positive composure, which he asserts is attained by about one in four dying in hospital, arises out of a meeting with the holy, even though this is not always consciously recognized and so is not expressed in words. To make one's death one's own, to commit oneself to death consciously and deliberately, is to surrender to the holy. Karl Rahner's analysis of the passion of Christ will help to show how this may be so.

The real miracle of Christ's death resides precisely in this: death which can be experienced only as the advent of emptiness . . . and which could be suffered, even by Christ, only as a state of being abandoned by God, now, through being embraced by the obedient 'yes' of the Son, while losing nothing of the horror of the divine abandonment native to death, is transformed into something completely different: into the advent of God in the midst of that empty loneliness, into the manifestation of a complete, obedient surrender of the whole man to the Holy God at the very moment when man seems lost and far removed from him.[31]

If we transpose this language, the point I am seeking to make should become clear: the 'yes' of the dying person, while losing nothing of the horror of abandonment, is transformed into the advent of the holy in the midst of the empty loneliness, into the manifestation of a complete surrender of the whole man to death, in and through which the holy is encountered.

By making his death his own, man achieves that dignity and authenticity which is inseparable from any meeting with the holy.[32] One has only to read the fictional account of the death of Don Quixote by Cervantes or the record of Samuel Johnson's decease by Boswell to see how this dignity can be displayed even in distressing circumstances.

So far I have written as if death were an entirely individual event, but a great number of people dying are in a situation of relationship to others. Consequently there can be an in-between which affects both the patient and those who minister to him professionally and his relatives and friends. This in-between can mediate the holy. There are occasions, for example, when at a death-bed those who have been at odds with one another are reconciled. For a dying person to enter into *shālōm* with a previously estranged loved one is for him to turn to the holy. The recreative activity of the holy then embraces both those who are shortly to be bereaved and the dying person. Here we see that the patient is not just a passive sufferer but an agent who is capable of vital interaction with others,[33] and by engaging in this in-between he achieves authenticity and full maturity, even in the process of dying.

It is regrettable that this possibility is often denied to people at the present day. The I-Thou relationship – it is of this that I am writing – rests upon an honest and open interchange. But when, for example, the pretence is maintained that death is not imminent, there is what Hinton has called a 'bereavement of the dying'.[34] Friends and relations cannot be open. This withdrawal only increases the suffering of a patient who cannot but notice the uncertain behaviour of others, their hollow cheerfulness and their halting conversation. Because there is no I-Thou, the possibility of meeting the eternal Thou is restricted.

This lying about the patient's condition is frequently associated with a restraint upon tears. But tears are just as natural as laughter and to share them is an authentically human act. To inhibit them until one has withdrawn from the bedside is unnatural. One can understand the desire not to make the patient unhappy by one's grief, but the denial of grief can reduce the relationship to a triviality and a sham and is in no sense a mediation of the holy.

When we turn to those who minister to the dying, the encounter with the holy is more evident and more simply formulated. In ministering to the dying, the doctors, nurses and staff are serving Christ. 'I was sick and you visited me. . . . When did we see thee sick? . . . As you did it to one of the least of these my brethren you did it to me.'[35] This – let me emphasize once again – is no devaluation of the human reality. The encounter with the holy through John Smith or Mary Jones is a serving of both, for the experience of the holy is always and at the same time the experience of something or somebody else.

Further, those who minister, either professionally or by being there in love, are encountering the holy whose presence is identified with the human suffering. To serve the brother in distress is an exercise in compassion, the etymology of which means 'suffering with'. This human compassion is the working in us of the compassion of God. So the mediation of the holy is reciprocal, both through the dying person and through those who minister. This identification in human suffering must not be 'spiritualized' until it is evacuated of meaning. To encounter the holy in the suffering person does not mean that he is just an *aide mémoire* of the passion of Christ, so that the connection is simply an association of ideas. Nor does it mean that this suffering is only an imitation, so that it resembles the passion but does not involve Christ himself. Rather, the suffering *is* Christ's suffering: he shares in the condition and identifies himself with it. To recognize the holy in this way is to become aware of the promise and to receive hope: 'I am the resurrection and the life.'[36]

The dignity and wholeness attained by the dying also affect those who attend on them. Hinton observes that there 'are times when the quality of content and acceptance that the dying man attains is a help to those about him'.[37] To be confronted by dignity and wholeness in the face of death is not to deny that these are human and remain so, but it is to affirm that, in accordance with the New Testament model, the holy is met through this dignity and wholeness. Just as the death of Christ profoundly affected those who witnessed it – such as the centurion and the repentant thief – so any man's death can witness to the multi-dimensional character of human life.

Sufficient has probably now been written to indicate how dying and death may be disclosure-situations in and through which the encounter with the holy is made possible. In conclusion, I wish to examine in some detail the account of a particular individual which will serve to illuminate and make more specific some of the generalizations above.

In *A Grief Observed*, which he published under the pseudonym of N. W. Clerk, C. S. Lewis provided a record of the weeks immediately before and following the death of his wife. It is a moving account, which matches that of Augustine's description of the passing of his friend, and is best presented by a series of extracts, to be followed, as in the last chapter, by comments.

Disclosure Situation – A Grief Observed

There is a sort of invisible blanket between the world and me. I find it hard to take in what anyone says. Or perhaps, hard to want to take it in. It is so uninteresting.[38]

Meanwhile, where is God? This is one of the most disquieting symptoms. When you are happy, so happy that you have no sense of needing Him, so happy that you are tempted to feel His claims upon you as an interruption, if you remember yourself and turn to Him with gratitude and praise, you will be – or so it feels – welcomed with open arms. But go to Him when your need is desperate, when all other help is vain, and what do you find? A door slammed in your face, a sound of bolting and double bolting on the inside. After that, silence. You may as well turn away. The longer you wait, the more emphatic silence will become. There are no lights in the windows. It might be an empty house. Was it ever inhabited? It seemed so once. And that seeming was as strong as this. What can this mean? Why is He so present a commander in our times of prosperity and so very absent a help in time of trouble?[39]

I cannot talk to the children about her. The moment I try, there appears on their faces neither grief, nor love, nor fear, nor pity, but the most fatal of all non-conductors, embarrassment. They look as if I were committing an indecency. They are longing for me to stop.[40]

The most precious gift that marriage gave me was this constant impact of something very close and intimate, yet all the time unmistakably other, resistant, in a word, real.[41]

Talk to me about the truth of religion and I'll listen gladly. Talk to me about the duty of religion and I'll listen submissively. But don't come talking to me about the consolation of religion or I shall suspect that you don't understand.[42]

Aren't all these notes the senseless writhings of a man who won't accept the fact that there is nothing we can do with suffering except to suffer it? Who still thinks there is some device (if only he could find it) which will make pain not to be pain?[43]

Gradually Lewis's grief moderated and he realized that it sprang from a desire to call his wife back, as if the past situation, before her illness and death, could be restored. As his sorrow lifted he found that a double barrier had been removed. The first was that between himself and his dead wife: as he mourned her less, he remembered her more vividly.

Indeed it was something (almost) better than memory; an instantaneous, unanswerable impression. To say it was like a meeting would be going too far. Yet there was that in it that tempts one to use such words.[44]

He contended that just as tears obscure one's ordinary vision, so one's grief prevents a true recollection of the deceased.

The second barrier removed was that between himself and God.

I have gradually been coming to feel that the door is no longer shut and bolted. Was it my own frantic need that slammed it in my face? The time when there is nothing at all in your soul except a cry for help may be just the time when God can't give it; you are like the drowning man that can't be helped because he clutches and grabs. . . . On the other hand, 'Knock and it shall be opened.' But does knocking mean hammering and kicking the door like a maniac? And there's also 'To him that hath shall be given.' After all, you must have a capacity to receive, or even omnipotence can't give. Perhaps your own passion temporarily destroys the capacity.[45]

Comments

Lewis's account takes the form of diary jottings, written down as each day passes. He is very concerned to be completely honest, and time and again he questions his motives, the correctness of his formulations and the extent to which he may be deluding himself. The result is a record of undoubted authenticity.

The description, of course, is not of dying and death as experienced directly by his wife, but as experienced by Lewis himself. Indeed the loneliness and sense of abandonment that characterize the major portion of the account are evidence in support of my previous statement that the death of a loved one can be an authentic experience of death for the bereaved. There is emptiness and the loss of any sense of the divine presence. 'My God, my God, why hast thou forsaken me?'[46]

But we have also to face the fact that Lewis's description suggests, in opposition to my thesis, that dying and death are not an encounter with the holy. To him the door appears to be slammed

and double bolted. Nevertheless, at the same time, apparently unconsciously, he reveals the reasons for this and, in so doing, supplies ground for endorsing my position. Lewis fails to encounter the
holy because he has allowed his grief to shut him up in himself. The
result of this self-enclosure, as he makes clear, is threefold. First, he
is cut off from the world: 'There is a sort of invisible blanket between the world and me.' Secondly, he is separated even from his
own children, so that he tells of a grief observed but not shared.
Thirdly, he is no longer conscious of 'otherness' – 'this constant impact of something very close and intimate, yet all the time unmistakably other' – after his wife's death. Now I have argued that the
encounter with the holy is in and through the world, that it requires openness to others, and that through the I-Thou there is a
meeting with the eternal Thou. Precisely because, in Lewis's case,
these circumstances no longer obtain, he does not and cannot encounter the holy. Nor, apparently, does he seem to appreciate the
extent to which death can be the consummation of the paschal pattern and see that, through his wife's decease, he too is involved in
this life through death.

Moreover, it is only as his grief subsides and he can recall his wife
clearly, that his meeting with the holy becomes once again real to
him. His wife had been a mediator of this encounter; when she was
removed, Lewis was unable, at first, to perceive the holy because,
being enclosed in himself, he did not allow any other mediation to
exist for him. If he had been able to share his grief with his children,
if he had not allowed himself to be cut off from the world, then he
could have said 'yes', and so, while losing nothing of the pain and
horror of the abandonment, he could have recognized the advent
of the holy in the midst of empty loneliness.

Lewis tells of a veiling of the holy in the face of death. But who
has lowered the veil? Lewis eventually recognizes that he is responsible for this. This means that the holy does not absent himself in
the face of dying and death, nor veil himself, but that man himself
lowers the curtain and then comes to believe that the holy has withdrawn. The veil, in Lewis' case, is created by his own natural but
self-centred grief and his consequent separation from the living
memory of his wife and from the world through which the holy is
apprehended. To say this is not to deny the existence of the veil
in Lewis' case, for that would be to call in question the reality of
his experience. That is certainly not my intention; it is, however,

my intention to draw attention to the veil for what it is and so assist those in a similar situation to remove it for themselves and encounter the holy.

Ultimately the restored meeting stems in Lewis's case from his own willingness to die to the past, and so to live according to the paschal pattern. He gives up the desire to re-establish the situation that obtained before his wife's illness and death, and this removes the barrier between himself and her and so, at the same time, between himself and the holy.

'Blessed are those that mourn, for they shall be comforted', says the Beatitude in its Matthean form.[47] 'Blessed are you that weep now, for you shall laugh' – this is the Lucan rendering.[48] The reference is not to those suffering from melancholia nor to those who bewail their sins, but to those in afflictions such as bereavement. But the blessedness has its source in the presence and activity of Jesus, the model of the holy. It is 'already' but 'not yet', eschatological but not apocalyptic – an element, therefore, in the present encounter.

It is only the person who has achieved the maturity of a caring, self-giving relationship to the other, dependable rather than dependent, who can accept the situation with grief but without anger, and say, like Job, 'The Lord gave, and the Lord hath taken away. Blessed be the name of the Lord.'[49]

8

The Holy and the Public World of Man

Since my subject is the encounter with the holy in the secular world, it is time to recognize that life in the secular world comprehends far more than personal relations. Man is involved in historical movements, in political, economic and welfare activities, as well as in work. All these are more or less institutionalized, so that he is faced with a multitude of organizations, some of great size and complexity, which have a profound effect upon his life. To restrict the locus of encounter with the holy to the sphere of the I-Thou would be to imply that many human beings spend the majority of their time in situations where no such meeting is possible. Indeed, as Graham Slater points out, because the holy 'is related to the world at many other levels than "I-Thou" encounter, personal models must be supplemented by others'.[1] Something, therefore, has to be said about economics, work, etc., each in its turn. But, first, by way of general introduction, there is a need to examine further the limits of the personalist approach and so to extend the criticism to which reference has previously been made when summarizing the I-Thou philosophy of Martin Buber.[2]

Buber himself acknowledges what may be called the fluidity of the worlds of I-Thou and I-It. By this I mean that the division between them is not absolute. Man cannot sustain indefinitely an I-Thou relationship, so that the other is constantly changing from being an object to a person and back to an object again. Moreover, objects are the essential basis of life as persons. They can be instruments of fulfilling relations between man and man. A nurse ministering to a patient uses syringes, bandages, ointments, and these things are essential to her personal service to the sick man. It is, of course, true that one cannot find a significance in things in themselves; they only have meaning if they are related to a consciousness. To find meaning in earthly realities is only possible in so far as they are involved in the destiny of man, promoting his humanization and maturity. From the Christian point of view one can even speak of a personalization of objects, since the eucharistic bread and wine are understood to be the means of an encounter with the holy.

Indeed, without a constant respect – one might also say reverence – for things, personal life itself can be put in jeopardy. The most striking contemporary demonstration of this is provided by the spectacle of the pollution of nature through technology and the consequent need for conservation. In 1970 an NBC documentary film was shown on television. It was entitled 'Pollution is a Matter of Choice'. It showed the fumes pouring from jet engines, the smoke from the factory chimneys, the gases from car exhausts, and the waste products spewed all around. It gave shots of rivers that had become open sewers, of fish dead and dying, of natural life gradually being choked out of existence. To see this film is to realize that the natural environment is being steadily poisoned; at the same time it is to appreciate, through this evidence from the world of I-It, our own responsibility and the need to preserve nature if mankind is to survive. Through confrontation with the impersonal world of natural pollution, we have to confess our responsibility and we experience judgment. The solution to the problem is by no means simple, when the choice is between starvation for some, because of lack of work or of a reasonable standard of living, and the building of a factory with all its accompanying industrial waste. It is easy for the affluent to declare that the environment must be preserved, but the poor need the work that modern technology creates. Nevertheless, to face the choice is to accept social responsibility for our actions, and this is to encounter the holy. In other words, through the impersonal world of polluted nature, the holy addresses us.

Yet the example I have just adduced must be treated with caution because it can so easily be misused. We have already noted, in the very first chapter, that as science advances, God, conceived as an explanatory hypothesis and as the power behind the scenes, becomes less and less credible. However, those whose thinking is still dominated by the sacral universe and who cling to beliefs in their traditional forms, seize upon unsolved problems that confront modern

man and the new problems such as pollution, as a basis for maintaining that there is still room in the world for God. So they sacralize
the secular reality.[3] The ecological crisis is no mystery; it is perfectly
understandable, and although it may not be easy to resolve, it will
not be overcome by recourse to the God of the sacral universe. In my
example, however, I have not used the holy to fill the gap in human
knowledge, but I have suggested that through pollution the holy
may address man.

But is this an encounter or, rather, a recognition? Is this a means of
knowing about rather than knowing the holy? Is this a mediated
and indirect meeting in contrast to a mediated and direct meeting
through personal relations?

Some modern novelists stress the impersonal aspects of the holy
itself. Sebastian, in Petru Dumitriu's *Incognito*, speaks of man's
constant effort to devise fantastic images of the holy in order to shield
himself from it.

> But the moment comes again when God snatches away the shielding
> fingers and forces us to see him and remember him. He gazes at us,
> living, inscrutable, terrible and unendurable, through the eye holes of his
> mask. The masks covering the wrath of God are very many. Those that
> I know are war, revolution, social upheaval, disaster, human arrogance
> and its inevitable humiliation, boredom, petulance and human stupidity,
> human folly and malice, and death.[4]

Similarly in *Zorba the Greek* we read:

> God changes his appearance every second. Blessed is the man who
> can recognise him in all his disguises. At one moment he is a glass of
> fresh water, the next your son bouncing on your knees or an enchanting
> woman, or perhaps merely a morning walk.[5]

There is some correspondence between this outlook and Tillich's
reminder that according to the trinitarian formulation the term
'person' was used for the three principles in the divine life and not
for God himself, and that 'personality' was never employed in this
connection at all. 'The idea of God in classical theology united personal and supra-personal traits, God was less and more than
personal, as well as personal; he was the unity of all potentialities.'[6]
It is only in comparatively recent times that God has been conceived
as an individual person and so become one among many. But if the
divine may be less than, as well as more than, personal, the possibility that there is an impersonal aspect to the holy must be admitted.
Nevertheless, I would still maintain with B. Häring that 'every

time the holy appears to us, it manifests itself as a personal Thou'.[7] This does not mean that the holy is not always more than our experience of him nor that the holy can be contained in our categories, not even the categories of personal relations.[8] It does mean that impersonal objects and events can mediate a direct encounter with the holy who thereby is present to human experience, if we respond to the address. I therefore accept Tillich's observation that 'in every religion the holy is encountered in personal images'.[9] But side by side with this must be set the further statement that 'in every religion the holy is mediated by some piece of finite reality'.[10] This may be an object; but when an object performs the function of mediating the holy, then it also receives what Tillich describes as 'a personal force', i.e. it becomes an element in personal encounter. The extent to which an object or an event can mediate this depends upon either the intensity of the relation to the object or the degree of involvement in the event. Hence the previous distinction – no more than hinted at – between encounter and recognition may be valid. Let us test it by a brief consideration of the holy and history.

The Judaeo-Christian tradition has consistently maintained that God is active in history.[11] In so doing it has affirmed the multi-dimensional nature of reality. The Exodus story may serve as an illustration. It is possible to describe this in at least two ways:

1. Moses led the Hebrews out of their slavery in Egypt.
2. God led the Hebrews out of their slavery in Egypt.

Both statements refer to a secular event within history; neither conflicts with the other nor renders the other otiose. If 1. is read in the light of 2., then Moses is understood as the agent and mediator of the divine action. If the reverse order is adopted, then God is understood to have acted through the agency of Moses.

Similarly, on the basis of the New Testament, one can produce another doublet:

1. Jesus was executed under Pontius Pilate.
2. He himself bore our sins in his body on the tree.[12]

The same secular event in history is referred to in each statement; both can be regarded as equally true, and for a full understanding of what took place both are necessary. Buber is therefore correct in declaring that the holy does not violate historical reality, rather it 'permeates history without divesting it of its rights'.[13]

Yet it is one thing to perceive, or recognize, the holy in history; it is another for this recognition to result in an encounter. I would suggest that this happens as and when man is fully involved in the action or movement in and through which he perceives the holy. Isaiah saw the Assyrians, ready to 'smite with the rod' as agents of the divine wrath.[14] To his contemporaries this recognition would have become an encounter when the Assyrians were at the gates of Jerusalem, and they had realized that this was the Holy One coming in judgment. Today the problem is to identify 'where, in the push and pull of human conflict, those currents can be detected which continue the liberating activity we witness in the Exodus and in Easter'.[15] This identification cannot be made genuinely by those outside the situation, hence M. M. Thomas asserts that 'only those who participate in the struggle of a people for fuller life receive the call to exercise the prophetic ministry of criticism. Only participants can be prophets.'[16] This is the role that he sought to fulfil in his study of *The Christian Response to the Asian Revolution*. In so doing he was in the succession of the Old Testament prophets who 'not only see God as active in past salvation events which are remembered and recorded, they claim that his hand is also *and equally* at work in the events of their own day.'[17]

As a distant and not directly involved observer, I can *recognize*, through the analysis given by M. M. Thomas, that the holy is operating in the historical movement, but only those who experience the moral compulsion towards active participation in the Far East can speak of encounter. In all forms of human effort, of course, I-Thou relations are possible and do take place. It is therefore not difficult to see how a meeting with a Gandhi or a Nehru may be an encounter with the eternal Thou, both through the in-between and by recognizing each as an organ of the divine action in history. But our concern is with more than this; it is with the public, as distinct from the private, life of man. To understand this in relation to the Asian revolution one has to leave it to a participant to speak for himself. The following extracts from M. M. Thomas's book summarize how he sees the political, social and economic upheaval in Southern Asia in terms of an encounter with the holy.

Through the revolution God in his providence is creating in Asia the basic conditions of greater human dignity, enhanced human creativity and maturer human living. Personal freedom and social justice and higher standards of living and a sense of national identity do not guarantee personal fulfilment in a responsible society, but they are necessary conditions for the same. . . . A new personal self-awareness has made new levels of interpersonal relations and community possible. . . . The vision of the Asian man of the new dimension of his humanity and fuller human existence is a gift of God through the Asian revolution. . . . Through the Asian revolution, God is judging and recalling the Church in Asia to repentance and renewal in a new way. It was Asian nationalism that broke the too close identification of the gospel with Western culture and Western imperialism and brought the awareness of the transcendence of the gospel over all cultures and historical movements and the possibility . . . of its relating itself positively, creatively and realistically to indigenous culture and national goals. The Churches are in search of a new self-hood, corresponding to the new self-hood of the nation. . . . Through the contemporary Asian revolution, God is judging and reforming his people, calling them to discover their being as witnesses within the Asian revolution.[18]

In making such statements Thomas is consciously fulfilling what he believes to be an essential part of the theologian's task.

The purpose of theology is not to find divine sanctions for a historical movement, but to help discern what is of Christ and what of the devil in that movement so that we may know the nature of our response in faith. True theology is not a means of enhancing self-righteousness and political messianism, but a spiritual source of constructive and discriminating participation. Certainly, we should not seek any new revelation of God in any historical event other than the Christ event, but faith in the divine revelation of Jesus Christ can be a key to understanding and discernment of God's creation, judgment and redemption in secular history. And at best the discernment is partial in character, for we see through a glass darkly. But if it is affirmed that what God does in secular history is absolutely hidden and that even a partial discernment is impossible to the eye of faith, then we are left without any guidance as to the nature or direction of our participation in secular affairs. . . . The result will be a divorce between faith and participation in life which creates a dangerous split between secular responsibilities and exercise of Christian spirituality and Christian mission.[19]

In effect Thomas is saying, in slightly different words, that Jesus is the model of the holy and that through the adoption of this pre-understanding we may discern the holy in the Asian revolution and indeed, possibly, in all the revolutions that are currently taking place in the world today.[20] It should, of course, not be too readily assumed that any and every revolution is necessarily beneficial and that the holy is always on the side of those who support them. Indeed, where the holy is not recognized, a reverse current may be set in action which is detrimental to man. So, for example, the establishment of a totalitarian state, which dismisses the sacred from public life, may result in the filling of the void thus created with a new holiness of its own – whether of race, blood, soil or of social class – which provides an ultimate concern other than that which is revealed by the New Testament model. The result, as evidenced both by Nazi Germany and by the USSR in the Stalinist era, is dehumanization.[21]

Whether we like it or not, those who would encounter the holy in the secular world cannot avoid political action. It does not matter whether we are opposing the sending of Jews to concentration camps or attempting to stop a racial riot or refusing to accept a one-party system. The Christian, in such circumstances.

understands to what extent the love of God and the love of men are no more than a single love and to what extent Christian faith, far from withdrawing us from the struggles of the earth, pours into our hearts sufficient hope to allow us to dare to risk everything in the struggle, even our earthly comfort and our life itself. It is in such circumstances that the Pascha of Christ leaves the realm of ineffective abstraction and historicism and becomes the present principle of our present saving boldness. So our struggle for the truth of man, lived for the love of man, makes the Pascha of Christ 'exist for us.'[22]

In the light of this, the plea of J. B. Metz for a 'political theology' becomes intelligible. He contends that Christianity must overcome the privatizing tendency to which it has become more and more subject over the past decades. He characterizes this trend in the following way:

The basic categories used in the interpretation of the message are preferably the intimate, the private, the apolitical. Charity, like all the phenomena of interpersonal relationships, is no doubt emphasized but as something that is *a priori* and almost obviously private and stripped of political meaning, a mere I-and-Thou relationship, an interpersonal encounter or a matter of neighbourliness. The category of encounter dominates. The real religious expression is mutual encounter, and the proper field of religious experience is the extreme of subjective freedom or the shapeless, inarticulate centre of the I-Thou relationship. The present prevailing forms of transcendental, existential and personalist theology seem to have one thing in common, the concentration upon what is private.[23]

In opposition to this, Metz calls for a reassessment of the relation between religion and society, involving informed social criticism in terms of the eschatological proviso, i.e. in the knowledge that every social situation has a provisional character. Social reality, as experienced in history, must be faced with a critical and dialectical attitude. In this way it may be possible to discover the signs of the times and so to recognize the holy. This is above all necessary in relation to institutions.

Today many regard individual man as an abstraction. Man only is in his social reality. This refers, in the first instance to his inter-personal relations, of which much has been said already. But, as a social being, man's co-operative efforts to achieve certain goals require the creation of institutions, and so his social reality includes, in the second instance, his institutional life. The quality of this life and the extent to which it may mediate the holy rest upon the institutions' relative freedom from or submission to reification. This term, with both sociological and philosophical overtones, refers to the apprehension of human phenomena as if they were things. According to Berger and Luckmann:

> Another way of saying this is that reification is the apprehension of the products of human activity *as if* they were something other than human products. . . . Reification implies that man is capable of forgetting his authorship of the human world. . . . The reified world is, by definition, a dehumanized world. It is experienced by man as a strange facticity, an *opus alienum* over which he has no control, rather than as the *opus proprium* of his own productive activity. . . . The decisive question is whether he still retains the awareness that, however objectivated, the social world was made by men – and, therefore, can be remade by them. In other words, reification can be described as an extreme step in the process of objectivation, whereby the objectivated world loses its com-prehensibility as a human enterprise and becomes fixated as a non-human, non-humanizable, inert facticity.[24]

Where this happens – and it is not infrequent in contemporary Western society – institutions assume an identity and a life of their own, which make them independent of the people who constitute them. They are then a reality produced by man which denies man. These reified institutions dwarf man quite as much as did nature in the sacral universe. One must, however, resist any move to sacralize them and regard them as part, if not of a divine at least of an un-changeable order, as did our medieval forbears. One must also recognize their ambiguity as human creations. Some of them, especially those that have become 'fixated as a non-human, non-humanizable, inert facticity', are a barrier to any recognition of the holy. They rob man of his authenticity and of his responsibility;

they become demonic and prevent growth in maturity. To be involved in such an institution, whether political or industrial, is to be
in a situation where to respond to the holy is possibly to strive for its
destruction and certainly for its transformation, so that it becomes
once again subordinate to human ends. The reality man has created
must be controlled and so shaped that it may be a channel for the
holy; otherwise it will reduce men to the status of things and deny
their freedom and being. So within a reified institution, which is itself a barrier to the encounter with the holy, the individual who acts
as an agent of change may himself become the bearer of the holy
and so mediate an encounter to others. Contrariwise, an institution
which has not succumbed to reification may itself be a medium for
the recognition of the holy in terms of humanization, freedom, etc.
Indeed, love and mercy are not just applicable to interpersonal relations; they can be embodied in institutions and structures.

Reification is especially evident in the world of technology and
industrial concerns. Technology itself is no more than an assortment of tools and techniques which extends the power of human
muscles and refines the perception of the human senses.[25] As such
it is a human creation, but its application to industry since the
Industrial Revolution has so changed the conditions of work that
the Protestant ethic, which gave a religious meaning to this activity
in the past, has ceased to carry conviction. Some preliminary consideration of this ethic is, however, necessary, not only because
traces of it still survive but also because, in its day, it did provide an
understanding of work that enabled it to be a means of serving the
holy.

The Protestant or Puritan ethic, sometimes called the 'Gospel of
work', was an amalgam which began to take shape in the Reformation reaction to certain medieval ideas and eventually comprised
elements from Luther, from Calvin, from the increasing individualism in the post-Renaissance period and from the changing economic
circumstances of the time. The medieval divines drew a formal
distinction between 'precepts' and 'counsels', and they based this
upon I Corinthians 7.25 in the Vulgate version: 'Concerning virgins
I have no commandment (*praeceptum*) of the Lord, but I give my
judgment (*consilium*).' It was argued that 'precepts' were commands
of God himself binding upon all men, while 'counsels of perfection' were recommendations for the few. So adultery was forbidden
by commandment to all, while celibacy was recommended by

counsel to a limited number. This was to introduce a dual standard; one, consisting of the commandments, for man living in the world, and the other, consisting of counsels, for those who had taken monastic vows. The latter state was regarded as the more meritorious and the term 'vocation' was applied to it. The way of holiness then lay through rejection of the world, by the practice of rigid asceticism within one of the religious orders and by obedience to both commandments and counsels.

Economic life was looked down upon, and indeed in the *Elucidarium* of Honorius of Autun it was regarded as little better than a struggle of wolves over carrion, those engaged in it being guilty of cheating and profiteering and having little chance of salvation.[26] Luther rejected the idea of a dual standard and applied the concept of vocation to man's calling in the world. Indeed, it has been said that he turned the whole world into a monastery. Calvin went further and used vocation of man's secular calling, whether it be baking or weaving or whatever. He stressed the need for men 'to prove themselves Christians by holiness of life',[27] and he regarded this latter phrase as applicable to the whole of earthly endeavour, including work. In similar vein, Richard Steele, a seventeenth-century English Puritan, declared that 'God doth call every man and woman ... to serve him in some peculiar employment in the world'.[28] So man is to serve God not only *in vocatione* but *per vocationem*. Work is indeed a form of ascetic discipline to be exercised in the punctual discharge of secular duties, and *laborare est orare* was interpreted to mean that labour is not a tedious necessity but an act of worship. Moreover, the wealth acquired by this diligent effort was held to be a sign of grace.

The effect of all this was to understand work not, as in the Middle Ages, as simply a means to maintain the individual and the community but as the way of holiness. The way was, however, conceived in intensely individualistic terms; one's relation to God was a private one, and its social context, which was still prevalent in Calvin's thought, was lost during the seventeenth century. As capitalism made the individual sovereign, so Protestantism pioneered in making the God-man relationship a vertical one centred on the individual rather than the community. The economic virtues now become all important: diligence, moderation, sobriety, thrift, prudence and industry. So, according to a treatise of 1690, workers were to be 'sober, patient, and such as believe that labour and industry is their duty towards God'.[29] There was thus created, in the words of Max Weber, 'a connection between the fundamental religions ideas of ascetic Protestantism and its maxims for everyday economic conduct'.[30]

Certain corollaries followed from this. In the first place, time-wasting was regarded as the deadliest of sins; not leisure but work is to the glory of God. In the second place, the poor were regarded as the victims, not of economic circumstances, but of their own idleness, of what the Poor Law Commissioners of 1834 called their 'individual improvidence and vice'. Their sufferings, as in the sweat factories or in terms of child labour, were therefore interpreted in accordance with the views of Job's comforters, and Job's own protest was conveniently forgotten. The comforters, it will be remembered, considered Job's loss of family and material possessions as a sure sign of his sinfulness.

This definition of the 'gospel of work', calls for some immediate comments. First, on the positive side, it should be recognized that Luther, Calvin and their followers did make a valiant attempt to see life in the world of work as a way of holiness and their effort, if not their solution, is in accordance with the main thesis of this book. Nevertheless, this teaching was more helpful to the bourgeoisie, consisting of shopkeepers and the heads of small industrial firms, than it was to the workers themselves. Moreover, there was a tendency to sacralize work and to gloss over the question of its human meaning. It is precisely here that this belief reveals its greatest weakness in terms of the contemporary industrial scene, which is characterized by a disenchantment with work, for if work loses its human meaning, what point has it at all? Again, it should be recognized that the basic concept of 'vocation' is quite contrary to the teaching of the New Testament. According to Alan Richardson:

The Bible knows no instance of a man's being called to an earthly profession or trade by God. St Paul, for example, is called to be an apostle; he is not called to be a tentmaker. . . . We cannot with propriety speak of God's calling a man to be an engineer or a doctor or a schoolmaster.[31]

Yet survivals of the Protestant ethic are to be detected on all sides. When a candidate for a university lectureship in theology explains that the reason for his application arises from his sense of vocation to the academic life, he is using a Calvinist, and not a New Testament, interpretation of the word and is rationalizing a perfectly normal human desire to undertake a role that he thinks will be more interesting and rewarding than his present occupation. When a person finds it difficult to relax and is of the opinion that he should be constantly on the go, he demonstrates a lingering acceptance of the idea that leisure is sinful or, at least, can only be justified as a time for recuperating from work in order to do more work. When the head of a firm endows the pursuit of his business with high moral purpose and expects from his employees the same devotion as he has himself, he is, probably unconsciously, still operating within the ambit of the Protestant ethic. But the fundamental weakness of this outlook lies in its failure to correspond with contemporary attitudes to work, and it is to these that we must next turn.

Analysis of work at the present day is by no means easy. Even the definition of the word bristles with difficulties. When an MCC team of professional cricketers plays an amateur Australian eleven, who is engaged in work and who is not? It has been suggested that work may be regarded as a purposeful activity directed towards ends that lie outside the activity itself, in contrast to play that is self-rewarding. Let us apply this to two academics, each writing a survey of Shakespeare criticism. The one may see his book as the by-product of an enjoyable exercise and as a means of clarifying his ideas; in this case the activity is self-rewarding, regardless of the ultimate acceptance of the completed book or the financial advantage that may accrue from its publication. The other may regard the writing of the book as a necessary means to securing promotion; he may find the task a hard grind and he may derive little satisfaction from doing it. Since both are performing the same kind of activity, it may be reasonable to conclude that the boundaries of work are subjectively indeterminate.

Indeed, even the boundaries between work and leisure are by no means clear. In 1959 M. N. Donald and R. J. Havighurst published the results of a survey which showed that most of the meanings ascribed to leisure were also ascribed to work, i.e. the chance to achieve something, to be creative, to serve or benefit society, as a means of passing the time, of making contact with friends, and as a source of interest, status and self-respect.[32]

Even the very carefully weighed definition by Sylvia Shimmin is not free from criticism. According to her, work is 'employment within the social and economic system which is pursued by the individual as his main occupation, by the title of which he is known and from which he derives his role in society.'³³ However, as she herself points out, there is now a widespread tendency not to regard work as a source of normative integration into society nor to see in it any personal significance, as illustrated by many individuals who, when asked about their jobs, do not reply with a title but simply say that they work at X's; i.e., their status and identification derive not from their work but from the organization for which they work. The days when Miller, Baker or Smith could be adopted from one's occupation as personal designations are passing.

The situation appears even more confused when one considers the very many different types of work. What has the lawyer in a magistrate's court in common with the man on the assembly line? The door-to-door salesman with the factory cleaner? The professional tennis player with the school teacher? There appear to be as many attitudes to work, however it is defined, as there are individuals. Those engaged in the so-called professions tend, by a large majority, to regard their work as a central life-interest, but 'most production-line jobs do not produce the kind of occupational involvement or identification necessary to make work a satisfying experience'.³⁴ Conditions of work differ from industry to industry and even within the same firm, and this affects interest in the task performed. Thus the making of waterproof clothes by the Wye Garment Company, described by Tom Lupton, involves a semi-mechanical set of movements, with each hand performing repeatedly the same limited range of actions – under these conditions the workers are frequently bored. At Jays' Electrical Components, on the other hand, each assembly sets the operator a different series of problems – under these conditions the workers are interested and see their role as a challenge.³⁵

That which one worker will find boring, another finds interesting. So there is the case of the girl inserting pieces of cork into the tops of toothpaste tubes. When asked if this was boring, she replied: 'Oh, no! They come up different every time.'³⁶ The same research worker was herself asked by another operator: 'Don't you get bored, just interviewing people all day?'

The upshot of all this is that one cannot generalize. This conclusion reveals a further weakness of the Protestant ethic, for it was a general theory applicable to all work in all circumstances. It would be vain to seek to replace it by another general theory. This means, therefore, that I have to be specific and discuss particular types of work, and not some universal and abstract concept.

In order to narrow the field of analysis, and keep the subject within the confines of this chapter, I must point out that I am not here concerned with those activities that are based upon I-Thou relations. In the light of what has been written previously, it should not be necessary to point out how the work of a doctor, a prison officer or a teacher can all provide opportunities for I-Thou relations and so for encounter with the eternal Thou. Nor is there any difficulty in appreciating that the context within which work is carried out, as distinct from work as a specific task, may equally provide such occasions. During one's time in a factory, there are the meetings at the tea break, the lunch hour and possibly in the evenings at union gatherings, and even on the job itself, if one works in a team, or alongside others and has regular contact with supervisors. It has indeed been asserted that workers are related to their work more by a gang-nexus or status-nexus than by a cash-nexus.[37] The different roles performed in a factory allow some workers to spend much of their time in this way, so that a foreman, for example, is as much concerned with the human as with the mechanical factors.

The importance of a group as mediating an encounter with the holy can be demonstrated from the experience of thirty women engaged in winding yarn. They worked in a long narrow room and their direct relations were confined to their immediate neighbours. The comment of one of them was to the effect: 'This is a dirty job; I do it and get off home.' Despite the bad lighting, the filthiness of the task and a somewhat bullying foreman, the women had remained loyal to the firm for some fifteen years without any protest. Then the room was redecorated and an electric fan was accidentally moved and left playing on to the head of one of the women. Despite representations, nothing was done and, after three weeks, the women unanimously decided to strike. The particular cause was not very important; only one individual was affected, but the group acted in unison. They repudiated the shop steward; they created a union and sought and gained an increase in pay. At the end of the episode, they had come to know each other well and a different relationship had been established between them – one of solidarity. Here we see an encounter with the holy in terms of responsibility and human dignity, of a growth in self-awareness and of interpersonal relations. Here is that solidarity, confidence and community of will that we have previously seen to be marks of a meeting with the holy. Nevertheless, we are still in the sphere of the I-Thou, and so we must limit our concern and, neglecting the total work-context, concentrate upon the performance of the work-task itself. Yet a further limitation is to be observed. We must concentrate upon the individual worker and especially upon those who work in mass production. I am fully aware that in so doing I am examining tasks that are not necessarily typical. It should be noted that between 1900 and 1956 the ratio of clerical, administrative and technical workers to manual workers changed from 1 : 12 to 1 : 4 in the manufacturing industry. Moreover, only a small proportion of manufacturing firms are actually engaged in mass production, and, even when they are, not all employees are on the assembly line.[38] Nevertheless, this limitation may be justified on the grounds that it is precisely there that the problem of work today can be seen in its sharpest outlines.

In their study of *The Man on the Assembly Line* (1952), C. R. Walker and R. H. Guest specified six characteristics of mass production:

1. Mechanical pacing of work
2. Repetitiveness
3. Minimum skill required
4. Preselection in the use of tools and techniques
5. Minute subdivision of product worked on
6. Surface mental attention.

The reaction of workers to these conditions has been widely documented. The incidence of the first item leads to such typical comments as: 'The work isn't hard, it's the never ending pace. . . . The guys yell "Hurrah" whenever the line breaks down . . . you can hear it all over the plant.'[39] The second characteristic may be illustrated by a remark reported by Lupton: 'You hear a lot of people complaining about youngsters nowadays having no interest in their work. It's not surprising when you look at it, the same thing day after day.'[40] The comparative ease with which some of the tasks may be learned is revealed by the statement: 'Only took a half hour to pick it up – then it's only a question of speeding up. Some men get it in less than half an hour.'[41] Predetermination in the use of tools and techniques inevitably cuts down the individual's freedom, while all these factors contribute to the dissociation of the worker from his job in that he does not require great concentration and so can engage in conversation or pursue his own thoughts in ways entirely unconnected with what he is doing. In literature the supreme example of this is provided by Arthur Seaton in *Saturday Night and Sunday Morning*. Working at his lathe, thoughts pass through his head in an unending stream.

So you earned your living in spite of the firm, the rate-checker, the foreman, and the tool-setters, who always seemed to be at each other's throats except when they ganged-up to get at yours, though most of the time you didn't give a sod about them but worked quite happily for a cool fourteen nicker, spinning the turret to chamfer in a smell of suds and steel, actions without thought so that all through the day you filled your mind with vivid and more agreeable pictures than those round about. It was an easier job than driving a lorry for instance where you had to have your wits about you – spin the turret and ease in the blade-chamfer with your right hand – and you remembered the corporal in the Army who said what a marvel it was the things you thought of when you were on the lavatory, which was the only time you ever had to think. But now whole days could be given up to woolgathering. Hour after hour quickly disappeared when once you started thinking, and before you knew where you were a flashing light from the foreman's office signalled ten o'clock, time for white-overalled women to wheel in tea urns and pour out their wicked mash as fast as they could from a row of shining taps.[42]

The constant effect of these characteristics is the alienation of the worker or group of workers from fellow-workers and also from the production of his/their work.[43] The subdivision of work reduces its importance as a centre of interest. The repetition and surface attention remove meaning and value.[44] The result is that nearly three-quarters of all workers are in a non-job-oriented category, i.e., their primary orientation is towards non-work activities and the real centre of life is found in areas other than work.[45] In complete accord with this is the remark of a miner in Alan Plater's TV play 'Close the Coalhouse Door'. He declares: 'Life begins for me when this activity ends; I do not regard labour as part of my life.' So there is a disengagement of self from the occupational role; personal ties with work are weakened; there is an absence of motivation provided by the task itself. The nature of work is such that money appears to be the only reward that can be obtained, and within an advanced capitalist society where monetary values increasingly prevail the only meaning of work is found in cash returns. Cynicism then becomes widespread about the value of work, and while many continue to regard it as necessary to a sense of responsible adulthood, only a minority have an interest in the jobs themselves.

To this somewhat grim picture should also be added the influence of the type of product being manufactured. When work was to obtain food, warmth and clothing, it had a human meaning; but if a factory is devoted to producing mink coats for dogs, it is not surprising that work should lose all moral content.[46]

No one, least of all the workers, can happily acquiesce in this situation, and no refurbished 'gospel of work' will do, if its intention is simply to encourage them to grin and bear it. One way sought out of this seeming impasse is to place greater emphasis upon leisure. Thus there emerges a split between unpleasant but necessary work and pleasant, personal fulfilment outside it. 'With an increasing drift away from recognizable individual contribution in the work context, the building up of a suitably acceptable identity in the non-work context becomes even more important.'[47] But in fact this would appear to be a vain endeavour and to be unrealizable because of two factors. First, there is the progressive commercialization of leisure. As this extends, it produces a uniformity of environment, materials and equipment and so standardization that falls short of personal achievement. In these circumstances the hope that leisure can lead to identity becomes more and more tenuous. Second, it fails to take account of the unity of work and leisure. According to S. Shimmin, 'Work and leisure are connected in that the conditions and demands of the one have a determining influence on the other.'[48] Horst Symanowski makes the same point when he says that work and leisure are closely connected with each other, since 'what we undertake *outside* our work depends to a great extent upon what we do *during* our work.'[49]* This is borne out by the evidence that certain industrial workers newly employed on an assembly line gradually became more and more passive in their leisure time and withdrew from roles in which they had previously exercised initiative.

It would appear, then, that it is the nature of work – or at least of some work – that has to be changed if man is to be an integrated being and find meaning in what he does. What, then, are those elements that provide job-satisfaction and so lead to a sense of personal involvement in one's work? Following Dr L. Klein, I would list the following:

1. Those that are intrinsic in the operation itself

    (*a*) Physical experience – absence from strain and noise; freedom to move about; pleasure in the materials; having one's own machine or tools.

    (*b*) Variation in speed.

    (*c*) Being free to do tasks in one's own way.

    (*d*) Having the opportunity to develop and use skills.

2. Social Factors

    Under this heading are included contacts with others, opportunities to gossip and to exercise one's independence.

3. Attendant circumstances

    (*a*) The social esteem of the product.

    (*b*) The acceptance of the aims of the organization.

    (*c*) The extent to which one feels that what one is doing is effective.

    (*d*) The possession of a knowledge of the results of one's work.[50]

Basically all the items under 1. can be comprehended under some such headings as relative freedom and independence, a sense of responsibility, self-expression and personal identity. All these, as will be abundantly clear by now, are aspects of the encounter with the holy. When these possibilities do not exist, the meeting is necessarily stultified. The 'social factors' do not need much comment, since they are related to the I-Thou relations, but certain aspects of the 'attendant circumstances' need expansion.

In this connection we have to recognize the importance of distinguishing between legitimate and illegitimate occupations. One may affirm that a painter of automobiles in a body-shop has a task which is legitimate, whereas if he is employed by a ring of car thieves to alter the colour of stolen vehicles, the purpose of the painting, which is technologically the same task as in the body-shop, is illegitimate. Indeed the goal of a particular task can be an extremely important differentiating factor. 'The clear recognition that an otherwise humdrum task has significant goals may make it exceedingly important to the job holder.'[51] This means, however, that the social esteem of a product, in terms of the values accepted, becomes a matter of central concern. Yet the movement in the West from a production to a marketing economy has had the effect of undermining human values.

Perhaps no clearer example of this could be adduced than the current promotion of vaginal deodorants. In many respects this sales campaign represents the complete denial of truth. Its basic premisses are three in number:

(i) Women are unconscious of unpleasant odours and should therefore be induced to take preventative steps to mask them;
(ii) The malodour is best overcome by deodorants;
(iii) Unless this is done the person concerned will be sexually offensive.

Each of these suppositions is false. The only body smell that human beings cannot perceive with relative ease is their own breath; others are readily detected. Further, if there is any unpleasant smell, this arises from one of two causes, either a lack of personal cleanliness or a discharge. The remedy for the first is a bath and for the second a visit to the doctor. Finally, the suggestion that a clean and healthy sexual odour is offensive denies the natural fact that it is attractive and is part of the stimulus and pleasure associated with sexual relations. If to these considerations be added the fact that the campaign is an anxiety-maker, in the sense of seeking to arouse fears about a supposed need not actually detected, it will be readily seen how unnatural the whole position is.[52] If one takes this view, then to work in a factory that manufactures these products is scarcely to be occupied in a legitimate activity. This means that in seeking to restore job-satisfaction one must not only alter the conditions of work and the nature of the task performed, but also one must attempt to change values in society as a whole, so that it ceases to be dominated by purely materialistic considerations and sees more in life than ever-increasing consumption.

It should be recognized that the transition from an economy related to production to one devoted to consumption has resulted in the creation of a new set of values that contrasts with those embodied in the Puritan ethic. These may be set out in parallel as follows:

1. (*a*) It is man's duty to work hard.
   (*b*) There are plenty of opportunities of making money without hard labour and good contacts may produce more lucrative results than earnest endeavour.
2. (*a*) Responsibility has to be accepted.

    (*b*) It takes a long time to secure work that calls for much respon-
        sibility.
3. (*a*) Loving relationships with people should be established.
    (*b*) Aggressiveness is needed if one is to forge ahead.
4. (*a*) The value of money is to be recognized.
    (*b*) Thrift is unnecessary, since if you want to make money you
        must look and act as if you had it.
5. (*a*) Perseverance helps to build a reputation as a good worker.
    (*b*) The way to advance is to be mobile; every move should be
        determined by the possibilities of better work and better pay.[53]

These new values require constant criticism, especially when unnecessary luxuries for an artificially created demand abound, as
then industry is not serving society but exploiting it. It cannot be
doubted that this is a characteristic of capitalism, based as it is on
acquisition and competition. Moreover, a society which idolizes the
material and so depersonalizes man, inevitably loses a sense of the
holy. Alienation is both a symptom of that loss and a cause of it.
Indeed it can be said:

> Work is experienced as something soulless, something without deeper
> purpose. People in the factory thus highlight again a general trend.
> The separation of the spheres of life and the relegation of industry into a
> sphere cut off from the universe of ethics and values destroys the whole-
> ness of life and alienates people from the ground of their being.[54]

This is to say, in different words, that such work separates man
from the holy.

But what of the nature of work itself? I am not, of course, com-
petent to comment *in extenso* on the changes that are possible, although there are three lines of advance about which a little may be
said. First, there is the possibility of reorganizing production so that
teams of men work on a particular article from beginning to end.
British Leyland, for example, is experimenting in this way, to enable
a gang to be responsible for one car at a time. In a sense this is a
return to a former situation. Previously man was related to a product; then, with the subdivision of work, he became related to a
pattern of production; in this new experiment he once again becomes related to the product as a whole.[55] Second, there is the move
towards what has been called the second industrial revolution. The
first replaced human power by machine power and eventually produced machines that included the worker as an essential part of the

cycle of operations. The second industrial revolution, brought into being by automation, is based on the assumption that the human operator can be eliminated from the production cycle as an essential link in doing the work. In work that is already largely mechanized this will not be too difficult, given the capital to modify or replace existing equipment, to substitute for the human operator. It will remove the highly repetitive and extensively sub-divided human task. Workers will still be needed to control the programming and to maintain the machines. These, however, will be highly specialized and not sub-divided tasks, and job-satisfaction could result.[56]

The third possible line of advance is not concerned with how the job is done, but with the status of the workers themselves and its relation to participation. Symanowski was prepared to concede that it would be sheer romanticism to suppose that work can always be meaningful and never monotonous, but he did affirm the need to alter the position of the worker. 'They do not want to be taken as a mere impersonal work force whose efforts are to be rewarded with pay. Rather, they want to be taken seriously as human beings, as persons who have a desire to think, act and decide together in their work.'[57] Consequently he repudiated the structuring of work on authoritarian lines, where all that is expected of the worker is disciplined obedience. Rather, there has to be co-determination in the work process, so that instead of being a passive 'hand' the worker shares in the formation, organization and evaluation of his work. 'Man can actualize his humanity only in the sort of work that allows him to be an acting subject, not a mere object that is acted upon. ... Even in the world of work, responsible co-operation belongs to the essence of human existence.'[58] It is doubtful, however, in the light of more recent studies, if this is the universal panacea that Symanowski assumed it to be. 'Joint consultation,' according to Dr Klein, 'is supposed to stimulate a sense of participation; on the other hand, nobody ever seems to get a sense of participation from it, and many people don't want a sense of participation.'[59] This is supported by a recent survey of Yugoslav enterprises in which, since 1948, all managerial decisions are subject to the approval of workers' councils, elected by the employees. It has been found that members of the councils were not markedly aware of exercising more power than other people and that job-satisfaction was not notably higher among these members than among the non-members. The research workers also concluded that the degree of satisfaction was determined by the correlation of the individual's own desire for power with the actual power he enjoyed.[60] Some workers manifest a different temperament and do not want power; they would not, therefore, find greater job-satisfaction through co-determination. That is not to say that advance along this line is not to be attempted, but caution should be exercised in assuming that it will achieve all that has been expected of it.

Whatever the future holds in store, whatever steps are taken in the quest for the humanization of organized work, it must be stated that the activity of the holy within the industrial scene is not to be reduced to a mere matter of pacification between contending parties. As we have seen,[61] the holy may be encountered in a strike, and certainly the holy is to be recognized in any movement towards the alteration of a system that makes men mere cogs in a technical apparatus. Society itself has to choose its values. Is man more important than production? Would it be right to slow the rate of production in order to introduce more freedom and flexibility? How far is man to be 'adjusted' to machines and how far is it possible to adjust and rebuild the industrial environment to fulfil the needs and personalities of men? These rhetorical questions do not imply the desirability of returning to the fifteenth century. A middle path has to be steered between the abolition of machines and the acceptance of every technological innovation as a blessing for all. Yet the questions do imply that certain aspects of industry may stand under the judgment of the holy, that this recognition may bring hope, for the present activity of the holy is not in order to enable men to endure passively but to change the present in the light of the future.

I have already stressed the impossibility of generalizing about work, and it would perhaps be as well, at this juncture, to reaffirm this by pointing to some particular attitudes discernible even within the factory setting. There are still many workers who do find a moral content in what they are doing. Two examples may be adduced, one from the aircraft and the other from the car industry. In providing these machines for human use, workers are fully aware that, if their skill falls short, they will be endangering human life. Workers on an aeroplane do have a pride in the result of their efforts and a concern about the future performance of the end-product. So there is the case of the man who came across a small crack in the part of an aircraft on which he was operating and proceeded to cover it over. His action, however, did not pass unnoticed. His workmates roughed him up and compelled him to make good the slight damage detected – all this without a word to the foreman or management. There is also the group of women performing a 100% check on brake pressings. Their task is to pass those that fulfil completely the necessary specifications and reject those that even to a small degree are less than perfect. Since what they are doing is vital to people's safety, the group has developed a sense of corporate responsibility. This has spilled over into their personal relations so that not only is there close co-operation on the job, but when one is sick or another known to be lonely they will take time out of work hours to visit them.

Evidence, too, is forthcoming of continued pride in work. Witness the thread-grinder who takes twenty minutes to complete only fourteen inches of screw and does so with the greatest of satisfaction in the precision of his achievement. Witness, too, the man in a nickle melting shop, operating a crucible of white-hot metal. When asked if he did not find the conditions over-hot, he replied: 'Yes; but there's something about this job. It burns the dross out of you.' It would be a mistake to lay too much stress upon this last example, as it suggests perhaps the attitude of the craftsman, and certainly the way forward is not by a rebirth of the arts and crafts movement with all its romanticism and its built-in antipathy to industrial processes. These processes are necessary to the material well-being of man; they are part of man's control of the natural world, the means whereby he can change material things and so emerge from the sacral universe. His life cannot survive without work nor progress apart from it.

The justification of work, however, is not to be sought in the supposition that it belongs to man's nature.[62]* The need to work is not rooted in human instincts like, for example, the inbuilt impulse in bees to create combs or in wasps to build nests. The need to work arises from the human condition; he has to work to subsist individually and to keep his community or society in existence.[63] It is only when work is creative – and much of it is not – that man, in the image of his Creator, fulfils his nature and by his work is able to create his own world. In other words, while work is not natural to man, in the sense that it is something he must do because of a built-in drive, it is the means by which he participates in a truly human world, in the sense that through work he creates that world. Work is meaningful to man, therefore, when it is seen to be socially useful. As such, it may be a means for him to attain personal identity, for this requires commitment to an end, to a socially desirable cause. Work then relates to wholeness; indeed, it has been argued that it is a fundamental activity in the retention of mental health.[64]

These several statements are so many ways of asserting that work may be a medium of encounter with the holy. But fundamental to the whole discussion is the question of motivation, for the meaning of any action lies in the motives behind it. I may, for example, paint my front door in order to preserve the wood or in order to impress my neighbour with its smartness. The activity is the same, but the motives are different and lead to different meanings. Motives, it should perhaps be emphasized, are to be distinguished from incentives. An incentive is something external to an action and is offered by someone else as an inducement. A motive is intrinsic to the action and is something I adopt myself, as my reason for doing what I choose to undertake. But what motive should be internalized in relation to work in order that it may mediate the holy? Here the precept to love one's neighbour as oneself is paramount. We should work in order to create a better world in which to live; we should work in order to serve others, and in so doing one serves the holy. There should be no false dichotomy between sacred and secular, leisure and work, for all spheres of human living are under one and the same Lord. We cannot limit our responsibility to one realm and neglect the other. The common factor that binds together all spheres of life, including work, is their potentiality for mediating the holy through the service of others. So even the world of I-It is under the holy, although, as we have seen, much of that world comes under judgment and has to be transformed so that it ceases to be an obstacle in the way of the encounter.

This involves a different attitude to things. Because there can be scarcely any configuration of human community that is not connected with material interests,[65] our understanding of the world of I-It is vital to our existence as persons. This requires a greater knowledge of scientific facts and principles than many possess. One of the consequences of man's virtual ignorance of these is that he

utilizes the products of science and technology in a purely possessive, exploitive manner without comprehension or feeling. His relationship to the objects of his daily use, the tap which supplies his bath, the pipes which keep him warm, the switch which turns on the light – in a word, to the environment in which he lives, is impersonal and possessive – like the capitalist's attitude to his bank account, not the art collector's to his treasures which he cherishes because he 'understands' them, because he has a participatory relationship to them. Modern man lives isolated in his artificial environment, not because the artificial is evil as such, but because of his lack of comprehension of the forces which make it work – of the principles which relate his gadgets to the forces of nature, to the universal order.[66]

If this ignorance be replaced by understanding and by the corresponding participatory relation to objects, the discernment of the holy becomes a possibility.

What now of the Protestant ethic in the light of the contemporary work-situation? I have argued that certain aspects of that situation require to be changed. Does this mean that if such an alteration were affected, the gospel of work would once again become relevant? I do not think so – at least, not in its complete form. In the course of the preceding discussion, certain essential elements in that form have been rejected. It is little short of wicked to regard the underprivileged as entirely responsible for their plight, due to their viciousness and idleness. It is absurd to continue to hold that leisure is sinful. The basic dichotomy presupposed between work and other activities denies personal integration. So far from prudence and sobriety being the supreme virtues, what is needed in today's world is rather zeal and revolutionary fervour. It is a mistake to regard salvation, in terms of wholeness, in individualistic categories. So far from endorsing the Protestant ethic, we must actively pursue the liberation of man from excessive work 'by emptying work of the almost neurotic compulsion and the religious mystery in which it has been enshrouded in Western Society'.[67]

Nevertheless, there remain two aspects of this ethic which are of value. The first of these is the recognition that the way of holiness is in the world and must include therefore one's work. The second, closely connected, is the understanding of work as service for others and therefore, at the same time, of the holy. This may be illustrated by a specific example.

How are we to understand the activity of engineers who are Christians, providing technical aid in, for example, North Africa? The motive of this should be love coupled with hope; the activity itself is a means of serving one's fellow human beings and so of serving the holy. Nevertheless *Christian* engineers, as heirs of a long tradition, naturally question what is specifically Christian about their work. Should they not use the opportunity to engage in preaching the gospel with the aim of conversion? Should they not be concerned for the 'salvation' of the inhabitants of the country in which they are at work? Technical aid is justified in and by itself; it is not to be undertaken in order to disseminate propaganda. The salvation involved in such an enterprise is not that of those whom the engineers are serving; it is the salvation of the engineers themselves, just as those welcomed into the kingdom are not the hungry, nor the thirsty, etc., but those who have given the hungry to eat, the thirsty to drink, etc. The salvation of the North Africans is only involved when, by the contagion of the disinterested love and hope of the Christians, they, in their turn, begin to serve others. There is, therefore, no dichotomy in the role of the Christian engineer. His work – the secular activity in which he is engaged – is an expression of that attitude of love through which is constituted and extended the Kingdom of God among men. He will only speak about his motive if asked, and then he will attempt to show the reality of the holy in the action itself,[68] as love in action and as a medium of hope – of hope, because to work for man's physical betterment is not just Christian *caritas*, but 'a practical proof of hope in the redemption of the body in this world'.[69]

In concluding this chapter I wish to extend the understanding of love embodied in service through work to the subject of welfare in general. There can be no question that where men are in dire want, it is very difficult, if not impossible, to achieve human dignity. Some seem able to rise above it, most cannot. The human bundles of rags that lie about the streets of Calcutta are scarcely examples of human dignity. So the church has to enter the lists in the struggle for welfare in order to witness in today's world to the compassion of Christ. This action is not to be limited to acts of charity towards individuals; it also embraces the transformation of institutions that threaten man's humanity. It must be effective in the associations and organizations that determine the direction of socio-economic development. Consequently the servants of the holy include those who work for economic growth as a means, and not an end.

It is a means to what we may call secular redemption: the eradication of the environmental factors that limit and falsify and corrupt the human spirit. Disease, ignorance, superstition, boredom and monotony – these are the cankers of the human spirit which economic and social development should strive to eradicate. Reduction in mortality and morbidity, the availability of higher education (in both technology and the

humanities) to all who want it, the satisfaction of a varied, challenging
and stimulating job – these are the redemptive ends of economic
activity. It is in these directions that the economist and the development planner can go a little towards the re-creation of the fullness of
man.[70]

On the basis of this statement, it is possible to make some further
affirmations. If it is taken seriously, it means that the redemptive
activity of the holy is discernible in the secular sphere wherever
disease, ignorance, etc., are being overcome. Hence the holy must
be recognized as working through secular agencies outside the
church, which is not then to be regarded as the exclusive or sole
instrument of redemption. The advance of science itself, with the
consequent removal of superstition, is also to be perceived as an
activity in which the holy is essentially redemptive. Indeed, since
the divine purpose is to lead men to fullness, whatever produces an
advance towards this is in accordance with his will. The human
agents of the holy cannot then be regarded as only those who call
themselves Christians.

Because redemption or salvation has been conceived for so long in
individualistic terms, Christians have failed to see signs of the working of the holy in society at large. To acknowledge this is to appreciate
the narrowness of certain concepts of salvation and also something of the cosmic scope of the divine activity. Moreover, it is to
realize that economists, development planners, community organ-
izers, may be agents of the holy. In other words, salvation is not to
be spiritualized (the saving of souls) but understood as restoration to
wholeness, as that which affects man in the totality of his worldly
existence. Nor is it something negative (salvation *from* the world,
hell, etc.), but positive in that it comprises the idea of a fuller life
now, although that is eschatologically understood in relation to promise. This enables the whole human enterprise to be kept on the
plane of relativity. It is at this level of the penultimate that we must
participate in the struggle for economic development and social justice.[71]

To say that work of this kind is a sign of the activity of the holy
is to make an affirmation of faith. The signs are ambiguous; they
consist of human work, but at the same time, without in any way
altering their nature, they can be perceived as a medium of the holy.
Wherever we take responsibility for our fellow men, wherever men
love one another and bear one another's burdens and disappoint-

ments, wherever they are ready to suffer for one another, there is the holy already at work.

9

Worldly Holiness

Is it possible for a modern man to be a saint? Can he who is at home within the secular universe pursue the path of holiness? These are the questions we are to examine in this concluding chapter of the first part of this study. The basic problem may be illuminated by reference to *Bread and Wine* by the Italian novelist Ignazio Silone. This tells the story of a communist who, though wanted by the police, returns to his native place in order to continue his battle for social justice. Pietro Spina, as he is named, adopts the disguise of a priest and meets a peasant girl, Cristina, who is devoutly religious. In his conversation with her, he raises the questions that concern us.

'If a *cafone* ever succeeds in overcoming his animal instincts, he becomes a Franciscan friar; if a girl ever suceeds in freeing herself from bondage to her own body, she becomes a nun. Do you not think that this is the source of many evils? Do you not think that this divorce between a spirituality which retires into contemplation and a mass of people dominated by animal instincts is the source of all our ills? Do you not think that every living creature ought to live and struggle among his fellow-creatures rather than shut himself up in an ivory tower?'

'Can a morality be purely contemplative? Are not morality and contemplation contradictions in terms? Is not practical, everyday life the very basis and foundation of morality, that is to say the virtuous life? Has morality any valid field of action but that?'

Cristina replies: 'You cannot serve two masters. Between spirit and matter there is an irreconcilable conflict.'[1]

Cristina voices the traditional outlook which stems from the sacral universe. Spina is unable to accept it; he seeks a unified life which does not separate the sacred and the secular. He refuses to withdraw from the world, but is aware that world-involvement denies that understanding of asceticism which hitherto had been regarded as the true path of holiness.

Traditional spirituality, with its emphasis upon rejection of the world, has had the effect of isolating Christianity from everyday life and confining it within a narrow religious enclave. 'It is a question, therefore,' comments Gabriel Vahanian, 'whether any rethinking of Christianity in contemporary terms can be relevant so long as no simultaneous attempt is made to dislocate and expel the habits of life-denial which have characterized it.' Indeed, Christianity has tended to prevent man attaining present maturity 'for the sake of a supernatural concern which is deleterious to human existence here on earth'.[2] It has denied nature in favour of supernature. This, in effect, is a re-echoing of Feuerbach's criticism of religion. He regarded it as something that cuts man off from the world and, in the last analysis, from himself. He contended that to divide reality into this world and the world to come and to direct man's attention exclusively to the latter is to produce a division in man's very being. 'Religion is the disuniting of man from himself; he sets God before him as the antithesis of himself.'[3]* If God exists, so Feuerbach argued, man is not himself, because he is then in an infantile state subject to a transcendental overlord and not free to develop. God, he believed, can only exist at the price of evacuating man of his humanity. 'To enrich God, man must become poor; that God may be all, man must be nothing.'[4] More recent attacks upon the theist position do no more than repeat Feuerbach's theses. So, for example, Goetz, the principal character in Sartre's play *The Devil and God*, denies God for the sake of man in words that faithfully reproduce the thought of Feuerbach. A more popularly expressed form of the argument is to be found in the description by a black American writer of his experiences in Folsom Prison, California. In *Soul on Ice*, Eldrige Cleaver writes:

All religions are phony – which made all preachers and priests, in our eyes, fakers, including the ones scurrying around the prison who, curiously, could put in a good word for you with the Almighty Creator of the universe but could not get anything done with the warden or parole board – they could usher you through the Pearly Gates *after you were dead*, but not through the prison gates *while you were still alive and kicking*. . . . Such men of God are powerful arguments in favour of atheism.[5]

In effect, Cleaver is saying that emphasis upon the supernatural is to the detriment of the natural.

However, to raise the question of worldly holiness is to take on Feuerbach at the very centre of his criticism. If worldly holiness is not possible, then his attack would appear to be justified. If worldly holiness is open to man, then Feuerbach cannot be regarded as having uttered the final word on the subject.[6]

But if Christianity is to be rethought in this respect, will it not involve the repudiation of the idea of a saint? Martin Buber believed that it would. 'There can be a saint living now, but he will not be a modern man – a man who bears in himself the contradictions of modern existence.'[7] Buber, is, of course, using 'saint' in the sense defined in a former age – the age of the sacral universe. Modern man, on the other hand, who remains in vital relation to the contemporary scene, cannot but share in the tensions and problematics of today. 'Such a man,' as M. Friedman points out, 'is excluded from a simple personal sanctity or a self-sufficient, spiritual perfection because the very wholeness of his personal existence includes his relationship to people and situations shot through with contradiction and absurdity.'[8]

However, in the light of all that has been said in the previous chapters, it should be evident that, since the holy is encountered in and through the secular world, we now have to seek a worldly holiness, i.e. sanctity is to be so understood that it is seen to involve acceptance of and involvement in the world, in the realms both of I-Thou and I-It.[9] Secular existence is the locus of the encounter – the holy gives it meaning and rescues it from sheer absurdity. Indeed, one cannot have a 'spiritual' life apart from one's life as a human being in the world, because 'God is at the heart of every human situation, summoning man to the Kingdom through the mediation of human objectives'.[10] Or alternatively, in the words of Martin Buber, 'it is here, where we stand, that we should try to make shine the light of the hidden divine life'.[11]

It is only in this way that modern man can pursue the path of holiness and, at the same time, avoid a divided existence. If sacred and secular are separated and yet the reality of both is affirmed, the result can only be a split mind: one compartment concerned with the holy and the other with the world. The result of this is the debasing of the disunited halves of the mind. Instead of each aspect completing the other, they develop autonomously and become insulated from reality in its entirety. Then, for example, sex becomes animality and union with the holy acquires an erotic ambiguity. Man no longer lives as an integrated being; he fails to achieve wholeness.[12] To reduce sanctity to one dimension – to an unmediated relationship with the holy – is, by implication, to assert that all other elements in human life have no such relationship, whereas the gospel, initially, was directed to and claimed the whole man. Hence to live a true 'religious' life means to live a truly human life, and this means to live a life truly responsive to the holy, and this, in turn, means to live a life truly responsive to man and to one's total situation.[13] The 'saint' today, then, is only a saint to the extent to which he neither reigns over his human nature nor delivers himself from it, but renders it more profound. The fulfilment of man is not distinct from his opening up to the holy. Indeed, if we define the words carefully, we can say that to be a fully mature man and to be a saint are the same thing.

O. A. Rabut formulates this as follows:

I do not think that there is any difference between the following terms:
– to develop according to the fundamental summons of one's own nature, or to realize one's self, or to be at one with one's self;
– to be in a right relation with reality;
– to be in a right relation with God;
– to approach God.[14]

So while traditional holiness cuts itself off, not only from sin, but often from the hopes and travails of the world, worldly holiness is achieved by responding to the summons of the holy to serve in the world. If this were not so, then baptism would initiate us into the monastic life and detach us from secular existence, whereas the ordinary Christian is called by the very logic of his baptism to engage in a quest for perfection under and within the very circumstances of his daily life. To ask whether a man can be a 'saint' today is to raise the question whether man can be God-related in and through the world.

Understood in this way, holiness is seen to fit with the New Testament model of the holy. The spirituality envisaged is in fact in accordance with the teaching of the Bible in general. 'While in other religions "spirituality" – man's relationship with God – is obtained at the price of a greater or lesser renunciation of the task of building up the human world, in the Bible man is bound to God – "the image and likeness of God" – by virtue of his responsibility for the transformation of the cosmos in which he lives and has his being.'[15]

In endorsing this statement I am taking a further step in the argument. In the past the struggle against evil, which is part of sanctity, was usually regarded as an internal one, against the forces of evil within. While this combat continues, its ground has shifted. The location of the conflict has moved from the private sector to the public one. According to Monica Furlong:

> To stem the tragedies of racialism or mass political movements which are careless of human suffering we may need a mutation of the traditional concept of holiness. . . . What will happen will be a moving away from the lovely and haunting vision of perfection in a tiny handful of men and women to a new understanding of how the seeds of wholeness might be coaxed to grow among a much wider section of the population.[16]

It is the readiness to give oneself up to the conflict for human values, freedom, dignity, etc., which reveals man's holiness. The goal of the old asceticism was the transcending of the self; today the ideal of service allows the achievement of the same end, for to be outgoing in concern is to cease to be self-regarding. To be committed to the holy is then not to betray the world. Indeed it is to accept responsibility for it, to be exposed and to be given over to it. Hence there is a certain solidarity with the world, although not an unquestioning conformism to it. Indeed, we have to challenge the present in the name of the promised future of God. Our responsibility for the world is a responsibility in hope so that, because of the eschatological proviso, we can never be satisfied. Even involvement in the world includes a protest against the slavery of what is simply present.[17] The encounter with the holy is to be found precisely in daring to imitate the unconditional involvement of the divine love for man. Only in this movement do we find the supreme nearness, the supreme directness of the mediated encounter with the holy.

The eschatological promises in the Bible are related to freedom, peace, justice and reconciliation. All these are social categories. So, for example, the peace of Christ is not the private inner peace of mind of the individual, nor a partial or special peace, but a peace (*shālōm*) for and open to all men. To accept these promises is to be directed to social responsibility and, indeed, to social criticism, in so far as the promises are not yet fully realized.

> The promises . . . are not an empty horizon of vague religious expectations, but a critical and liberating imperative for our own present time.

They are a spur and a task to make them effective in the historical conditions of our time and thus 'to make them true'. Our orientation towards these promises therefore constantly changes anew our present historical awareness. It brings and forces us constantly into a critical and liberating position towards the social circumstances about us.[18]

To say this is to recognize that holiness is not to be conceived in individualistic nor in moralistic terms. Buber is certainly right when he contends that Christianity created a dualism between life in God and life in the world, when, after New Testament times, it replaced the idea of a holy people by that of personal holiness,[19] so that holiness became an individual goal and possession. Such a view is only possible when holiness is seen as a state of being to be attained by the individual apart from the society to which he belongs. The norm of holiness in all aspects of existence then ceases to occupy a central position; it is only the individual, apart from the world, who can attain it. Asceticism follows from this – and so Christianity came to desanctify the elemental and created a world alien to the spirit and a spirit alien to the world. If, however, the encounter with the holy is in and through the secular world, mediated by I-Thou relations and through the realm of I-It, holiness is to be sought in the world and not outside it. Indeed, one must endorse this statement by W. Rauschenbusch, written as long ago as 1917:

The mystic way to holiness is not through humanity but above it. We cannot set aside the fundamental law of God that way. He made us for one another, and our highest perfection comes not by isolation but by love. The way of holiness through human fellowship and service is slower and lowlier, but its results are more essentially Christian.[20]

Similarly, a further statement by Monica Furlong is entirely valid and apposite at this stage of the argument.

In all Churches, there has been a tendency to think of holiness almost exclusively in personal and inward terms, so that it has been much easier for a nun to be canonized than a great theologian, and much easier for a theologian than a great statesman. But this surely is to value the integrity and wholeness of life given to God in prayer and silence, at the expense of the different kind of integrity and wholeness which is to be found in one who has sought to serve God through all the vicissitudes of a long life of intellectual effort or political combat, lived in the midst of the affairs of the world. It is to restrict the meaning of holiness too narrowly to one type of holiness.[21]

Holiness, too, is not to be equated with that which is morally good. Sonia in *Crime and Punishment* is a prostitute and hence immoral, but her condition is forced upon her as the only means to save her brothers and sisters from starvation. Despite her manner of life, she is still essentially pure. So Raskolnikov kisses the ground before her feet, and in this way Dostoevsky presents her as a holy person, since to be holy, i.e. related to the divine, is far more than accepting or living up to a moral code.[22] Of course, when holiness is regarded as synonymous with moral righteousness, a saint by definition must be a morally righteous person. Whether or not someone is a saint is then determined by the extent to which he manifests virtues and conforms to a certain ethical ideal. It is, however, possible for a man to be a saint, i.e. God-related, while not living in exact accord with a particular code of morals. The holy man is in fact the God-related man, and no one can possess such infallible insight that he can lay down absolute rules for deciding what forms that relationship may take within the ambiguities of life in the secular universe. 'What is sanctity in a creature,' asks de Chardin, 'if not to adhere to God with the maximum of his strength?'[23]

Holiness is not, then, a personal quality but a relationship involving being-for-others. This is the identical conclusion that we reached after examining the New Testament understanding of holiness, viz., that it is a life-style, characterized by a relation to the holy which is actualized in loving self-giving.[24] This, too, is similar to the Hasidic outlook. The rabbi of Kotzk commented on the text: 'And you shall be holy men unto me.' He said: 'You shall be holy unto me, but as men, you shall be humanly holy unto me.'[25]

It is time now to pass from generalization to specific examples of the life-style that reveals the 'humanly holy'. This is all the more necessary in the light of one further consideration. The word 'holiness' has certain affinities with other terms such as 'usefulness'. We cannot see 'usefulness' with our eyes as we can, for example, see 'greyness', but discernment of it is nevertheless possible. So we may acknowledge the usefulness of a lawn-mower in good working order, but it only reveals its usefulness when someone is actually employing it for its proper purpose. It would cease to be useful if no one ever used it. In other words, our perception of the usefulness of a lawn-mower requires our seeing the object, then understanding its purpose and finally witnessing its employment. Similarly, holiness cannot be seen with the eyes, but discernment of it is nevertheless possible. A person reveals his holiness when he is actually living out his God-relatedness. In other words, our discernment of holiness requires perception of the person, the understanding of his intentions and evidence of his actions to fulfil those purposes.[26]

Because holiness is not a quality that inheres in a person, but a relationship, we can only understand what it is all about by descriptions of such relationships, and the more concrete the description the better. Hence the remainder of this chapter will be devoted to short accounts of four people whose life-style is evidence of the relationship called holiness. These are men who may be considered to have revealed what worldly holiness is all about. I should perhaps hasten to add that I am not presuming to issue certificates of sanctity; I merely illustrate what being humanly holy may involve. I shall select only certain facts from the biographies of these men – for complete portraits the reader should consult the many excellent fulllength studies that have been published.

The Statesman

It was in the autumn of 1953 that Dag Hammarskjöld became a world figure upon his appointment as Secretary-General of the United Nations. From then until his death in a plane crash in the Congo on 17 September 1961, he was to play an outstanding role in international affairs and to be acclaimed universally as a great statesman and a brilliant leader. Cosmopolitan, cultured, wideranging in his interests and knowledge, possessed of a keen insight and political acumen, he was admired as a fully mature man of the twentieth century and as a distinguished public servant of integrity and stature.

Among his personal effects in his New York apartment was discovered a short manuscript, with a covering note addressed to a close friend. The friend was informed that these entries in a diary 'provide the only true "profile" that can be drawn' and that he could publish them if he thought it right to do so. Hammarskjöld entitled his notes 'Signposts', or 'Markings' – they were like the piles of stones that a climber leaves to mark his progress up an uncharted mountain. He further described them 'as a sort of white book concerning my negotiations with myself – and with God'.

In terms of his religious development and outlook, according to a statement made on a radio programme arranged by Edward R. Murrow, shortly after he became Secretary-General, Hammarskjöld appears to have passed through three stages. In his early youth he accepted traditional Christianity; he then went through a period when he challenged it intellectually, and then ultimately came to endorse what he had naturally criticized. In some respects even his mature belief was traditional. He spent much time in prayer and meditation and in Bible-reading. He read widely in the medieval mystics, especially in the works of Meister Eckhart. However, his understanding of the mystics was very idiosyncratic. He scarcely noticed their negative attitude to the world, and instead observed that they had helped him to see how 'man should live a life of active social service in full harmony with himself as a member of the community of the spirit.'[27] Hence, in one important particular, he was a new type of Christian, in that he rejected the *via negativa* and conceived his secular role in terms of Christian discipleship. If his public acts as Secretary-General are set side by side with the corresponding entries in his diary, this pattern of life becomes evident.[28]

On 1 April 1953, Hammarskjöld in Sweden was informed of his election as Secretary-General. On 8 April he left for New York, to be inducted on the 10th. In his diary under 7 April, he noted his response to the news and to the challenge it offered.

When in decisive moments – as now – God acts, it is with a stern purposefulness. . . . When the hour strikes He takes what is His. What have *you* to say? – your prayer has been answered, as you know. God has a use for you, even though what He asks doesn't suit you at the moment. God, who 'abases him whom He raises up' . . . What had befallen me and seemed so hard to bear became insignificant in the light of the demands which God was now making. . . . Not I, but God in me. . . . Maturity: among other things, a new lack of self-consciousness – the kind you can only attain when you have become entirely indifferent to yourself through an absolute assent to your fate.[29]

He then quotes from Thomas à Kempis:

Their lives grounded and sustained by God, they are incapable of any kind of pride; because they give back to God all the benefits He has bestowed on them, they do not glorify each other, but do all things to the Glory of God alone.

Hammarskjöld's comment on the passage reads:

I am the vessel. The draught is God's. And God is the thirsty one.[30]

So Hammarskjöld interpreted this purely secular act – his election as Secretary-General – as a divine act: the holy at work in and through the world. He also understood his fulfilling of this political function as his way of discipleship. It is from this perspective that he constantly saw all that he did in the service of the United Nations.

You are dedicated to this task – as the sacrifice in a still barbarian cult, because of the divine intention behind it: a feeble creation of men's hands – but you have to give your all to this human dream for the sake of that which alone gives it reality.[31]

So the pursuit of international harmony was Hammarskjöld's encounter with the holy.

He had no need for the divided responsibility in which others seek to be safe from ridicule, because he had been granted a faith which needs no confirmation – a contact with reality, light and intense like the touch of a loved hand: a union in self-surrender without self-destruction, where his heart was lucid and his mind loving.[32]

Upon his induction for a second term of office, 10 April 1958, Hammarskjöld wrote:

In the faith which is 'God's marriage to the soul', you are *one* in God, and God is wholly in you, just as, for you, He is wholly in all you meet.[33]

There are three further elements in his understanding of his task that should be noted. First, he sees the holy as being mediated to him through other persons.

In the presence of God, nothing stands between him and us – we *are* forgiven. But we *cannot* feel his presence if anything is allowed to stand between ourselves and others.[34]

Second, he saw his work as essentially a service to and for others.

The only value of a life is its context for *others*. Apart from any value it may have for others, my life is worse than death.[35]

Third, he conceived his life-style as necessarily sacrificial and therefore in accordance with the paschal pattern. Hence Aulén summarized his view to the effect that 'the way of self-surrendering sacrifice is the road to sanctification which passes through action'.[36]

To pursue the path of holiness is to be oneself a medium for the revelation of the holy. So Hammarskjöld compared the sanctified man to a lens which focusses and diffuses the light of the holy.[37] For a lens to operate properly, however, it must be entirely transparent and not interpose anything of itself between the light and the observer. Similarly, the human mediator of the holy – the human in-between – must surrender self and transcend egotism through sacrificial acts for others. The service of men is also at the same time the service of the holy, and so the way to sanctification passes through action. Union with the holy is then to be achieved in the world through self-giving.[38]

> Then I saw that the wall had never been there, that the 'unheard-of' is here and this, not something and somewhere else, that the 'offering' is here and now, always and everywhere.[39]

There is no need to labour the points further. Hammarskjöld's life and his own understanding of it are an impressive demonstration of the truth of his own dictum: 'In our era, the road to sanctification necessarily passes through action.'[40] This fits exactly both the New Testament model of the holy and its interpretation of holiness, and sheds light upon the meaning of worldly holiness.

The Revolutionary

Dag Hammarskjöld's path of holiness was related to world peace – indeed he gave his life for it. The path followed by Camilo Torres was a different one, even though it, too, ended with the surrender of his life.[41] So far from seeking to decrease tension, Torres was eventually committed to violence; he did not act on the world stage – though what he did has become known throughout the world – but within the confines of a relatively small Latin-American country. The story of his life can be briefly told.

Born on 3 February 1929 of well-to-do parents – his father was at one time Columbian ambassador in Berlin – he was educated at a German school in Bogota and then, when this closed in 1941, transferred to a Catholic school where he studied law. Much to the annoyance of his mother, who regarded the political struggle as man's central concern, he decided to seek ordination. He was sent to Louvain to study political and social science, and at the end of his three-year course he stayed a further twelve months as Vice-Rector of the College for Latin America.

Upon his return to Colombia in 1958 he was nominated as chaplain to the National University at Bogota and in this capacity he sought, with the aid of students, to improve conditions in the slums; he founded a pilot farm and established some schools. He was not, however, easy about his status, regarding his privileged position as making him a delegate of the religious and civil powers of which he was becoming more and more critical. He therefore asked to be relieved of his post and, with the approval of Cardinal Luque, became a professor in the Faculty of Sociology and the School of Economic Sciences, where he taught until September 1962. He then transferred to the School of Public Administration where he served until May 1965.

Torres' pronouncements on political and social issues now led to a clash with the church authorities. Cardinal Concha Cordoba condemned his platform as 'pernicious and erroneous'. Torres accordingly asked for laicization. He continued to strive for a union between students, peasants and city workers and organized a new political movement – the United Front. Eventually he decided to join the Army of National Liberation (ELN), and two months after becoming the member of a guerrilla group he was killed, on 15 February 1966, in the town of El Carmen by government forces.[42]

More important than the bare outline of Torres' life are the answers to two basic questions. Why did he do what he did do? How did he understand his actions?

The answer to the first question is to be sought in the socio-political and economic conditions in Columbia. Columbia, which is typical of many Latin-American countries in this respect, is the scene of a dual confrontation: between a society of transition and a new type of community, and between popular forces on the one hand and a minority élite that exercises supreme power on the other. The majority of the population, which increased from some nine million in 1939 to something near nineteen million thirty years later, is in dire straits. 61% of the ground belongs to 3.6% of all landowners, and 4.6% of the population receive 40.6% of the national income. Of 150,000 entering the labour market each year, only 12,000 find jobs. The infant mortality rate is at 10%; there are 2.5 doctors for every 10,000 people and each year 25,000 children die of malnutrition.[43] Confronted with this situation, Torres saw the necessity for radical change in the basic social and economic structures. Seeing the human degradation and suffering that underlay these bare statistics and convinced that the oligarchy would not freely surrender its power, Torres saw no alternative but to work for its overthrow. But he also believed that he was committed to this course of action by the gospel he had accepted. It is here that we find the answer to the second question relating to the way in which he understood his actions.

On 3 August 1965 he issued 'A Message to Christians'. He began this by affirming the necessity for his fellow Catholics to remain steadfast in the essentials of their religion. He then declared that the basic Christian precept is to love one's neighbour. He continued:

> For this love to be true it must seek to be efficacious. If beneficence, alms, a few free schools, a few nursing programmes, in a word, what has been called 'charity', does not suffice to feed the majority of the hungry, to clothe the majority of the naked, to teach the majority of the ignorant, then we must look for more effective means of ensuring the welfare of the majority.

Torres next affirmed his conviction that the majority in power would not do what was required, since this would oblige them to sacrifice their privileges.

> It is necessary, therefore, to take power away from the privileged minority and give it to the poor majority. This, if it is done quickly, is the heart of a revolution. The Revolution can be peaceful if the minority does not resist with violence. The Revolution is, therefore, the way to get a government which will feed the hungry, clothe the naked, teach the ignorant, comply with works of charity, and make possible a true love for our neighbours. This is why the Revolution is not only permitted but is obligatory for all Christians who see in it the most effective way of making possible a greater *love for all men*.

Finally Torres explained his own position:

> I have put aside the privileges and duties of the clergy, but I have not stopped being a priest. I think I have given myself to the Revolution out of love for my neighbour. I have stopped offering Mass to live out the love for my neighbour in the temporal, economic and social orders. When my neighbour no longer has anything against me, and when the revolution has been completed, then I will offer Mass again, if God so wills it. I believe that in this way I am following Christ's injunction. 'If you bring your offering to the altar and there remember that your brother has something against you, leave your offering on the altar and go and be reconciled first with your brother, and then return and offer your gift.' (Matt. 5.23f.)
>
> After the Revolution we Christians will have the peace of mind which will come from knowing that we established a system which is grounded in the love of neighbour.
>
> The struggle will be long. Let us begin today. . . .[44]

In a further message, this time addressed to the Communists, in which Torres made it quite clear that he himself was not a Communist although prepared to co-operate with all men who sincerely sought the improvement of the Columbian situation, he has some additional remarks to make about his own stance.

My role as a priest, even though I am not exercising its prerogatives externally, is to lead all men to God. The most effective way to do this is to get men to serve the people in keeping with their conscience. I do not intend to proselytise among the Communists and to try to get them to accept the dogma and teachings of the Catholic Church. I do want all men to act in accordance with their conscience, to look in earnest for the truth, and to love their neighbour effectively.[45]

Torres also contended, in a paper entitled 'Crossroads of the Church in Latin America', that:

When Christians live fundamentally motivated by love and teach others to love, when faith is manifest in life and especially in divine life, in the life of Jesus and the Church, then the external rites will be the true expressions of love within the Christian community; then we will be able to say that the Church is strong, not in economic or political power but in love. If a priest's temporal commitment in political struggles contributes to this end, his sacrifice would appear to be justified.[46]

It is not my concern, however, to attempt to justify Torres' decision to join the guerrillas. Remote from Latin America and Columbia in particular, it would be presumptuous as well as beyond both my competence and knowledge to pass a judgment on the rightness or wrongness of his action. It is, however, possible to understand it. But what is particularly relevant to my concern is to see how Torres incarnated almost every aspect of holiness that was reviewed in general terms in the opening pages of this chapter.

First, here, without question, was a man who bore in himself the contradictions of modern existence. François Houtart, his friend and former teacher at Louvain, has expressed the tension in this way. He was torn between the exercise of his priesthood in a church which was joined to a socially unjust power and his participation in the struggle for the liberation of man. Houtart suggests that the way he chose was perhaps the contemporary form of 'preaching the good news to the poor and proclaiming release to the captive'.[47] What this means may be brought out by reference to a fictional character of whom Torres had probably never heard. In *The Fratricides*, by Nikos Kazantzakis, we encounter a certain Nicodemus who is a one-time monk turned communist. Nicodemus reveals the contradictions that he experienced as a monk and which led him to repudiate his vows.

To whom shall I turn? To Christ as the Church has degraded him, or to those who want to shape a new world – a more just world, without Christ? I used to go to church, I fasted, I prayed, I called to God, but

I found no relief; God never answered me. I realized in time that prayer is not the way, that neither is retreat; once, they were; they brought earth to heaven, but no more. Now they alienate us from earth, they do not carry us to heaven – they leave us halfway, in mid-air.[48]

Is it fanciful to suggest that if someone like Nicodemus had heard of Torres he would be in a better position to understand the good news in its contemporary form?

That form, in the considered view of another revolutionary priest, Alipio de Freitas, may be defined in this way:

The gospel of our age is to bring about agrarian reform, educational reform, urban reform, and reform for the workers in industry, to fight against political and economic imperialism, to fight against all forms of oppression.[49]

Houtart also finds the significance of what Torres did, not in the particular solution he sought to bring about by an immediate revolution, but in his prophetic stance. He quotes from Amos:

Therefore because you trample upon the poor,
    and take from him exactions of wheat,
You have built houses of hewn stone,
    but you shall not dwell in them;
You have planted pleasant vineyards,
    but you shall not drink their wine.
For I know how many are your transgressions,
    and how great are your sins –
you who afflict the righteous, who take a bribe,
    and turn aside the needy in the gate. . . .

Hear this, you who trample upon the needy,
and bring the poor of the land to an end. . . .
saying, 'We may buy the poor for silver
    and the needy for a pair of sandals,
    and sell the refuse of the wheat.'
The Lord has sworn by the pride of Jacob:
    'Surely I will never forget any of their deeds,
Shall not the land tremble on this account,
    and every one mourn who dwells in it,
and all of it rise like the Nile,
    and be tossed about and sink again,
    like the Nile of Egypt.'[50]

The prophet is he who recalls the injustices of a society. This is what Torres did, and it is in this sense that his action is prophetic.[51] This is also to recognize him as an agent of the holy who confronts men in judgment. One can say, therefore, that he was also an instrument of God's peace in the sense defined by Alan Paton:

> To be the instrument of God's peace is not to confine oneself to the field of personal relationships, but to concern oneself also with the problems of human society, hunger, poverty, injustice, cruelty, exploitation, war.[52]

As a channel of the holy, Torres was attempting to restore dignity to human life; he accepted his responsibility for transforming the world in which he lived; he acted to further the realization of the eschatological promises which, as we have seen, are all social categories. His path was one of outgoing in concern, prompted by love of neighbour, which he understood not as a general sentiment but as a passion impelling him to force the embodiment of that love in social and economic structures. As a God-related man, his holiness also involved sacrifice. I refer not just to the hardships of a guerrilla life nor to his eventual death, but also to his request for laicization. His letter to the cardinal, in which he put this request, shows how great an act of renunciation and of sacrifice it was, even though his surrender of the exercise of his priestly functions was necessary, in his view, in order that he might be truly faithful to his priesthood.[53] All this embodies an ideal of worldly holiness within a very specific situation – worldly holiness because his life reveals a pattern of political development that was *at the same time* a spiritual one. But for the last word let us return to Ignazio Silone's character, Spina. Writing to Cristina, he says:

> What a great revolution there is in the world when persons who possess such spiritual riches as you possess, almost as a natural gift, cease expending them upon religious symbolism and devote them to the collective life. Thus a new type of saint is born, a new type of martyr, a new type of man. I do not believe there is any other way of saving one's soul today. He is saved who overcomes his individual egoism, family egoism, caste egoism, does not shut himself in a cloister, or build himself an ivory tower, or make a cleavage between his way of acting and his way of thinking. He is saved who frees his own spirit from the idea of resignation to the existing disorder. Spiritual life has always meant a capacity for dedication and self-sacrifice. In a society like ours a spiritual life can only be a revolutionary life.[54]

The Urchin

Mario Borelli was born in 1922, the son of a labourer in the slums of Naples and one of ten children. At the end of the Second World

War he was ordained as a priest and worked in a parish in his native city. The social and economic conditions were very grave; unemployment was high, while sickness, disease and starvation were rife. Large numbers of uncared-for and unwanted children roamed the streets, pimping and stealing for money and food. In 1950 Borelli obtained an interview with Cardinal Ascalesi and sought his permission to give up his parochial duties and go and live on the streets with these *scugnizzi*. He wanted to understand the outcasts, then to learn how they thought, to make himself their friend and ultimately, perhaps, to bring them to live with him. Borelli's attitude at the time is revealed by his own statement:

I was angry. I was bitter. I knew that I could not remain a priest, unless I did something worthy of a priest. I could not stand at the altar and hold the body of God in my hands while the bodies of his children slept in the alleys and under the barrows of the Mercato.[55]

The cardinal was touched by Borelli's zeal, but he was hesitant to approve of his sharing the life of these urchins and said that he would take ten days to reach a decision. Borelli spent the time in the company of a photographer for a Neapolitan daily. They walked the city taking shots of all they saw, and when Borelli came back to the cardinal he brought with him a sheaf of prints illustrating the wretchedness which grieved him so much. Permission was granted, on the understanding that Borelli did not work alone but had a friend to assist him. He chose another young Neapolitan priest named Spada.

Removing his clerical garb and donning the rags and tatters of the urchins, Borelli went to the Piazza Mercato to establish contact. He was successful and was accepted into the gang and adopted their ways of keeping alive. As a member of a gang he had to make his contribution, accept their risks and their devious code of honour.

So the moralist became an associate of thieves.

When the more agile were scaling balconies to steal washing or tools or the pitiful jewellery of the poor. Borelli kept watch and whistled the warning signals. When the proceeds were sold to the fence, Borelli added his voice to the chaffering and held out for a better price. When the boys were chased by angry householders or the police, Borelli carried his share of the spoils and ran like a hunted animal. He ate the bread that was bought with money stolen from Church poor boxes. He peddled the cigarettes that were smuggled through the customs or filched from the glove-boxes of American cars.

The celibate joined the pimps.

He was one of the dancing groups that edged the foreign soldiers closer and closer to the casino. When the girls came out to sun themselves on the balconies or at the doors of their shabby rooms, he talked with them and joked with them. He took his share of the money that was paid in commission by the whoremasters and by the private practitioners.

The priest became a beggar.

He stood with the boys outside the tourist agencies whining for cigarettes. He carried bags and jostled for tips. He collected trodden butts and teased out the tobacco for the back-alley manufacturers. He opened car doors outside the theatre and was jostled and pushed by the fine gentry who were affronted by his filth.

When midnight came and the commerce of the day and the night was done, he squatted with the *scugnizzi* over a fire of twigs and warmed his scraps of food and talked with them in the argot of the streets. He slept huddled against them for warmth, under the stairways or in the corners of the courtyard where the wind was less.[56]

Morris West, from whose account I have taken this description, asked Borelli how he squared his conscience with his actions as an urchin. The priest replied:

'It was my endeavour, so far as possible, to withdraw myself from the strict act of sin. For instance I never stole, personally. I never solicited directly for a girl. I participated, certainly, in the act, but I tried so far as possible to make my participation a matter of appearance, to withdraw it, as much as I could, from the substance of the act.'

'But in fact you did participate?'

'Yes.'

'And you did share in the fruits of the act?'

'Yes.'

'Was that justifiable in law and conscience?'

'Much of it was justifiable, yes. Much of it was, shall we say, on the razor edge between right and wrong. But I was committed, you see, I could not turn back. I could only make my own judgment and commit it to the mercy of God. Even so . . .

'Even so?'

'Even so, there were many moments when I was a *scugnizzo* and not a priest.'[57]

Borelli had two objectives when he entered the world of the urchins. He wished, first, to understand and then to help them by giving them a home and a hope. He became convinced that these derelicts of society were in need of love and that their condition was itself the result of a lack of it. He began to appreciate how in consequence of their being unloved they had become what they were. The *scugnizzi* became vain and boastful, because there was no love to affirm their real value as human beings. They became cunning because there was no love to protect them from the malice of others. They became cheats and liars because honesty would make them the prey of those who had no love for them. Nervousness, instability, physical underdevelopment – all these followed.

Borelli hoped to open a home for these boys, but he soon became aware that it would have to be of a special kind. They would not be shut up in an institution; the rigid discipline of the classroom and a time-table would be intolerable; to talk about religion and morals would be unintelligible. He determined to provide them with food and shelter, to give them security with freedom so that they would return willingly to the centre he envisaged. While Borelli sought to understand, Spada was attempting to find the physical means to care for the boys. Eventually he secured the use of an abandoned church and then began to collect mattresses, blankets, etc.

The critical stage in Borelli's mission could now no longer be postponed. He had to declare himself to the *scugnizzi* and invite them to accompany him to the shelter. The danger was that they would either reject him or refuse to believe him. He prepared for this disclosure by having more photographs taken, this time of himself as an urchin with the gang. He then resumed his priest's habit and went to meet his friends. At first they refused to accept that he was the same person, until their doubts were dispelled by the photographs. Then they suspected that it was simply a trick to have them shut up. Finally, on the assurance that they were free to use or not the home he had found for them, they followed him to the old church. There, eventually, they settled down. The story of their gradual rehabilitation is told by Morris West and need not be repeated here.

When this account is read with the previous discussion of holiness in mind, there emerges clearly a point-by-point correspondence with the various aspects of Borelli's life. The course that he adopted was his path to integration. As he himself said, in the quotation already given, he could not minister at the altar and hold the sacramental body of Christ in his hands while the bodies of his children were so afflicted. There is a parallel here with Torres' cessation of the offering of mass – both men were concerned to unify the holy and the secular. Borelli had to be responsive to human needs, to give himself to the service of others. Undoubtedly he was 'coaxing the seeds of wholeness to grow'. His path of holiness was through human fellowship with the *scugnizzi*. Here was involvement in the world in protest against the virtual slavery of these children; at the same time, what he did was replete with promise and eventually brought hope. So Borelli's achievement was to bring dignity into the lives of the urchins. To accomplish this is to follow the New Testament model of the holy. Hence Alan Paton, speaking of Jesus' followers in Galilee, remarks that 'they were given a new sense of their value as persons. Especially was this true of women. One can hardly describe the joy of the first disciples, who were given by Jesus such a sense of their significance in the world.'[58]

Borelli's involvement went to the length of identification, just as again, according to Christian belief, in Christ the holy identified himself with the human condition. So, as Harvey Cox puts it, 'He allows his word to be heard in the ghetto only when those who speak it share the existence of those who hear it.'[59] Father Yanaros, another character in Kazantzakis' *The Fratricides*, has this to say:

Today prayer means deeds. To be an ascetic today is to live among the people, to fight, to climb Golgotha with Christ, and to be crucified every day. Every day, not just on Good Friday. . . . Christ remained in the wilderness only forty days. Then he descended from the summit of solitude, he hungered, he pained, he struggled along with the people, and was crucified. What then is the duty of the true Christian? I say it and I repeat it: to follow the pattern of Christ here on earth.[60]

To accomplish this duty today is to share in contemporary tensions and problems, even to the extent of being guilty of what may be regarded as immoral acts. The commission of such acts, while one does not consent to them, does not place one under sin, for sin is not primarily a moral category but a religious one, i.e. a man is in sin when he is separated from the holy. Borelli, on the other hand, was not so estranged, despite his participation in the gang's activities. Indeed, the holy is known in life where evil and good, despair and hope, the power of destruction and the power of rebirth dwell side by side. According to Martin Buber: 'The divine force which man actually encounters in life does not hover above the demonic, but penetrates it.'[61] Hence the holy is met in the tensions, and not apart from them. Elsewhere Buber records a saying of the Baal-Shem:

For the sinner who knows he is a sinner, and therefore considers himself base – God is with him, for he 'dwelleth with them in the midst of their uncleannesses'.[62]

Here let us note two other aspects of the New Testament model of the holy which are reproduced in the life of Borelli. First, there is that serving love which embraces even the unlovable – certainly, no one could say that the *scugnizzi* were an attractive lot; they were closer to the publicans and sinners of Jesus' day than to many another group, but Borelli loved these untouchables and outcasts. Second, Borelli showed complete openness and indeed exposed himself in his active fight against evil. It is not surprising that what he did – and in particular his somewhat compromising identification with the urchins – has led some to be offended by him. His relationship with the boys who came to live in the disused church was a further factor in the spreading of *shālōm*. As L. J. Collins says: 'Integrity in personal relations is the true end of holiness.'[63] Borelli undoubtedly attained this, and that is why I have chosen to retell his story as an example of worldly holiness.

The Double Agent

Few subjects have received more attention over the last two decades than the life and theological teaching of Dietrich Bonhoeffer. It is not my intention to attempt to reproduce yet another biography, even in an abbreviated form. The reader has to hand the sensitive narrative by Mary Bosanquet and the magisterial and detailed account by Eberhard Bethge.[64] Bonhoeffer, however, raised at an early date and in a remarkable way the question of worldly holiness, and to illustrate this I propose to concentrate solely upon his activities as a member of the *Abwehr* or German Military Intelligence.

The Bonhoeffer of the war years was a different person from the young theologian of the early 1930s. Then he was disposed towards pacifism, being attracted to the ideas and practice of Gandhi and, like many German Christians, tended to separate politics and religion. With the German invasion of Poland, he changed considerably. Bethge formulates the contrast in this way:

The year 1932 had put Bonhoeffer into a world where things were comparatively clear-cut, where it was a matter of confessing and denying, and therefore in his case of the one Church for the whole world and against its betrayal to nationalist particularism. . . In 1939 he entered the difficult world of assessing what was expedient, of success and failure, of tactics and camouflage. The certainty of his calling in 1932 now changed into the acceptance of the uncertain, the incomplete and the provisional. The new call demanded quite a different sacrifice, the sacrifice even of a Christian reputation.[65]

Bonhoeffer joined the *Abwehr* as a double agent under Admiral Canaris. He was supposed to use his ecumenical contacts for military intelligence; instead, he used his position to help the resistance group within the *Abwehr* and to plan the downfall of Hitler, and he accepted 'treason' as true patriotism.[66] Once engaged on this path, his position was equivocal and he risked the loss of trust by his ecumenical friends. Our concern is not with the details of his many missions, with the secret meetings, with hopes raised and dashed, with plots and counter-plots, but with his own interpretation of what he was doing and how this was related to his Christian faith.

In 1942 Bonhoeffer wrote down a series of reflections which he entitled 'After Ten Years'. In the course of this he said:

Are we still any use? We have been silent witnesses of evil deeds; we have been drenched by many storms; we have learnt the arts of equivocation and pretence; experience has made us suspicious of others; intolerable conflicts have worn us down and even made us cynical. Are we still any use? . . . Will our inward power of resistance be strong enough, and our honesty with ourselves remorseless enough, for us to find our way back to simplicity and straightforwardness?[67]

So Bonhoeffer recognized that the path he was following carried with it the danger of inner corruption; this he faced and this he accepted. His underground activities, involved him in lying, in forgery and in consent to assassination. Time and again he retailed untruths because, in order to fulfil what he believed to be his task, he had to remain *persona grata* to the Nazi authorities and demonstrate his usefulness to the war machine.[68] At his interrogation he roundly asserted that he had made an 'offering of all my ecumenical connections for military use'.[69] To protect his fellow-conspirators he produced false documents, as when in November 1942 he copied a letter and backdated it to 1940 in an attempt to cover their tracks.[70] Incessantly he accepted compromise. So when France fell, he and Bethge were in a cafe together where all the patrons rose in jubilation at the news. Bonhoeffer gave the Hitler salute and said to his friend: 'Raise your arm! Are you crazy? . . . We shall have to run risks for very different things now, but not for that salute!'[71]

Bonhoeffer was quite ready, not just to plot the death of Hitler, but to be himself the killer. This decision was not lightly reached. Wolf-Dieter Zimmermann reports a conversation at Werder in

November 1942. Amongst those present was Werner von Haeften, a
staff lieutenant of the Army High Command. Von Haeften suddenly asked Bonhoeffer: 'Shall I shoot? I can get inside the Führer's
headquarters with my revolver. I know where and when the conferences take place. I can get access.' In reply Bonhoeffer argued
that the liquidation of Hitler would in itself be of no use; it would
be justified only if something were gained by it, a change of circumstances, of the government. The careful pre-planning of what
was to happen after the assassination was essential before any
attempt was made. Bonhoeffer exhorted von Haeften to be discreet,
to plan clearly and to envisage all unforeseen complications.[72] It was
precisely because, eventually, a total plan was devised that Bonhoeffer supported the plot. He considered, however, that before he
was fully involved to the extent of actually killing Hitler he would
have to resign formally and officially from the church, because the
church could not shield him, nor did he wish to claim its protection.[73] He reached his decision in the full recognition that what he
was proposing to do 'may prevent me from taking up my ministry
again later on'.[74]

With his brother-in-law Hans von Dohnanyi he discussed the
application of Matthew 26.12 to themselves as would-be assassins:
'All who take the sword will perish by the sword.' He believed that
they had to acknowledge that they were subject to that judgment,
but that there was now need of such men as would accept the
validity of it for themselves.[75] He was prepared to act in accordance
with what he wrote in his *Ethics*: 'The structure of responsible
action includes both readiness to accept guilt and freedom.... If
any man tries to escape guilt in responsibility, he detaches himself
from the ultimate reality of human existence, and what is more he
cuts himself off from the redeeming mystery of Christ's bearing
guilt without sin and he has no share in the divine justification
which lies upon this event.'[76] So he went into the conspiracy with
his eyes open and ready to accept the consequences of his action. He
therefore had to abandon all outward and inner security; he was
ready to sacrifice his reputation within the church and as a theologian. He knew that when his complicity came to light, he would
probably be rejected by the church, and indeed when he was arrested
the Confessing Church refused to place his name on the intercession
lists.[77]

Bonhoeffer had no thought of self:

The ultimate question for a responsible man to ask is not how to extricate himself heroically from the affair, but how the coming generation is to live. It is only from this question, with its responsibility towards history, that fruitful solutions can come, even if for the time being they are very humiliating.[78]

A few months after his arrest and his confinement in Tegel, he wrote:

At first I wondered a good deal whether it was really for the cause of Christ that I was causing you all such grief; but I soon put that out of my head as a temptation, as I became certain that the duty had been laid on me to hold out in this boundary situation with all its problems.[79]

In some respects this was an echo of what he had written in his *Cost of Discipleship*, published in 1937:

It is important that Jesus gave his blessing not merely to suffering incurred directly for the confession of his name, but to suffering in any just cause.[80]

This agrees entirely with one of his remarks, recorded by Hans-Werner Jensen: 'Secular freedom, too, is worth dying for.'[81]

Bonhoeffer attempted no self-justification; he indulged in no self-pity; indeed, Bethge describes a visit he paid him in Tegel prison in June 1944 as an occasion of gay discussion.[82] Bonhoeffer was indeed a martyr of a new kind: a non-religious martyr. He did not suffer *directly* for the Christian faith, but because he acted on behalf of justice and humanity. When asked, during exercise in the Tegel yard, by a fellow-prisoner how he could reconcile joining in active resistance with being a Christian, he replied in the form of a story.

If he, as a pastor, saw a drunken driver racing at high speed down the Kurfürstendamm, he did not consider it his only or his main duty to bury the victims of the madman, or to comfort his relatives; it was more important to wrench the wheel out of the hands of the drunkard.[83]

Yet, one can say that in acting on behalf of justice and humanity, as he understood them, he was following the path of holiness and therefore suffered for it. Such a view is not shared by all churchmen. According to W. Nicholls:

Conservative churches in Germany after the war refused to honour his memory in church because he did not die for the cause of the churches but for the political cause of resistance to Hitler. He did not give his life for religion or even for the God of religion. He died, alongside humanists and secularists, who had been his fellow conspirators, in the common human cause. This was how he saw participation in the sufferings of God at the hands of a godless world.[84]

Bonhoeffer was a modern man and his activities raise again the question with which this chapter began: is it possible for a modern man to be a saint? The fundamental issue here was formulated in 1951 when Helmut Gollwitzer visited the ruins of Flossenburg castle where Bonhoeffer had been executed on 9 April 1945. Gollwitzer noted that there was nothing there nor in the village church to recall the event, and he initiated discussion about the possibility of erecting a commemorative tablet. 'The question was raised whether Bonhoeffer had really died as a martyr of his faith or only for his political convictions.'[85] To Bonhoeffer himself such a distinction would have been meaningless, since he held that his political responsibility belonged to the wholeness of life which he owed to Christ.[86] Gollwitzer asserted that 'political resistance, under such a government of murderers, is a consequence of being a Christian, a fruit of faith and a subject of pastoral counselling.'[87] Indeed, if the holy is to be encountered in and through the world, one cannot have a split allegiance. Service of the holy is in and through the secular; it is vain to reject the political realm and withdraw into some so-called spiritual sphere. Hence if that part of the secular reality concerned is the political one, this means that the service of the holy is in and through one's political responsibility. There cannot be – there should not be – any division. Bonhoeffer did not serve two masters but one, since his service was in the world and not apart from it. He manifested wholeness – holiness – precisely because he lived not a divided but an integrated life. He is, in fact, a supreme example of worldly holiness – a fully mature man and so a saint. This is so not only because he unified the different dimensions of his existence, but also because he displayed many of the characteristics that belong to the path of holiness.

He fully identified himself with his fellow-conspirators. This identification was, for him, a basic principle, as indicated, in a slightly different context, by his remark to one of his pupils, Ferenc Lehel: 'We must think with the doubter, even doubt with him.'[88] But this involved him in bearing the tensions of the modern scene. 'One noticed at once,' reports Gerhard Jacobi, 'what a sensitive person he was, what a turmoil he was in, and how troubled.'[89] He gave himself up to the conflict for human values; he struggled against evil; he worked in the present in hope of the future; he was throughout and to the end a God-related man. His final years were one long sacrifice – of truth, honour, reputation and, at the last, of his life-blood. He accepted freely his responsibility for what he was doing and his guilt for the part he played. The paschal pattern is clearly evident. In his life-style he was humanly holy.

Bonhoeffer was the first to coin the phrase 'the man for others' to describe Christ. He never presumed to use this of himself, but others may. As a man for others, Bonhoeffer was Christlike and to be Christlike is to be on the path of holiness.

Very little is needed by way of conclusion to this chapter. Perhaps I should re-emphasize that I am not presuming to issue certificates of sanctity. This means that in the definitions and examples of holiness given above the word 'saint' has been employed in a way that differs from the traditional concept. A 'saint' has been regarded as one who has achieved heroic virtue and who has performed miracles, or whose cult has resulted in miracles. He is also one who has been canonized; i.e., through the official organs of the church he has been declared to have entered into the eternal glory. In contrast, I have been using 'saint' more in the sense given to it by Paul. Frequently he begins his letters with a salutation 'to the saints who are in ...' When we examine the letters we find that these 'saints' (*hagioi*) are a somewhat mixed lot. The Corinthians, for example, who 'are called to be saints'[90] include a number of contentious groups, and their behaviour at the Lord's Supper is little short of scandalous. Nevertheless, Paul sees them as God-related. It was not until much later that the church limited the term to a particular category of people, but to a category that it is almost impossible to specify. After all, who can know who has entered into the eternal glory? Who can have the knowledge to determine degrees of sanctity? It does seem possible to me, however, to recognize God-relatedness.

There is a further aspect of holiness today that emerges from the descriptions given above. It is a way that passes through the world and not apart from it. Moreover, it may involve conduct that some would regard as morally suspect. Two of the four examples adduced were committed to violence and bloodshed: Torres the guerrilla and Bonhoeffer the would-be assassin. Two of them engaged in deception and lies – Bonhoeffer again and Borelli. All of them saw the locus of encounter with the holy as being the world. Hammarskjöld's

dictum indeed applies to each and every one: 'In our era, the road
to sanctification necessarily passes through action.'

The list of examples illustrating holiness as a contemporary life-
style could have been much extended. One thinks, for example, of
Danilo Dolci, but to mention his name is also to note a further
characteristic of many modern saints – they are frequently looked
down upon by the church or are even outside it. Torres was condemned by members of the hierarchy; Borelli was regarded by many
as not quite respectable; and Bonhoeffer's activities are still regarded
by some German churchmen as reprehensible. Dolci himself eventually left the church.

Dolci began as an orthodox believer, although his social concern
was evident at an early stage. While he was at Nomadelphia, looking after a colony of homeless children, he wrote this poem, which
was published in 1951:

> In order to live I must be brother to You
> And father
> And wipe Your dripping nose
> Support Your faltering steps
> Build You a strong house of stone
> Solid and upright, and revive You
> When Your helpless forehead
> Burns on my knees
> And get bread for You, soup,
> And the honey and fruit You like:
> This is my worship.[91]

When later Dolci began his work in Sicily, he found his efforts
constantly criticized and even blocked by the Catholic hierarchy. It
seemed to him that the church was anti-humanitarian; it so stressed
the other-worldly that this world was left out of account; it so
affirmed supernature that human nature was being denied its fullness – and so he left. In his thinking a central concept is that of
creativity.

'To create' – how do we create? It can be 'by the will of God', and
if there's no fatalism involved then this is also creative in an educational
sense. But for me this isn't enough. Man must also intervene to try to
change things, to modify and perfect, and this is outside the traditional
religious concept. St Paul says man must be a *co-creator* with God –
which is the same idea, though Paul doesn't expand it.[92]

I do not propose to retell Dolci's struggles – they are well known

– but, he, too, follows the path of holiness in the sense that I have defined it.

The old priest, Don Benedetto, in the novel by Silone, from which I have already quoted, asks the question:

Might not the ideal of social justice that animates the masses today be one of the pseudonyms the Lord is using to withdraw himself from the control of the churches and the banks?[93]

The ways of encountering the holy in the secular world are many.

There is one final comment to be made by way of conclusion to the first part of this study. This comment takes the form of a contrast, between the Israel of the Old Testament and the church of the New. Israel's vocation was to be a holy people,[94] i.e., it was to be a people whose life was patterned after the very being of its holy God. What this meant for Israel was therefore determined by its understanding of the holiness of God, and eventually led to the concept of separation. The church's vocation is also to be a holy people,[95] but in the New Testament this is understood, not in terms of the Old Testament concept of the holy, but in terms of the divine revelation in Christ. Hence for Christians to pattern their lives upon the very being of the holy God revealed in Christ is to accept a pattern of service in the world, of death and resurrection, etc.; hence their holiness is not to be conceived in terms of separation but of involvement in the world.

Of course, if holiness is taken necessarily to mean 'apartness', then the God of the New Testament cannot be properly styled holy, for he is anything but separate, since the focus of attention is directed towards his active presence, through Christ and in the Spirit, in, with and for man in his worldly existence. Again, whereas in the Old Testament the holy is ultimately that which is enshrined in the temple where honour is paid through the cultus, according to the New Testament the holy walks the lanes of Palestine, hangs on a tree, and is known in the breaking of bread, and the celebration of the holy takes place in the ordinary living-room of a house. These final words, relating as they do to worship, point forward to Part II, in which this subject is to be examined.

PART TWO

The Holy and Worldly Worship

10

The Crisis of Worship

The Fourth Assembly of the World Council of Churches, which met in Uppsala in June 1968, was the first in the history of the ecumenical movement to address itself to the subject of worship. It did so, in the words of its report, because of the widespread recognition that 'there is a crisis of worship'.[1] Using terms that will now be familiar from the first part of this study, I would describe this crisis as the result of the passage from the sacral to the secular universe. The forms of worship in general use in the major Christian denominations, even allowing for liturgical revision, are essentially those that were created in a former age – the era of the sacral universe. It is not surprising, therefore, that in the context of the secular universe more and more people should find these forms less and less meaningful.

Worship, whatever else it is, is certainly understood by Christians to be an encounter with the holy. However, as long as it retains the forms it adopted in the sacral universe, it will function as an emphasizing of the dilemma of modern man and as an intensification of his divided existence. This explains why it is necessary for me to add a second part to this book. The acceptance of a model of the holy that enables contemporary man to meet the holy in and through the secular universe is not sufficient to overcome the dichotomy between the sacred and the secular if worship itself continues to operate as a divisive factor. When worship proclaims the separation of the holy, no amount of talk about the encounter with the holy in the hominized world will carry conviction. Consequently it is necessary to take the model of the holy, that has been presented in the previous chapters, and apply it to worship. This could lead to a twofold result: first, if it can be done, it is a further demonstration of the model's 'empirical fit', and second, it may enable us to appreciate the possibility of a new understanding of worship which is based upon world-involvement instead of world-rejection. The way would then be clear to seeing life, including worship, as one whole, and the encounter with the holy in the secular world would be understood to comprise worship.

In support of my contention that our inherited forms of worship stem from the sacral universe, let us consider three passages from documents of widely differing dates. The first, from the liturgy of Theodore of Mopsuestia, takes us back to the patristic period.

Above, to the exalted height, to the aweful place of glory, where the waving of the wings of the Cherubim ceases not, nor the Alleluias and sweet chanting, the Holy, Holy, Holy of the Seraphim – thither lift up your minds.[2]

The second is from the first exhortation in the communion rite of the 1662 *Book of Common Prayer*.

Repent you of your sins, or else come not to that holy table, lest, after the taking of that holy sacrament, the devil enter into you, as he entered into Judas, and fill you full of all iniquities, and bring you to destruction both of body and soul.

The third quotation is from the concluding words of the Liturgy of the Lord's Supper published in 1966 by the Standing Liturgical Commission of the Protestant Episcopal Church of the United States.

Go forth into the world in peace.

From these statements three conclusions may be drawn about worship:

1. It is a drawing apart from the world.
2. It is an entering into the sphere of the sacred or holy.
3. It is a means of encountering an other-worldly reality, indeed of participating in the life of heaven.

Worship, according to this view, is an activity whereby we retire for a time from the secular world and, leaving all that is common behind, penetrate into another, sacred, world, where we enter the presence of the all-holy God and sing his praises in company with the heavenly choir of angels, archangels and saints. So worship is a special, religious activity, performed in special holy buildings; it may strengthen us to fulfil the divine purpose within our daily lives but is, in itself, something separate from our daily lives in the world. All this, be it noted, is not just what Christians have believed in the past. The citation from the American source indicates that it still survives. Moreover, some of the Orthodox churchmen at Uppsala declared that 'the Liturgy has always been understood primarily as an act of withdrawal from the world'.[3]

It is also to be noted that the concept of the holy that underlies these ideas is that of the numinous – which is a further demonstration of the extent to which these forms belong to the sacral universe. I know of no better illustration of this association of worship and the numinous from a non-liturgical source than a passage in *The Wind in the Willows*. Mole and Rat have been led to an island by the music of a pipe.

'This is the place of my song-dream, the place the music played to me,' whispered the Rat, as if in a trance. 'Here, in this holy place, here if anywhere, surely we shall find Him!'

Then suddenly the Mole felt a great Awe fall upon him, an awe that turned his muscles to water, bowed his head, and rooted his feet to the ground. It was no panic terror – indeed he felt wonderfully at peace and happy – but it was an awe that smote and held him and, without seeing, he knew it could mean that some august Presence was very, very near. With difficulty he turned to look for his friend, and saw him at his side cowed, stricken, and trembling violently. . . . Perhaps he would never have dared to raise his eyes, but that, though the piping was now hushed, the call and the summons seemed still dominant and imperious. . . . Trembling he obeyed, and raised his humble head; and then . . . he looked in the very eyes of the Friend and Helper . . . and . . . as he looked, he lived, and still, as he lived, he wondered.

'Rat!' he found breath to whisper, shaking. 'Are you afraid?'

'Afraid?' murmured the Rat, his eyes shining with unutterable love. 'Afraid! of Him? O, never, never! And yet – and yet – O, Mole, I am afraid!'

Then the two animals, crouching to the earth, bowed their heads and did worship.[4]

Kenneth Grahame has conveyed in a remarkable way that blend of awe and delight, of fear and fascination, which is said to be induced by the numinous and to demand worshipful obeisance. This same note is to be found in certain liturgies, and it is important to discover when and why the numinous found a place in Christian worship.

The date of the incorporation of a sense of the numinous in the liturgy can be determined with considerable precision. The evidence has been carefully sifted by Edmund Bishop in an appendix which he contributed to an edition of the liturgical homilies of Narsai published in 1909. Since this was eight years before Otto invented the word 'numinous', Bishop referred to the phenomenon as the awe, fear or dread attaching to the eucharistic service. Bishop was able to demonstrate that this became prevalent in some quarters by the middle of the fourth century.[5] The first reference he could find was in the *Mystagogical Lectures*, attributed to Cyril of Jerusalem, although Cyril gave expression to it only as if in passing. Writing of the canon, he says:

> After this the Priest cries aloud, *Lift up your hearts*. For truly ought we in that most aweful hour to have our heart on high with God, and not below, thinking of earth and earthly things.[6]

The Greek word, *phrikodestatēn*, translated 'most aweful', really means that which causes shuddering and horror,[7] and it was used again by John Chrysostom to refer to 'the most awesome sacrifice'.[8] By contrast, there is nothing of fear or dread in the prayer book of Serapion nor in the writings of the Cappadocian Fathers,[9] while in the *Apostolic Constitutions* there is only one brief hint: 'Let us stand upright before the Lord with fear and trembling.'[10] By the time of Narsai, who founded the school of Nisibis *c*. 547, the sense of awe was all-pervading. So, immediately after the kiss of peace, we read: 'Great is the mystery . . . the dread mysteries, lo, are being consecrated; let every one be in fear and dread while they are being performed. . . Entreat earnestly and make supplication to the God of all in this hour which is full of trembling and great fear.'[11] Again, before the Invocation: 'Then the herald of the church (i.e. the deacon) cries in that hour: "In silence and fear be ye standing. . . . Let all the people be in fear at this moment in which the adorable Mysteries are being accomplished by the descent of the Spirit." '[12]

This sense of the numinous is repeatedly inculcated in the liturgies both of St Basil and St Chrysostom, but rather than weary the reader with more examples, I would simply draw attention to three features in Orthodox worship which P. Eudokimov regards as vital to our understanding of the holy. He notes that many of the patristic writers declare that in the eucharist 'you are partaking of fire', and that the spoon used for the administration of communion is called the tongs (*labis*). He also points out that, at the communion, the priest kisses the rim of the chalice and says: 'Lo, this hath touched my lips; and mine impurity shall be taken away, and my sin purged.'[13] Each of these three relates to Isaiah's vision in the temple.

Then flew one of the seraphim to me, having in his hand a *burning coal* which he had taken with *tongs* from the altar. And he touched my mouth and said: '*Behold, this has touched your lips; your guilt is taken away, and your sin forgiven.*'[14]

The numinous is clearly present in Isaiah's vision, and the application of this to the eucharist is further proof of the incorporation of the same understanding of the holy.

In the West the numinous aspect of the liturgy, in terms of awesomeness, was less to the fore, but it was nevertheless there. Thus, for example, Fulbert of Chartres, who died in 1029, wrote in one of his letters:

Let us now go on to the venerable sacrament of the body and blood of the Lord, which is so terrible to speak of as the mystery is not of earth but of heaven, not to be weighed by human understanding but to be wondered at.[15]

In similar vein, Stephen of Autun, who died in 1139, has this to say in his treatise *On the Sacrament of the Altar*:

O wonderful miracle! O marvellous and most divine sacrament! What mind fears not? What intellect fails not? Every sense is dull; all processes of reasoning disappear. Let the searchings of dialecticians be gone. It is proved and acknowledged by faith alone that the food of angels becomes the food of men.[16]

The attitude to the sacramental species themselves reflects further this numinous aura. So the Council of Cologne, which met in 1280, laid down the following provisions:

If any part of the blood or body of the Lord has fallen on the covering of the altar, that part is to be cut out and burnt, and the ashes are to be placed in a sacred place or the piscina. And, if a part of the corporal has been stained with the blood, it is to be carefully washed three times, and the water is to be taken by the priest or some other religious person fasting. And after being washed the aforesaid cloth can be used as before. Also, if a drop of the blood has fallen on a vestment, that part is to be cut out and burnt, and the ashes are to be placed in a sacred place, as was said before. If the blood has fallen on wood or stone or solid earth, that part, if it can conveniently be, is to be licked by the priest, and afterward scraped, and what is scraped off is to be placed in a sacred place or the sacred piscina.[17]

Various ritual changes were also, in part, the outcome of this emphasis upon the numinous. Amongst these are to be noted – noted only, since a full discussion is not necessary – the practice, found in both East and West, of saying certain prayers secretly: i.e., they were so closely associated with the fearful mystery that they were not made audible to the congregation. Again, there was the turning of the minister's back to the people, the withdrawal of the cup from the laity and the infrequency of communion itself. This last practice is also to be interpreted in the light of the numinous as that which brings creature-feeling, a sense of abasement and un-worthiness. This was also responsible for the insertion of a con-fession of sin into the mass immediately before communion, while several prayers testify to the feeling of dependence and nothingness. One example will suffice, viz. the prayer that follows the Litany of the Saints in the Stowe Missal.

> I stand, O God, before the sight of thy divine Majesty, who presume to call upon thy holy Name; have mercy upon me, O Lord, a man, a sinner, sunk in the mire and refuse of uncleanness; pardon, O Lord, thy unworthy priest by whose hands this Oblation seems to be offered; spare, O Lord, a sinner polluted with the taint above all of mortal sins, and enter not into judgment with thy servant, O Lord, for in thy sight shall no man living be justified: we indeed are weighed down by the weak-nesses and desires of the flesh: remember, O Lord, that we are flesh, and that there is none other to be compared to thee; in thy sight even the heavens are not clean, how much more we that are men, earthy and un-clean like a filthy rag. We are not worthy, Jesu Christ, that we should live, but thou who willest not the death of a sinner, grant unto us who are set in the flesh pardon, that through the labours of penitence we may enjoy eternal life in the heavens.[18]

Why, then, did this note enter the liturgy in the latter half of the fourth century, to become more and more accentuated as the years passed? Since this is not an historical study, no more is required here than an outline answer to the question. Among the factors that brought about the change are to be noted the following, al-though they are not listed in any order of priority.

First, there was the influence of the Old Testament. The New Testament has relatively little to say about worship *per se*; con-sequently when the early church came to elaborate its forms, it had recourse to the Old Testament and, in the process, accepted its understanding of the holy. Second, the great basilicas that were erected to provide for the new liturgical forms were regarded as imitations of the Jerusalem temple as well as replacements for pagan shrines; hence they were considered to be holy places – holy again being conceived as the numinous.[19] Third, in its competition with paganism, Christianity did not hesitate to take over some of the categories of the latter, and added to the splendour and numinous aura of its acts of worship in order to impress the multitude and to check their unseemly conduct during services. In the struggle with Arianism, which taught that Christ was only a creature, emphasis was placed upon the absolute divinity of Jesus, and his Godhead was stressed in all its awefulness. Then there was a growing concentration upon the 'real presence' in the eucharist, and the corollary of this was an insistence upon man's unworthiness to be in such a terrible presence. The developing cult of the saints, with the enclosure of relics in altars, also served to intensify the sense of the numinous, as did the incorporation into the liturgy of several features of the imperial court ceremonial.

All these factors contributed to sacralize worship and set it apart from everyday life. At the same time there was a development of the rationale of worship on the basis of the Epistle to the Hebrews. Ambrose and Augustine were the pioneers in this movement. They linked the action of the eucharist with the exercise by the risen and ascended Christ of his high priesthood in the heavens.[20] The communion service thus introduced the worshipper into heaven itself, and in time this was associated with the concept of the two worlds: the one divine, holy, supernatural and Christian, and the other worldly, profane, natural and un-Christian. According to Bonhoeffer:

This view becomes dominant for the first time in the Middle Ages, and for the second time in the pseudo-Protestant thought of the period after the Reformation. . . . In the scholastic scheme of things the realm of the natural is subordinate to the realm of grace; in the pseudo-Lutheran scheme the autonomy of the orders of this world is proclaimed in opposition to the law of Christ, and in the scheme of the Enthusiasts the congregation of the elect takes up the struggle with a hostile world for the establishment of God's kingdom on earth.[21]

The function of worship, when defined in the light of a belief in these two antithetical realms, is to lift the congregation temporarily from one into the other. The *Sanctus* – itself based on the numinous passage in Revelation 4 – expressed and still expresses this otherworldly reference of the liturgical action. Worship, thus conceived, divides reality into two parts and affirms the dichotomy of the holy and the secular. It is the means of withdrawal from the latter into a sacred, liturgical realm which allows access to the heavenlies. It was Bonhoeffer who emphasized the falseness of this outlook. There is no such concept in the New Testament. Rather, the apostolic writings are

concerned solely with the manner in which the reality of Christ assumes reality in the present world, which it has already encompassed, seized and possessed. There are not two spheres, standing side by side, competing with each other and attacking each other's frontiers. If that were so, the frontier dispute would always be the decisive problem of history. But the whole reality of the world is already drawn into Christ and bound together in him, and the movement of history consists solely in divergence and convergence in relation to this centre.[22]

Bonhoeffer goes on to analyse the consequence of this two-worlds view and to affirm, instead, the oneness of reality.

... the cause of Christ becomes a partial and provincial matter within the limits of reality. It is assumed that there are realities which lie outside the reality that is in Christ. It follows that these realities are accessible by some way of their own, and otherwise than through Christ. However great the importance that is attached to the reality in Christ, it still always remains a partial reality amid other realities. The division of the total reality into a sacred and profane sphere, a Christian and a secular sphere, creates the possibility of existence in a single one of these spheres, a spiritual existence which has no part in secular existence, and a secular existence which can claim autonomy for itself and can exercise this right of autonomy in its dealing with the spiritual sphere... So long as Christ and the world are conceived as two opposing and mutually repellent spheres, man will be left in the following dilemma: he abandons reality as a whole, and places himself in one or other of the two spheres. He seeks Christ without the world, or he seeks the world without Christ. In either case he is deceiving himself. Or else he tries to stand in both spaces at once and thereby becomes a man of eternal conflict, the kind of man who emerged in the period after the Reformation and who has repeatedly set himself up as representing the only form of Christian existence which is in accord with reality...

There are not two realities, but only one reality, and that is the reality of God, which has become manifest in Christ in the reality of the world. Sharing in Christ we stand at once in both the reality of God and the reality of the world. The reality of Christ comprises the reality of the world within itself. The world has no reality of its own, independently of the revelation of God in Christ. One is denying the revelation of God in Jesus Christ if one tries to be 'Christian' without seeing and recognizing the world in Christ. There are, therefore, not two spheres, but only the one sphere of the realization of Christ, in which the reality of God and the reality of the world are united.[23]

I have reproduced these passages at length because they highlight the crisis of worship today. Because we live in a secular universe, the numinous is no longer a meaningful category. Because we live in a secular universe, the idea of two worlds has little or no relevance. But, since worship, in the classical forms that persist virtually unchanged today, rests upon this twin basis, it has become emptied of content.

Alternatively expressed, it may be said that worship traditionally has come to be based upon the idea that there are two worlds: the one is the everyday world in which we live and work and play, while the other is a spiritual realm where God and the things of the Spirit are supreme and with which we have contact through worship. Worship is then understood as the bridge between these two worlds, as the means of access from the world of man to the realm of the divine.

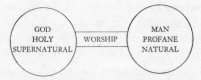

Now, as Bonhoeffer affirms, there is no basis whatsoever in the Bible for this distinction. The Old and New Testaments know only of *one* world. They know nothing of the division of reality into a sacred world and a secular one, nor into a divine world and the world of man. To them there is only one world which is God's. The New Testament does speak of a difference between the present age and the age to come, which in common speech is often loosely and inaccurately represented as a distinction between this world and the next, but the biblical contrast is not between an earthly existence and eternity in heaven; it is between life in rebellion against God on the one hand and the Kingdom of God on the other. This Kingdom has broken in through the ministry of Jesus, so that even in this present age we may taste the powers of the age to come.[24] This, however, allows of no distinction between two worlds. And if there is only one world, worship cannot be interpreted as a bridge. So yet another element in the present crisis of worship is precisely the apparent meaninglessness of cultic acts, once we have rejected the two worlds and affirm only one. Moreover, if we persist in thinking in terms of this division, we are splitting reality into two areas, and in so doing we are reducing God to the status of a tribal deity. The divine being is then envisaged as an object of devotion to be worshipped and encountered within the religious enclosure alone; he is sovereign only over the religious world, while from the secular his presence and activity are largely banished.

In terms of classical Christian doctrine, the incarnation itself gives the lie to this kind of thinking. Through Jesus 'it becomes clear that the transcendent God is not to be sought apart from human life, for he has himself lived a human existence'.[25] The history of Jesus is an episode in secular history; so the holy is now encountered in and through the secular. This encounter does not require, indeed cannot require, separation from the world, nor does it need special holy buildings for its location; anywhere can be the place of his presence. He may be met by the member of a caravan on the road to Damascus or by an itinerant preacher in the desert between Jerusalem and Gaza; the result of such a meeting was not the erection of shrines but the acceptance of the service of the holy in the world.

In thus rejecting the older concept of worship which rested on the dichotomy between two worlds, and affirming another one, I am doing no more than return to the insights of the New Testament. Indeed, in New Testament times 'worship', conceived as the joyful response of Christians to God's action in Jesus Christ, was not defined first and foremost in terms of what happened in a certain *place where* and at a certain *time when* Christians assembled. What happened on those occasions was understood 'within the context of response to God in their total existence'.[26] Worship is then celebration of life in the one world; it is a coming to awareness of and response to the holy in and through that which is human and secular.

It follows from this conclusion that there can be no escape from the present crisis by means of liturgical revision. Revision is usually taken to involve adding to and subtracting from and otherwise altering something already in existence, very much as the Revised Version of the Bible was essentially the Authorized with some changes. But this is to evade the real issue. Worship is a vital test-case to decide whether or not the encounter with the holy involves a divided or a unified existence. There would have been little point in reaching the conclusion at the end of the last chapter, that the service of men and the holy in the world are not distinct activities, if it were also to be maintained that the service of the holy in worship is apart from the world and necessarily involves both the acknowledgement of the numinous and participation in a cult celebrated in heaven. The results of a liturgical revision, which simply updates the language and rearranges the units of forms of worship devised in and for a sacral universe, are just not acceptable to modern man. It has not solved the problem of worship in a secular age and, instead, has created an expectation of renewal that it cannot fulfil and has irritated people by producing forms that are neither ancient nor modern. While it has enabled some Christians who were wavering in their allegiance to continue to worship, revision has often amounted to no more than a temporary rehabilitation of the old forms.[27]

In this situation it has been suggested that the choice before us is only between the ghetto and the desert. The terminology is that of Charles Davis who, in a recently published article, has certainly illuminated the present crisis, although, for reasons that will become apparent, I cannot share his view about where we go from here.

Davis takes as his point of departure the sociology of knowledge, in particular as elaborated by P. L. Berger and T. Luckmann and previously summarized by me in '*Excursus A*'.[28] These two authors affirm that what man takes as real is that which is endorsed by a society as a whole. Knowledge is socially shared and socially confirmed; it has a social dimension and is dependent upon social experience. This knowledge and this reality are accepted in so far as they rest upon a specific plausibility structure, which is provided by the social base and social processes required for their maintenance.[29] This does not mean that all that is taken for granted is true. Ancient Babylonian society, for example, regarded astrology as part of reality – a view that we would not endorse today. It does, however, mean that those who differ in their outlook from the majority of the fellow members of the society to which they belong are deviants; they constitute a cognitive minority and they can claim only a weak plausibility structure. Christians today, in the view of Charles Davis, are such a minority. Their inherited beliefs and forms of worship are not part of the socially shared and confirmed reality of the modern secular world. 'As believers and worshippers we step outside the dominant secular culture as social deviants.'[30] He is therefore led to the conclusion:

There is no modern way of being a Christian, precisely because the modern world is not Christian. Likewise the problem of worship is not that of finding modern forms of worship to replace outdated forms. It is that worship itself is outdated. There is no modern form of public worship because the modern world is secular.[31]

It is in the light of this analysis that Davis sees only two possibilities open to Christians today: the ghetto or the desert. By 'ghetto' he means the preservation of a sub-culture – at odds with the prevailing secular culture – within which alone worship can have any meaning. It involves the creation of a counter-community, i.e. a community within the larger secular community, that has its own distinct knowledge, language, symbols, attitudes and emotional responses. By 'desert' he means the recognition that Christians today are without any appropriate cultural forms in which to express their faith and worship. They live in an uneasy tension between the antiquated mould of traditional Christianity and contemporary dynamic society. 'For the Christian there is a cultural hiatus, a break, a discontinuity: he has to live for a period in the desert.' Nevertheless, Davis looks forward to a future 'when present secular culture will be redeemed and rendered open to Christian faith';[32] then, and only then, will the wandering in the wilderness cease.

We are bound to ask: is this analysis correct? Are these two options the only ones open for Christians today?

I find myself in entire agreement with several of the points that are advanced by Davis. First, I do not see how anyone can doubt that knowledge is socially conditioned – although there are limits even to this. Second, I would not deny that Christian belief and worship, as formulated in the context of the sacral universe, are at odds with the secular universe. Third, it follows that those who adhere to the inherited traditions are deviants. Consequently I also agree with Davis that those who engage in liturgical revision have failed to appreciate the true nature of the crisis of worship today and have, probably without being aware of it, chosen the ghetto. So far we are at one – but I cannot follow Davis in the conclusions that he draws precisely because he does not allow for the possibility of a new understanding of the holy, nor does he appreciate the extent to which the New Testament model of the holy – as distinct from the numinous of the sacral universe – can be related to the secular world in terms of empirical fit. The whole of Part I of this present book is an attempt to show what is involved in 'the modern way of being a Christian' within a secular society. The previous chapters are an extended endeavour to indicate that there are cultural bridges between 'secular' Christianity and the contemporary scene. In so far as I have been successful – and the reader will judge that for him-self – Davis' stark options cannot be regarded as the only alterna-tives. Moreover, his characterization of the desert appears to me to rest upon a vain hope; in effect he waits for a restoration of Christen-dom, when 'present secular culture will be redeemed and rendered open to Christian faith'. My contention is that it is already open, if Christian faith is centred in the New Testament model of the holy. He substitutes his own tension – Christianity versus secular culture – for the real tension between the 'already' and the 'not yet', and so waits for the future instead of living out of it in the present.

It is precisely because Davis is not radical enough in his theolo-gical thinking – taking 'radical' to mean 'going back to the roots' – and still operates within a sacral context that he fails to suggest any other viable option. Further, he accepts that Christian worship should essentially be a *cultus publicus*, and so reveals an inability to recognize that this is only one way of understanding worship which did not emerge within Christianity until the time of Constantine and the inception of Christendom. Logically his position, in relation to this, implies that prior to Constantine, and so for some three cen-turies, Christians were not really worshipping at all. Within the logic generated by his own definitions Davis is cogent, but if one does not accept his stereotype of either the Christian or worship, then one does not have to endorse his conclusion. The ghetto and the desert are indeed possibilities, but if I am to be consis-tent with what I have written previously, then a third way must be found.

Nevertheless, this brief survey of Davis' essay has been of value. On the one hand, it helps to illuminate the true nature of the crisis – and indeed Davis is one of the few modern writers who has not evaded the problem – and, on the other hand, if one refuses to accept either the ghetto or the desert, it demands the formulation of a third possibility. It is to this task that the remaining chapters will be devoted.

There is, however, one further point in the essay we have been examining of which note should be taken before passing on. On several occasions Davis refers to a 'Christian culture'. I very much doubt if such an entity has ever really existed or ever can exist. In-deed, it is reasonable to hold that it was precisely the acceptance of this idea that produced such dire consequences for Christianity in both Africa and India. The nineteenth-century missionaries assumed that the gospel was indissolubly wedded to Western culture. Consequently they made little or no attempt to indigenize Christianity; they did not see the need to adapt Christianity to the different prevailing cultures in the lands to which they went and, instead, sought to replace those cultures with that which was current in Europe. The gospel was, therefore, and remained, a foreign importation into an alien environment. But if Christianity is to have any permanent validity, it must be adaptable to all ages and cultures. Western technological society represents a new culture within which Christianity has to indigenize itself or perish. This is not to say, however, that the complete identification of Christianity with secular culture is required. Because of the eschatological proviso, any and every culture is relative; no one form, past, present, or future, is to be absolutized. It is one thing to discern cultural bridges which may allow the possibility for modern man to engage in meaningful acts of worship; it is another for Christianity to give up its critical role and conform itself entirely to the society in which it is present.

I would certainly not wish to claim to be the first to raise these issues. There is a widespread recognition of the need to find what, for want of a better description, one might call secular forms of worship. This may be illustrated by taking three quotations from contemporary writers.

'Liturgy is secular before it is religious activity because liturgy is always celebration of life' – these are the words of an American Roman Catholic.[33]

'Too often efforts at liturgical renewal have been concerned only with public worship, whereas it also involves the renewal of one's stance *vis-à-vis* the world' – this is the reasoned conclusion of a Methodist.[34]

'Worship as a separate section of man's life has been destroyed' – this is the assertion of a Roman Catholic professor.[35]

From these statements we may draw three conclusions about worship:

1. It is *not* a drawing apart from the world, but is itself a worldly activity.
2. It is *not* an entering into a sacred realm.
3. It is therefore *not* a means of encountering an other-worldly reality, but is concerned with how the holiness of the common is made manifest.

Worship, according to this view, is an activity which springs out of life in the world; it is a celebration of that life. Instead of involving a divorce from the secular, it takes the secular or common as its basis, and so the cultic action is a means whereby we express the unity of the sacred and the secular. It does not need holy shrines for its performance, and while it is essentially a coming to awareness of and a response to the holy, this is achieved through that which is human and secular.

These conclusions are in direct opposition to those that stemmed from the three passages cited from liturgies ancient and revised at the beginning of this chapter, and they demonstrate a movement in modern theological thought on the subject of worship. Yet the statements made are frequently too general and too cryptic to be of real assistance. 'Yes, we agree, of course, that worship is a worldly activity . . .' But then one is prompted to ask: but what exactly does this mean? I hope that the succeeding chapters will in part provide an answer to this question and spell out a 'new' understanding of worship. Indeed, in face of the present crisis many are seeking what is called a 'renewal' of worship. Renewal, however, is not just the restoration of things as they were. When Paul writes to the Corinthians about the new creation and the passing away of the old,[36] and when, in Revelation, he who sits on the throne says, 'Behold, I make all things new',[37] the reference is not to a return to a previously existing *status quo*. The theme is new creation; it is a matter of dynamic and continuous creativity. Hence the 'newness' which is brought about by renewal is not something merely later in time; it is qualitatively new. Paul exhorts the Romans to be 'transformed by the renewal of your mind';[38] so renewal is a transformation towards something always fresh and not yet known.

It should be evident by now that in my view this renewal of worship is not equivalent to liturgical revision. Liturgical revision – the evidence is abundant – is generally dominated by the study of past forms of worship.[39] The 'why' of a particular element in any revised service is almost always determined by reference to previous liturgical tradition. But if renewal is, as I have defined it, a transformation towards something always fresh, this line of approach is doomed to failure from the start; the result can only be a modified restoration of a previously existing *status quo*. This will be of interest to the liturgical expert, but it will not mean a great deal to the men and women in the congregations, or outside them, who cannot see why, for example, having the Lord's Prayer before communion is all that better than having it, as previously in the *Book of Common Prayer*, after it. One meets many lay people who are concerned about the renewal of worship; there are few who find liturgical revision an inspiring and worthwhile activity.

In the light of Part I of this study, the starting point of renewal must be sought in 'life, not liturgy. Roots of liturgy are in society, rather than in the Church.'[40] Again, 'sacramental celebrations are liturgical actions reflecting and building up the life we already have . . . worshipful high points of an already blessed, free and Christian way of life'.[41] Indeed, we may say that 'liturgical renewal is splendid, but it comes as a part of the complete renewal of the Church and not as a single aspect'.[42]

The point at issue here is a vital one. The Dutch Roman Catholic writer Robert Adolfs has argued that the church today is like the Indians in the United States.

Their way of life could not be made to fit into modern American society and they have consequently been put into special reservations where 'they cannot do any harm'. So it is with the Church. She has become a 'religious reservation' with its own patterns of life.[43]

Within this enclave – this ghetto – the church has its own esoteric cultic acts, which are 'religious' practices divorced from the world. Because it is out of touch with and largely irrelevant to the twentieth-century world, the church cannot expect its worship not to be the same, i.e. equally out of touch and irrelevant. Relevance and meaning will not be achieved by liturgical revision, as generally understood; the renewal of worship will be an expression of the renewal of the church as she enters into dialogue with the world, and once again becomes world-centred, as is the God she claims to serve, who 'so loved the world that he gave his only Son . . . not to condemn the world, but that the world might be saved through him'.[44] We have to acknowledge that the temptation of Christianity is always to fall back into the security of a religious realm of existence where the holy is guaranteed. Too often the Christian today

uses his religion to create for himself a chimeric shangri-la where the unholy realities of his city-world cannot penetrate. He tends to the heretical notion that 'only the holy is holy'. He conditions himself to hear God only in organ music and to smell God only in incense. Not only does he, in this artificial escape-world, ill prepare himself for seeing God or meeting God in the city, but his response to God within his other world becomes artificial, stereotyped, and as unreal as the God he fashions for himself.[45]

Only when we take the secular world seriously, only when the church sees its part in the mission of the holy as an entering into the struggle for human existence and welfare, witnessing to the compassion of Christ, only then will worship begin to be renewed. In other words, the renewal of worship is and will be a by-product of the renewal of the Christian community. To attempt to deal with this aspect of the subject in any depth would involve too long a digression from my principal concern, but a brief indication of what this may involve is necessary if the renewal of worship is to be set within its full context.

The report of the Nottingham Faith and Order Conference was entitled *One Church Renewed for Mission*. I believe that this title reveals a fundamental misconception. It conveys the idea that only if the separated churches will unite, and only if they will renew their lives together, can they engage in mission. But in the Acts of the Apostles, which is above all a document about mission, we are not presented with a church which first spends its time in introspection and carefully builds itself up, and only then, when it considers itself to be ready, moves out in mission. From the moment of the descent of the Spirit, the church was in mission, ready for it or not because it was subject to the sovereignty of the Spirit. So the church according to Acts, renews itself and finds its unity in mission. By 'mission' I understand the divine activity in the world, and I would maintain that for the church to be true to its calling it must share in that activity in the world.[46] It must then cease to be preoccupied with its own ecclesiastical concerns; it must cease to be a church for itself and become a church for others. It must give up pretensions to dominate after the medieval pattern and become once again, after the New Testament model of the holy, a servant church, outgoing in concern for all mankind, seeking, according to its resources, to meet human need in all its forms. If the church would save its life, i.e. make it whole or renew it, it must be prepared to lose it in disinterested service to others[47] – only then will renewal become a real possibility.

The crisis of worship, which arises as a consequence of the transition from a sacral to a secular universe, is made even more acute by three other factors. The first of these is related to the loss by religion, at least in the West, of its previous social role; the second of these concerns the function of worship interpreted in terms of that social role. The third element is the transformation of social relations within an urban and technological society. For light on the first and third of these, one has to seek the assistance of sociologists, on the second the help of social anthropologists – and this, in part, is what will occupy us in the succeeding chapters. However, from this introductory chapter the outline of a programme of investigation emerges. We have to consider what the social role of religion is or could be in a secular society and the effect of this upon the function of worship, and also the modification of forms of worship demanded by changed social relations. All this has to be brought into relation to the encounter with the holy in the one world and in a unified life-style, comprising worship and everyday life but not putting the sacred and the secular asunder. This seems to me a possible way forward, which may enable one to reject both the ghetto and the desert.

11

Worship and Ritual

The study of ritual is a necessary exercise for the understanding of worship, since worship is offered formally according to fixed rites. Even in so-called 'free' worship, there is normally to be detected an underlying structure, which is reproduced on each occasion, and to that extent it, too, is to be classified as ritual. The precise definition of ritual is, however, by no means simple. Liturgiologists usually distinguish it from ceremonial. The latter refers to the prescribed and formal actions that constitute worship, while the former denotes the set pattern of words. So, for example, the use of incense falls within the category of ceremonial, whereas the eucharistic prayer is within that of ritual. But in common usage the two are interchangeable, with ritual as the more frequently employed, especially in the writings of social anthropologists.

Some social anthropologists, however, have attempted to substitute a different distinction between ceremonial and ritual for that just indicated. According to Monica Wilson, ritual is 'a primarily religious action . . . directed to secure the blessing of some mystical power', whereas ceremonial is an 'elaborate conventional form for the expression of feeling, not confined to religious occasions'.[1] Max Gluckman, following Monica Wilson, defines ritual as that which refers to actions and beliefs addressed to spiritual beings or some ultimate view of destiny, while ceremonial covers 'any complex organization of human activity which is not specifically technical or recreational and which involves the use of modes of behaviour which are expressions of social relationships'.[2] This leads him to distinguish between 'ceremonious' and 'ritual', the latter referring to suprasensible phenomena.

Mary Douglas, on the other hand, rejects such a separation and contends that to give a different name to these activities and then to study them in isolation is to be guilty of a methodological error.[3] What is significant about this disagreement is that Mary Douglas is concerned with tribal societies, in which there is undoubtedly a continuity between secular rituals (ceremonial) and religious rituals, whereas Gluckman illustrates his contrast by reference to the October Revolution parade in Moscow as 'ceremonious' and to a Corpus Christi Day procession as ritual. In other words, he chooses his example from contemporary, non-tribal, society and in so doing emphasizes the problem with which we are concerned, viz. the separation of worship from everyday life in the world and its apparent irrelevance to secular existence. Hence a dilemma emerges. If one follows Gluckman, despite the fact that he acknowledges that these categories 'shade into one another',[4] one has already in part predetermined the outcome of any investigation into the re-lationship of worship and the secular: by definition they are already largely distinct, ritual, i.e. worship, having been *by definition* differentiated from ceremonial, i.e. secular activity. If one pursues the path laid down by Douglas, one is operating within the context of the sacral universe, and the possibility of discovering a bridge to the present situation appears remote.

Goody, on the other hand, as quoted by Gluckman, occupies a midway position between these two views. He defines ritual as 'a category of standardized behaviour in which the relationship between the means and the end is not "intrinsic", i.e. is either irrational or non-rational'. He is prepared to use 'ritual' of all human activities, and in so far as any distinction is to be made, it can be denoted by adding the adjective 'religious' whenever the ritual is believed to be related to some mystical power.[5] But this is not satisfactory in relation to the perspective of this present study. If the holy is encountered through the secular, one cannot drive a wedge between the two by the simple expedient of adding the qualification 'reli-gious'. Rather, the essential distinction is between ritual as a human activity, which includes worship, and worship itself, which makes use of ritual as its necessary basis and vehicle.

This divergence of view suggests that our starting point should not be, after all, a definition, but rather an examination of ritual patterns to discover their meaning. In other words, the purpose of this chapter is to define the meaning of what people do when they perform certain rites and then to consider if this meaning is valid today.

If it has proved difficult to produce an agreed definition of ritual,[6] it is even more difficult to formulate an accepted classification. There is a multiplicity of rituals. There are rites of separation, of transition and of incorporation. When the last is regularly repeated it assumes the character of a rite of intensification. There are rites, too, of protection, of regulation, of participation. There are rites of reintegration and of commitment. There are negative and positive rites; there are magical and religious observances. There are rituals of celebration and of affirmation. As a means of entry into this bewildering confusion, one may begin by recognizing that rites can belong to any one of three types:

1. Rites whose object is to establish an intimate contact between man and the holy in order that he may control the divine power.
2. Rites whose object is to isolate man from the holy which is regarded as dangerous.
3. Rites whose object is to facilitate man's contact with the holy in such a way that he may be preserved and at the same time enter into a relationship with the source of his being.[7]

Rites of the first type belong to the sphere of magic. They provide the means to dominate and manipulate the holy. They enable direct contact with the holy for man's own ends. They preserve the secular by keeping it away from the sacred and so tend to undermine the settled order and involve the surrender of the normal human condition. These rituals set the individual apart from ordinary humanity; he then becomes a being who is unlike the majority of mankind. This is deemed necessary because 'the purpose of magic is to bring about a fusion with the numinous power by a kind of renunciation of the human condition'.[8]

Rites of the second type correspond to negative ones and relate to impurity, being often connected with the idea of taboo. Such rituals are an attempt to regulate the holy and so, to a certain extent, to control that which is regarded as abnormal. When the holy is perceived as that which threatens the human condition, steps are taken to hedge it in and so to direct it in the interests of the continuation of human life and social cohesion. Negative rituals of this kind constitute a set of rules to protect man from the numinous. They allow the creation of a world apart, closed in on itself, where every-thing is ordered and from which the extraordinary, which may upset the equilibrium of the human situation, is kept out. Hence man says to himself, as it were: 'If we observe the rules embodied in these rituals, we know where we are and we have nothing to fear.' This type of ritual clearly arises out of a dialectic between the sacred and the profane.[9]

For obvious reasons, neither of these two types is our immediate concern. Meaningful worship within a secular universe cannot be related to the practice of magic nor, since we are looking for an understanding of worship in which the holy and the secular are integrated, are we interested in the isolation of man from the holy. Nevertheless, elements from both of these types are to be found inter-woven with the third category.

The final classification, given above, refers to those rituals that seek to create a synthesis between the human situation and the holy.[10] Primitive man finds himself in a dilemma. He desires to enter into contact with the numinous as a source of power, but this is 'coun-tered by the fear of being obliged to renounce the human condition' as by magic.[11] Hence he devises rites to reconcile the numinous with the normal order of things, with the rules.[12] Such a synthesis between the sacred and the secular is in part based upon the two worlds' concept to which attention was directed in the previous chapter. Rites are then understood as so many bridges between the profane world of man and the sacred realm of God.

This synthesis can only be achieved by means of symbols which are able to represent the order of the human situation and, at the same time, possess the power of that which goes beyond that order, of that which is not limited by it. These symbols must guarantee the rules of the human universe and yet have the form and figure of that which is extra-human. The holy participates both in that which is regular and that which is exceptional.[13]

Consequently rites of this third type tend to borrow elements from the other two. They are concerned, like magic, to establish contact with the holy, but not with the same end in view, i.e. not in order to exploit it or make it subservient to man's desires. They are also concerned, like negative rites, to preserve both the human reality intact and the holy uncontaminated, without either being absorbed in the other or being denied in favour of the other. The nature of this synthesis will become clearer if we turn to van Gennep's classification.

In his outstanding study *The Rites of Passage*, van Gennep distinguished three categories: (1) Rites of separation; (2) Rites of transition; (3) Rites of incorporation. Since they are all related to the idea of crossing a threshold (Latin *limen*), he also called them: (1) Preliminal; (2) Liminal; (3) Postliminal. If this classification be applied to Christian initiation, in its classical Western form, the distinction and interweaving of these elements can be made plain. Schematically presented, the structure may be set out in this way:

1. *Rites of Catechumenate (Preliminal)*

   (*a*) Exsufflation and exorcism = rites of separation
   (*b*) Sign of cross on forehead = rite of separation and incorporation
   (*c*) Placing of salt on tongue = rite of incorporation

2. *The Catechumenate (Liminal)*

   (*a*) Occupation of a special place at the back of the church and withdrawal before the beginning of the eucharist proper
   (*b*) Repeated exorcisms
   (*c*) *Effeta*, unction, renunciation of Satan, recitation of creed (in these three, separation and incorporation are intertwined.)

3. *Initiation (Postliminal)*

   (*a*) Baptism
      (i) Removal of clothing = separation
      (ii) Baptism in water (death and resurrection) = separation, transition and incorporation.
      (iii) Putting on of white clothes = incorporation
   (*b*) Confirmation
      This marks a further stage of the incorporation into the community
   (*c*) Eucharist
      This is the consummation of the process of incorporation.[14]

A similar structure may be discerned at the basis of the eucharist itself, in the form it assumed from the fourth century onwards. This can be demonstrated more briefly. The dismissal of all but the initiated is a rite of separation, the same function being performed

by the later practice of a confession of sin. The recital of the creed
is a sign of adherence. The communion is regarded as uniting the
believer with Christ in his death and resurrection (a very close
parallel with baptism), while the whole rite is a community meal
and therefore one of incorporation. In a sense the eucharist is a
periodic renewal of initiation.[15]

It should now be apparent that traditional religious rituals have
both a negative aspect, which serves to safeguard the holy, and a
positive, which allows participation in the holy. They thus constitute a bridge and a synthesis which enables the human to share
in the holy, and so they integrate the sacred and the secular. Nevertheless, there is a tendency for religious rites to degenerate in either
of two ways. They can overstress the negative aspect. By suggesting
that a complete transformation is required in the individual, they
can divide the sacred and the secular, and so the rite tends to intensify the dichotomy. Conversely, they can border on magic, involving
both the abandonment of the human condition and the manipulation
of the holy as a source of power. Both of these deviations could be
illustrated from the history of Christian worship.

Van Gennep believed that rites of passage involved a movement
between the profane world and the sacred world. The incompatibi-
lity between them is conceived to be so great that passage from one
to the other is regarded as impossible without the provision of some
sort of intermediate state. One cannot arrive at the postliminal from
the preliminal without going through the liminal. If this is so – and
there is no reason to doubt the accuracy of his observation – then it
poses the question whether such rituals can have any meaning
within a secular universe in relation to an understanding of the
unity of the sacred and the secular within the one world. A re-
definition of ritual – if possible – then becomes necessary. This conclusion indicates that the analysis so far has served the negative
purpose of throwing the present crisis of worship into even greater
relief. It does, however, assist one to recognize more fully some of
the essential aspects of the problem with which we have to deal.
The problem becomes yet more complex if we go on to consider the
social dimension of ritual, to which van Gennep paid little attention,
but which has been developed in more recent studies by social
anthropologists.

According to Max Gluckman ritual is 'a stylized ceremonial in
which persons related in various ways to the central actors, as well

as these themselves, perform prescribed actions according to their
secular role, and . . . it is believed by the participants that these
prescribed actions express and amend social relationships so as to
secure general blessing, purification, and prosperity for the persons
involved in some mystical manner which is out of sensory control.'[16]
In agreement with this is the contention of A. R. Radcliffe-Brown
that the social function of religion, and so of ritual, is to contribute
to the formation and maintenance of social order.[17] How does it
achieve this? It does so in the following ways:

1. *Ritual provides the means of containing and overcoming anti-
social drives*

Within any society there are conflicts between individuals and/or
groups. Egocentricity and diversity of interests can produce disorder.
In the ritual process these emotions and divergent concerns can be
divested of their divisory character. Through a fellowship meal, for
example, the unity between the members of society can be re-estab-
lished. Similarly, the marriage ritual unites dissimilars and curbs
excess, while penance reintegrates within the social order those who
have been deviants.[18] The ritual does not necessarily settle the disputes that arise nor remove them, but it does enable the parties to
accept one another again and to act together. It is even possible to
put the forces of disorder at the service of social order, as when
the cross is made central to the Christian cultus.

2. *Ritual maintains social equilibrium*

This function is in part a corollary of the first, but it is listed as a
distinct item because it also involves the understanding of certain
rituals as rites of intensification between the members of the group
and so preservers of stability.[19] They provide a dramatic representation of the habitual relationships of the individuals and so keep those
relationships upon an even keel.[20] They help to restore contact between individuals who occupy positions in the structure of society.
Within that structure there is a tendency for the individual to be lost
behind the social *persona* (the functionary); rites of intensification promote person-to-person encounter and increase the unity of the group.

3. *Ritual distinguishes roles and permits transference from one to
another*

Much of the ritualization of tribal societies arises from the multiplicity of undifferentiated and overlapping roles. Ritual is then a

process whereby role-playing, an essential part of life in any society, is clarified and the possibility of a change of roles emerges.[21]

4. *Ritual is the means whereby religion itself functions as the guarantor of society*

Religion in primitive societies was the support of the state, the protector of the social order and the medium of social cohesion and integration. Rituals were necessarily related to all this. Since peace and welfare depend upon the gods, the proper worship due to them must be offered in order to preserve society as a whole. When, under Constantine, Christianity became the official religion, it inherited the role of offerer of the former public cult of the gods. Sacrifices might have ceased, but the Christian sacrifice was now pleaded on behalf of the ruler and the empire. Society continued to have a religious goal, and Christianity assumed responsibility for its realization.[22]

5. *Ritual symbolizes values and leads to commitment*

According to Monica Wilson: 'Rituals reveal values at their deepest level . . . men express in ritual what moves them most, and since the form of expression is conventionalized and obligatory, it is the values of the group that are revealed.'[23] Consequently in any act of worship there is not just an amalgam of separation, transition and incorporation, as van Gennep argued; there is also an accompanying moral commitment to the values declared. In other words, ritual requires the assumption by the group of a range of responsibilities. There may be a vesting with rights, but there is also an acceptance of responsibilities. Through ritual a person may be presented with a role as a member of society, but at the same time it imposes accountability for the proper exercise of that role. Every part that a man plays in society has some instrumental or utilitarian end, but each carries with it a dimension of responsibility. Ritual serves to enjoin, sanction and symbolize this aspect and so places the status or role in the moral order.[24]

6. *Ritual ensures continued orientation to the socially accepted reality*

Ritual is an instrument to 'remind' society of the divine order upon which it is believed to be based. Further, it 'makes present' the fundamental definitions of reality and their appropriate legitimization. It does this both verbally, by enunciating them, and in action to restore the continuity between the present moment and the societal tradition, 'placing the experience of the individual and the various groups of the society in the context of a history (fictitious or not) that transcends them all'.[25] So Christian worship recalls the action of Christ and reaffirms the gospel as the basis of reality.

7. *Ritual gives coherence to life-experience*

Worship is a social rite which symbolizes the totality of what is meaningful to the people involved. It provides for encounter with socially shared symbols that unify human experience in the world, invest it with meaning and relate it to ultimate concern.

It will be apparent that these seven ways in which ritual contributes to the formation and maintenance of social order are all closely interwoven. Together they provide a comprehensive definition of ritual, from its functional aspect, in terms of social relations – using 'social' here to mean 'of society as a whole'. The definition, however, stems from past and/or primitive tribal societies.[26]* Even Christianity, as it developed, did not escape from this matrix. The empire, in a sense, was one large tribe, welded together by common citizenship, a common allegiance to the ruler and a common religion. In medieval Europe the 'nations' were still tribes writ large. At the Reformation, the acceptance of the principle *cujus regio, ejus religio* shows the persistance of the same concept. At the present day, the survival of an established Church of England or of Scotland, and of the folk churches in Germany and Scandinavia, rests upon this tribal basis. Nationalism, whether in its Nazi form or in its 'white' variety in South Africa, are further examples. By accepting this social reference, as part of its almost unavoidable response to historical circumstances, Christianity underwent a certain degree of tribalization. In fact, it tended towards social henotheism rather than radical monotheism. The terms are those of Richard Niebuhr. He defined henotheism as 'that social faith which marked a finite society, whether cultural or religious, the object of trust as well as of loyalty';[27] in other words, society itself became the centre of value, and religion and ritual its support.

The bearing of this upon the problem of worship today is twofold. First, the inherited ritual, being implicitly henotheistic, compromises the character of the Christian faith as universal. A tribal religion is inextricably bound up with the society of the tribe, whereas a universal religion is primarily independent of any specific social group or types of group. For the universal religion the social universe is no longer primary.[28] Consequently, a religion whose ritual is largely understandable in relation to a particular society cannot be universal without a transformation of its worship.

Second, society has changed; it has become pluriform. In a state which numbers among its citizens Christians, atheists, agnostics, adherents of Islam, Hindus, etc., no one religion can claim to be the goal of the social order. Moreover, we no longer believe that the welfare of society depends upon the continuing goodwill of the gods. Again, citizens today are not linked by social necessity and a greater freedom of choice lies open to them. Relations are looser, more objective and functional. So the tendency is for religion to become a private concern and therefore to be socially irrelevant. In this situation, to define ritual in terms of social relations becomes virtually impossible.

There are other characteristics of the secular society which, together with those just mentioned, undermine the validity of the previously existing social functions of worship. Because of the privatization of religion, Christian commitment has become reduced to social homogeneity. According to Gibson Winter: 'The service of worship proclaims the sacredness of association by similarity in economic performance symbolizing the insulation of one social rank against another rather than mutual dependence of rich and poor, insider and outsider, strong and weak, leader and led.'[29] Consequently the first two social functions of ritual listed above, viz. the overcoming of anti-social drives and the maintenance of equilibrium, can no longer be executed. Indeed, in modern society conflicts are dispersed, e.g. disputes about politics or economic matters or about the distribution of wages and profits are conducted in isolation from one another and also from family relations. One does not need ritualization to contain and overcome these stresses.

Further, in a modern city the various roles of individuals are segregated from one another, since they are played in different places, e.g. work in a factory, recreation somewhere else and dwelling also elsewhere. So there is no need of ritualization to achieve the third function, viz., the distinction of roles and transference from one to another.

Ritual, and even ceremonial, tends to drop into desuetude in the modern urban situation, where the material basis of life and the fragmentation of roles and activities of themselves segregate social roles. Etiquette and conventions exist, but they do not pass into that mystical association by which tribal peoples often believe that breach, default, and misdemeanour, and even vicious feeling, will bring misfortunes on one's fellows, so that ritual dealing with mystical forces and beings is necessary to redress the equilibrium at any alteration of social disposition, or to establish a new equilibrium in changed relations.[30]

This means in effect that the types of ritual examined by van Gennep are more or less incompatible, in their pristine form, with the structure of modern urban life.

The loss by religion of its former role as guardian of society necessarily involves the abandonment of the fourth function of ritual as a means of guaranteeing the state. Similarly, in a 'permissive' society commitment to certain values through ritual cannot be equated with the acceptance of social norms (function 5). Moreover, the apparent unrelatedness of worship to the problems in the daily lives of people means that it can neither have relevance to social experience nor give it cohesion (functions 6 and 7).

It would appear that this analysis of ritual has brought us to an impasse. If ritual rests necessarily upon the distinction between a sacred and a profane world and so, instead of unifying human existence, splits it asunder, and if its previous social dimension has gradually disappeared, is there anything to be said for the continuation of ritual practices? Is not worship, as Charles Davis has asserted, outdated in the modern era? In other words, although this account of ritual has served to sharpen the problem and so to bring it into focus, continuing the elucidation of the crisis of worship begun in the last chapter, where do we go from here?

First, we would do well to remind ourselves that, despite the present impasse in which worship seems to be confined, ritual would appear to be natural to man. When even birds and animals engage in it, as for example in sex play, it is not surprising to discover that human beings generally regard it as a necessity. Such activities as trooping the colour, the bearing of the torch and the ceremonial lighting of the Olympic flame, the standardized behaviour of football crowds – all these testify to man's predisposition towards formalized celebrations. Indeed Mary Douglas can say:

As a social animal, man is a ritual animal. If ritual is suppressed in one form it crops up in others, more strongly the more intense the social interaction. Without the letters of condolence, telegrams of congratulations and even occasional post cards, the friendship of a separated friend is not a social reality. It has no existence without the rites of friendship. Social rituals create a reality which would be nothing without them. . . . It is impossible to have social relations without symbolic acts.[31]

Such statements do not allow the re-intrusion of the religious *a priori*, as if they meant that man *must* worship by his very nature, so that there has to be a divinity to answer to this inherent need. This would only be the case if I were identifying ritual and worship, whereas I am arguing that ritual can be and is a vehicle of worship. Ritual becomes worship, as it were, when it brings the holy to our awareness. Because man is a ritual animal, worship has its foundation in ordinary human behaviour, but man's ritual activities attain the level of worship only when they are a focusing mechanism to sharpen the perception of the holy.

Ritual, too, is based in the human world. A rite is not an action other than one which a man can and usually does perform; it is a formalization of that which is quite often and commonly done non-ritualistically. The raw material of ritual, therefore, is nothing but ordinary actions, of which certain features are emphasized by rhythmical repetition or in some other way.[32] Hence, to quote Mary Douglas again:

No experience is too lowly to be taken up in ritual and given a lofty meaning. The more personal and intimate the source of ritual symbolism, the more telling its message. The more the symbol is drawn from the common fund of human experience, the more wide and certain its reception.[33]

Rituals are therefore not artificial compositions but have their basis in the natural order and in the sphere of human action, just as baptism, for example, rests upon water and washing. In worship it makes a great deal of difference what a thing may naturally signify. The meaning of a rite cannot be divorced from natural symbolism without its degenerating into either superstition or magic. Thus the secular actions are not indifferent, as if in becoming ritualized they have been invested with an arbitrary connotation. So L. Bouyer says of the eucharist that 'the words of institution simply gave a new meaning to rites already charged with meaning. And the new meaning was not forced upon the natural meaning but rather amplified and enriched it.'[34]

Of course, when worship is divorced from everyday life, as exemplified by our inherited Christian forms which are no longer at home in a secular universe, it ceases to be rooted in the world and a crisis of meaninglessness is created. This suggests that the way forward must involve the rediscovery and the reformulation of the secular basis of worship. This task will be undertaken in a later chapter, but attention has been drawn to it here in order to indicate that the present impasse is not necessarily one in which to remain. Nevertheless, consideration must now be given to the two factors described above which have contributed so markedly to its creation, viz., the understanding of ritual in terms both of the dialectic between the sacred and the profane and of social relations.

The problem in relation to the first is this: if, in the light of Part I, we discard the category of the profane, and so dispose of the dialectic upon which worship has been based, what other foundation can be provided in its place?

The third type of ritual defined above, viz., that which facilitates contact with the holy, has not persisted unaffected by the other two types and in particular by the second category, with its primary emphasis upon separation. The truth of this statement has already been demonstrated by the previous analysis of the structure of Christian initiation in its classified form. If baptism were to be divested of its liminal and postliminal aspects, how would it be understood? A brief answer to this question will show the kind of reformulation needed if a particular ritual is to be defined in terms of the unity of the holy and the secular instead of the dialectic of the sacred and the profane.

Since, as I have argued, the holy is not incompatible with the human condition, baptismal ritual only has a negative aspect in so far as it requires the abandonment, not of secular reality, but of everything that mars or degrades human nature. Baptism has always been understood as a death to sin, i.e. as a casting off of that which makes man less than human. It does not therefore alienate, but raises to maturity. It does not involve rejection of the world but commission to serve in the world, otherwise it would no longer be a medium of integrating the holy and the secular. Instead of baptism being seen as a setting apart – which implies a magical rite – it should be interpreted as conveying the fullness of humanity which is available to all. It is then the instrument of making explicit the unity of the sacred and the secular; it includes an acknowledgment that the holy is a dimension of the whole of life and so it opens up the secular to the holy.

Because we live in the 'already' but 'not yet', because, that is to say, the present situation is one in which the discernment of the holy is always mediated, men need – to use baptismal terminology – to be enlightened, i.e. they need to have the situation illuminated so that they can perceive the holy in and through the secular medium. Baptism thus enables man to be truly secular, since it liberates him from distortions and the deification of the secular order to see it as it is and so engage in it. To understand baptism in this way means that the baptized know that they continue to live and work in the same world as before, 'what happens is simply that they begin to treat this external world in the right way, which means that they now serve those with whom they come in touch rather than exploit them. . . . Baptism points beyond itself to the relationships into which it brings the baptized. It is the reverse of the acquisitive attitude. . . . It points outward to the neighbour, i.e. to service which is still to be done for the benefit of the neighbour'.[35] But this service, as I have repeatedly emphasized, is an encounter with the holy.

So short and incomplete an analysis[36]* is not sufficient to demonstrate fully how the replacement of the dialectic of the sacred and the profane by the affirmation of the unity of the holy and the secular affects our understanding of ritual. In effect I am saying that worship should not be interpreted as that which facilitates contact with the holy, but should rather be comprehended as that which assists us to find the holy in everyday life. Hence I agree with Harvey Cox that 'the matter of Christ's presence in worship opens our eyes to the way he is present in the world'.[37] Of course, if worship is cut off from worldly existence, it cannot provide the help that is required. It cannot 'sensitize' us to the encounter with the holy in the secular. A sacral cultus over against a profane world does not allow for any bridge. It simply constitutes a liturgical life which runs parallel to one immersed in the secular and so never touches it. Instead of this, however,

Religious action – cultus – like religious knowledge, must create its forms out of the experiences of the daily life and the actual situation. The cultus is supposed to give an ultimate meaning to the daily life. It is not so important to produce new liturgies as it is to penetrate into the depths of what happens day by day, in labour and industry, in marriage and friendship, in social relations and recreation, in meditation and tranquillity, in the unconscious and conscious life. To elevate all this into the light of the eternal is the great task of cultus, and not to reshape a tradition traditionally.[38]

Using somewhat more traditional terms, John Macquarrie makes the same point when he writes:

The sacrament of the altar, like the incarnation itself, which it re-presents, becomes a focus of interpretation for the material world as well. This is seen as a sacramental world that has become transparent to the God who has made it and put himself in it.[39]

If, however, one of the functions of worship is to sharpen our perception of the holy, then the concept of the holy embodied in the ritual will affect that perception. The numinous element in present services thus predisposes us to recognize the holy in everyday life in the form of the unexpected. But this, as I have argued at length, is a misconception which both warps and renders useless the sensitivity envisaged. It is useless because its character, by definition, precludes encounter with it outside the liturgy, apart from a limited number of unusual experiences related to fear and trembling and creature-feeling. If, however, we change our understanding of the holy, our understanding of worship must be altered also.

This may be expressed in a slightly different way. Culture is dumb and does not itself disclose the holy. Hence the need for worship, which will necessarily adopt a cultural form, to enable man to perceive the holy in and through cultural activity. This means that worship cannot be cut off and regarded as the exclusive sphere of the holy. But that is precisely what has happened. Our forms of worship emphasize separation in order to affirm transcendence, which is equated with the holy. The traditional plan of a church, with sanctuary apart from the congregation, is regarded as a proper expression of this. So there are those today who object strongly to the siting of the altar in the midst of the people, because they understand the spatial distance previously obtaining as the affirmation of the necessary apartness of the holy. Similarly, a modern writer can argue in favour of a screen on the grounds that it adds 'a certain sanctity'.[40] Here the numinous appears once more; the holy is the 'wholly other' and must be isolated. This is to reject the New Testament model of the holy, whereby it is identified with mankind, so bridging the gap. To equate the holy with separation is to deny the Incarnation and to affirm that the gulf has not been bridged.

By confining the holy to the cultic area and by making it exclusively a realm apart, the sacred has been uprooted from its vital humus, from its earthly attachment, from its existential values, from the whole of human existence which in its depths has a window, more or less open, upon the beyond in all its personal and collective experiences. . . . If one wishes to remove the holy from existence in time, if one makes it an enemy of the necessary and proper autonomy of the secular, it is not surprising that there is a loss of the sense of the sacred. It is no longer provided with daily nourishment by earthly realities which themselves have a sacred signification, in no way in contradiction to their secularity, their existence or their own end, if we understand the sacred and the secular as twin existential dimensions present in every reality.[41]*

So the dialectic between the sacred and the profane has to be replaced by another dialectic, i.e. that between secular life in and through which the holy may be encountered and ritual acts on a secular basis in and through which the encounter is made explicit.

In this last statement we have in part an answer to a possible question: if the holy is met in and through the secular, what is the point of specifically religious activities? Yet the question is really misconceived. There are no 'specifically religious' activities. Worship is as much a secular event, with a dimension of the holy, as is political activity. This does not mean that the ritual acts are gaps in our secular existence; they are acts beside, but related to, other acts. Just as someone having a bath cannot at the same time be a guest at a dinner party, so when worshipping we do not, at the same time, work on the assembly line or prepare a school lesson. It is the relation of the ritual acts to the rest of life that is vital. Thus conceived ritual does not involve a rupture in man's being; it is not the celebration of a sacred schizophrenia. It is the celebration of the secular, in and through which the meeting with the holy takes place. It is not an interruption in secular living, but part and parcel of it, making explicit that meaning which is to be discovered in the whole of life. Hence ritual is not to be considered in itself nor for itself, but only within the totality of life. Worship, says Roqueplo, 'is not authentically sacramental unless it refers meaningfully to our whole existence which itself contains the "reality" signified and actualized by the sacrament.'[42]

This essential unity of sacred and secular, of worship and life, may be clarified by reference to a concrete situation. In 1968 the Bishop of Birmingham conducted a service of thanksgiving to mark the completion and the opening for use of SS Philip and James, Hodge Hill, which he had previously commissioned the Institute for the Study of Worship and Religious Architecture in the University of Birmingham to build; this new 'church' embodies and expresses the unity of the sacred and the secular.[43] It does so because in design and use the so-called nave area is the scene both of worship and of such secular activities as dancing, table-tennis, eating, etc. The Hodge Hill plan has unified the sacred and the secular in spatial terms. But if the unity is to be a true one, it must also be achieved in terms of time. To employ the same space for worship and for a modern play is to unify spatially the sacred and the secular, but there may still remain a temporal dichotomy. So the identical space may at one time be employed for sacred use and at a later hour for secular use. The separation is then not completely overcome. To overcome it, we have to unite the sacred and secular in all our activities. There is, however, a danger here which, if not guarded against, could result in the sacralizing of the secular. To begin a performance of a modern drama with a few prayers might seem to unite sacred and secular, but in fact it is merely to sacralize the secular. The way out of this temporal dichotomy is, in part, to secularize worship, i.e. to recover the secular basis of ritual so that through its cultic acts the congregation learns to appreciate the unity of the sacred and the secular. If this is achieved, then all activities can be known and experienced as extensions of or aspects of this worshipful response to the holy on the basis of the secular. The play or dance need not then be sacralized; they stand on their own as secular activities, but they become infused with a spirit which sees in these secular acts the presence of the holy, because in worship the perception of the holy in and through the secular has been sensitized.

Hence there is no need to make special arrangements in connection with secular activities (such as prefacing them with a prayer) in order to discern the holy in and through them; the holy is there in any case. One is living the unity of the sacred and the secular just as much by special acts of worship on a secular basis as by engaging in a specifically secular activity in which one meets the holy. The unity is a fact; we do not create it; we do have to discern it. Secular worship is to make the unity explicit and sensitize us to the holy in and through the secular.

Now there has been some imprecision in my use of terms so far in this analysis based upon SS Philip and James. It will be evident that I do not accept either the separation or the antithesis between the sacred and the secular. I do, however, accept a distinction between them, but I only know them in their unity, since the one mediates the other. Hence to talk of 'sacred' activities is meaningless; and to talk of 'secular' activities is equally misleading. Every activity is at the same time both sacred and secular. Our mistake as regards worship is to conceive of it as a specifically 'sacred' action. To ensure that it is so, we isolate it from the secular and in so doing make it unreal. Any so-called 'sacred' activity *per se* is without meaning and relevance. By endorsing the view that there are 'sacred' activities distinct from secular ones, we deny the unity manifested in Christ; we then create a make-believe world which has nothing to do with the everyday world, and in effect we turn aside from the holy.

All this means that we have to state that sacred and secular are two aspects of a unified experience. Every activity is *at the same time* secular, i.e. a human activity, and also sacred, i.e. a divine activity. The distinction in analytical thought enables us to appreciate the dual character of experience, although that experience is itself a unity. So there are not separate sacred experiences and secular experiences, sacred activities and secular activities; there are only experiences and activities possessing this twofold character. Thus to say that worship is a sacred act but dancing is a secular one is incorrect. Worship is a sacred/secular act and so is dancing. Consequently, for the worship at Hodge Hill to correspond with what its architecture is saying there should be a spatio-temporal unification of the sacred and the secular; this means that the secular dimension of worship should be evident and the sacred depths of secular activities should be perceived.

This way of thinking can be further illustrated from the eucharist, which is the supreme model of this perspective. It is an act of worship and it does involve eating and drinking. If it is regarded as an entirely sacred act, then the consumption of food is sacralized. If the consumption of food is seen as an entirely secular act, then a necessary dimension of the service as a whole is lost. The eucharist is a sacred/secular ritual; it has a dual character, since in it sacred and secular are united. Because this is its nature, the eucharist can be a means whereby we are enabled to appreciate this unity and so recognize it in the whole of life. It is a key to secular living. In a sense every meal is a eucharist, as is, of course, strongly emphasized by the Quakers. I would, however, contend that without the sacrament this understanding could soon be lost. Even the Quakers, who see all life as sacramental and therefore deny the need for a specific sacrament, would be unlikely to perceive the sacramental nature of life if there had not been sixteen hundred years of sacramental practice before they came into existence and if they had not before them the New Testament witness to the eucharist to help them to preserve this insight. Just as the Last Supper was not an isolated incident but was the culmination of the many meals which Jesus had with his disciples, leading on to the Lord's Supper of the early church, so the eucharist is not an isolated act but the culmination of many meals throughout the week.

Perhaps sufficient has now been said to support the validity of ritual in a secular universe on a basis other than that of the sacred/profane dichotomy. Further consideration of this can be postponed until later, as we turn to examine the second element in the current impasse, viz. that which concerns the social dimension of ritual.

The problem in relation to the social dimension of ritual is this: what is to be done when, because of social change, ritual loses its meaning? Ritual, as we have seen, has been developed to provide for social interaction. However, when society undergoes a radical transformation, as in its passage from a sacral to a secular universe, the social action in which the ritual inhered no longer exists and so worship has no basis.[44]

It is as well to recall that the social dimension of ritual, as analysed by the anthropologists, has not always been, and so need not always be, the same. In the pre-Constantinian era Christian worship was not an expression of social relations, using 'social' here again in the sense of 'society as a whole'. Indeed, membership of the Christian community cut across social relations – witness the equality within worship of slaves and freemen. Of course, the understanding of Christian ritual in the Middle Ages is impossible without taking into account these relations because Christianity was the religion of the entire society and its rituals, e.g. the coronation service, were embedded in the tribe or nation. The situation before Constantine was entirely different. The early Christians were concerned about society, for example they prayed for the emperor, but their ritual was not an expression of their roles within pagan society. This indicates that worship has been, and therefore should be, possible in what may be called a dispersion situation. Hence what is needed at the present day is an understanding of ritual in this new context. This cannot be achieved simply by adopting the perspective of the modern anthropologist whose material derives largely from those societies where society and 'church' are one. His emphasis upon social relations is both legitimate and necessary in relation to the subject with which he is dealing, but it does not provide the key to interpreting Christian ritual in the early church nor to reconceptualizing it in contemporary secular society.

At the present day, there is a tendency for church leaders to continue to regard Christianity, probably unconsciously, as a tribal (or national) religion and to cling to the existing structures in the hope that the nation will once again return to the faith of its forefathers. This is a vain hope, but the alternative is not to retribalize Christianity in terms of contemporary society, but to perceive its role as a universal religion in relation to society. The role of a universal religion must obviously differ from that of a tribal religion. It sits loosely in relation to the society in which it is present because, unlike tribal religion, it is not primarily concerned with the maintenance of social order. Indeed frequently it sits in judgment upon the existing social order. When Christianity supports the *status quo*, and forgets the eschatological proviso, it acts as a tribal religion and compromises its universal character. While the principal role of a tribal religion is to contain change and provide through its ritual for its accommodation, Christianity, as a universal faith, should be concerned to promote change – change, not for its own sake, but for the sake of humanization.

The loss of its former social role has involved Christianity in a crisis of identity, simply because the world in which it is present is a social world. Failure to realize this has resulted in the complaints of conservative churchmen that many modern theologians are undermining the old certainties. Whereas these scholars, and the present book, are simply accepting the fact that the old certainties have in any case been eroded and are seeking to discover the identity of their faith in a changed situation, believing that 'whoever would save his life will lose it'.[45] But if the social role of religion is altered, the function of its ritual has also to be changed, otherwise the Christian will experience a conflict between himself as a believer and a worshipper and as a member of secular society. Those who continue to worship according to the old forms will find their cultus less and less socially relevant and therefore ultimately meaningless.

This new or rediscovered social role has a dual aspect. It involves, as we have seen previously, both social criticism and outgoing concern to those in need. The former task immediately produces a contrast with inherited ritual. According to Cazeneuve, 'the primitive seeks to enclose himself in a system of rules which can define for him a human condition free from anxiety and so, to a certain extent, assure him an ideal situation of inertia'.[46] Ritual then operates as a sedative and preserves social equilibrium. But when the early Christians worshipped the holy in the crucified Jesus, they were in fact overthrowing the nerve-centre of the political religion and the religious politics of their time. Similarly, today, the worship of the holy in the crucified Jesus calls in question the *status quo*. Worship in fact is revolutionary and is the means whereby the hoped-for future is brought into practical contact with the present.[47]

There are, of course, Christians who would reject this role of social criticism and stand apart from the political struggle. They believe that the church should not take sides. But as Jürgen Moltmann puts it, 'This is the old ecclesiastical triumphalism in modern dress. . . . Here the church is always "the third power", a "neutral platform" for peace and reconciliation, a "place for meeting and negotiation".'[48] But the church cannot be reticent when the humiliation and slavery of men is in question. It is not a heavenly arbiter amidst the world's strife, and must soil its hands and identify itself with those who struggle for humanization, in the knowledge that in so doing it will lose the support of many. Yet even in relation to those movements that are devoted to humanization, Christianity, as a universal religion, stands somewhat loosely, since it has also to attack the infection of presumption and of resignation amongst the various groups directed towards freedom and social justice *as well as* in itself. To exercise social criticism in this way is not to claim to be more revolutionary than the revolutionaries, for this task can only be accomplished through involvement. But while being alert to what is possible in the present, the church must also investigate and seize new historical possibilities.[49] To execute this role, the church cannot consist of gatherings of like minded people. While there is a common task, its accomplishment requires a variety of professions and representatives of all social levels.

Ritual today, then, is concerned with responsibility; it has to express the responsibility of Christians in the social, political and economic spheres.

The Church's worship must express a critical attitude to social evil. It must inspire political commitment which is needed and personal dissent from what is evil in our society, both at the national and international level.[50]

So worship becomes a celebration of hope and a centre of stimulation for the active reshaping of the world. Unless this is achieved, it will be abstracted from human life in the world; it will have no point of contact with the problems in the lives of individuals nor with their social experience. Unless it so accommodates and modifies its product, Christianity will simply entrench itself in a ghetto. It will take refuge in the temple as a place of liturgical security. It will display a spirituality founded upon the numinous.

God would not be God if he were not efficaciously present 'always and everywhere'; in particular, God would not be God if he were not present 'here and now'. This means that a spiritual attitude which always seeks God 'elsewhere' or 'apart from' the concrete circumstances of our existence – as if these very circumstances were not themselves mysteriously invested with his presence – constitutes in my view an attitude that is intrinsically contradictory and so mortal.[51]

The second aspect of the social relatedness of ritual today involves outgoing in concern. Worship should be a source of creative and inventive imagination in the service of love. One might perhaps suggest that it should be something like an amalgam of a gathering of Alcoholics Anonymous and a branch meeting of radicals! Certainly the ones with whom Jesus ate and drank were the social outcasts of his day, i.e. those who were marginal to society and in need of love. This concern for others should find its focus in ritual which is understood in terms of community or fellowship.

Worship is indeed personal, but this does not mean, of course, that it is just the concern of individuals. It must be experienced in the first place in personal terms, but it is about people and their relations with one another and their neighbours outside – in a word, its context is essentially communal.[52]

So worship is the liturgical expression of the love of neighbour, and its point of reference is always beyond itself in the world of human need. Nevertheless, much depends upon how we understand community, as distinct from society as a whole – for this, too, has vastly changed under the impact of the technological revolution. It is on this subject that we must concentrate in the following chapter.

12

Community, Fellowship and Worship

The intimate connection between community and worship has long been recognized. It would be relatively easy to produce a whole series of statements to the effect that worship is the central act of the Christian *community* or that worship is the principal means of building up the Christian *community*. Nevertheless, such affirmations are highly ambiguous, since it is frequently impossible to discover how the word 'community' is understood. Its meaning is assumed rather than defined; the presupposition is that everyone knows what community is and so, because it is self-evident, no explanation is required. Upon a little reflection, however, one soon realizes that the matter is not so simple. The term is used in many different contexts and in many different ways. One speaks of the 'international community', which presumably refers to the desired solidarity between all human beings, no matter what their race or colour. One points to the 'academic community', presupposing a common concern and even a fellowship between the various scholars and students which scarcely exists, and probably can never exist, in view of the constantly increasing numbers involved in higher education of this kind. Again, it is possible to employ community of a small group based upon interpersonal relations. Clearly the term is not being used in the same way in these several contexts.

It would appear that when theologians and churchmen speak of the Christian community, many of them frequently have in mind the medieval village unit. Indeed, church structures in the West, based as they are upon the parochial system, embody this very concept. What, then, were its characteristics?

A village was a social unity; it was a territorial area of restricted dimensions within which everyone knew everyone else. Its population found its residence, its work and its play all within its boundaries. There was an unavoidable interchange which promoted interest in other people, over and above any utilitarian project in which they may have been engaged. Conversation was the chief means of communication. Indeed, the development and coherence of the community depended upon it. The spoken word was the instrument of cultural diffusion; news was passed from mouth to mouth; it exercised social control and provided the principal means of distraction. Through personal relations the community was integrated, but certain professions contributed more to this than others: e.g., the barber in his shop was a focus of meeting and a centre for the sharing of information.[1]

Worship, in this situation, was the occasion when those who knew one another gathered together and strengthened the ties that bound their already existing community, i.e. it was an assembly of a pre-existing community. The Sunday service was an important occasion for going out of the house and encountering one's fellow villagers; hence the importance, too, of conversation and interpersonal contacts before, during and after the service. This pattern of life favoured stability, respect for tradition and for nature, and it allowed the development of primary relations.

With the onset of urbanization, this rural model was applied to the towns. Towns were conceived as aggregations of village units. Each parish, therefore, had to have its central church, its hall and often its school. Worship was the occasion when those who lived within its boundaries and knew one another as neighbours came together to strengthen their ties as an existing local community.

The principal sociological character of the parochial structure has always been its correspondence with a social group or its being a constitutive element within it. When a particular area formed the basis of a group, the parish was organized on that basis. The village constituted the unity of rural life and to each one there corresponded a religious unity. Towns in the preindustrial era were characterized by a social life strongly structured by neighbourhoods, and so parishes were adapted to each one of them.[2]

This model had certain disadvantages. The village community tended to be an enclosed one, and so it often displayed an inability to integrate newcomers and an ability to foment discord when disputes arose. Nevertheless, it would be a mistake to sit in judgment upon it, as if the values embodied were false. Experience of community and its expression in worship were valid. Its proportions were according to a human scale, so that man did not feel himself dwarfed. He was able to achieve identity and find meaning in his life. He could enjoy face-to-face encounters. In this web of interwoven I-Thou relations, he could and did meet the holy.

Because of its positive features, this concept has remained for many the implicit ideal of community and is used as a yardstick to measure other 'communities', i.e. they are praised or condemned to the extent to which they correspond to the village model. In much theological writing, where community is applied to the church, it is precisely this connotation – of the village community – that is given to it. This, as we have just noted, has determined ecclesiastical strategy in the great conurbations, which are regarded as agglomerations of village communities. It still continues to operate, in that new housing areas are deemed to need a church and new towns themselves are divided up into parishes. The advocates of the 'Parish Communion', the supporters of 'Parish and People' in England, and indeed the Liturgical Movement in general have worked with this model as their implicit and unquestioned basis. Unfortunately the model no longer corresponds with social reality – this is particularly evident in the industrialized West, and is becoming prevalent in all countries where the move to the towns appears to be an irreversible trend.

In the rural situation the community was based upon the locality, all social functions being united in one and the same geographical area. In a town, however, due to specialization and diversification, these functions are dispersed over a very wide area indeed. The husband goes to work in one quarter, the wife may shop in another, the children may go to school in a third, while the family as a whole will seek entertainment elsewhere. So individuals neither work where they live nor spend their leisure-time there. The consequence is that in a residential area personal relations may be non-existent, and without this direct contact and sharing of interests, ideas and news, there exists no *local* community within which anyone can be integrated. Specialized functions, such as work, social welfare and health, are based in institutions which create their own centres, and it is to these that people come from all over town. In some of them, e.g. a factory, men and women may spend a large proportion of their time and so establish relations beyond the boundaries of the parish in which they have their home. A new social life now opens up to the town dweller, however important his house and family base may remain. Community based upon locality then has meaning only for those who are non-active – the aged and the infirm – or are otherwise tied to the place of residence – mothers with young children.

The consequence of this transformation is that relations between fellow citizens become less and less primary, i.e. face-to-face, and more and more functional. One chooses one's doctor because he is the best available and not because one hopes to make him a family friend. One prefers supermarkets because the extent of personal engagement with the staff is minimal. Many workers favour large industrial concerns because they wish to claim rights with greater ease than is possible in small firms where personal relations with management are close. This functional dimension of urban living changes the types of relations between individuals and the basis of those relationships. Those relations no longer perform the role that they did in the village, where they were the means of ensuring the unity and continuity of social life. In the city they are replaced by mass-media. The newspapers and the television provide information and news. They now operate, side by side with the newly created institutions, as instruments of socialization. Social homogenization ceases to depend upon conversations with other people, nor does support of a good cause require personal interaction – one can respond separately to a radio appeal.

Urban man becomes mobile man, changing his abode and travelling hither and thither to perform different functions. He no longer belongs to a single uniform group, but to a multiplicity of groups, based on work, leisure, etc. Recreation itself is catered for by a specialized entertainments industry, so that one can, for example, visit a cinema without the necessity of knowing anyone else who happens to be there at the same time.

The positive value of this new situation is that the individual now has a greater freedom of choice and a certain autonomy. He can create his own social universe. He does not have to engage in conversations with everyone he meets nor need he seek intimate knowledge of his neighbours. He is liberated to foster relations with people whom he himself has selected. The requirement to give assent is replaced by the freedom to consent. In the village the self-determination of the individual was swallowed up in the all-embracing unity of the group. He was subordinated to the community which was concerned not so much to foster his welfare as to maintain and strengthen its own life. The individual was a means, and he was only an end as part of the whole. The urban situation favours the rise of the personality to conscious self-determination and enables him to transcend his social ties. Yet there is a concurrent danger.

While 'social groups lose their power to crush and to mutilate personality, they also lose their power to create and protect it'.[3] With the breakdown of the village-type community under the impact of urbanization, there arise conditions that favour social disintegration,

in which first the community and then the personality is deprived of its spiritual substance. But, since there is no vacuum in social life any more than in nature, other powers enter the space left by the disintegration of the original social unity, especially economic factors, psychological mechanisms, sociological constellations. The personality, after having undermined the community, is undermined itself, even though it be legally recognized and even though it is aware of ethical demands. The present situation gives abundant evidence of this statement.[4]

Before proceeding to consider this further, let us look at the effect of the demise of the neighbourhood-based community upon worship. Clearly worship in an urban context can no longer be understood in terms of the gathering of a pre-existing village type community. Moreover, the freedom of choice, to which reference has just been made, is bound to influence the individual's liturgical practice. On the one hand, he will feel at liberty to go to whatever service – if any – in whatever place he likes. On the other hand, because the circumstances of city life encourage a certain distance from one's neighbours, he may not wish to become too closely involved with them, and to preserve his autonomy will worship away from his place of residence. In so far as the Christian is a man of his age, he cannot be expected to seek relations that decrease his freedom and inhibit his choice. It must be expected that he will seek the experience of worship in more than one place, and there is no reason why he should participate in the cultus in his parish church. This outlook, too, has both advantages and disadvantages.

On the positive side, it compels us to look again at the understanding of liturgy as the act of pre-existing community. In so doing we become aware that this interpretation can produce erroneous results.

It tends to make the rite no more than an expression of contemporary culture and so the prisoner of it; then worship becomes simply a means of sacralizing society. The liturgy is not creative of community, but just sacralizes one that is already in being. Indeed the new context within which worship has to take place today can liberate it, too, and enable us to examine it afresh apart from the perspective of Christendom. In the Middle Ages the cultic assembly was the celebration of a community that was already in being, but this was not the situation in the pre-Constantinian era. Then individuals did exercise their freedom of choice; they associated together because they consented to do so. The fact that the early Christian congregations were not natural communities indicates that neither at the present day do worshipping groups have to be such. It is only if we allow ourselves to be mesmerized by the medieval pattern that we think that there can be no credible alternative. If this is positive gain, we also have to acknowledge that the present outlook has a disadvantage. If, following the argument in Part I, one of the primary loci of the encounter with the holy is I-Thou relations, anyone who attends a liturgical assembly consisting of so many unknown individuals will find himself in a situation where such relations do not exist. Without some sort of community – in the sense of a series of interlocking I-Thou encounters – worship will lack any basis in human reality and will progressively seem more irrelevant. This means that we have to pursue the quest for community within the urban situation and examine further the undermining of community which, according to the quotation given above, Paul Tillich believes is evident at the present day.

The lack of community within a technological civilization may be illustrated shortly by reference to four diverse subjects. First, there is the condition of many old people. Reports are now frequent of the finding of the dead bodies of the aged, undiscovered for days because they lived alone and no one cared for them. No more poignant nor pathetic example could be adduced of the extent to which loneliness is a factor to be reckoned with today; such loneliness is the result of the absence of community. The hippy movement may provide a second example. Its adherents are very much exercised about community, even though they are frequently naive about the structure necessary for its preservation. They have a strong sense of personal encounter and a shared concern and commitment. Stuart Hall observes of them that they desire to recreate 'the peace and gentle cohesiveness of the tribal community', and so oppose individualism and competition in favour of a new kind of togetherness.[5] Their existence is in part a demonstration that what they want, viz. community, they have not found within existing urban society, and have therefore sought to create it for themselves.[6]

For a third example, one may turn to the many small sects which are currently proliferating. Cardinal Suenens observes that

one of the reasons for the attraction which small sects exercise over their members ... lies precisely in their nature as sects, small groups, where everybody knows everybody else. They are personal societies. ... Can we not say that this paradoxical example proves with urgency how necessary it is for us to reduce our ecclesial communities to a size which is human?[7]

My fourth illustration is the phenomenon of the sit-in. To observe this, within a university, is to become aware that, whatever the immediate pretext for the action, the effect upon the participants is to give them a sense of unity which they did not have before. As student discusses with student about their common concern, often held with a passionate moral fervour, across the academic disciplinary barriers that previously separated them; as they talk with members of the staff, with whom they may not have exchanged a word hitherto, the predominant functional relations are temporarily replaced by face-to-face encounters. For a short time community exists because I-Thou relations are formed. The disappointment when the sit-in ends and the previous functional relations reassert themselves is evidence of the felt lack of a communal dimension in their lives. They have a need, although it is not often articulated, for I-Thou relations; i.e., their experience shows their subconscious recognition that a person comes into being only in relation with other persons and that this requires something more than just functional relationships.[8]

Nevertheless, 'functional relations are not necessarily humanly poorer. They can be more in evidence in certain situations, and the city tends to favour them, as they provide a climate of greater autonomy.'[9] But this does not mean that personal relations are not valued. The questions are: where are they to be found and how are they to be fostered?

Certainly the city itself cannot be regarded as either an aggregrate of village units nor, taken as a whole, as a community based upon personal relations with everyone knowing everyone else. Yet there would appear to be something in such statements as: 'I am a

Parisian. . . I am a Londoner.' These affirmations mean more than that I happen to live in Paris or in London. They suggest that Paris has a character of its own and so has London. This character derives in part from the buildings, but also from the inhabitants. So one may speak of a city *community* as long as one is aware that in so doing one is using the word in a sense different from that which can be applied to the village of medieval times. The city community depends upon a multiplicity of more or less autonomous groups which allow both for the development of personal life and for the promotion of practical projects for the common good. It is by this means that a diffuse solidarity is achieved. Collective symbols support this identity, e.g. public buildings of which one is proud, a city centre full of animation or a repertory theatre with a national reputation. Inter-city sporting activities also reinforce this community spirit.

However, it is to the groups that we must now turn our attention as possibly viable forms of community, which support the larger city 'community' and enable individuals to feel that they have a part in the whole.

It is customary to divide groups into those that are primary, i.e. involving the members in direct relationships, and those that are secondary, i.e. the members being indirectly related. If we concentrate upon primary groups, we find that these may also be divided into various categories, such as 'socio-group' and 'psyche-group'.[10] For the purposes of this present study, however, the most helpful distinction is that between affective and instrumental groups. Affective groups are those that express the emotional life of individuals and contribute to its security. They give a meaning to existence and provide a model with which to identify. Examples of this type include the family, a revolutionary cadre, a fan club, or even a research team which has engaged the devotion of its co-workers.[11] Such a group may also be called a reference group, i.e. it is the one which a member may take as his point of reference, identifying with it and seeking to imitate it.

In an instrumental group participation is determined as a function of the objective to be attained. So a group devoted to the improvement of housing in a particular locality may include various experts, such as a lawyer, a social worker, a town councillor, etc., each of whom will contribute from his specialized knowledge to the production and implementation of the plan. The affective group tends to find its place outside public life, although it can provide a centre of reference to one who is temporarily a member of an instrumental group devoted to a project which is related to public life. In order to have a communal dimension, both groups have to provide – and indeed by definition as primary groups do provide – a high degree of social interaction. The size of each group has therefore to be restricted, for studies have shown that the larger the group, the more the individual feels inhibited. Indeed, there appears to exist a general principle that as the size of a group increases an increasing number of people is reduced to silence.[12] Social interaction is then limited and face-to-face relations are correspondingly minimized in large gatherings. This means that a contrast has to be drawn between those groups that foster 'community' and those that, by their very nature, do not allow it to develop. In other words, one must differentiate community from aggregate or collectivity.[13]

Various terms are used to point to this distinction. In sociology, the word 'community' was introduced in Germany in the nineteenth century by Tonnies in opposition to 'association'. The latter is defined as a group which has deliberately constituted itself to pursue a particular objective; it corresponds, therefore, to the instrumental group, in which relations are based upon rationality, i.e. upon a calculation to obtain the maximum effect with the minimum effort.[14] This is not to say that an instrumental group may not involve face-to-face encounters, but that is not of its essence.

A 'statistical' group is one of which the members have the impression that they have no influence upon the proceedings as a whole.[15] Thus the audience at a theatre may be said to constitute such a group, in that any one of those sitting in the stalls or circle could absent himself without this affecting the performance in any way. Alternatively, such a collection of people may be termed an 'aggregate'; i.e., those present are in physical proximity but there exists virtually no relations between them. In contrast, a community must involve active participation, a sense of solidarity and a sharing in the fulfilment of a common task.[16]

Consequently community means participation. Indeed participation is impossible apart from others; when an individual can achieve an objective on his own, he does not speak of participation. So, for example, if I light a cigarette with a match from a box that I possess, I am in no sense participating in anything. But if I lack a match and someone else strikes one of his for me, he is participating in the lighting of my cigarette. Participation, therefore, refers to a collective action in which the individual has his part to play, and it therefore involves interaction between people in order to bring to a successful conclusion an action which could not be accomplished in isolation.[17]

Participation is the greater the more one is affectively identified with a group. Moreover, active participation in decisions reached requires full discussion of all problems. The participation will only have meaning if one also knows that there exists the possibility of influencing the outcome. Here again, the size of the group is important. The smaller it is, the greater the chance of active participation. The structure of a group, too, affects participation, for if it is dominated by one individual, who is accorded a position of supreme authority, the participation will be minimal.

J. Rémy distinguishes four aspects of participation:

1. Cultural participation: individuals can only participate fully in a group if they are at home with its language and customs.
2. Affective participation: this refers to the individual's identification with the group and his sense of being an integral and responsible member of it.
3. Decision-making participation: the members consider that they can influence the decisions that will determine the group's future. The exact form this may take, e.g. discussion by all or by one's representative, may differ from group to group.
4. Intellectual participation: the individuals inform themselves about and understand what is happening.[18]

So far this analysis has been presented exclusively in sociological terms; now it is time to add a more philosophical understanding of community. For this I turn to the thought of Martin Buber. Buber contrasts community with both individualism and collectivism.

Individualism sees man only in relation to himself, but collectivism does not see man at all, it sees only 'society'. With the former man's face is distorted, with the latter it is masked.[19]

Collectivity is not a binding but a bundling together.... Community is the being no longer side by side but with one another.... Collectivity is based on an organized atrophy of personal existence, community on its increase and confirmation in life lived towards one another.[20]

Buber regards collectivism as typical of the present age in giving the appearance but not the reality of relations. It denies the dialogue between man and man so that each remains essentially isolated. Instead of his alienation from his fellows being overcome, he is overpowered and numbed. Man is not *with* man but *alongside* man. Separation persists so that man is, as it were, smothered as a sound may be drowned out by noise.[21] The collective threatens man with the loss of personality, because, in the words of Ronald Gregor Smith, 'collective man is the man without a face, with only a number'.[22]

This situation has been very clearly delineated by Moses Herzog in Saul Bellow's novel of that name. Herzog descends into the New York subway.

He dropped his fare in the slot where he saw a whole series of tokens lighted from within and magnified by the glass. Innumerable millions of passengers had polished the wood of the turnstile with their hips. From this arose a feeling of communion – brotherhood in one of its cheapest forms. This was serious, thought Herzog as he passed through. The more individuals are destroyed (by processes such as I know) the more their yearning for collectivity. Worse, because they return to the mass agitated, made fervent by their failure. Not as brethren, but as degenerates. Expressing a raging consumption of potato love. Thus occurs a second distortion of the divine image, already so blurred, wavering, struggling.[23]

In opposition to this, Buber bases his understanding of community upon his I-Thou philosophy, not restricting community to dual relations only, but seeing it as constituted by a series of interlocking I-Thou relations. So he speaks of an 'essential We.' By this he means 'a community of several independent persons, who have a self and self-responsibility. . . . The *We* includes the *Thou*. Only men who are capable of saying *Thou* to one another can truly say *We* with one another.'[24] He also contends that:

Community is the being no longer side by side (and, one might add, above and below) but *with* one another of a multitude of persons. And this multitude, though it moves towards one goal, yet experiences everywhere in turning to, a dynamic facing of, the others, a flowing from *I* to *Thou*. Community is where community happens.[25]

The I-Thou relation, as we have previously seen,[26] involves a recognition of the boundlessness of the other; it respects the freedom of the Thou, encounters with whom require complete openness, a surrender of becoming for being, of dissimulation for frankness, and a refusal to dominate. 'True community among men cannot come into being until each individual accepts responsibility for the other.'[27]

It is time, now, to face the question: what does all this mean for worship?

Worship is, in part, to be defined as a means of sensitizing man to the holy. It may, therefore, be understood as a focusing mechanism whereby experience is selected and provided with a frame for concentrated attention. This attention is directed towards the holy as it is mediated through the secular. Expressed christologically, one can say that he 'is the person who comes to definition as the community's self-awareness – an awareness of relatedness to the course of the community's life'.[28] Using slightly different phraseology but making precisely the same point, Ernst Bloch affirms that prior to Jesus 'God had been a mythical periphery, now he has become the humanly adequate, humanly ideal centre, the *centre of the community wherever* it may be gathering in his name'.[29]

Since, however, the primary locus of encounter with the holy is in and through I-Thou relations, worship can fulfil this function only where such relations exist. But, as we learned from the opening pages of this chapter, such relations exist in primary groups, which must be relatively restricted in size to allow a high degree of interaction. This immediately calls in question the value of the large liturgical assembly. Such, of course, does continue to exist, particularly in the United States, where congregations of three to four hundred are not uncommon, and at celebrations of the mass in Roman Catholic churches in Europe. Indeed many churchmen hope for a return to the pews, and an incumbent who increases attendance into the hundreds is considered to be eminently successful. Yet in many respects large assemblies are in conflict with the essential basis of worship in community. The justification for this statement is to be found in certain of the characteristics observable in any large group at the present day.

1. Within the urban situation, large *communities* no longer exist, and so worship in a great assembly cannot be the expression of a pre-existent community.

2. Because of their size, there is an inevitable decrease in the sense of personal responsibility and involvement. Indeed the clericalization of worship in the past was, in part, due to this increase. There is a limit to what the members of a large congregation can be given to do, and so there necessarily arises a distinction between principal actors and spectators. Not everyone can be an actor, otherwise the result would be chaos.

3. Size also inhibits the development and exercise of personal relations.

4. The result is that the large assembly really belongs to the category of a statistical group; i.e., individuals can absent themselves at will, in a way that is impossible in a small group, without their being missed and without affecting what takes place – it will continue as usual. So to give a contemporary illustration, a Christian may attend mass in his local church at 7, 8, 9, or 10 a.m. It does not matter to which he goes, nor if he chooses to be present at different times on successive Sundays. Because he is simply one of a statistical group, his presence or absence does not affect the cultic act.

5. When the worshippers do not know one another, the assembly becomes a collectivity of faceless ones. Worship then is a celebration of alienation because the trans-personal reality of the holy is denied. The large liturgical assembly may proclaim the absence of God.

6. Such aggregates either remain ineffective or, if they are to become single-minded and engage in dynamic action, they have to give way to mob psychology. The mob requires the temporary suspension of individual differences; it has to be adjusted intellectually to its lowest common denominator and there is a surrender of individual responsibility. All this is entirely contrary to the concept of community.

The combined result of these several factors has been a change in the nature of Christian worship. So the eucharist, which initially was a domestic affair patterned upon a meal shared in common by friends, has now become closer to the model of a cafeteria. In the latter, all may have the same food but they are there as isolated individuals; they constitute a collectivity and not a community. Mutuality does not exist. The I-Thou is absent. The locus of the encounter with the holy is not provided.

Contrast all this with the small group. This increases the sense of personal responsibility because each has his role, and the absence of any will affect the efficacy of the whole. It facilitates the establishment and development of personal relations, is the medium of face-to-face encounters and intensifies the sense of belonging. Small groups, in other words, function in an entirely different way from large assemblies and, in so doing, the former correspond more closely to community than the latter.

Lest it seem that I am about to write off the large liturgical assembly forthwith, let me hasten to acknowledge that even small groups have their dangers. They can easily become turned in on themselves. They readily become closed, concerned with the creation of a universe of affective security, and so develop into so many refuges from life. They may intensify social estrangement and attract only those who are already suffering from it. Then they themselves become socially irrelevant, and are often centres of social stagnation. These dire results can be counterbalanced in two ways. On the one hand, each affective group can be made at the same time an instrumental group, so that an outward-looking aspect is built in in terms of tasks to be accomplished. On the other hand, they may be related to a large gathering, so that the particularity of the one is offset by the universality of the other. Indeed it is time to recognize the positive, as distinct from the previously defined negative, aspects of the large assembly.

1. The dissociation between belonging to a small group and belonging to a large 'community' can be a practical sign expressing a coming together which is compatible with the existence of many forms of social belonging. This very dissociation symbolizes the universal character of the assembly.
2. By diminishing the sense of dependency upon the small group, the large one allows the individual freedom of action and choice. By exercising this autonomy, he increases his sense of belonging to the community as a whole, since he freely chooses to be there.
3. Because in a large gathering much has to be on an impersonal level, it can be an open group.
4. The large assembly can transcend and contain the stresses and conflicts that could break up a smaller unit.

Nevertheless, in saying this I have in mind a new model of the large assembly. Hitherto it has generally been regarded as an aggregate of individuals. I am now suggesting that it should become a meeting of groups. This is in accordance with Buber's view, as exemplified by his statement that 'a nation is a community to the degree that it is a community of communities'.[30] Hence the church is not built up of individuals but of communities; or, one can say, slightly transforming Buber's sentence, that 'the church is a community to the degree that it is a community of communities'. In other words, the small group is a key factor in promoting participa-

tion in the large group. The latter becomes effective if it consists
of a gathering of small units in which individuals have had an
active part to play. Participation in the assembly is then achieved by
having participated in the smaller groups, and the coming together
allows for integration in the larger whole.

This in part is an answer to the possible objection that emphasis
upon a multiplicity of groups may be divisive. Let us be realistic.
Division is already a fact. There is, for example, the generation gap.
Further, it would be an illusion to suppose that the church is not
like other human institutions which are all based upon class. In
many countries the church consists in the main of the bourgeousie.
A diversity of groups celebrating worship would take this class
differentiation seriously and build upon it, instead of pretending
that it does not exist. In other words, it is not just a question of a
generation gap, nor of a gap between cultural sub-groups within
classes, but also a question of class and cultural distinctions. To
recognize this and to encourage liturgical creativity within this
diversity is not necessarily to produce disunity, since these many
groups would come together – once a month, once a quarter – to
confess and declare their unity in Christ. This is one way of relating
to a pluriform society.

This model may be further illustrated from a hypothetical theological seminary in the Philippines. One of the problems which
faces that country at the present time is the discovery of a national
identity, and a great impediment to this is the co-existence of different cultures and different languages. We will suppose that our
hypothetical seminary has drawn its students from three areas and
consists of a third from the Mountain Province, a third from the
Visayas and a third from Mindanao. It would be reasonable in this
situation to divide into three for the purposes of group worship.
To retort that this would deny the very nature of the seminary which
is intended to be one community misses the point. Community has
to be created. The divisions exist. It would therefore be realistic
to build upon three divisions – to use them in fact – by encouraging
liturgical creativity within the several cultural and language groups.
These groups should then come together, since one of the tasks of
a seminary is to provide training in worship, once or even twice a
week, to manifest and experience their oneness in Christ. Such a
strategy would have the added value of assisting the seminarians to
become familiar with the dialectic between groups and the large

liturgical assembly and to enable them to experiment with this when they go out to exercise their ministry.

This integration of the groups within the large liturgical assembly will only be achieved if three conditions are observed. First, each group must preserve its cultural originality. Second, each must have an equal chance to express its own point of view and to undertake with others some action in common. Third, each must feel that it shares in a universal responsibility.[31] Clearly the implementation of these will affect the forms of worship suitable for a large assembly of the kind envisaged. But the impersonality of the assembly can be overcome to the extent to which it consists of participatory groups in which inter-personal relations have been fostered. So the complexity of the urban situations should not be regarded with regret; it provides the opportunity for Christians to break out of a limited experience of fellowship and worship into a far wider range of experiences.

Moreover, it should be stated that intimacy is not a *sine qua non* of personal encounter. It will be recalled that in analysing the disclosure-situation about the convict,[32] it was noted how Olgi was illuminated and met the holy through a fleeting glimpse of a fellow prisoner. He had no personal knowledge of the other; he had not seen him before, did not know his name and never saw him again. Yet, while sounding this cautionary note, I am bound to emphasize that personal intimacy can and does facilitate I-Thou relations. Of course, on occasion such knowledge may act as a barrier, e.g. if one knows the other so well that he or she is taken for granted. Nevertheless, the norm must certainly be that formulated by Macmurray: 'Community can only be actual in direct personal relations, since we can only be actually in fellowship with those whom we know personally.'[33] Or, as he says elsewhere, 'to create a unity is to make friendship the form of all personal relations'.[34] These relations normally have to be direct and not indirect, and therefore require primary groups. It is therefore upon these that we must concentrate in the remainder of this chapter.

Briefly summarizing the argument to date, it can be said that for a group to have a communal dimension it must possess the following characteristics:

1. It must be a primary group.
2. It must be a reference group.

3. It must be engaged in the pursuit of common tasks.
4. It must be restricted in size.
5. It must rest upon interpersonal relations.
6. It must allow for a high degree of interaction and participation.
7. It must involve a sense of responsibility.

However, these factors do not exhaust all aspects of the subject: some of them need further investigation and additional ones have to be specified. The previous stress upon interpersonal relations also serves to focus attention upon personalization and identity. Community may be understood in terms of a function of bringing to maturity. The more united the community, in contrast to the collectivity of the hive or ant hill, the greater the differentiation between the members.[35] This is so because wholeness does not depend upon my relation to myself but upon my participation in human relations. It is precisely because community belonging assists this to take place that the breakdown of community leads, as Tillich declared in the quotation given previously, to the undermining of the personality. Within a group, however, each person can recognize the other as the limit of his freedom but also as the necessary agent of its fulfilment.[36]

By identity I am referring to that, not of the individual, but of the community itself. According to Roger Mehl: 'Every human being experiences and needs to experience a certain pride in his past; he needs to be joined to a tradition, to a line of ancestors.'[37] The same applies to a community if it, too, has an identity. It is in this way, for example, that a nation comes to an awareness of its own identity. Where this has been compromised, a turning to the past can assist in its rediscovery. So in the years immediately after World War II, German composers of opera drew upon their national history for their themes, as did Hindemith for *Mathis der Maler* and Berg for *Wozzeck*.[38] Similarly, television presentations in England of the lives of Henry VIII and Elizabeth I provide, not a means of escape from the present, but a point of reference for awareness of identity. Community therefore involves both encounter *and* transmission. Hence R. L. Howe asserts that

The Church as a 'tradition-bearing community' contains both poles and does not want to subordinate one to the other. When the content of the tradition is lost, the meaning of the encounter is lost, and in the end even the encounter itself. And when encounter is lost, tradition becomes idolatrous and sterile. Both are necessary to the faith community and both are dangerous and meaningless if separated.[39]

This means, too, that community is concerned with an interpersonal unity of experience. This unity represents the funded result of many individual experiences and the interpretation which has been shared and compared for the purpose of separating the well-based from evanescent or incidental experience. J. E. Smith illustrates this by reference to the story of Joseph and his brothers. This is a record of jealousy, revenge and forgiveness.

By the Jews these experiences came to be accepted as a model of what is perennial and repeatable within the experience of each member of the community. . . . Through the community as a medium for sharing and comparing experience, the individual members discover for themselves the representative character of Joseph's experience, since they too experience jealousy and revenge and are capable of showing the redeeming power of forgiveness. This isolated individual may have whatever experiences you please, but he cannot know how representative or perennial they are until he has had an opportunity to share and compare his experience with the experience of others. As a result of the intersection of distinct experiences within a community of shared experience the idiosyncratic experience gradually becomes distinguished from what is pervasive.[40]

This sharing of experience is a normal feature in human relations. Even the solitary angler likes to tell of 'the one that got away'. In the act of sharing, each one reaffirms his own personality and, at the same time, relives his experience in common with others, so joining his life with that of the group. In this way an acceptable identity is discovered and maintained, both at the individual and group levels.

If, however, community is not to stagnate, it must both allow for conflict and be open to the future. Conflict is a necessary element in change; without it there is no movement whatsoever. It is a central element in social dynamism. Because it has this positive aspect, any community must make provision for it, but in such a way that, instead of being destroyed, it benefits from it;[41] i.e., means have to be found to regulate it so that it profits the community and does not tear it asunder. When it is regarded as a normal feature, it loses its dramatic character and can therefore be faced calmly. It can then become an element of transformation and collective dynamism.[42] Hence, while the past may provide a point of reference, conflict in the present is necessary in order to open the way to the future. By this means a community can be safeguarded from petrification and social irrelevance within a society in rapid change. Without roots it is difficult to find a shared identity, but without a shared hope one remains either imprisoned in the past or under the tyranny of the present. The result can be self-assertiveness which is focused on the here and now. To transfer one's interests and emotions to another time, past and future, is to pass beyond the self. This participation in something other than the present inhibits self-assertiveness and encourages the unfolding of self-transcending tendencies.[43]

At this juncture it is important to note that the English versions of the Bible do not contain the word 'community'. The noun that most nearly corresponds to this, in the sense I have been defining, is *koinōnia*. This is variously translated as fellowship and communion, and could also be rendered by participation. This *koinōnia* has all the characteristics I have tabulated on the basis of a sociological and philosophical analysis. But it is also an eschatological fellowship, i.e. it lives out of the future. The addition of this qualification is essential, for fellowship need not affect society as a whole but only a few groups, and often its objective is simply to decrease loneliness and isolation. Hence even fellowship can be no more than a device for adjustment which allows one to bear the burdens of a present situation. Once add the adjective eschatological and this type of community is seen to be concerned to mediate the dynamic of its hope to society.[44] Because, in the light of the eschatological proviso, the present is not what it should be, Christian community must witness to its hope for the world by a creative contradiction of existing patterns. This hope, as we have seen, is not other-wordly, but is concentrated upon the secular universe. So to the sociological and philosophical understanding of community we have to add this theological interpretation, and we have to see what all this means for worship.

In effect, our concern is with the reality of worship today and, in this chapter particularly, with its basis in community and/or fellowship. Reality, according to the Oxford English Dictionary, is the quality of having an actual existence. In this sense it may appear absurd to talk about the reality of worship, since in countless churches services are being held, and so worship has an actual existence; we can both observe it and engage in it, if we are so inclined. But I suspect that when one refers to the reality of worship today, what one is speaking about in fact is its intelligibility and its relevance to human existence, and that, conversely, when modern Western man rejects worship as unreal he means that he finds it both unintelligible and irrelevant.

It was one of Paul's liturgical principles that everything said or sung during a service should be understandable not only by the members of the Christian community but even by outsiders. 'If,' he wrote to the Corinthians, 'I do not know the meaning of the sound the speaker makes, his words will be gibberish to me, and mine to him.'[45] Further, 'If you bless with the spirit, how can anyone in the position of an outsider say the "Amen" to your thanksgiving when he does not know what you are saying? . . . If, therefore, the whole church assembles and all speak in tongues, and outsiders or unbelievers enter, will they not say that you are mad?'[46] Paul was, of course, referring to glossolalia, but his thesis is quite plain: whatever language is used must be meaningful. It does not require much comparative study to become aware that most churches have long ceased to follow Paul in this matter. An extensive list of words, phrases and sentences could easily be compiled which only survive in liturgical use and are no longer part of the living language of man today. This is true even of those churches that do not have fixed forms of liturgy, since their *patois* is usually modelled upon archaic translations of the Bible.

We must also recognize that this vocabulary often relates to concepts that are no longer intelligible. The old ontological way of thinking (about what a thing *is*) has given way to a functional manner of thinking (about what a thing *does*). Such Hellenistic ideas as God's omnipotence, omniscience and omnipresence refer to qualities of being which we today do not really understand, yet it is often this manner of thought that has found expression in our forms of worship, while the really fascinating insights into what God has done and is doing in history are left out.[47] The point I am seeking to make can be conveniently summarized in the words of one of the recommendations in the *Report of the Theological Commission on Worship*, 1963, to the Faith and Order Conference of the World Council of Churches.

The Church's traditional worship is frequently expressed in an inherited language and world view which modern man regards as belonging to the mythology of a past generation. Such language and such ideas do not, it is claimed, correspond to any objective reality, and are largely unintelligible to those who live within the modern technical and scientific culture. Thus the whole traditional pattern of worship seems to constitute a serious obstacle to any attempt by the Church to confront modern man with the challenge of the gospel.

We therefore recommend to the Faith and Order Conference that it should promote further study of the problems arising from this discrepancy between the biblical world-view and the language of liturgical tradition on the one hand, and the contemporary language and world-view on the other.[48]

Persistence in employing outdated words and concepts reinforces the impression that worship is an activity of an in-group and has little to do with the contemporary world, for a really outward-looking community would presumably not cling to its own dialect, but would seek to express itself in the common speech of mankind. Indeed it is difficult to deny that most acts of worship are essentially church-centred. An examination of many service books reveals that the majority of prayers are for the Christian community: i.e., the church assembles to pray for itself; the 'real' world, as modern man sees it, seldom falls within its purview.[49] Consequently, to many, worship has an air of unreality, which is often intensified by what is actually done.

There are churches in which wafers are used at the communion service; there are churches where a non-alcoholic beverage is consumed; there are churches where no drink whatsoever is given to the congregation at the eucharist or where a mere moistening of the lips is deemed sufficient. What kind of world is this? Is it not a world of make-believe, where bread is not bread, wine is not wine and drinking is not drinking?

Both language and action declare that worship is something apart and that to engage in it is to move out of the secular world into a sacred one which is ecclesio-centred. Our church buildings proclaim the same message: they are holy shrines which must be reserved exclusively for cultic performances by the Christian community and must be guarded from profanation by worldly activities. This means that the problem of the reality of worship is not simply that of bringing archaic words, actions and concepts, up to date; it goes much deeper than that. The problem is to rediscover the unity of the sacred and the secular, which was the theme of Part I of this book, while, at the same time, preserving the integrity of the secular. In relation to the subject of this chapter, this last remark refers to the communal dimension of worship.

The reality of worship depends upon the extent to which the worshipping body is truly knit together in person-to-person relationships. Unless this is so, we do not have a community, but a collectivity – a mere aggregation of separate individuals. For worship to be real, therefore, it must be corporate, and its corporateness is to be understood in terms of the I-Thou. Much stress has indeed been laid in the recent past on the corporate nature of Christian worship, but little attempt has been made to define what this means, except along negative lines: i.e., corporate worship is said to be not the coming together of private persons who say their own prayers in isolation; it is something we *do* together. But how is what we do together a corporate action? It is a corporate action if it is rooted in the I-Thou, in mutuality, reciprocity, in relation.

In the light of the previous discussion of community, it is now possible to affirm that the reality of worship is to be sought, not in the coming-together of a pre-existent community, but in the action of a primary group within which interpersonal relations are fostered. Through the saying of 'we' by those who are *with* one another in a series of I-Thou relations, the eternal Thou is to be encountered. Real worship, i.e. worship that is intelligible and relevant to human existence, may then be a possibility. It is a corporate activity if all are participating, i.e. corporate worship is participatory worship. This participation is not simply an appreciation of what is taking place, as an audience at a concert may be said to participate by listening. The appropriate form of participation in an act of worship is that which involves person-to-person contact. If worship is represented as the means of entrance into a sacred world, then participation becomes a sharing in heavenly things, which are unreal to many people. But if participation is sharing in the human reality, it may become a means of encountering the holy who is to be met always through the secular.

At the same time we must recall the four aspects of participation distinguished by J. Rémy. Both cultural and intellectual participation require a common language which is intelligible to all, with actions that everyone regards as fitting and with a common understanding of what is taking place. Affective participation is also possible in the small group, for each and everyone is able to recognize his responsibility for what happens. Participation in decision-making, too, may be an element in worship.

If worship is not comprehended as a means of fostering the interpersonal, it becomes otiose. The excessive individualism of the last few centuries has devitalized worship because it has led to the absence of the I-Thou and so of the reality of the holy. The individual does not need the other to worship when worship is conceived as a private communing with God; but then, enclosed in his selfhood, he cannot be aware of any reality to encounter. So the 'function of corporate ritual is to provide a means of entering into the world of relation. . . . It is a confession and demonstration of the truth about men, their need for, and fear of, self-revelation in the presence of others.' It is 'to demonstrate the embodied and concrete nature of human interpersonal experience'.[50]

Other conclusions follow from the preceding analysis. The problem of community is not just a problem for the Christian; man needs community, but Christians cannot create one as a meta-historical formation; they can only do so in the midst of the socio-political process.[51] The constitution of traditional society has become involved in a crisis which threatens disintegration. The church, too, is caught up in this same situation. As past social structures decay and break down, so the social structure of the church falls apart. The old relationships are dissolved, and the church has to seek new forms and adapt its structure accordingly if worship is to have any meaning today. This is one of the reasons why it must be related to the world and find its expression and reality in new human groupings.

The family cannot provide the model that is required, although this has often been supposed.[52]* The idea was naturally inferred from certain New Testament passages which speak of Christians as children of God, of Christ as 'the first-born of many brethren'[53] and of God as Father. But 'family' is an imprecise category. It may be extended or nuclear; it may be matriarchal or patriarchal. It can foster domination and exploitation. It often keeps conflicts latent for too long, so that there is stagnation and no development. The model is rather, as I have argued, the task-oriented group, which is also an affective one. Such a community, as the locus of worship, is to be sought within the socio-political process. Its primary social functions are service and social criticism.

At the same time such a community is a fellowship. In this connection it has been said that 'worship is most real when it is not God-directed but constitutive of genuine fellowship at the human level',[54] but this either/or approach should be repudiated. To constitute a genuine human fellowship is *at the same time* to be God-directed, since 'where two or three are gathered in my name, there am I in the midst of them'.[55] Yet in *Christian* worship this should be not just implicit but explicit, if it is to act as a sensitizing medium of the holy. Not that the nature of the shared experience is modified by the perception of the holy; on the contrary, it is illuminated by it and provided with a category of interpretation and so of meaning.

It is to this end that ritual has an important function to perform, because it is a method of mnemonics, i.e. it enlivens the memory and links the present with the relevant past. So when we tie a knot in our handkerchief, we are not practising magic but bringing our memory under the control of an external sign. In this way, ritual aids and even changes perception because it alters the selective principle. Similarly 'liturgy grows from our own life together, but a life enriched by overtones from the past'.[56] In this way the model of the holy is constantly brought before the members of the community, who are thereby assisted to perceive the holy in the world at large. Worship is a disclosure-situation. By pointing to the holy in and through the secular reality which is its basis, worship helps man to perceive and encounter the holy throughout the secular world. This reference to the holy, as embodied in Jesus, assists self-transcendence by directing attention to a different time and place in the past and forward to the one who is to come.

13

Secular Rituals

One of the conclusions reached at the end of the last chapter was that worship is, or should be, a disclosure situation which sharpens the perception of the holy by the participants and so assists them to recognize and to encounter the holy in and through the world. It is to the world that I now turn for disclosure situations, but I am looking for a different kind from those that concerned us in Part I. I am seeking those that have the nature of worship or ritual. However, just as I had previously to describe a model of the holy to enable it to be perceived, so, too, it is necessary here to formulate a mental set that will make possible the recognition of worship within secular activities. The principal features that may constitute this proto-knowledge have indeed been outlined already in the first three chapters of Part II. On the basis of this discussion, it is now possible to make various statements about worship.

Worship is an activity that springs out of life in the world; it is a celebration of that life and is based upon world-involvement and not upon world-rejection. It is an encounter with the holy and expresses and makes explicit the unity of the sacred and the secular, by showing that the holy is a dimension of the whole of life. Worship opens up the secular to the holy and assists us to find the holy in everyday life. So it gives coherence and meaning to social experience. Worship has a communal basis, involving face-to-face encounters, social interaction, participation, mutuality, reciprocity and corporateness. It fosters interpersonal relations and functions in terms of personalization and communal identity. Worship is a shared activity, which is both intelligible to all and relates to the past. It celebrates hopes, brings the hoped-for future into contact with the present, and provides a stimulus for reshaping the world. It points to the service of others; it expresses the love of neighbour and it comprises commitment and the acceptance of responsibility for one another.

This last aspect – love expressed in the service of others – serves to remind us that if worship is an encounter with the holy, then its nature is also to be understood in terms of one's model of the holy. This means, in the light of Part I, that worship is concerned with humanization, with the restoration of dignity, wholeness and the establishment of *shālōm*. It relates to the ordinary and the unexpected, to openness and exposure, to suffering and judgment. Yet there is a limitation imposed by the material I have to review. If a making-explicit of the holy is a necessary element in worship, we should not expect to find this in secular rituals. To that extent they are not completely adequate as patterns for the future, although in so far as the holy is implicit in them they may give some pointers to the way forward.

Secular rituals, according to Rosemary Haughton, have as their purpose the expression of 'the underlying nature of what is going on'.[1] So let us consider an event which took place at Tewkesbury in Gloucestershire on 17 June 1970 to discover what was its underlying nature. On that day a by-pass was opened around this country town. The Ministry of Transport, which was ultimately responsible for the construction, would not do anything to mark the occasion, so the inhabitants arranged their own celebration. This consisted of the mayor of Tewkesbury being driven along the by-pass in a 1912 Renault, after which everyone drank a glass of wine at the roadside. This was a ritualization of a secular event. To the residents at Tewkesbury, delighted that the town was to be relieved of the burden of traffic passing through, filling the air with noise and fumes, and turning a pleasant centre into a clutter of vehicles, the ceremony was meaningful. It expressed their joy; it marked the beginning of a new era. They were celebrating their life in the world; they were giving coherence and meaning to their social experience. They were engaging in face-to-face encounters. They shared in an activity which was intelligible to all. It was related to the past, with its traffic chaos, and to the future with its hoped-for freedom.

Although the participants would not have interpreted it in this way, this activity was one of worship. Implicit in what they did, but not explicit, was the recognition of the holy who brings whole-ness and establishes *shālōm*, and is known in interpersonal relations. Such an event would not have the same meaning for, say, the citizens of Worcester, whom it affects marginally, and only on those occasions when they travel to Bristol and are grateful to avoid, on the way, a previous bottle-neck with consequent traffic-jams and delay. If one goes further afield, it is to be acknowledged that the people of the Outer Hebrides would certainly not be interested in this event and would scarcely appreciate 'the underlying nature of what was going on'. In other words, ritual must be directly related to the concerns of those people who celebrate it.

For a second example I return to *The Transfer*, by the Italian novelist Silvano Ceccherini. We have already met the chief charac-ter Olgi, the convict, who is being moved from one prison to another. The background to the incident to be reproduced here is Olgi's discussion with a young man about his girl friend. Marcello has decided to break off his engagement with Mara, because he thinks it unfair to keep her bound to him when he has years still to spend in prison. Olgi, however, realizing the extent to which Mara is dependent upon Marcello's love, persuades him to write to her, after a long period of silence, to reaffirm his devotion. A few days later, after the dispatch and receipt of the letter, Olgi enters his cell to find there a meal sent by Mara as a token of her gratitude.

Olgi took out the contents of the bag: there was a small pot contain-ing soup. The soup smelt of chicken. There was a fine piece of boiled meat, roast rabbit and chips, a piece of cheese, two pears and two apples. And there was half a litre of wine, a fine clear red wine.

He had laid it out on the bed, and with rather sorrowful tenderness looked at those things that expressed more than the physiological need of nourishment. This was how men ate. Food that cost sweat, and then meant gaiety.

I'm eating what they're eating, Olgi thought. And he saw them all gathered round the table, the eternal human family: Mara's father, the pensioned-off railwayman, his wife Ersilia, Duccio and Piero, Mara's brothers, Giovanna, Duccio's wife, their children Teresa and Giacomo; and Mara. Eating the food they were eating, it was as if Olgi were sitting at the table with them, a member of the one inalienable family. The break was finally mended, the long expiation over. Beyond the law, in spite of the law. In the brotherhood of the human heart.[2]

The novelist has himself provided a key to the understanding of this secular ritual, for immediately before coming back to his cell Olgi had attended mass. He was asked if he believed in God.

'I don't know,' Olgi replied, 'But I don't refuse anything. I leave the door open, and when you least expect it a welcome visitor may come in.'[3]

By this device, Ceccherini indicates that the meaning of the mass is to be found in the meal in the prison cell, which is therefore an act of worship. After twenty years in prison, Olgi has come to terms with life and has developed a deep love for living and for people. He has lost his life, but now he finds it. The meaning of the meal restores him to life – 'the break was finally mended, the long expiation over' – and at the same time it is a commentary on the meaning of the more formal act of worship that preceded it. That meaning rests upon the human reality of fellowship. That meal is a celebration of life in the world which finds its basis in physical nourishment and human community. At the same time, a 'visitor' has come, the Holy One who brings dignity, wholeness and *shālōm*. Further comment seems superfluous, for the story itself enunciates its own meaning with force and clarity. My only cavil would relate to the imagery used, viz. that of a visitor coming, which does suggest a *deus ex machina*. The incident would more completely correspond to the perspective of this study were it to have been described in terms of the recognition of One who had been there all the time.

Norman Mailer's *Armies of the Night* supplies a third example. This is a moving account of the mass demonstration of protest in Washington in October 1967 against the Vietnam war. The demo began on the Thursday evening with a meeting in the Ambassadors Theatre – it was not a very successful exercise. On the Friday afternoon there was a gathering on the steps of the Palace of Justice. Speeches were delivered and then talk was transformed into action, and indeed into ceremonial, as one after the other people came forward and surrendered their draft cards.[4] They announced their names, declared the college or area they represented and gave the number of the cards they were handing over. The students were followed by university teachers who, having given advice, felt equally involved and equally responsible.[5]

The next main stage was the march on the Pentagon itself on the Saturday. Mailer describes the incredible assortment of folk involved: of all ages and physiques, of all backgrounds, of all costumes, advancing along the Arlington Memorial Bridge to the centre of the American war effort. He helps the reader to appreciate the humour and the pathos of what was taking place: the singing together; the chanting of slogans; the determination to press on whatever the cost in terms of personal suffering. He brings out clearly the ritualistic nature of the event. There never was any hope of bringing the Pentagon to a standstill. This was not a movement of revolutionaries with guns and bombs, prepared for bloody battle, whose success or failure would be measured by the extent of the damage inflicted on the Pentagon. It was a symbolic act to proclaim the evil of the war effort, itself symbolized by the five-sided, more or less faceless, building. This symbolic character becomes very evident in the rites of exorcism which were performed in the parking lot close to the main edifice. The theatrical medium for this was a pop group known as the Fugs who provided a musical accompaniment to the chanting of exorcist formulae. The meaning of the happening was spelled out in a mimeographed paper which was handed round and affirmed that they were there to exorcise and cast out evil so that the Pentagon could once again serve the interest of God manifest in the world as man.[6]

There followed the attempt to penetrate the ranks of soldiers and militia; the arrests; the removal of many to detention centres; the summary hearings, the verdicts and the fines. Mailer believed that the participants shared a confidence that politics had again become mysterious and that the gods were at work in human affairs.[7] If this partakes a little of the numinous, this may be understood as the author letting his pen run away with him rather than as an expression of his considered verdict which he reserves until the final pages of his book when he gives an account of the assembly on the Sunday morning. There he describes how he experienced a sense of liberation, of freedom from dread, of happiness and compassion – to him all this was to be interpreted as meaning precisely the same as what Christians are referring to when they speak of Christ within them. Finally Mailer went to the microphone and declared that they had all been engaged in a symbolic protest against the war in Vietnam and that what was taking place in that ravaged country was tantamount to the burning of the body and blood of Christ.[8]

There is a number of obvious points of contact between this account and the model of worship outlined above. There is ritual in the surrendering of the draft cards and in the symbolic act of exorcism. There is openness and exposure to suffering. The act is one of massive social criticism, which is at the same time a blow in the struggle against evil. There is the recognition that the response to the holy may involve political action. There is a shared compassion for both the American service men and the natives of Vietnam. There is a sense of liberation. Each one knows himself an an individual person, discovers afresh his identity, and yet all are aware of their unity. The process corresponds most nearly to the large liturgical assembly, which has previously been defined as a gathering of small groups – here too groups from all walks of life were involved and their existing inter-personal relationships made the entire effort one that expressed and actualized community. What is perhaps most striking in Mailer's final paragraph is his testimony to the extent to which the event was a means of sensitizing the participants to the holy, as embodied in Christ, in the secular world.

My fourth example has some affinity with the last in that it, too, is concerned with Vietnam and the call-up; it relates, however, to an event of much smaller proportions. A certain American was a conscientious objector. He decided to dramatize his refusal to be enlisted by reporting to the induction centre, but then not taking the symbolic step forward. He determined further to ritualize his action. To this latter end he arranged with his girl friend to bring fresh bread and strawberry jam, balloons, flowers and banners, and to have a band in attendance. The event then became one of celebration. Instead of promoting feelings of fear and hostility, possibly resulting in an ugly scene, the young man gained some understanding for his refusal. 'In this case,' comments Harvey Cox, from whom I have taken this description, 'the "no" to an unjust war was expressed firmly but as a minor note in the major theme of saying "yes" to life, and peace.'[9] This account serves to draw attention to a feature of secular ritual which has not previously been mentioned, and that is the idea of a 'feast'. Cox has made this the central theme of a recent book, but it had previously been subjected to phenomenological analysis and had been related to Christian worship by Frédéric Debuyst.[10] Drawing on these various sources, it is possible to distinguish the main aspects to be comprehended under the category of a 'feast' or 'celebration'. The following characteristics are apparent:

1. *It is exceptional.* So Debuyst states that it breaks up the normal pattern of time and space and opens a window in the wall of our daily life. Hence, for example, it is not every day we have a birthday party. Cox dubs this aspect 'juxtaposition', which he defines as involving a contrast so that the feast is notably different from everyday life and breaks ordinary routine.

2. *It is superabundant.* Debuyst draws attention to the display of unnecessary elements: china, silver, crystal, flowers and candles; special dishes; salmon instead of cod, poultry rather than a joint, wine for water. Cox uses 'conscious excess' to refer to this characteristic and relates it to revelry and joy.

3. *It is linked to a value or event of especial importance.* Debuyst defines a feast as 'an external, expressive, symbolic manifestation whereby we make ourselves more deeply conscious of the importance of an event or of an idea *already important to us*.'[11] Cox denotes this by 'celebrative affirmation'. It is a saying 'yes' to life, or, in the words of J. Pieper, it is a living out of 'the universal assent to the world as a whole'.[12] In saying *yes* to one single moment of our existence – the event celebrated – we are affirming our entire existence and even existence as such. Nevertheless, not every event is worthy of such celebration; not every detail of ordinary living merits this special treatment. It has to mark such happenings as a victory or a success or a stage in life accomplished.

4. *It is a phenomenon of love, joy, unanimity and participation.* Debuyst brings this out very clearly by reference to a research project undertaken under the auspices of the University of Louvain. The subject to be investigated was how children experience the phenomenon *feast*. A group of children were shown three drawings, each being a different representation of a birthday feast. The first depicted a child standing before a table laden with presents. The second showed a child sitting with his father and mother at a table bearing cakes, ice-cream, etc.; one solitary present was at his feet. The third represented a child sitting at a table with many other people – parents, grown-ups and other children. The table itself was laden with food and both it and the walls were lavishly decorated. There were, however, no presents in the picture. The children were then asked which of the three feasts they would choose for their own. 72% of the boys and 69% of the girls selected the third drawing. In other words, a feast to them is a symbol of love, where everyone is happy and there is a communal spirit of joy. It is an occasion when all participate – there can be no wallflowers, standing aloof from the action or ignored by others. Even if a stranger comes in, he is to be welcomed, for otherwise the sense of community and togetherness would be dampened.

5. *It has a reference to time past, time present and time future.* The celebration may be of a past event. 'Festivity is a human form

of play through which man appropriates an extended area of life, including the past, into his own experience. . . . Festivity, by breaking routine and opening man to the past, enlarges his experience and reduces his provincialism.'[13] So the event is 'a way that accepts the past without being bound by it, that views past history not as a prison to escape or as an antique to be preserved but as a dimension of reality that enlarges and illuminates the present'.[14]

The celebration is, too, in itself a present event, and its accompanying revelry expresses delight in the here and now. It also looks forward to the future. Cox associates this future reference with his concept of fantasy. This is perhaps a somewhat journalistic use of terms, but the point he is making is a valid one. He defines fantasy as 'the faculty for envisioning radically alternative life situations'.[15] It therefore widens the possibilities for innovation and links the feast with social criticism. But this future reference is also to be associated with the anticipatory nature of a feast. I am not merely referring to such things as a New Year's Eve Party which celebrates a coming event, for even a silver-wedding reception is an anticipation of a future unity that has not been fully realized in the past. Yet such a party does celebrate the past years of life together, being a form of thanksgiving for their successful conclusion and a recognition of their relevance to the present; it is, at the same time, a rejoicing in the here and now and a looking forward to the continued union of the couple in possibly new and untried ways.

6. *It involves order and spontaneity*. So Cox describes it as a liberating ritual that 'provides the formal structure within which freedom and fantasy can twist and tumble'.[16] The order is a necessary limit to unlicensed chaos and the condition for free interaction, but it should never be predominant nor a pervading feature to which everyone must rigorously conform, otherwise the festive note will be absent. The ritual of celebration therefore provides a set of connections through which emotion can be expressed, rather than repressed. This is neither superficiality nor frivolity, but what Debuyst calls a symbolic dialogue between charm and order, spontaneity and unity.[17]

7. *It involves sacrifice*. This is an emphasis pecular to Debuyst who affirms that a feast requires a gift of time and 'a renunciation of work and money-earning in order to introduce us into the inexhaustible freedom and richness of creation itself'.[18]

8. *It is a symbolic action and is concerned with meaning*. The

feast itself is a symbol of love and of joy. Its meaning is intrinsic to itself. Yet, at the same time, this meaning may be made explicit. So Debuyst points out how most feasts include a speech, whether a simple toast or an elaborate address. This always has a specific purpose: to express the inner meaning of the feast. This can be related to Cox's statement that 'the Christian dimension of ritual can add depth, universality, and compassion to secular celebration. They are only properly introduced, however, if they unlock, challenge and reassure.'[19]

In listing these characteristics of the feast I do not wish to suggest that I am in agreement with them all, in the sense of finding each one equally valuable as a pointer to future patterns of worship. In particular, the emphasis, by both Debuyst and Cox, upon the 'exceptional' nature of the feast could be unfortunate. Indeed I suspect that Cox himself has not yet completely moved out of the sacral universe. So he finds something of value in hippy cults, etc., the adherents of which he names neo-mystics and says that they reveal man's desire 'to taste both the holy and the human with unmediated directness'.[20] But this desire is neither to be condoned nor is it realistic. I have repeatedly stressed that while the encounter with the holy is direct it is always mediated. 'Immediate directness' smacks of the numinous – and much of the writings of LSD addicts breathes this same atmosphere. They are not modern men, but then they have opted out of contemporary society. Moreover if worship, as festive, is exceptional, there is the danger that it will be cut off from everyday life. The result is not unity. Indeed Cox's choice of the word 'juxtaposition' in reference to the notable difference from everyday life that he perceives is itself a denial of union. It recalls Nestorius who, rightly or wrongly, was charged with teaching a union of juxtaposition of the human and divine in Christ, and this the church at large decided was not a real unity. A unity of juxtaposition is exemplified by a sackful of wheat and barley; the grains are side by side, juxtaposed; they constitute a unity of juxtaposition, but in fact there is no vital relationship between them. If the feast is simply juxtaposed, it becomes a hiatus in secular living, and then we have an understanding of worship in groups corresponding to a theology of the God of the gaps. This fissiparous tendency has to be resisted, otherwise worship will continue to be understood as a drawing apart, and the separation of the sacred and the secular will persist.

I would rather describe the feast as a highlight within living. The substance of feasts is, after all, not dissimilar from what is to be found on ordinary occasions. One may eat rather special food – but it is still food. One may put on one's best clothes – but they are still clothes. One may decorate the space in which the celebration is being held – but the items used are still the products of nature and of the world of man's industry. In other words, festivity finds its basis in the secular world, in life in the world lifted to its highest level. It is not discontinuous, nor juxtaposed. It does not open a window into the wall of daily life as if from outside, but its context is daily life itself, so that it too may be lived as the locus of encounter with the holy.

However, on the basis of this analysis and taking my reservations into account, it is possible to suggest a further definition of worship and to use this as a tool to discover other cultural bridges or secular equivalents. Worship may be defined as that which celebrates, expresses and/or actualizes community or fellowship and makes explicit a relationship to that which is of ultimate concern, viz. with the holy as embodied in Christ.

This definition does raise a problem. Much of human life is related to penultimate concerns rather than to the ultimate. Man works, for example, to obtain the wherewithal to live – his immediate concern is a penultimate one. How, then, is it possible to discover cultural bridges in terms of ultimate concern? The answer to this, arising from the discussion in Part I, is to be found in the thesis that the holy is to be encountered in and through the world. Phrased more directly in terms of the question just asked this means that the ultimate is to be encountered in and through the penultimate. How this may be so has already been illustrated from Mailer's account of the events at Washington. The participants in the march on the Pentagon had a penultimate objective, viz. to protest against and possibly to bring to an end the war in Vietnam. Mailer's own summing up, however, shows how this was also to be related to the ultimate. What in the world, then, corresponds to the definition of worship just formulated? The list could be very extensive indeed, but my purpose will be served by the provision of a limited number of representative examples, using the disclosure situation described in chapters 5 and 6 as a starting point.

Secular events corresponding to the definition of worship given above may include the following:

1. Involvement in a protest action relating to social justice. This has been previously illustrated by Mailer's account and disclosure situation X entitled 'The Demo'.
2. Engagement in a common task. An example of this is provided by 'The Strike', disclosure situation XI.
3. Discussion in depth in an attempt to reach mutual understanding – e.g. 'A Theological Conference', disclosure situation XIV.
4. Sexual relations between two persons in love. Several examples were provided in chapter 6 on 'The Holy and Sexual Relations'.
5. Mutual forgiveness, cf. 'The Mother and the Naughty Child', disclosure situation VI.
6. Loving service of others – 'Old People', disclosure situation VII.

To these half dozen may be added a further four not previously illustrated, but whose relevance is self-evident.

7. Friends eating and drinking together, sometimes involving a party or celebration.
8. Shared silence.
9. Drama in which the audience becomes involved as participators.
10. Group life and activity.

The next step in the argument is to define the characteristics that underlie these actions or activities. Such an analysis leads to the following list:

1. Commitment.
2. The sharpening of critical discernment or awareness of oneself and of the world.
3. Openness to one another leading to enlightenment.
4. Intellectual integrity.
5. Physical activity.
6. Love, as a quality defining human relationships.
7. Celebration or festivity.
8. Actualization of community.
9. Silence.
10. Participation.
11. Freedom for spontaneity.
12. Restoration to wholeness.
13. The recognition of both the unity and diversity of men and society.

14. The making explicit of a relationship to that which is of ultimate concern.

My contention is that these characteristics suggest the real possibility of cultural bridges – so that the choice is not simply between the ghetto or the desert. Worship, which has some or all of these characteristics, can then be comprehended in its necessary relationship to the world – the dichotomy between the sacred and the secular, emphasized by our traditional forms, can then be overcome.[21]*

14

Mission and Worship

The quest upon which I have embarked in Part II of this study is for an understanding of worship in relation to the world. This has led us to seek insights from sociologists and from anthropologists as well as from novelists and other creative writers. The subject can, however, be approached in another way, viz., by considering the relationship between mission and worship. Such an examination is not an interlude in the present discussion, but constitutes an alternative perspective from which to approach it.

The question before us then, is, this: what is the relationship between mission and worship? This is not the first time that this question has been raised. I myself raised it in a book entitled *Worship and Mission* which was published only a few years ago; but that book was no more than a tentative essay in a comparatively new area of study and I would be the last to claim that the subject has been exhaustively treated. In this chapter I shall not reproduce an abbreviated account of what is already available in print, but rather attempt to carry my examination of the relationship further.

I propose to begin by drawing a contrast between the Old Testament understanding of Israel's vocation and the role that worship has to play within that vocation and the New Testament understanding of the vocation of the church and the role that worship has to play within that vocation. Briefly put, Israel's vocation is to be a holy people,[1] i.e. a people whose life is patterned after the very being of its holy God. In so far as this is achieved, Israel then becomes a 'light to the Gentiles'; it is a witness before the nations to Yahweh in order that the nations themselves may come to acknowledge his universal Lordship. The function of worship in relation to this vocation is to enable Israel to be holy; it is a means of sanctification for the chosen people, who are set apart for the worship of Yahweh.[2] The Temple cultus both guarantees of the purity of Yahwism and is the centre to which the nations are to come.

> It shall come to pass in the later days
> that the mountain of the house of the Lord
> shall be established as the highest of the mountains,
> and shall be raised above the hills;
> and all the nations shall flow to it,
> and many peoples shall come and say:
> 'Come let us go to the mountain of the Lord,
> to the house of the God of Jacob;
> that he may teach us his ways
> and that we may walk in his paths.'[3]

It will be noticed that Israel's vocation is interpreted centripetally; Israel is not *sent* to the nations; instead they are to *come* to it, attracted by its life of worship and devotion. In exact conformity with this, Israelite worship is understood centripetally; it has its true centre in a single place, viz. the Jerusalem Temple, and it is to this that all the nations are to come.

The New Testament presents a contrast – indeed, an antithesis – to this view, in that this centripetal attitude is discarded and is replaced by a centrifugal one. The church's vocation is to go out; it is to participate in the divine mission. 'Go therefore and make disciples of all nations.[4] . . . As the Father has sent me, even so send I you.[5] . . . You shall be my witnesses . . . to the end of the earth'[6] in order that the nations may acknowledge the universal Lordship of Christ. The church's vocation is then to join in God's action in the world as he continues his movement of humanization, assisting man towards that maturity or fullness that is embodied in Christ. The function of worship in relation to this vocation is to celebrate God's action in the world and so 'to proclaim the Lord's death until he comes', this being involved in the eating of the bread and the drinking of the cup at the eucharist.[7] Thus just as the church's vocation is interpreted centrifugally, so is its worship; it does not have a centre in a single place; anywhere is the place of encounter with God in the context of everyday life, and in so far as any temple continues to exist, this is not a building of stone but a community living in the world.[8] Hence the Old Testament is consistent in understanding both the vocation and the worship of Israel centripetally, while the New Testament is equally consistent but understands both the vocation and worship of the church centrifugally.

To this contrast must be added a further one, viz., the contrast between the general understanding of Christians today of their vocation and worship and that which we have just noted in the New Testament. As a consequence of the great missionary awakening of the eighteenth and nineteenth centuries, many Christians now understand the vocation of the church centrifugally, but they still persist in viewing their cultic acts centripetally. They thus give up the logical consistency that is to be found in both the Old and New Testaments, and attempt to combine the New Testament centrifugal concept of vocation in terms of mission with the Old Testament centripetal concept of worship in terms of ingathering. Hence the relationship of mission and worship has for decades been defined in terms of gathering and sending. The next logical step in our argument, then, is to examine this definition, before proceeding to consider in greater detail what a centrifugal perspective in relation to worship itself may be said to involve.

The idea of gathering and sending was prominent in German missiological thought at the end of the last century and it is often re-presented at the present day. According to this, worship is an occasion for the gathering together of the Christian community in order that its members may be strengthened to engage in mission; through their sharing in the life-giving body and blood of Christ in the eucharist, Christians are enabled to go out into the world as men and women charged with missionary participation. These cultic acts and this missionary activity can then be compared to breathing in and breathing out, which are both necessary for life, and so both worship and mission – gathering and sending – are essential for the church. The analogy is a plausible one, and it is doubtful if it would have persisted so long if it were not, but is it accurate? In effect it merely associates centripetalism – breathing in – with centrifugalism – breathing out – and therefore fails to resolve the basic tension between them. Moreover, it involves the idea that the cultic acts are interruptions in the church's participation in mission. When the church ceases its centrifugal action in mission, for however brief periods, in order to engage in centripetal actions of worship, it is no longer being missionary during those cultic actions

– in terms of the analogy, you are breathing either in or out: you cannot do the two at once. Whereas if mission and worship are to be truly united, the cultic assembly must be understood within the context of mission; the coming together takes place in mission and it is not preparatory to mission. The church is the church when it is participating in the mission of God; if it is to fulfil its role constantly, it cannot disengage itself from mission in cultic activity. Church services must then not be conceived as halting places *in via* nor as iron rations on the way; they are an essential part of being on the way. So while the gathering and sending analogy does point to a relationship, it is more one of juxtaposition than of real unity, and this is precisely what we have to rediscover if we are to be true to the New Testament. Worship then is not a means to mission; nor is it a preparation for mission, since we worship in mission. The inadequacy of the analogy under consideration should, however, become more apparent as we go on to examine what worship means from a centrifugal or missionary perspective.

Worship, as it is presented to us in the New Testament, is the joyful celebration of life in the world; it is the response of man to what God has done and is doing in history. Three examples will serve to illustrate this.

In Luke 17, we are told how Jesus is met by ten lepers who ask him to have mercy on them. He accedes to this request and they are made whole. One of them, who is a Samaritan, recognizes here the act of God and accordingly he worships – 'praising God with a loud voice, he fell on his face at Jesus' feet, giving him thanks'.[9] The man does not draw apart from the world in order to worship; the basis of his act of worship is his response to God's action in the world – his restoration to wholeness by Christ – and this takes the form of expressing thanks and giving praise. Similarly in Acts 4, we are informed how Peter and John are arrested and how, after trial before the Sanhedrin, they are eventually released. They then 'went to their friends and reported what the chief priests and the elders had said to them'.[10] The reaction of the group to this was to join in prayer, i.e. they worshipped together on the basis of an incident which had taken place in the secular world. The Lord's Supper itself, throughout the apostolic age, was also essentially a secular act, since it was an everyday meal, although one which, while not ceasing to be a source of bodily nourishment, was at the same time a vehicle of worship. Indeed the meaning of the eucharist 'cannot be understood without reference to the normal physical functions of eating and drinking'.[11] Christians met from house to house, breaking bread together, presumably in the main living or dining room.

Here we have worship interpreted from a centrifugal position. Just as the world is understood to be the sphere of mission, so it is also the sphere of worship which is to be offered in terms of the Christian's total existence. The church of the apostolic age does not, then, withdraw from mission in order to engage in cultic acts which prepare it for mission; it never ceases to be in mission in the world whether it is preaching, serving or worshipping. There can therefore be no great centre of worship, corresponding to the Jerusalem Temple. Cultic acts take place *in via* – they are centrifugally conceived in complete unity with mission itself. In the words of Gerhard Bassarak, which he uses of the present day but which apply equally to the New Testament period: 'The reality of the congregation materializes in the gathering of the two or three rather than through church-going.'[12] Hence worship is a spontaneous response to God's action in the world and it does not involve *reculer pour mieux sauter*.

To speak of God's action in the world is, however, to refer to mission, for mission is not something that the church does; it is a divine movement in which the church has to be involved if it is to be true to its calling. The church's role is to facilitate, to identify and to participate in this movement, and the function of worship as response is to be understood within this totality. Worship is not, therefore, just historical commemoration, in the sense of the thankful remembrance of what God has done and, in particular, of what God has done in Christ in Palestine two thousand years ago; it is also the celebration of what God is doing in contemporary history. This, of course, is only possible when we are able to perceive the signs of the divine activity and this, in its turn, we can do only if we acknowledge the possibility and the reality of secular redemption. By 'secular redemption' – to which previous reference has been made[13] – I mean God's redemptive action through secular activities in the secular world. This means that the holy can and does work through secular agencies outside the ecclesiastical structures and that Christians, while called to be participants in the divine action, are not the sole agents of it. This conclusion serves as a corrective to our concept of redemption or salvation. In the past Christians have tended either to think of this in highly individualistic terms, and have therefore failed to recognize the signs of the divine activity in society at large, or they have spiritualized the concept so that salvation has been taken to refer to the saving of souls, and they have therefore failed to appreciate that it is essentially restoration to wholeness, i.e. that it concerns man in the totality of his worldly existence. In contrast to the older, though not the New Testament, negative view that salvation is *from* something, e.g. from the world, from hell, etc., we now have a positive understanding that it comprises the achievement of a full life now.

Christian worship, in terms of the older concept, has been the celebration of the Christians' redemption; Christian worship in terms of secular redemption is the celebration of the divine redeeming act in the world at large, of the fact that God in Christ was and is reconciling the world to himself. Of course, to say this is to make an affirmation of faith. The signs are ambiguous. Overtly they are human efforts, but Christian faith enables us to discern the divine activity indissolubly united to these efforts and apart from which it cannot be perceived. Worship can then be defined as 'a social acknowledgment of the primacy of God's action' in and through the secular world.[14]

This social acknowledgment also involves the exercise by the church of its prophetic role. The Old Testament prophets 'not only see God as active in past salvation events which are remembered and recorded, they claim that his hand is also *and equally* at work in the events of their own day'.[15] Worship, as joyful celebration of God's activity in the world, is thus a prophetic proclamation of the meaning of those secular events which provide the basis for the cultic assembly. Unless worship and mission are united in this way, our church services cannot but remain unreal and indeed irrelevant to modern man, being no more than esoteric reunions by the members of an inward-looking fellowship of the righteously like-minded.

If we listen to what modern man is saying, instead of eagerly proclaiming a gospel which he does not understand and which he cannot see has any relation to his situation, then we cannot but endorse the line of thought I have been pursuing and which I venture to suggest stems from the New Testament. This is the kind of thing modern man is saying: 'The churches and chapels are not part and parcel of the struggle in which we are involved' . . . 'The postulates of God and eternal life are external and superimposed on

life, not an intrinsic part of it.'[16] There is truth in these remarks, if
we persist in adhering to outmoded concepts of mission, of salvation
and of worship. But the truth of the gospel impels us to move forward in our understanding of worship and mission as both concerned essentially with life in the world. We Christians are not
to be purveyors of 'pie in the sky when we die', nor perhaps can
we provide as much pie as is needed on earth now, but at least we
can promote hope out of God's future, based upon a recognition of
his ceaseless struggle for the humanization of our race. This, after
all, is the message of the Incarnation which is 'the humanization
of God for the sake of the humanization of man'.[17]

Let us now call a momentary halt to our ongoing argument and
survey the progress so far. In so doing we shall have the opportunity to examine certain other aspects of our subject. My thesis is
that according to the Old Testament the vocation and worship of
Israel are to be understood centripetally, and both are concerned with the sanctification of the chosen people, whereas
according to the New Testament the mission and worship of
the New Israel are to be understood centrifugally and both are
concerned with humanization. Does this mean that the church is
not also to be a holy people? Clearly the author of I Peter believes
that the church is to be a neo-levitical community and he has no
hesitation in applying to it Lev. 11.44: 'You shall be holy, for I am
holy.' Like the people of the old covenant, the people of the new
are to pattern their life on the being of God. But a shift of meaning has taken place that we have to recognize. Holiness in the Old
Testament is closely associated with the idea of ritual or cultic
cleanliness centred upon the Jerusalem Temple; holiness in the
New Testament, as we have seen previously,[18] is associated with the
person of Christ in relation to life in the world. Christians, according to I Peter also, are to take Christ as their example and to follow
in his steps,[19] i.e. they have to pattern their lives on his. But Christ's
life was one of service of others unto death; ours must be likewise,
i.e. it must consist in service. This service is to be directed towards
our fellow men because only in this way can it be directed towards
God. That this is so becomes evident when we remember that
according to the New Testament there is no rule that requires us to
do to Christ what he has done for us; rather we have to render to
others the service he has rendered to us. So according to the narrative of the *pedilavium* Christ says: 'If I have washed your feet,

you also ought to wash [not mine but] one another's feet,'[20] i.e. Christ's action is aimed at us, while our action is to be aimed at our neighbour and only in so far as it is can it be at the same time for Christ. We must not, therefore, divorce mission, which is a sharing in the divine activity on behalf and in the service of man, from worship, as if the latter were something apart directed to God alone. Worship is the celebration of a relationship which is always two-way; it is a relationship with the holy and man – with the holy because it is with man and with man because it is with the holy.

Here we have yet another contrast with the Old Testament cultus. One of its chief purposes was the maintenance or restoration of good relations with God because man's well-being was understood to depend entirely upon such relations.[21] According to the New Testament, however, right relations with God are impossible without right relations with one's neighbour. This relationship rests upon life together in the world, of which the cultic acts provide, as it were, so many highlights. In terms of Christian worship this means that, like mission, it must be dialogical. Because 'man becomes man in personal encounter',[22] i.e. through dialogue, our worship must be dialogical in order that it may function as an instrument of humanization. We have to break away from the idea of monological and hieratically structured forms of worship. We must no longer regard them as sacred reserves but as offered in dedication to the world, to the actual joys and sorrows, labour and sufferings of man. The inner reality of worship and of mission is indeed self-offering, and we emasculate both if we separate one from the other or either from the practice of sacrificial service.

So far in this chapter I have been discussing the relationship of mission and worship in general, seeking to work out a theoretical basis for understanding their essential unity. The reaction of many people to this is likely to be acceptance of the logic of the reasoning, followed by an immediate demand about what it all means in practical terms. 'Yes,' they say, 'we agree – but . . . what must we do?' Such a specific question requires an equally specific answer. But here we encounter a difficulty. A specific answer can only be discovered within a specific situation. Further, each situation is different and so there is not one universally valid answer, but as many answers as there are situations. What one group of Christians may do in one situation is not regulative for what another group should do in another situation. There can, in fact, be no single scheme of strategy; there is no way we can escape the burden of our freedom and of our responsibility to respond to the holy *where we are*. We have to act as adults, making decisions in terms of *our* situation; and we should not expect others to make decisions for us and provide blueprints from outside the situation. Nevertheless, it is possible on the basis of all that has been written in this second part to formulate certain principles which could be embodied in rites of modernization. To these we turn to the next chapter.

15

Rites of Modernization

The title of this chapter is identical with that of a study by a social anthropologist named James L. Peacock. I have selected this deliberately, partly because it expresses precisely the theme which I now wish to develop and partly because I propose to begin by drawing upon the insights that Peacock has himself put forward.

Much of the work undertaken in the recent past by social anthropologists in analysing the role of religion in society has been dominated by functionalism. This means that, when considering ritual, emphasis has been placed upon the way in which it performs the function of reinforcing traditional social ties, preserving equilibrium and maintaining stability. In effect, its chief concern has been with the role of religion in the explanation of society, rather than with religion as such.[1] It was this kind of thinking that was examined in chapter 11 in terms of ritual and in chapter 12 in terms of religion. But this approach is not of great help in dealing with the relationship between ritual and social change, and it has, indeed, certain disadvantages. In the first place, it tends to focus attention upon institutions as data given at a moment of time, but this is to observe the realized potentialities of yesterday and to exclude the potentialities that exist today and may be realized tomorrow. In the second place, by its very nature it neglects any disfunctional aspects of religion and ritual. It does not concern itself, for example, with the ways in which religion, and its ritual expression, can transform or even destroy social structures as well as preserve them.[2] Yet it is precisely this that requires consideration, since the crisis of worship today is in part the outcome of social and cultural change.

If worship is to have meaning, it has to be understood in relation to this process of change; its characteristics must, therefore, be apprehended as different from those of rites which are preservative in intent.

Fortunately for my purpose this comparatively new aspect of social-anthropological studies has formed the basis of the field-work reported by Peacock in the book to which I referred in the opening paragraph. Consequently by drawing upon his research it will be possible to begin to provide the phrase 'rites of modernization' with content.

In order to appreciate the import of what Peacock has to say it is necessary to know something of Javanese society, which provides the background to his work. As in nearly every other country in both East and West, Java is undergoing urbanization, with all its accompanying features. Rural folk are leaving the villages and flocking to the towns. They are moving out of a pre-existent, closely-knit society, with its face-to-face relations, into the wider 'community' of the city with its mobility, specialization and functional relations. Initially many of these new town dwellers live in *kampungs*, which are so many urban slums or shanty-town neighbourhoods with many of the features of a rural Javanese village.

Within the Javanese village the principal ritual observance is the *slametan*. This consists of a feast among neighbours which may take place, for example, at the erection of a house or the celebration of a birth or in connection with a funeral. The female members of one family produce specially prepared dishes which are set out on mats in the living room. Invitations are issued to the male heads of eight to ten contiguous households. After a speech, explaining the spiritual purpose of the occasion, each man takes a few mouthfuls of food, wraps the remainder in banana-leaf baskets and returns to his house to share it with his relations. The *slametan* serves to sanctify the bond among neighbours by making them joint participants in a sacred feast; it rests upon a pre-existent community, promotes its harmony and equilibrium and strengthens neighbourhood solidarity.[3]

When these peasants move to the city, they continue to hold *slametans*, but the pressures of modern life – all that is involved in urbanization – are leading to the breakdown of the *kampung* and so the *slametan* is less frequently held. In effect what is happening is that the role of the *kampung* within the lives of its inhabitants is shrinking, and consequently the *slametan*, which sustained it and functioned as an integrating device, is similarly losing its relevance.[4]

It will be immediately apparent that this process in Java corresponds to what is happening in Western Europe in relation to Christian ritual. *Slametan* and *kampung* are parallel to parish eucharist and neighbourhood. We have already seen how within the urban situation in the West the residential neighbourhood plays a diminishing role in the life of man in a technological society and how this results in the devaluation of worship as the act of a pre-existing community.[5] The correspondence is exact. *Slametan* in the Javanese countryside parallels the celebration of the eucharist in the villages of Western Europe. The *kampung* is equivalent to the village-type community transferred to the city, which is mistakenly envisaged as an aggregrate of such village units. The dissolution of this form of community evacuates both eucharist in the West and *slametan* in Java of meaning. This conclusion supports to the full Mary Douglas's thesis that rituals cease to make sense when 'the social action in which they inhered no longer exists'.[6]

The result of all this in Java has been not the disappearance of ritual; instead *slametan* is being replaced by *ludruk*, which is a form of ritual drama more attuned to the contemporary situation than the *slametan* for which it is being substituted. Hence to examine *ludruk* is to become familiar with a 'rite of modernization'.

Ludruk reflects and promotes certain trends in contemporary Javanese society.[7] The simplest way to demonstrate this is to contrast the plots of the traditional plays with those of *ludruk* itself. Traditional plots present the idea that social mobility is virtually impossible – the proletarian never becomes a member of the élite. The plots are cyclic, emphasizing that though things may appear to change they really remain the same. They stress permanence and tradition; they are concerned with institutional equilibrium, which may be broken for a short time but is always restored in the end. Modern plots present the idea that it is possible for a proletarian to marry an élite person and set up a new household. They therefore foster and encourage social mobility. Their climax is the emergence of a situation which has not previously existed. They concentrate upon individuals and their successful attempts to achieve different status.[8] These two contrasting types of plot thus present different concepts of social action, and *ludruk* itself is an innovative ritual directly related to social change. Apparently each performance of four or more hours involves a high degree of audience participation, with those present reacting to the characters, and not infrequently they eat a meal in their seats during the proceedings.

In describing *ludruk* as a rite of modernization, Peacock is able to specify a number of the features that justify this title. In the first place, it directs attention away from the *kampung* to the wider urban society and even beyond to the nation as a whole. It does this by denigrating *kampung* life and idealizing extra-*kampung* society. In the second place, *ludruk* seeks to perform for this heterogeneous wider community what the *slametan* once did for the village; i.e., it points to a harmony, but to one that includes the greater diversity of the larger social unity or city. It trains the participants to operate in large-scale, non-face-to-face society, to empathize with strangers and to cope with unfamiliar situations. In the third place, *ludruk* desacralizes community by replacing magical concepts by rational goals. This means that the older view that a magical force pervades all objects now gives way to the idea that objects are means to an end. To this extent *ludruk* is anti-traditional. Fifthly, *ludruk* encourages the decline of traditional relationships and their substitution by ones freely entered into; so, for example, it fosters friendship and romantic love.[9] Finally, it expresses social and political criticism through the medium of the accompanying songs, the lyrics of which are pungent comments on the contemporary scene.[10]

The emergence of *ludruk* in Java demonstrates that it is possible to have a ritual action related to social change and to replace traditional forms with new ones that are meaningful within the context of modern life. This brief account of what is taking place within a different culture and in terms of different religious beliefs from those that obtain in the West and among Christians encourages one to think that a viable understanding of Christian worship today within a secular society should be possible. But Peacock's analysis not only provides grounds for optimism in pursuing such a quest, it also gives some specific indications of what may be involved in a Christian rite of modernization.

Such a Christian rite should:

1. Direct attention away from the congregation itself to the wider urban society in which it lives and indeed to the world;
2. Point to and manifest a unity within multiplicity;
3. Promote empathy with strangers and encourage new relationships;

4. Be a vehicle of social and political criticism;
5. Be a means of assisting the participants to accommodate to and cope with change.

The large liturgical assembly, being a gathering of groups, is well suited to achieve the first three of these goals, while the fourth can apply both to the assembly and to small groups. This social criticism could take the form of discussion or be embodied in hymns, so that songs such as 'We shall overcome' would replace the traditional lyrics which so often breathe an atmosphere of escapism and of other-wordliness.[11]*

Once the function of religion is understood to be not support for the *status quo* but the pioneering of change, then the social role of Christianity today can be defined in terms of hope. This means that each worshipping group faces its present experience of the world with trust in God and with hope for the future of this self-same world. The result will be discontent and dissatisfaction with the existing situation. Because of this hope, the Christian community should be a constant disturber within human society; it ceases to be an accommodating group, and living within the horizon of eschatological hope resists both quietism and ready acquiescence in the present. Of course:

People are tempted to use the Church's traditions as a supernatural argument to unite people in opposing change. Rather than leading its people to follow a life meaningful for the future, the Church thus can become an escape for those who want to stay forever in the past.[12]

But I am contending that worship is no longer to be regarded simply as a source of social adjustment, but as a creative force. By behaving in this manner, it demonstrates its realism. For 'hope alone is to be called "realistic", because it alone takes seriously the possibilities with which all reality is fraught. It does not take things as they happen to stand or to lie, but as progressing, moving things with possibilities of change.'[13] The function of worship can then be redefined as the celebration of hope and of change. It should assist the participants to understand change, to join in it and to adapt to it.

But worship of this kind cannot avoid conflict. Too often in the past the church has regarded conflict as culpable; it has sought to prevent its open expression, and its cultic acts have therefore assumed the character of a spiritual sedative. But without conflict there is no movement, no progression. It is only when the normality of conflict is recognized that its dramatic character can be removed and it can be utilized for good. The discussion relating to the world of politics and economics that would form part of an act of worship directed towards change would inevitably produce conflict, but if this is allowed for and contained, the dynamic of worship could be given full rein and the cultic forms themselves could mediate the dynamic of hope. The relevance of the previous discussion of instrumental groups needs to be recognized in connection with this. An instrumental group, it will be recalled, is one that has a particular objective to be achieved. When several groups come together, as in the large liturgical assembly, conflict can be contained if they are united in the pursuit of a common task. 'Hostility gives way when groups pull together to achieve overriding goals which are real and compelling to all concerned.'[14] This is not to say that conflict may not also have an evil aspect, especially if it arises out of unbridled self-interest. But recognizing this, one has to discover its creative elements and help people to face the alternatives. Conflict, indeed, is essential for life and change: only a graveyard is a place of perfect peace, but then it is occupied by the dead. Conflict can be a sign of health and provide the context for the inbreaking of newness.[15]

Such conflict is likely to be present in the large assembly, consisting of so many different groups, but it is in the latter that the reality of worship must first be rediscovered before the assembly itself can once again become viable. Indeed it can be said that the problem of worship is not that of discovering meaningful forms, but of rediscovering units of personal relations to celebrate it – hence the relevance of the previous discussion of the nature of groups.

It is at this juncture in the argument that we have to consider the relevance to Christian worship of the fifth element in a rite of modernization derived from Peacock's analysis, viz. that it should be a means of assisting the participants to accommodate to and cope with change.

There is no question that human beings are remarkably adaptable. They can live under the most diverse circumstances; they can survive in the most adverse conditions. They can inhabit spheres on the ocean bed or walk on the moon in their protective space-suits. Nevertheless, there is now a considerable body of evidence to indicate that there is a limit to man's capacity to respond to change. The amount of change the human organism can absorb is not infinite. Unless there is a balance between the rate of change and the rate of human response there result stress, anxiety, hostility, violence, physical illness and apathy.[16] These are symptoms of what Alvin Toffler has designated 'future shock', because, as he formulates it, 'change is the process whereby the future invades our lives'.[17] Future shock is experienced by individuals when they have to face too much change in too short a time.

However, while change carries with it this undoubted risk of breakdown, it may also be an opportunity and a challenge to creativity. It is for this latter reason that I have argued previously that the church should promote change, although not for its own sake but for the sake of humanization.[18] From this aspect I have suggested that worship, including provision for conflict, may be understood as the celebration of change and should assist the participants to understand it. But, what is the relation of worship, if any, to future shock, i.e. to the negative and destructive effects of change?

Toffler has specified numerous ways of coping with change so that overstimulation may be offset. He stresses the importance of 'stability zones', i.e. of certain enduring relationships that are carefully maintained despite all kinds of other change.[19] He draws attention to the need for some degree of continuity and quotes J. Gardner to the effect that 'mesmerized as we are by the very idea of change, we must guard against the notion that continuity is a negligible – if not reprehensible – factor in human history. It is a vitally important ingredient in the life of individuals, organizations and societies.'[20] Toffler also contends that to adapt to change one needs a framework within which new experiences can be assimilated.

It will be readily apparent that worship could fulfil each of these three functions. To spell this out is to advance further in our quest for a modern understanding of worship in relation to social change. As regards 'stability zones', clearly the meetings of primary groups, consisting of individuals in face-to-face relations, provide such opportunities, not to resist change but to manage it. As regards continuity, this may be secured through liturgy if the act of worship assists community identity by relating to tradition, by the real reaffirmation of common roots and by the acceptance of an agreed point of reference, viz. the model of the holy presented by Jesus.[21] In terms of a framework, ritual involves in part repetitive behaviour, which, 'whatever else its function, helps give meaning to non-repetitive events, by providing a backdrop against which novelty is silhouetted'.[22] Worship may also assist adaptation if it is itself related to specific events. For example, one drastic change experienced by many is the death of a loved one. Such a serious alteration in lifestyle may be more easily faced and accepted through an act of worship which helps the bereaved to come to terms with the new and unavoidable situation. The sharing of worries and concerns, the celebration of changes of employment – these and many other daily occurrences can be the substance and vehicle of worship, and should be if worship is to help adaptation to future shock. Moreover, if worship is a celebration of hope, bringing the hoped-for future into contact with the present and providing a stimulus for reshaping the world, it may be defined as a means to promote future-consciousness, and this in itself furthers the adaptative reaction.

In the past, as we have seen,[23] ritual has functioned as a 'change-buffer'. Indeed, it has been a bulwark against change. I am not suggesting that this cluster of previous functions be reasserted, so that worship is again understood as maintaining the social order, but rather that worship should be conceived as a means of assisting the participants to accommodate to and cope with change without avoiding it or opting out of history. In other words, worship should cease to inoculate against change; it should not be an escape mechanism, but instead, should assist adaptation.

Several of these points now require further elaboration. First of all, it should be recognized that 'community', even as a 'stability zone', is not an end in itself. A group of human beings may meet to accomplish a common task, but if their purpose is nothing more than community itself they will soon dissolve, because they have no objective beyond themselves to unite them.[24] As O. and I. Pratt express it: 'A group that comes together simply for the purpose of coming together, that has no definite purposive context in which to celebrate its liturgy, is inevitably a rather artificial unit' – and so is its worship.[25] Nevertheless, while the need for each group to have its instrumental aspect is thus stressed, it must not be forgotten that worship is symbolic action. It is directed towards the creation of moral ideals and concepts of reality. It is therefore not simply to be identified with technical action, which is action directed towards the achievement of specific economic, political and social ends. Of course, the symbolic action may have political or other consequences; it may, for example, express and inculcate a concept of social action – this concept then becomes a determinant of social action outside the actual time devoted to worship. Social life is then apprehended as the sphere within which those who have participated in the ritual strive to actualize the ideals it has expressed. Worship, as symbolic action, then becomes an active agency within society as a whole; it helps the participants to understand society and both what they do and have to do within it. It can therefore assist modernization in the sense that it enables the worshippers to adopt new perspectives, to adapt to change and to become agents of change. It teaches attitudes by drawing people into empathy with its action, and so there is a correlation between what is expressed and the worshippers' daily conduct.

However, the continuing life of any group depends upon the extent to which its acts of worship are a ratification and reinforcement of intimate human love. In other words, Christian worship is a special kind of symbol 'precisely because it wishes to say something special about the nature of human relationships'.[26] It declares that love is the fundamental reality at the basis of life. But this symbol loses much of its impact in the large assembly of the traditional individualistic type where those present are virtually strangers. Within the nexus of I-Thou relationships, however, ritual can be perceived as a sign and means of a shared life. Hence 'liturgy . . . will be done only from love. This means it will not be done at all unless it is really meaningful.'[27]

Certain corollaries follow from this, which can be summed up in four words: meaning, accountability, identity and tradition. By 'meaning', I refer to the function of worship as the expression of a conviction about the inherent structure of reality. It serves to explain that reality to us and to help us to see how we ought to live in order to be in harmony with that reality; it provides a framework within which the new experiences can be assimilated. The worshipper thereby acquires an interpretative scheme,[28] and is enabled to perceive meaning in life in the world by being sensitized to the presence of the holy in and through the secular. This perception makes the act of worship a rite of accountability in the sense that it demands a response to the meaning and life-pattern expressed. One accepts responsibility for life in the world in the service of the holy through the service of one's fellow-men. Worship is then the symbolization of

values and commitment, and so is a liturgical expression of the love
of neighbour. Further, it provides a frame of reference for behaviour
and so promotes the achievement of identity. In the ritual of small
groups there is both an interpersonal acknowledgment of separateness and of personhood as well as the establishment of the identity of
the self. In the ritual of large assemblies the same may be accomplished
as regards the greater comunity's own sense of identity. It is at this
point that tradition has its part to play. Tradition is funded experience, which has to be repossessed by each person, for 'the truth of
Christianity is not a timeless truth but the truth of an event or events
in history. Hence the need for the community to preserve the
memorial of those events, to remain in touch with this past, and to
make the link between this past and the rest of history.'[29] In this
way continuity is preserved.

The essential tradition for Christians is, of course, contained in
the Bible, which itself provides the model of the holy upon which
this whole study is based. This statement raises the question of how
the model is to be applied to worship. In effect this application
involves the affirmation of the secular reality of worship and, at the
same time, the perception of that reality as mediating the holy.
Worship then does not presuppose the absence of the holy whose
presence it is its object to effect. Again, celebrations of the cultus
are not so many occasions for the church to provide sacred spaces
for the divine invasion of the secular.[30] On the contrary, worship
is based upon the unity of the sacred and the secular, otherwise
there is a fragmentation of experience and the holy has no means
at its disposal through which it can be mediated. Hence worship
must be a celebration of everyday life and not a series of isolated
acts. Unless it is understood in this way, both Christian faith and
practice become no more than 'a hot-house plant unable to survive
except in the artificially controlled atmosphere of a churchly environment'.[31] It is indeed apposite to note that in Western Europe, where
certain acts of worship do still spring from daily life – baptism
in relation to birth, matrimony in relation to marriage and funerals
connected with death – there persists a relatively popular observance
of it.

It is for this reason that the symbols employed have to be rooted
in the world of nature and of human relationships. Such symbols
belong to the sphere of finite reality and, as symbols, express man's
relationship to the infinite. Nevertheless, these symbols are not to be

selected in an arbitrary manner in such a way that their secular nature is denied or is regarded as alien to ultimate reality. So, for example, water is used in baptism because it has its own natural properties, i.e. of cleansing and even of bringing death. It is this natural power that makes it suitable to be the medium of the holy. Similarly the bread and wine in the eucharist are not fortuitous; they represent the natural powers that nourish the body. Moreover, food is intimately associated with our first experience of love. The giving of food to a hungry infant by its mother mediates her love to her offspring. This feeding is, or should be, an expression of love, and so food and love are associated for the child. The nourishment 'becomes for him a sacrament of his *being* and of his relationships. In every culture that we know anything about, we see this sacramental relation between food and fellowship.'[32] Howe goes on to state that 'the ultimate of this association is to be seen in the Holy Communion, which we may truly regard as the sacrament of the common food and the uncommon love.' It is precisely because of this connection of food and love that the eucharist can be a meaningful vehicle of fellowship. It is indeed worthy of note that one of the earliest sayings ascribed to Jesus is: 'Man shall not live by bread alone,'[33] while one of his latest is: 'This is my body.'[34] Here we see the dual character of reality, which is at the same time a unity. Bread alone is not enough; equally, nourishment for the spirit is insufficient. It is bread that both provides energy for man as a physical being and is also the body of Christ which is the basic human diet and mediates the holy through the secular.

Eating together is both a biological and a social event; when it is ritualized it transcends the biological process in importance and significance, while never ceasing to rest upon and include that physical basis.[35] Further, as a social event, celebrated within a fellowship, it manifests the eternal Thou and, at the same time, functions as a rite of integration, binding the co-diners closer together with one another and with the holy. Indeed the eucharist, understood from this perspective, declares the unity of the sacred and the secular and would be impossible without it. It also discloses the unity of the worlds of I-Thou and I-It.

The eucharistic species are inanimate objects which are personalized to become the medium of union with Christ. Things are thereby shown to be instruments of fulfilling relations between man and man and between man and the holy.[36] In so far as they serve this sacramental purpose, they have a part in the process of humanization. So the essential meaning of the eucharist is, in part, to be found in communion and community, not in individualistic salvation. If this is not the meaning and effect of the celebration, then the act of worship is depersonalized and what is primarily sacramental is made of no effect. Instead of the species being instruments for fulfilling relations, they become mere things to be used, e.g. for the individual's supposed spiritual profit. Communion, after all, means 'union with'. If we ask, 'Union with whom?', the answer is with one another and therefore with the holy.

As symbols, then, the bread and wine refer to the relations between persons, between persons and objects and between persons in terms of objects.[37] Instrumental the objects are, in the sense of mediating the holy through transpersonal encounter, but 'if the faithful have come to think of rites as means to health and prosperity, like so many magic lamps to be worked by rubbing, there comes a day when the whole ritual apparatus must seem an empty nothing.'[38]

Nevertheless, it is a mistake to hold, as some do, that the essence of the eucharist resides exclusively in the celebration itself. In the words of Rosemary Haughton,

For a certain kind of theology it may be sufficient to describe the eucharist in terms of the presence and action of Christ. But this presence is not something on its own, unrelated to the people who take part in the celebration. At some point, somebody must ask, what does this presence and action mean in terms of the experience of people taking part? What is happening to them? What results should it, does it, produce?[39]

To answer these questions we have to begin by recognizing that the eucharist has two poles, neither of which is part of the ritual observance itself. These two poles are: 1. the sacrifice of Christ on the cross; 2. that love which is at the heart of human existence in all its secularity. The eucharist actualizes the identity of these two poles, for it 'realizes' the presence of the Holy One within our daily life.

The Christian life is one of sacrifice, i.e. it should reproduce the pattern of the life of Christ. But as we have seen previously,[40] all life in its movement towards fullness is paschal in character. The eucharist is related to this in that it is the means whereby we are enabled to sacrifice ourselves each day, i.e. to reproduce in our daily lives that paschal pattern. As a cultic act it does not constitute an interval in daily living; it is co-extensive with the whole of our existence. It helps to conform the Christian to the model of the holy and so to involve himself in human society in service.

This interpretation of the eucharist is identical with that formulated by Søren Kierkegaard, who argued that it consecrates the communicants to sacrifice. He contended that Christians do not live off the sacrifice of Christ, but are drawn into it so that their lives may be self-offerings. In his view this insight had been completely obscured by the contemporary church. 'Their whole business is based upon *living off* the fact that others are sacrificial, their Christianity is *to receive sacrifice*. If it were proposed to them that they should themselves be sacrificial, they would regard it as a strange and unchristian demand.'[41] This sacrificial understanding is fundamental in Kierkegaard's view and he supported it by a lively, if by no means certain, exegesis of two of the sayings of Jesus, viz. the one about 'fishers of men'[42] and the other about 'the salt of the earth'.[43] According to Kierkegaard, Christ's summons to be fishers of men was a call to sacrifice. He admitted that from the point of view of common sense this may seem absurd. 'Can one think of anything more topsy-turvy than that sort of fishing, where fishing means being sacrificed, so that it is not the fishermen who eat the fish but the fish who eat the fishermen?' Hence the real meaning of the summons was changed and understood to refer to man-fishing. 'It was quite simply arranged. Just as one company is formed to speculate in the herring-fishery, another in cod-fishing, another in whaling, etc., so man-fishing was carried on by a stock company which guaranteed its members a dividend of such and such a per cent. And what was the result of this? . . . The result was that they caught a prodigious number of herring, or what I mean is men, Christians; and of course the company was in brilliant financial condition.'[44] Similarly as regards the salt of the earth; 'Christ required "followers" and defined precisely what he meant: that they should be salt, willing to be sacrificed. . . . But to be salt and to be sacrificed is not something to which thousands naturally lend themselves, still less millions.'[45]

One is reminded of Dostoevsky's Grand Inquisitor, who argues that the demands of Christ are too stern and that the church had consequently to replace them with a programme of giving mankind what it wants. In contrast to this, the paschal pattern *must* embrace the whole of life, including the eucharist.

The second pole relates to human love, and directs attention to the understanding of the eucharist as a meal which ratifies and reinforces intimate human love and so provides a model for relationships among all men.

If the Church goes through a ritual that expresses the 'fellowship' of love, and does not show fellowship and love in its secular actions – not just the actions of individuals but the corporate activity that expresses in secular terms the transforming purpose – then this is nonsense.[46]

So this pole of love joins the first of suffering, in that the cross is the demonstration of supreme love, while suffering is found only where one loves; it springs from the passion of love and directs Christians outwards away from the church and themselves.[47] Nothing of this could be achieved through the eucharist were the holy not already present within human secular existence. Indeed, if the world does not in itself mediate the encounter with the holy, then the 'salvation brought by Christ could only be effected by turning us away from earthly realities which then become theologically incomprehensible'.[48] Worship is not withdrawal from the world, because it is in and through the world that we meet the holy. Rather worship, as expressed in the eucharist, makes explicit the sacramental and paschal nature of the whole of life; it illuminates human life from within and enables us to become conscious of its true character and purpose. Hence one may speak of the representative character of sacraments pointing to the universality of the sacramental principle, i.e. 'the bread of the sacrament stands for all bread and ultimately for all nature.'[49] This is not to say that it helps us to experience more vividly what we would have experienced anyway. Here we should heed the warning of Mary Douglas.

Ritual is not merely like the visual aid which illustrates the verbal instructions for opening cans and cases. If it were just a kind of dramatic map or diagram of what is known it would always follow experience. But in fact ritual does not play this secondary role. It can come first in formulating experience. It can permit knowledge of what would otherwise not be known at all. It does not merely externalize experience, bringing it out into the light of day, but it modifies experience in so expressing it.[50]

So worship is a focusing mechanism, enabling us to interpret worldly experience in terms of the model of the holy. Indeed all ritual has an exemplary model-making character. Eucharistic worship displays the model of the holy, assists in the formulating of a mental set and so enables the participants to come to awareness of the holy and to respond to the holy in their daily lives. Worship is then a means of assisting those who take part to become or remain reality-oriented. It helps men in the world to 'see beneath the surface of worldly things and everyday relationships to the holy depths that given meaning and worth'.[51]

So far in this chapter I have been concerned with the substance of worship – its meaning and possibility in a secular universe – and I have said little about its forms. This has been quite deliberate, and is intended to supply a lack to which Hovda and Huck have drawn attention by their observation that 'experimental liturgies to date have in the main concentrated on the "how" and have substituted a few generalizations for the "what"'.[52] However, the argument may be further advanced if I now attempt to outline a possible structure for eucharistic worship which could embody the understanding previously worked out. The question immediately arises: where do we begin?

Whenever the church has been true to its biblical inheritance, it has taken its agenda from the contemporary world. Since authentic theology arises from an interplay of the gospel and the world, we have to take the world seriously; we have to take its questions to heart; we have to let it tell us what its agenda is so that we can write the gospel into it. This was the procedure adopted by the early Christians, and indeed by Christ himself, when he and they created our first liturgical forms. When the early Christians celebrated the communion service they would appear to have repeated the Last Supper *en toto*. They began with a blessing, breaking and distribution of bread; then followed the meal, and they ended with a blessing and the distribution of wine. So they took their ritual practice from the world of Judaism – the pattern of a meal, and thereby affirmed the unity of the sacred and the secular. Just as the Jewish father in his home began a meal by saying grace over a loaf, breaking and distributing it, so did the leader of the Christian fellowship. And just as the Jewish father at the Passover meal explained what he was doing in terms of God's action at the Exodus, so Christ first, and after him his representatives, accompanied the familiar actions with an explanation: This is my body . . . this is my blood. The agenda of the world was accepted and its inner meaning made clear, as the early Christians gathered around a table in the house of one of their fellow believers. This was over nineteen hundred years ago.

If we adopt this same approach now, in order to have a point of departure, then we have to consider the phenomenology of the meal at the present day, and then, in the light of this, decide what restructuring of our eucharistic meal is called for. We are, in fact, seeking the human reality of a meal in order that it may provide the basis of the reality of our eucharistic worship. The type of meal I propose to examine is the family meal on formal occasions, i.e. not the everyday lunch or dinner, but the feasts with which a family, together with some friends, observes birthdays and similar anniversaries.

In most households a meal usually begins with the handing round of bread to be eaten with the first course, e.g. with the soup. In England this is likely to be in the form of either complete rounds from a pre-sliced loaf or pieces cut according to taste from a loaf on the table. Sometimes crusty French bread may be provided and, since this is a family occasion and one does not stand on ceremony, it is likely that, as in France itself, this kind of loaf will simply be broken into chunks by hand. The bread in any case is passed round on a plate or board and each helps himself.

The next common item is the provision of a drink and, as this is a special occasion, probably of wine or beer. If a red wine is being served, this may have had the cork drawn beforehand and it may have been decanted. If a white suits the menu, it is likely to be brought from the refrigerator and the cork pulled. After tasting it, to see if it is in good condition, the father, or one of the family at his request, will fill the glasses. The first drink is usually taken together, and since this is a celebration, a toast will probably be called for. During this time conversation is taking place, which should not be a monologue by the father, otherwise he is likely to bore the others, nor will the contributions be primarily didactic; and since some friends are present, it would be rude to indulge in private language or swop family jokes in which they cannot share.

To this pattern may be added two features from other kinds of contemporary meals represented by Rotary lunches or dining-club dinners. These invariably begin with a grace and end with the reading of a paper and a discussion upon it. It may be said that a grace is merely a superstitious survival; it is, however, very tenacious – at none of the secular meals I attend, whether a sailing-club annual dinner or the meetings of a graduates' club, would they think of beginning without one – and in any case an expression of gratitude is not unbecoming civilized adults.

The meal thus described is clearly to be distinguished from those taken in a cafeteria, where one frequently eats alone and at one's own pace. Such a meal is a convenient modern device for obtaining individual sustenance quickly, but it has little to do with fellowship, whereas a family meal is essentially an occasion for expressing and experiencing fellowship, unity, a sense of community, love and, unless one is very self-centred, outgoing concern.

Here, then, is the human secular reality of the meal, the structure of which may be summarized as follows:

1. Grace.
2. Sitting down at table.
3. Taking of bread and preparation for distribution, if not pre-sliced, by cutting or breaking.
4. Helping oneself to bread.
5. Eating bread.
6. Taking of wine.
7. Pouring of wine into glasses.
8. Toast.
9. Drinking of wine.
10. Address.
11. Discussion.

If this structure is now re-expressed in terms of the eucharist, we obtain the follow outline:

1. All standing, a prayer of thanksgiving, during the course of which God is blessed, and the absent members of the family unable to be present and those in need are remembered.
2. All sit round the table.
3. The president takes the bread and breaks or cuts it according to local usage.
4. A plate is passed round containing the bread and each helps himself.
5. The bread is eaten together.
6. The president takes the wine.
7. The wine is poured into the several glasses.

8. A prayer is offered, being a further blessing of God.
9. The wine is drunk by all together.
10. There is an address.
11. There is a concluding discussion.

This pattern embodies the majority of the characteristics, specified at the end of chapter 13[53] as corresponding to worship, that it is possible to discern within secular events. Thus it comprises physical activity (characteristic 5) and participation (no. 10), while being a celebration (no. 7). By means of the discussion provision is made for spontaneity (no. 11) and the sharpening of critical discernment (no. 2), both of which require openness to one another (no. 3), and the maintenance of intellectual integrity (no. 4). The address, as well as the dialogue, can make explicit the relationship to ultimate concern (no. 14), leading to commitment (no. 1). All of this is envisaged as an expression of love (no. 6), an actualization of community (no. 8) directed towards the restoration of wholeness (no. 12).

It will be obvious that this pattern does not correspond to any eucharistic service celebrated at the present day by the churches; some of its features are found in some of them but no one church has every one. We normally have the address or sermon at the beginning and not at the end, and seldom does any discussion follow. We do not generally sit around a table, although this was the practice in former days in Scotland and is still so in some Dutch Reformed churches. We do not help ourselves to the bread but have it given to us, as if we were not adults but children. In many churches, through not in all, we drink, or rather sip, from a single wine-glass or chalice and, completely oblivious of hygiene, we do not have separate ones. In those churches where individualism is rife and the corporate or transpersonal nature of the community is not appreciated, the impression given is that of a help-yourself cafeteria. Where large congregations are concerned, as in some Roman Catholic churches, only a small proportion of those present know each other. Conversation, in the sense of dialogue, is lacking; monologue is the norm. The prayers, especially those that stem from the Reformation, are excessively didactic, and the language is full of allusions and terms which only the initiated of long standing can appreciate. It is little wonder that the human reality of our worship has been lost.[54]*

The structure that I have just outlined, being what it is, is no more than the bare bones of a possible form of eucharistic celebration. In order to fill it out a little, it is necessary to recall briefly some of the points already made in this chapter and add others. Because of the relation of a rite of modernization to social and political criticism, it would be reasonable to suppose that this would find a place in the conversation, address or discussion, and could be further articulated in song. Let us not forget that the Last Supper itself included all these elements. Further, since this may issue in a divergence of view, we should expect conflict to be present – as indeed it was also present in the Upper Room[55] – and it will have to be faced openly. Again, the pattern of the meal is that of a special observance, such as a birthday. Similarly, the eucharist must be the celebration of life in the secular world; this means that it should be related to a specific task or tasks which the group has undertaken and should spring out of the life of that group. It should not, then, be possible to say of Christians what Peter Brook has said of the theatre: 'We do not know how to celebrate, because we do not know what to celebrate.'[56] Tradition and the re-presentation of the model of the holy also have their part to play in developing the identity of the group, relating to history and to the world. This may be achieved by the inclusion of a reading from the Bible.

In relation to this last item, it may be helpful to provide an illustration from experience on a housing estate in Germany,[57] and to link this with our previous consideration of mission and worship.

Leonberg-Ramtel is the newest district in the county town of Leonberg, not far from Stuttgart. It now has a population of 5,000, two-thirds of whom are Protestants. The Christians living in the area soon came to the conclusion that their task was to be a church for others – they were there not to serve themselves but the community as a whole. They understood the church centrifugally, not as a come-structure but as a collection of service units. It was at this point in their understanding of mission that the subject of worship had also to be faced. I quote from a first-hand account:

What is the role of the Sunday service in a parish consisting of service teams? Could it not become no more than the refuge for a sheltered pietism? And how does it correspond to the New Testament's unequivocal declaration that the proper worship of a Christian is new obedience in everyday life? These were among the questions which the voluntary workers pondered for a whole year before concluding that a congregation closely associated with real life needs worship, and that it is precisely this congregation within the housing estate which can discover the true function of its worship, and above all new and varied forms.

The monopoly of the Sunday service must be abolished. Bible discussions in house groups, Communion celebration for the service-teams, discussion evenings dealing with factual problems in a theologically responsible manner, theological seminars – all these must be raised to the level of worship and be prepared with care. The Bible reveals its power when studied in relation to concrete issues. Thus the congregation came to appreciate the fact that some people were in the working groups but not in church on Sundays, and they gradually stopped arranging Bible classes where texts were taken up in a continuous sequence, because it was seen that Bible study does not create a group but that an already existing group begins to study the Bible. This Bible study is then no longer a leisure activity for devout people, but an indispensable function in the life of the group.

Worship must not only take various shapes; it must be intensified. This calls for dialogue and serious participation by the non-theological members. Otherwise no answer can be given to the thousand-and-one questions arising from actual situations. Worship is the place where these questions are met, where mutual correction and encouragement takes place and new bearings are found. . . . No one felt these services to be extravagant. Their functional suitability was recognized. The significance of worship for every day became clear.

Here, on this housing estate in Germany, I venture to suggest that they have not only acknowledged the unity of mission and worship; they are living it and thereby witnessing to it. A centrifugal concept of mission, wedded to a centrifugal practice of worship, is making sense. Moreover – and this is the principal reason for citing this example – the Bible study is not an alien element artificially inserted in the cult; it arises out of the life of the group itself.

Continuing with the further examination of the structure outlined above, we next observe that it demands festivity, whereby, without leaving daily life behind, its banality is transcended, just as Jesus turned what he had himself done into a festival.[58] This is to be associated with joy, which is the concomitant of hope. So Alan Paton says: 'When one brings joy, and when one experiences joy in bringing it, one has what I can only describe as an experience of God.'[59] Hence the holy, mediated through worship, is not an object to be used; he is not necessary in the sense that he exists simply to meet human need; he exists to be enjoyed; he is an active presence in which to rejoice. The festive celebration is then to be understood as a sharing of happiness, an appreciation, renewal and deepening of fellowship and an acknowledgment of the divine activity in history. It marks an occasion and is a thanksgiving for joys and sorrows shared. This involves the rediscovery of that eschatological note which characterized the gatherings of the early Christians who are said to have taken 'their food with gladness'.[60]

Within the give and take of such I-Thou relations, there is clearly no place for feelings of superiority or inferiority. Indeed ascendance-submission relations are not true interpersonal relations.[61] This immediately affects our understanding of the holy as it is sensitized through worship. It is possible to think of man's relation to the holy as that of a vassal who has to make periodic acts of homage to his Lord. But if the presence of the holy in our life situation is a constant factor, whether we are conscious of it or not, and if everything we do is capable of placing us in a relationship with the holy, then the problem is different. We do not settle any debt of honour to the holy by interrupting our activity as human beings; we have to maintain an attitude to every action, including worship, which sees it both as the service of the holy and as the fulfilment of our role as human beings.[62] To follow the pattern under consideration is to be liberated from the numinous.

It should not, however, be supposed that I am advancing this pattern as an absolute norm or indeed as a norm of any kind. In the first place, it is too obviously modelled upon the social habits of the well-to-do British middle class to be of universal application. Not only could other social practices be utilized, e.g. a cheese and wine party as suggested by O. and I. Pratt[63], but the patterns of working-class celebration would be different, and social rituals, in any case, are not the same in every culture and in every country. Moreover, this particular structure may suit one type of group; it is doubtful if it could be adapted to the large liturgical assembly. What is suitable for a domestic occasion may be out of place at a more public gathering. Thus a Regimental Sergeant Major who acted as such in his own house would be regarded as both pompous and laughable; but if he behaved on the parade ground with the same informality which he adopted at home, he would be considered slovenly and would soon be demoted. The proper balance of informality and stylization differs according to the nature of the group or community which is meeting. This suggests that more than one structure is required. Indeed liturgical uniformity, which seems to some so desirable, can be regarded as entirely out of place in a pluriform society and as, in any case, 'an aspect of the church's form of power, because it is the principle underlying the control of humanity as a mass'.[64]

Ritual is a necessary basis for good manners; it can facilitate rather than impede personal relations.[65] In time, however, ritual practices may become outdated, and so eventually they have to be changed. Similarly, in relation to worship, ritual is a mechanism to foster personal exchange, but in a society in change it is bound to have a provisional character.

This is not to say that a eucharistic celebration is to be equated with a 'happening'.[66]* Of course, the purpose of a happening is to turn observers into participants; it thus shares one aspect of eucharistic involvement, but, as David Martin has pointed out: 'Ritual not merely mechanizes meaning but maintains it, whereas an attempt to concentrate meaning in one spontaneous totally genuine moment is just self-defeating.'[67] Hence the vital necessity of worship, for 'it is impossible to maintain the holy merely as an idea or a general pervading spirit; actual celebration is required so that, in so far as the holy coincides with religion, religion must take on a positive and visible form – a cult and church'.[68]

Moreover, a continuing series of happenings could eventually drive away the less creative and, since they have usually to be pre-planned, those responsible could be manipulating the large gathering and so denying free response.

Yet unless worship grows from below, rather than being imposed from above, and unless it starts from occasions that belong to everyday life, it will not be relevant to man in the secular universe and so will not have meaning. The result would then be a shrinkage in human experience. Without the encounter with the holy in life and worship, man undergoes an impoverishment.

My task is nearly accomplished. In this second part we have passed from an analysis of the crisis of worship today, by way of sociological and socio-anthropological insights and with the aid of secular rituals and a theological understanding of the dialectic of mission and worship, to rites of modernization. In this concluding chapter I have sought to give an understanding of worship which is in accordance with the model of the holy presented in Part I. I have given one single example of a possible structure for contemporary worship. I believe that this shows that the choice before us is not only between the ghetto and the desert.

Of course, the subject could have been approached in many other different ways. It is perfectly legitimate, for example, to begin with current experimental forms – of which there are not a few – expounding and analysing them.[69]* This task, however, is best executed by those who themselves are involved in this liturgical creativity, and for that reason I have not attempted it. Instead, let me describe two more overtly 'religious' celebrations which in themselves break no new ground.

It is 6 a.m. I am in the dining-room of a semi-detached house on the outskirts of Leeds. There are six of us around the table: the vicar of the parish, a trades-union official and his wife, two neighbours and myself. The vicar is dividing up the round of bread which the wife has provided. We eat and drink. I am acutely conscious of a fellowship which binds us together. Although all but the vicar are unknown to me (apart from a brief introduction a few minutes before), and although there are barriers of class and education that divide us, I am aware of a sense of the in-between, of unity, of *shālōm*. I am given a glimpse of the holy as that which knits men together and overthrows walls of separation.

It is 6.30 p.m. A large prefabricated concrete hut in one of the side streets of Santa Cruz, Bolivia. It is filled with Bolivians, some very dark-skinned, revealing their Indian ancestry; many have tattered clothes, others are evidently in their colourful best. I rise to speak. What can I say? My carefully prepared notes are useless. These are simple people, not given to theological analysis in the form habitual to an academic. I speak about the humour of Jesus, about the joy at the heart of the Christian life in the world, of the joy that was in the heart of Jesus even in the shadow of the cross. I have a sense of shame – I experience a judgment – in the presence of these underprivileged folk – I who have come from an affluent society, who spend more on tobacco in a week than many can earn in a month. Their language I can understand when it is spoken slowly, but my English sounds odd to their ears and my talk has to be translated sentence by sentence. Through the barriers of race, speech, privilege, I know myself to be one with these people, and this sense of unity carries with it anguish at my own incapacity to assist them to rise above a sub-human standard of living. They laugh as I retell the jokes of Jesus; their joy is infectious. I am in the presence of the holy mediated through the persons of this little Bolivian congregation of Methodists. I have glimpses of the divine joy, of that presence that brings joy. There is no discontinuity between the divine and human rejoicing; they interpenetrate each other and the human joy discloses the divine depths.

In each of these incidents, the interpersonal – the medium of the holy – breaks through, despite my lack of previous acquaintance with those present. This does not conflict with my former emphasis on the need for face-to-face groups – it only shows that the holy is not always confined by our social limitations.

Finally, there is a quotation that speaks for itself. It is from a sermon delivered by Dean Charles Buck on the first Sunday after Christmas, 1963, in Boston's St Paul's Episcopal Cathedral.

Last Thursday night some of you attended a Freedom Rally in this church. Two busloads of Negro high-school children from Williamstown, North Carolina, participated in that rally. They sat on folding chairs in the chancel. They prayed. They sang. They clapped hands. At one point they marched up and down the aisles in a rhythm unlike anything in the hymnal. Nothing remotely like it, I am prefectly certain, has ever happened here before.[70]

Notes

Books listed in the Bibliography are referred to by section and number

Preface

1. Marinoff (V.17).

2. Davies (V.8).

1. Exit from the Sacral Universe

1. The effect of this transformation upon social relations is mainly considered in Part II in terms of community and worship.
2. The *confessio* is the shrine housing the relics of a saint or martyr.
3. The reference is to St Anthony's Fire, which has been traced to poisons generated in corrupt rye bread.
4. Quoted by Coulton (IV.2), 2f.
5. *Ibid.*, 155.
6. Quoted by Poole (IV.7), 41f.
7. *Ibid.*, 42ff.
8. Quoted by Heer (IV.5), 300.
9. Coulton (IV.2), 71.
10. I am indebted to Dr W. H. Scott of Trinity College, Quezon City, Philippines, for this information.
11. Coulton (IV.2), 151.
12. *Ibid.*, 26–9.
13. Poole (IV.7), 44f.
14. Davies (IV.3), 92.
15. This is the argument of James Ussher, Archbishop of Armagh (1625–56), cf. More & Cross (IV.6), 691ff.
16. *Henry VI Part II*, Act IV, Sc. 7, quoted by Poole (IV.7), 8 n.4.
17. Moltmann (XII.43), 306; (XII.45), 131–4.
18. *Odes* III.6, quoted by Moltmann (III.18), 10.
19. Houtart & Rémy (XI.11), 20.
20. *Ibid.*, (XI.12), 36.
21. *Ibid.*, 193.
22. Eliade (VIII.1), 285.
23. James (VIII.5), 134–40.
24. Brightman (XIII.4), 119, 127, 159, 168.
25. Wordsworth (XIII.28), 31, 84.
26. Dawson (IV.4).
27. de Margerie (V.16), 391.
28. von Rad (I.14), 111.
29. Robinson (XII.59), 11ff.
30. *Ascent of Mount Carmel*, I. iv.4
31. J. M. Gonzalez-Ruiz in Taylor (V.28), 190.
32. First German edition 1917; quotations taken from the English translation and from the edition of 1939.
33. Otto (V.21), 5.
34. *Ibid.*, 19.
35. *Ibid.*, 113.
36. *Ibid.*, 10.
37. *Ibid.*, 14.

38. *Ibid.*, 26.
39. *Ibid.*, 28.
40. Durkheim (XI.7), 37ff.
41. Editorial in *Maison-Dieu*, 17, 1949, 7.
42. Caillois (V.4), 11.
43. I am here reproducing some sections from Davies (V.8), 214f.
44. van den Leeuw (VIII.7), 47.
45. Eliade (V.10), 24.
46. Caillois (V.4), 58.
47. Heer (IV.5), 40.
48. Davies (V.8), *passim*.
49. Heer (IV.5), 38f.
50. Metz (XII.42), 144.
51. Houtart & Rémy (XI.12), 37.
52. Gorer (II.5).
53. Cf. Martin (V.19).
54. Metz (XII.42), 85.
55. Some writers contend that the Renaissance was largely responsible for the shift from God to man; this is both an oversimplification (cf. Bainton (IV.1)) and an underestimation of the effect of the technological revolution.
56. Vahanian (XII.72), 78.
57. Houtart & Rémy (XI.11), 193.
58. Altizer & Hamilton (XII.2), 52.
59. Nicholls (XII.46), 228.
60. Gregor Smith (XII.64), 75.
61. Esslin (VI.16), 57.
62. Eliade (VIII.3), 59f.
63. Altizer & Hamilton (XII.2), 40.
64. Acquaviva (V.1), 56.
65. *Ibid.*, 61f.
66. *Ibid.*, 65.
67. Hamilton (XII.25), 53.
68. Keen (XII.32), 90.
69. Hamilton (XII.25), 41.
70. Koestler (VI.28), 100.
71. Mehl (XI.19), 78.
72. Grand'maison (V.11), vol. II, 33.
73. Buber (IX.7), 28.
74. Cox (XII.14), 4.
75. Watzke (XI.25), 93.

2. *The Nature of Perception*

1. Gombrich (VII.4), 157.
2. Beloff (VII.1), 44.
3. Cf. Macquarrie (XII.40), 149.
4. Langer (VII.6), 58.
5. Douglas (X.4), 36.
6. Malraux (VII.7), 20f.
7. Gombrich (VII.4), 61ff.
8. *Ibid.*, 62.
9. *Ibid.*, 73.
10. Quoted *ibid.*, 11.
11. Wilson (VI.45), 232.
12. Gluckman (X.8), 9.
13. Turner (X.14), 8f.
14. Popper (VII.10), 280.
15. Dubos (VII.3), 93f.
16. Russell (IX.28), 32f.
17. Argyle (XI.1), 115.
18. John 20. 11–16.
19. Cf. Schillebeeckx (XII.61), 53.
20. Koestler (VII.5), 72.
21. Ogletree (XII.50), 48.
22. Dretske (VII.2), 4–77.
23. *Ibid.*, 154.
24. Berger & Luckmann (XI.4), 199.
25. Mucchielli (VII.8), 12.
26. Luke 7. 36–50.
27. Piaget (VII.9), 365.
28. E.g. Hick (IX.21).
29. Dretske (VII.2), 201.
30. For many other examples see the fascinating experiments described by Toch & Smith (VII.11).
31. *All Religions are One.*
32. *Auguries of Innocence*, 107 – 110.
33. *Everlasting Gospel*, d, 98–101.
34. *Marriage of Heaven and Hell*, 14.

35. Silone (VI.40), 105ff. 36. Cf. John 1.35–51.

3. *The Model of the Holy*

1. Ramsey (IX.26), 17, 78.
2. Eichrodt (I.5), 274f.; Ringgren (I.15), 74.
3. I. Sam. 2. 2.
4. Amos 4.2//6.8; cf. Heb. 3.3.
5. Jacob (I.6), 86.
6. Isa. 40.25.
7. Isa. 5.24; Ps. 71.22.
8. Ringgren (V.25), 9.
9. Jones (V.15), 149.
10. Hos. 11.9.
11. I Sam. 6.20.
12. Ringgren (V.25), 107.
13. Gen. 18.27.
14. Gen. 28.16f.
15. Ex. 3.6.
16. Isa. 6.5.
17. Isa 8.13.
18. Ps. 111.9; cf. 99.3.
19. Pedersen (I.12), vol. III–IV, 266.
20. Lev. 10.10.
21. Ezek. 42.20.
22. Deut. 20.5ff.
23. Lev. 18.8–20.
24. Lev. 11.29.
25. Lev. 11.20f.; cf. Douglas (X.4), 52–6.
26. Ringgren (V.25), 20.
27. Pedersen (I.12), vol. III–IV, 271f.
28. *Ibid.*, 288f.
29. von Rad (I.14), vol. II, 42.
30. Jacob (I.6), 92.
31. Deut. 4.7.
32. Hos. 9.15.
33. von Rad (I.14), vol. I, 207.
34. Otto (V.21), cap. 10, 74–84.
35. *Ibid.*, 205; Eichrodt (I.5), 277.
36. To reach this conclusion is not to write off Judaism, which has not stood still since the closure of the OT canon. The movement known as Hasidism has produced many new insights upon which I shall be drawing later in this study.
37. I Cor. 2.11.
38. I. Cor 12.10.
39. Heb. 1.17.
40. Mark 1.23.
41. Cf. von Allmen (I.1), 166.
42. Luke 1.35.
43. Mark 1.24.
44. John 6.69.
45. Rev. 3.7//6.10; cf. Proksch in Kittel (I.7), vol. I, 101f.
46. Rev. 4.8.
47. John 17.11.
48. von Allmen (I.1), 166.
49. I John 1.1f.
50. Hick (IX.22), 144.
51. Col. 1.15.
52. Matt. 1.23.
53. Acts 17.27.
54. Luke 7.16.
55. Malraux (VII.7), 224.
56. Nineham (I.11), 447f.
57. Luke 5.8.
58. Mark 4.40.
59. Mark 6.50.
60. Luke 24.37f.
61. E.g. Gen. 15.1.
62. Mark 9.6.
63. Luke 9.34.
64. Matt. 17.6.
65. Otto (V.21), 88.
66. Davies (V.8), 227f.
67. Mark 14.33.
68. Nineham (I.11), 391.
69. van den Heuvel (XII.27), 52
70. Ex. 19.16.
71. Spicq (I.17), 404; Manson (I.9), 148.
72. Montefiore (I.10), 237.
73. II Cor. 5.11.

74. Phil. 2.12.
75. Rom. 11.20.
76. Rom. 8.5.
77. I John 4.18.
78. I John 4.16.
79. Tit. 2.14; cf. Gal. 1.4;
I Tim 2.6.
80. Luke 22.27.
81. Martimort (V.18), 51.
82. Rom. 14.14.
83. Luke 11.41.
84. Mark 7.19.
85. Acts 10.14f.
86. Acts 10.28.
87. Gal. 4.10.
88. Col. 2.20f.
89. Heb. 1.3.
90. Tit. 2.14.
91. II Cor. 6.16.
92. Zech. 14.20ff; see above p. 50.
93. Num. 14.21; see above p. 50.
94. Eliade (VIII.4), 133.
95. Buber (IX.14), 28.
96. de Chardin (XII.11), 66.
97. See below p. 120.
98. Roguet (V.26), 19–31.
99. I Thess. 4.3; Rom. 6.19, 22.
100. I Peter 1.15.
101. Bultmann (I.3), 219.
102. *Ibid.*, 223.
103. *Ibid.*, 101.
104. Jones (V.15), 144f.
105. Luke 7.13.
106. Luke 23.34.
107. Jenkins (V.14), 79.
108. Mark 6.3.
109. Heb. 2.17.
110. Marinoff (V.17), 27.
111. Jung (VI.22), 388.
112. Matt. 11.29.
113. Phil. 2.8.
114. Mark 7.37.
115. II Cor. 4.6.
116. Rom. 8.15.
117. Luke 19.5ff.
118. Luke 10.17, 21
119. John 10.10.
120. Lambourne (XII.36), 90–111.
121. Matt. 5.48; Bultmann (I.3), 224.
122. I. Cor. 14.20; Phil. 3.15.
123. Cf. Davies (XII.16), 13f.
124. Pedersen (I.12), vol. I-II, 264.
125. Kittel (I.7), vol. II, 402.
126. Pedersen (I.12), vol. I-II, 313.
127. I am here reproducing my analysis from (XII.16), 29ff.
128. Macquarrie (XII.40), 209.
129. *Ibid.*, 210.
130. Matt. 15.12.
131. Matt. 11.6.
132. Cf. Matt. 7.21f.
133. John 3.17.
134. John 9.39.
135. Matt. 25.31–48.
136. Robinson (XII.58), 125.
137. *Ibid.*, 142.
138. Matt. 6.14f.
139. Mackenzie (I.8), 33.
140. J. E. Smith (IX.31), 60.
141. See above p. 49.
142. Moltmann (XII.43), 100.
143. *Ibid.*, 22.
144. Cf. *ibid.*, 202.
145. Metz (XII.42), 89.
146. Corwin (I.4).

4. *The Place of Encounter*

1. See above p. 32.
2. J. E. Smith (IX.31), 17.
3. Cf. *ibid.*, 151.
4. Hick (IX.21), 103.
5. J. E. Smith (IX.31), 12f.
6. *Ibid.*, 81.
7. Hick (IX.21), 115.
8. Niebuhr (XII.47), 45.
9. Tillich (XII.69), 5.
10. Buber (IX.5), 99.
11. Grand'maison (V.11), vol. I, 48.
12. Schillebeeckx (XII.60), 50f.
13. I Cor. 13.12.

14. Acts 25.16.
15. II John 12; III John 13.
16. Buber (IX.14), 231.
17. Sermon at Barcelona on 15 April 1928, quoted by Bethge (XII.4), 81.
18. Sermon at Advent 1928, quoted *loc. cit.*
19. Kazantzakis (VI.23), 253.
20. *Ibid.*, 381.
21. Buber (IX.9), v.
22. Matt. 25.31–46.
23. Bonnard (I.2), 366f.
24. Roqueplo (V.27), 176f.
25. *Ibid.*, 194.
26. Schillebeeckx (XII.61), 46. See also p. 215 below on Feuerbach.
27. Mark 12.30f.
28. I John 4.20f.
29. Baillie (IX.3), 139.
30. Stauffer in Kittel (I.7), vol. I, 46.
31. Antoine in Martin and Antoine (V.20), 81.
32. Matt. 5.23f.
33. Gonzalez-Ruiz in Taylor (V.28), 197.
34. Baillie (IX.2), 180.
35. John 14.6.
36. Tillich (XII.68), 242.
37. Hamilton (XII.25), 87.
38. Cf. Dewart (XII.17), 18.
39. Rom. 15.26.
40. Vincent (V.29).
41. Mark 2.9–11.
42. Vincent (V.29), 99.
43. Luke 19.9.
44. Vincent (V.29), 127ff.
45. *Ibid.*, 115.
46. Luke 12.16–21.
47. Luke 6.20–26.
48. Luke 16.13.
49. Vincent (V.29), 117.
50. *Ibid.*, 121.
51. Buber (IX.11), 92.
52. Niebuhr (XII.48), 52.
53. Schillebeeckx (XII.61), 61.
54. Buber (IX.14), 174, 126.
55. Buber (IX.9), 4.
56. Buber (IX.15), 305.
57. *Ibid.*, 179.
58. *Ibid.*, 170.
59. Buber (IX.14), 31.
60. Buber (IX.5), 52.
61. Buber (IX.4), 233.
62. Buber (IX.8), 46.
63. Buber (IX.6), 171.
64. *Ibid.*, 121.
65. Buber (IX.15), 235.
66. *Ibid.*, 128.
67. Schlipp and Friedman (IX.29), 733f.
68. Buber (IX.16), 229.
69. Buber (IX.14), 43.
70. Buber (IX.16), 231.
71. Cf. Tillich (XII.70), 194.
72. Cf. Boros (XII.9), ix.ff.
73. Demetillo (VI.13), 2, 4.
74. Roqueplo (V.27), 201.
75. Schlipp and Friedman (IX.29), 35.
76. Buber (IX.5), 204.
77. *Ibid.*, *loc. cit.*
78. Buber (IX.10), 14.
79. Buber (IX.12), 68.
80. Buber (IX.10), 39.
81. *Ibid.*, 6.
82. *Ibid.*, *loc. cit.*
83. Buber (IX.5), 110f.
84. *Ibid.*, 62.
85. Howe (XII.29), 105f.
86. Buber (IX.5), 168.
87. Schlipp and Friedman (IX.29), 24.
88. *Ibid.*, 206.
89. Buber (IX.7), 89.
90. Buber (IX.10), 137.
91. Buber (IX.9), 122
92. Buber (IX.10), 5
93. *Ibid.*, 9.
94. Cf. Friedman (IX.18), 52.
95. Grand'maison (V.11), vol. II, 127.
96. Metz (XII.42), 107ff.
97. Pannenberg (XII.52), 95f.

98. Metz (XII.42), 119.
99. Roqueplo (V.27), 182.
100. In his preface to Ward (III.32), 6.
101. Roqueplo (V.27), 183.
102. Buber (IX.10), 7f.
103. Schlipp and Friedman (IX.29), 709.
104. See below pp. 186–213.
105. Bayley (VI.4).
106. *Ibid.*, 147.
107. Anderson (VI.2), 34.
108. *Ibid.*, 58.

109. Quoted by Esslin (VI.16), 273.
110. *Ibid.*, 192, 227.
111. Adamov (VI.1), 19, 45. (quoted by Esslin (VI.16), 66f.).
112. Esslin (VI.16), 58.
113. Eliot (VI.15), 87, 89.
114. *Ibid.*, 187, 189.
115. *Ibid.*, 118.
116. Schillebeeckx (XII.62), 72.
117. Wilson (VI.47), 56.
118. Cf. Zahrnt (XII.74), 325–8.

Excursus A

1. Chavchavadze (V.5), 13–21.
2. *Ibid.*, 147.
3. Berger and Luckmann (XI.4), 174.
4. Berger (XI.3), 7.
5. *Ibid.*, 18.
6. *Ibid.*, 65f.
7. *Ibid.*, 114.
8. Berger (XI.2), 177.
9. Ramsey (IX.25), 81.
10. *Ibid.*, 151; cf. Smart (IX.30), 130–66.
11. II Sam. 12.1–7; Ramsey (IX.25), 113.
12. *Ibid.*, 119.
13. Cf. V. Buckley, 'Specifying the Sacred', in Gunn (VI.18), 53–67.
14. Wilson (VI.45), 248, 251.
15. Wilson (VI.46), 10.
16. *Ibid.*, 47.
17. *Ibid.*, 270.
18. Wilson (VI.48), 46.
19. *Ibid.*, 35.
20. *Ibid.*, 74.
21. *Ibid.*, 69.
22. Wilson (VI.45), 187.
23. Nagel (XI.20), 173.
24. *Ibid.*, 187.
25. Cf. Glasser (III.10), 128–34.

26. Hepburn (IX.20), 206f.
27. Baillie (IX.3), 213f.
28. Acquaviva (V.1) , 55; cf. Kee (XII.31), 9–13.
29. Acquaviva (V.1), 60.
30. Watzke (XI.25), 93.
31. Oman (XII.51), 474.
32. *Ibid.*, 308.
33. Baillie (IX.2), 241; cf. his previous criticism in (IX.1), 246–55.
34. Baillie (IX.2), 245.
35. Reid (XII.57), 69.
36. Otto (V.21), 116.
37. Munz (IX.24), 82.
38. Cf. Hamilton (XII.24), 50.
39. Altizer and Hamilton (XII.2), 52.
40. Cf. Davidson (V.7), 195.
41. Altizer (V.2), 45.
42. Altizer and Hamilton (XII.2), 143.
43. Altizer (V.2), 23.
44. *Ibid.*, 27.
45. *Ibid.*, 23.
46. *Ibid.*, 40.
47. Martin and Antoine (V.20), 36, 51.
48. Tillich (XII.70), 61.

Excursus B

1. Audet (V.3); Roguet (V.26).
2. Roguet (V.26), 32.
3. *Ibid.*, *loc. cit.*
4. *Ibid.*, 20.

5. Tillich (XII.68), 240.
6. For another essay in terminology see Schmidt (XIII.22).

5. *The Holy and Personal Relations*

1. Kazantzakis (VI.25), 286.
2. For the importance of story telling in relation to theology see Keen (XII.33), 82–105.
3. Hamilton (XII.23), 137.
4. J. E. Smith (IX.31), 119.
5. Buber (IX.11), 82.
6. Ramsey (IX.26), 17, 38.
7. Gregor Smith (XII.64), 130.
8. Buber (IX.5), 11.
9. Koestler (VII.5), 191.
10. Hick (IX.21), 117.
11. de Chardin (XII.11), 46.
12. Gregor Smith (XII.64), 94.
13. Buber (IX.11), 83.
14. Ceccherini (VI.11), 118f.

15. Brod (VI.9), 195.
16. Tillich (XII.67), 185.
17. Kessel (VI.27).
18. Rikhoff (VI.35), 259f.
19. Friedman (IX.19), 304ff.
20. Tillich (XII.67), 214f.
21. Cf. Howe (XII.30), 132–7.
22. *Jerusalem*, 66, 56.
23. *Gates of Paradise*, prologue.
24. Habe (VI.20), 96f.
25. Lane and Roberts (XI.14), 104f., 167, 232.
26. Updike (VI.42), 296.
27. Bonhoeffer (XII.8), 181.
28. Sharp (VI.37), 120f.

6. *The Holy and Sexual Relations*

1. Paul (XII.55), 194f.
2. Tax (III.29), quoted by Mailer (VI.34), 37.
3. For a more positive appreciation of Miller see Mailer, *op. cit.*
4. Tillich (XII.67), 125.
5. Solzhenitsyn (VI.41).
6. Macmurray (XII.39), 172.
7. Brock (VI.8), 259ff.
8. *Holy Sonnets* XVII, lines 5f.
9. Lawrence (VI.30), 10.
10. *Ibid.*, 87.
11. *Ibid.*, 89–92.
12. Rolph (VI.36), 71.
13. *Ibid.*, 102.
14. *Ibid.*, 150.

15. Lawrence (VI.31), 361.
16. Dumitriu (VI.14), 315.
17. Wilson (VI.48), 66.
18. Bellow (VI.6), 185f.
19. Quoted by Paul (XII.55), 180.
20. Cf. Moltmann (XII.43), 105.
21. Tillich (XII.70), 64.
22. Bonhoeffer to Bethge, 18.12.1943 (XII.6), 168.
23. Lawrence (VI.29), 185.
24. I am drawing here on a previous study which the passage of time does not appear to have rendered invalid; Davies (XII.15), 211–20.
25. Berdyaev (XII.3), 295.

26. Butler-Bowdon (XII.10), cap. 3.
27. Doms (XII.18), 26.
28. *Ibid.*, 43ff.
29. Irenaeus, *adv. Haer.*, 1.26.3.
30. *Jerusalem*, 27.

31. Kazantzakis (VI.24), 77.
32. Schlipp and Friedman (IX.29), 733f.
33. Keen (XII.33), 159.

7. *The Holy and Death*

1. Bonhoeffer to Bethge, 30.4.1944 (XII.6), 282.
2. *Ibid.*, 25.5.1944, 311.
3. J. E. Smith (IX.31), 151.
4. *Ibid.*, 60.
5. Bellow (VI.5), 78.
6. Kazantzakis (VI.25), 266.
7. Cf. Hinton (II.6), 88.
8. A. N. Wilder in Scott (II.9), 23.
9. Cf. B. Murchland in Lepp (II.7), x.
10. Ebeling (XII.19), 85.
11. Jung in Feifel (II.4), 6.
12. Lepp (II.7), 39.
13. Buber (IX.5), 61.
14. Hammarskjöld (VI.21), 136.
15. Aulén (VI.3), 132f.
16. Aries (II.1), 57–89.
17. Gorer (II.5), 17.
18. Berger (XI.2), 5.
19. A. Toynbee in Toynbee *et al.* (II.10), 64f.
20. Yeats (VI.50), 476.
21. Lepp (II.7), 119.
22. Feifel (II.4), 128.
23. Quoted by Bethge (XII.4), 566.

24. Rahner (II.8), 51.
25. Hinton (II.6), 104.
26. *French Revolution*, 192f.
27. Rahner (II.8), 125.
28. So Hinton (II.6), 72.
29. Augustine, *Confessions*, 4.4.
30. Hinton (II.6), 103.
31. Rahner (II.8), 78.
32. Cf. L. Tyler in Cope (II.3), 28.
33. Cf. Wilson (II.11), 114–23.
34. Hinton (II.6), 81f.
35. Matt. 25.36f., 40.
36. John 11.25.
37. Toynbee *et al.* (II.10), 45.
38. Clerk (II.2), 7.
39. *Ibid.*, 9.
40. *Ibid.*, 11.
41. *Ibid.*, 18.
42. *Ibid.*, 23.
43. *Ibid.*, 29.
44. *Ibid.*, 37.
45. *Ibid.*, 38.
46. Mark 15.34.
47. Matt. 5.4.
48. Luke 6.21.
49. J. Mathers in Cope (II.3), 42.

8. *The Holy and the Public World of Man*

1. Slater (XII.63), 21.
2. See above pp. 101–4.
3. Cf. Schillebeeckx (XII.61), 5ff.
4. Dumitriu (VI.14), 276.
5. Kazantzakis (VI.25), 217.
6. Tillich (XII.67), 61.
7. Häring (V.12), 58.
8. Cf. Macquarrie (XII.41), 65.
9. Tillich (XII.69), 26.

10. *Ibid.*, 22.
11. For an analysis of what this may mean see Ogden (XII.49).
12. I Peter 2.24.
13. Buber (IX.11), 91.
14. Isa. 10.5, 24.
15. Cox (V.6), 242.
16. Thomas (III.30), 108.

17. Perrin (I.13), 161.
18. Thomas (III.30), 29–33.
19. *Ibid.*, 22.
20. Cox (III.6), 29f.
21. Cf. Mehl (XI.19), 250.
22. Roqueplo (V.27), 311f.
23. Metz (III.16), 4.
24. Berger and Luckmann (XI.4), 106.
25. Allen *et al.* (III.2), 275.
26. ii. 16.
27. From a letter to the Protector Somerset of October 1548, quoted by Tawney (III.28), 115.
28. Quoted *ibid.*, 216.
29. *Ibid.*, 191.
30. Weber (III.34), 155.
31. Richardson (III.21), 35f.
32. Donald and Havighurst (III.7), 357–60.
33. Shimmin (III.24), 197.
34. Smigel (III.25), 89.
35. Lupton (III.14).
36. Klein (III.13), 1.
37. Sargant Florence (III.9), 83.
38. Klein (III.13), 9.
39. Walker and Guest (III.31), 51.
40. Lupton (III.14), 35.
41 Walker and Guest (III.31), 56.
42. Sillitoe (VI.38), 25.
43. *Work in Britain Today* (III.35), 51.
44. Dubin (III.8), 187f.
45. Glasser (III.10), 145.
46. Smigel (III.25), 31.
47. Glasser, *loc. cit.*
48. Shimmin (III.24), 200.
49. Symanowski (III.27), 140. The relation of work to leisure differs with the occupational group concerned. Three types of relationship have been distinguished: (1) the *extensive* pattern, where leisure activities are similar to work; (2) the *neutrality* pattern, where leisure activities are different from work but are regarded as complementary to it; (3) the *opposition* pattern, where leisure activities are unlike work (Parker (III.20), 162–5).
50. Klein (III.13), 3–7. For a fuller discussion see Child (III.5), 64–76.
51. Dubin (III.8), 51.
52. Alexander (III.1), 93ff.
53. Miller and Form (III.17), 548ff.
54. Blum (III.4), 321.
55. Schuller (III.22), 18f.
56. Dubin (III.8), 191–6.
57. Symanowski (III.27), 141.
58. *Ibid.*, 129f.
59. Klein (III.13), 2.
60. Account in *New Society*, 21 January 1971, No. 434, 111, of the paper by J. Obradovic, J. French and W. Rodgers in *Human Relations*, 23.5, 459. For a fuller discussion of participation and a bibliography see Weber (III.33), 182–96.
61. See above pp. 149–52.
62. This is affirmed by Symanowski: 'Work belongs to man's nature and he must actualize his nature in his work. If his work becomes a necessary evil for him, a mere appendage to his proper life, a matter of "lost time", then he will lose himself' (III.27), 140f.
63. *Social Attitudes to Work* (III.26).
64. Jacques (III.12).
65. Pannenberg (XII.52), 118.
66. Koestler (VII.5), 264.
67. Cox (V.6), 190.
68. Cf. Roqueplo (V.27), 223–7.
69. Moltmann (XII.44), 104.

70. C. Elliott in Munby
    (III.19), 340.

71. M. Lopez in Matthews
    (III.15), 18.

9. *Worldly Holiness*

1. Silone (VI.39), 79f.
2. Vahanian (XII.72), 97f.
3. Feuerbach (IX.17), 33. Cf.
   Bloch (IX.4. 153–65) who
   insists upon the numinous as
   the primary religious reality
   and then proceeds to argue
   subtly and convincingly
   from this to atheism.
4. *Ibid.*, 26; cf. Mottu (IX.13).
5. Cleaver (VI.12), 5.
6. Cf. Pannenberg (XII.53),
   184–200.
7. Friedman (IX.19), 21.
8. *Ibid.*, *loc cit.*
9. Cf. Macquarrie (XII.41), 66.
10. Roqueplo (V.27), 295.
11. Buber (IX.14), 173.
12. Cf. Koestler (VI.28), 101f.
13. Cantwell Smith (IX.32), 80.
14. Rabut (V.24), 9f., 62.
15. J.-M. Gonzalez-Ruiz in
    Taylor (V.28), 191.
16. Chavchavadze (V.5), 32.
17. Metz (XII.42), 103.
18. *Ibid.*, 153.
19. Buber (IX.7), 138.
20. Rauschenbusch (XII.56), 104.
21. Charchavadze (V.5), 41.
22. Pelikan (V.22), 81.
23. de Chardin (XII.11), 66.
24. See above p. 64.
25. Buber (IX.15), 181.
26. Jones (V.15), 16–26.
27. Foote (XII.20), 24.
28. The correlation of *Markings*
    with events in
    Hammarskjöld's life has
    been admirably accomplished
    by H. van Dusen (VI.43).
29. Quotations from *Markings* are
    taken from the translation by

L. Sjöberg and W. H. Auden
(VI.21), Occasionally I have
used as more accurate the
rendering given by Aulén
(VI.3). This present quotation
is from p. 87 of (VI.21).

30. *Ibid.*, 88.
31. *Ibid.*, 100, but Aulén's
    translation.
32. *Loc. cit.*
33. *Ibid.*, 139.
34. *Ibid.*, 110.
35. *Ibid.*, 79, Aulén's translation.
36. Aulén (VI.3), 101.
37. *Markings* (VI.21), 133.
38. Cf. Aulén (VI.3), 128f., 133.
39. *Markings* (VI.21), 90f.
40. *Ibid.*, 108, Aulén's translation.
41. For further information about
    Torres see Guzman (VI.19)
    and Gerassi (XII.22).
42. See the introduction to Garcia
    and Calle (XII.21).
43. *Ibid.*, 7f.
44. *Ibid.*, 72ff.
45. *Ibid.*, 75f.
46. Gerassi (XII.22), 331f.
47. Houtart and Rémy (XI.11),
    287.
48. Kazantzakis (VI.26), 63.
49. Quoted by Gerassi (XII.22), 11.
50. Amos 5.11f.; 8.4, 6ff.
51. Houtart and Rémy
    (XI.11), 383f.
52. Paton (XII.54), 24.
53. Houtart and Rémy
    (XI.11), 382.
54. Silone (VI.39), 287f.
55. West (VI.44), 83f.
56. *Ibid.*, 95f.
57. *Ibid.*, 97f.
58. Paton (XII.54), 20.

59. Cox (XII.14), 109.
60. Kazantzakis (VI.26), 21.
61. Buber (IX.7), 31.
62. Buber (IX.9), 72.
63. Collins (XII.13), 16.
64. Bosanquet (VI.7); Bethge (XII.4).
65. Bethge (XII.4), 582.
66. *Ibid.*, 579.
67. Quoted *ibid.*, 580.
68. *Ibid.*, 199.
69. *Ibid.*, 719.
70. *Ibid.*, 688.
71. *Ibid.*, 585.
72. Zimmermann and Smith (VI.51), 190f.
73. Bethge (XII.4), 656.
74. *Ibid.*, 585.
75. *Ibid.*, 530.
76. Bonhoeffer (XII.7), 209f.
77. Bethge (XII.4), 700.
78. *Ibid.*, 702.

79. Bonhoeffer to Bethge, 18.11.1943 (XII.6), 129.
80. Bonhoeffer (XII.5), 102f.
81. Zimmermann and Smith (VI.51), 154.
82. Bethge (XII.4), 732.
83. Zimmermann and Smith (VI.51), 82.
84. Nicholls (XII.46), 231.
85. Zimmermann and Smith (VI.51), 143.
86. *Ibid.*, 129.
87. *Ibid.*, 144.
88. *Ibid.*, 69.
89. *Ibid.*, 72.
90. I Cor. 1.2.
91. Quoted by McNeish (VI.32), 33f.
92. *Ibid.*, 239.
93. Silone (VI.39), 239.
94. Lev. 19.2.
95. I Peter 1.15f.

10. *The Crisis of Worship*

1. *The Uppsala Report* (XII.71), 78.
2. Underhill (XIII.25), 35.
3. *The Uppsala Report* (XII.71), 84.
4. Grahame (VI.17), cap. 7, 161ff. I am indebted for this reference to Pratt (V.23), 62.
5. Connolly (XIII.6), 92–7.
6. *Catech. mystag.* 5.4.
7. Lampe (XII.37), 1490.
8. *De Sacerd.* 6.4.
9. See passages listed by Bishop in Connolly (XIII.6), 94.
10. 8.12.
11. Connolly (XIII.6), 10f.
12. *Ibid.*, 22.
13. Chavchavadze (V.5), 148.
14. Isa. 6.6f.
15. *Ep.*5 (*PL* 141.201), quoted by Stone (XIII.24), 242.

16. Cap. 13 (*PL* 172.1293), quoted *ibid.*, 281.
17. Quoted *ibid.*, 355.
18. West (XIII.26), 82f.
19. See Davies (V.8).
20. For a summary see Kelly (XII.34), 453ff.
21. Bonhoeffer (XII.7), 168f.
22. *Ibid.*, 170.
23. *Ibid.*, 169f.
24. Heb. 6.5.
25. G. Moran in *Worship in the City of Man* (XIII.30), 90.
26. F. W. Young in Shepherd (XIII.23), 88.
27. See 'Worship Today' (XIII.29), 129–41.
28. See above p. 112.
29. Berger and Luckmann (XI.4), 174.
30. C. Davis, 'Ghetto or Desert' (XIII.10), 17.

31. *Ibid.*, 11.
32. *Ibid.*, 22.
33. J. DeWitt in *Worship in the City of Man* (XIII.30), 154.
34. White (XIII.27), 109.
35. G. Moran in *Worship in the City of Man* (XIII.30), 90.
36. II Cor. 5.17.
37. Rev. 21.5.
38. Rom. 12.2.
39. Cf. Davies (XIII.8), 42–35.
40. DeWitt in *Worship in the City of Man* (XIII.30), 154.
41. J. Moore, *ibid.*, 159.
42. White (XIII.27), 109.
43. Adolfs (XII.1), 107f.
44. John 3.16f.
45. S. Altman in *Worship in the City of Man* (XIII.30), 137.
46. I have discussed what this means at greater length in (XII.16).
47. Mark 8.35.

11. *Worship and Ritual*

1. Wilson (X.17), 9.
2. Gluckman (X.8), 22.
3. Douglas (X.4), 65.
4. Gluckman (X.8), 22.
5. *Ibid.*, 21f.
6. See further Goody (X.10), 142–63.
7. Cazeneuve (XIII.5), 262f.
8. *Ibid.*, 163.
9. *Ibid.*, 34–9.
10. *Ibid.*, 134.
11. Eliade (VIII.2), 35.
12. Cazeneuve (XIII.5), 236.
13. *Ibid.*, 261.
14. van Gennep (X.15), 94f.
15. Cf. Davies (XII.15), 123–34.
16. Gluckman (X.8), 24f.
17. Radcliffe-Brown (X.12), 154.
18. Turner (X.14), 52f., 93.
19. Chapple and Coon (X.3), 398–402.
20. *Ibid.*, 507.
21. Gluckman (X.8), 34.
22. Moltmann (XII.44), 110f.
23. Wilson (X.16), 241.
24. Gluckman (X.8), 62, 86.
25. Berger (XI.2), 21.
26. I am aware that there is a lack of precision in my use of the term 'tribe', but I believe my general meaning will be clear without further discussion.

For modern studies of the concept of tribe see 'Essays on the Problem of Tribe' (X.6) and Southall (X.13).
27. Niebuhr (XII.48), 11.
28. Bohannan (X.2), 328.
29. Winter (XI.26), 61.
30. Gluckman (X.8), 38.
31. Douglas (X.4), 62.
32. Munz (IX.24), 76.
33. Douglas (X.4), 114.
34. Bouyer (XIII.3), 64.
35. Winter (XI.26), 152.
36. Cf. also Davies (XIII.8), 72–92. The various statements made on those pages about baptism in terms of mission all involve a new, secular, understanding of it.
37. Cox (XII.14), 97.
38. Tillich (XII.67), 219.
39. Macquarrie (XII.41), 136.
40. Cf. P. B. Bond in Cope (II.3), 86.
41. Grand'maison (V.11), vol. 1, 187f. I have altered in two places the original 'profane' to 'secular' to preserve a uniformity in the use of terms.
42. Roqueplo (V.27), 387.
43. Davies (V.9).
44. Cf. Douglas (X.5), 144f.

45. Mark 8.35.
46. Cazeneuve (XIII.5), 123.
47. Moltmann (XII.44), 137ff.
48. *Ibid.*, 120.

49. *Ibid.*, 121.
50. Pratt (XIII.20), 6.
51. Roqueplo (V.27), 347f.
52. Pratt (XIII.20), 4.

12. *Community, Fellowship and Worship*

1. Rémy (XI.21), 78f.
2. Houtart and Rémy (XI.11), 59.
3. Tillich (XII.67), 126.
4. *Ibid.*, *loc. cit.*
5. Stuart Hall in Nagel (XI.20), 180.
6. Cf. P. Goodman in McGuyan (XI.17), 229f.
7. Suenens (XII.66), 159f.
8. For a study of how social interaction is necessary for the emergence of the 'I' see Mead (XI.18).
9. Rémy (XI.21), 82.
10. Jennings (XI.13).
11. Houtart and Rémy (XI.12), 188.
12. Sprott (XI.23), 116f.
13. Houtart (XI.10), 58.
14. Rémy (XI.21), 86.
15. Houtart and Rémy (XI.12), 180.
16. *Ibid.*, 349.
17. *Ibid.*, 175.
18. Rémy (XI.21), 100.
19. Buber (IX.5), 200.
20. *Ibid.*, 31.
21. G. Marcel in Schlipp and Friedman (IX.29), 42.
22. Gregor Smith (XII.64), 87.
23. Bellow (VI.6), 176.
24. Buber (IX.5), 210.
25. *Ibid.*, 51.
26. See above pp. 97f.
27. Buber (IX.11), 47.
28. Haughton (XII.26), 191.
29. Bloch (IX.4), 184.
30. Buber (IX.13), 136.

31. Houtart and Rémy (XI.12), 230f.
32. See above p. 133.
33. Macmurray (XII.39), 189.
34. *Ibid.*, 198.
35. de Chardin (XII.12), 56f.
36. Pannenberg (XII.52), 88.
37. Mehl (XI.19), 157.
38. Pratt (XIII.19), 86.
39. Howe (XII.30), 114f.
40. J. E. Smith (IX.31), 160.
41. Houtart and Rémy (XI.11), 251f.
42. *Ibid.*, 278. On conflict as a positive force see Scheller (XI.22).
43. Koestler (VII.5), 363.
44. Moltmann (XII.44), 118.
45. I Cor. 14.11, NEB.
46. I Cor. 14.16, 23.
47. van den Heuvel (XII.28), 85f.
48. *Report of the Theological Commission on Worship* (XIII.21), 22.
49. Davies (XIII.8), 150ff.
50. Grainger (XIII.13), 20, 64.
51. H. Schmidt in Smith (XII.65), 220.
52. I therefore disagree with John Macmurray who contends that the family is 'the norm of all community' (XII.39), 155.
53. Rom. 8.29.
54. Hamilton (XII.24), 47.
55. Matt. 18.20.
56. DeWitt in *Worship in the City of Man* (XIII.30), 156.

13. *Secular Rituals*

1. Haughton (XII.26), 248.
2. Ceccherini (VI.11), 219.
3. *Ibid*., 215.
4. Mailer (VI.33), 76.
5. *Ibid*., 77f.
6. *Ibid*., 120f.
7. *Ibid*., 86.
8. *Ibid*., 213f.
9. Cox (XIII.7), 118.
10. Debuyst (XIII.11) and (XIII.12), 5–9.
11. Debuyst (XIII.11), 12f.
12. Pieper (VIII.6), 23.
13. Cox (XIII.7), 7, 12.
14. *Ibid*., 32.
15. *Ibid*. 7.
16. *Ibid*., 75.
17. Debuyst (XIII.11), 14.
18. *Ibid*., 15.
19. Cox (XIII.7), 81.
20. *Ibid*., 102.
21. I am indebted for the substance of this and the preceding paragraph to the report of Group II of a Consultation on 'Worship in a Secular Age', which was held in Geneva, September 1969. Some, but not all, sections of the report of this group, of which I was a member, were embodied in the final Report 'Worship Today' (XIII.21), 129–41.

14. *Mission and Worship*

1. Lev. 19.2.
2. Ex. 19.6.
3. Isa. 2.2f.
4. Matt. 28.19.
5. John 20.21.
6. Acts 1.8.
7. I Cor. 11.26.
8. II Cor. 6.16.
9. Luke 17.17.
10. Acts 4.23.
11. Gustafson (XI.9), 18.
12. Matthews (III.15), 380.
13. See above p. 211.
14. A. Adegbola in Bennett (III.3), 185.
15. Perrin (I.13), 161.
16. Busia (XI.6), 92, 109.
17. Lehmann (XII.38), 24.
18. See above p. 63.
19. I Peter 2.21.
20. John 13.14.
21. Rowley (I.16), 123.
22. Howe (XII.29), 65.

15. *Rites of Modernization*

1. See M. E. Spiro in Banton (X.1), 122.
2. Geertz (X.7), 32.
3. *Ibid*., 35f.
4. Peacock (X.11), 218.
5. See above p. 285.
6. Douglas (X.5), 145.
7. Peacock (X.11), 103.
8. *Ibid*., 122.
9. *Ibid*., 217–33.
10. *Ibid*., 40.
11. For examples of liturgies related to political and social themes see Hovda and Huck (XIII.15).
12. Illich (III.11), 94.
13. Moltmann (XII.43), 25.
14. Sherif (III.23).
15. Lee and Marty (XI.15), 5.
16. Toffler (XI.24), 290.
17. *Ibid*., 3.
18. See above p. 280.

19. Toffler (XI.24), 335.
20. So J. Gardner (XI.8), quoted by Toffler (*ibid*.,) 348.
21. Toffler (*ibid*.,) 144.
22. *Ibid*., 349.
23. See above p. 267.
24. Greeley (XIII.14), 68.
25. Pratt (XIII.20), 120.
26. Greeley (XIII.14), 62.
27. Pratt (XIII.19), 10.
28. Greeley (XIII.14), 59–63.
29. Mehl (XI.19), 81.
30. Cf. Williams (XII.73), 37.
31. Hamilton (XII.24), 20f.
32. Howe (XII.30), 84.
33. Luke 4.4.
34. Luke 20.19.
35. Malinowski (XI.16), 23.
36. Howe (XII.30), 22.
37. Cf. Chapple and Coon (X.3), 482.
38. Douglas (X.4), 174.
39. Haughton (XII.26), 267.
40. See above p. 95.
41. Kierkegaard (XII.35), 207.
42. Mark 1.17.
43. Matt. 5.13.
44. Kierkegaard (XII.35), 203.
45. *Ibid*., 34.
46. Haughton (XII.26), 264.
47. Moltmann (XII.45), 148.
48. Roqueplo (V.27), 220.
49. Tillich (XII.67), 111.
50. Douglas (X.4), 64.
51. Macquarrie (XII.41), 65.
52. Hovda and Huck (XIII.15), 30.
53. See above p. 317.
54. I have reproduced this analysis from a lecture given at the Annual Meeting of the Church Service Society in Edinburgh in 1967. It is printed in full with the title 'The Reality of Worship' in (XIII.9), 3–13.
55. See the interesting analysis by Una Maguire (XIII.18), 640–5.
56. Brook (VI.10), 47.
57. A full description is given in *Monthly Letter about Evangelism*, Sept.-Nov., 1967.
58. von Allmen (XIII.2), 23.
59. Paton (XII.54), 92.
60. Acts 2.46; cf. Davies (XII.15), 107.
61. Dewart (XII.17), 204f.
62. Rabut (V.24), 61.
63. Pratt (XIII.19), 51ff.
64. Adolfs (XII.1), 133.
65. Cf. Goffman (X.9).
66. What is meant by a happening is illustrated by Harvey Cox's account of the one in the Judson Memorial Church in Greenwich Village, which was one of the events of the New York International Congress on Religion, Architecture and the Visual Arts, 1967. (Hunt (V.13), 216–19.)
67. Martin (V.19), 73.
68. Smith (IX.31), 62.
69. A useful survey is contained in 'Living: Liturgical Style' (XIII.17): this includes a stimulating account of two new expressions of worship by W. J. Hollenweger (pp. 45–55). See also Huck and Hovda (XIII.15), 82–125; Bloy (XIII.2) and Killinger (XIII.16).
70. Bloy (XIII.2); the whole of the final chapter – The Celebration of Life – is well worth reading.

Bibliography

Except where otherwise stated, the place of publication is London

I. BIBLE

1. Allmen, J. J. von, ed., *Vocabulary of the Bible*, Lutterworth, 1958
2. Bonnard, P., *L'évangile selon Saint Matthieu*, Delachaux et Niestlé, Neuchâtel, 1967
3. Bultmann, R., *Theology of the New Testament*, II, SCM Press, 1958
4. Corwin, C., *Biblical Encounter with Japanese Culture*, Christian Literature Crusade, Tokyo, 1967
5. Eichrodt, W., *Theology of the Old Testament*, I, SCM Press, 1966
6. Jacob, E., *Theology of the Old Testament*, Hodder & Stoughton, 1958
7. Kittel, G., ed., *Theological Dictionary of the Bible*, I, II, trans. G. W. Bromiley, Eerdmans, Grand Rapids, 1964
8. Mackenzie, J. L., *Vital Concepts of the Bible*, Burns & Oates, 1968
9. Manson, W., *The Epistle to the Hebrews*, Hodder & Stoughton, 1951
10. Montefiore, H., *A Commentary on the Epistle to the Hebrews*, A. & C. Black, 1964
11. Nineham, D., *Saint Mark*, Penguin, Harmondsworth, 1963; Seabury Press, New York, 1968
12. Pedersen, J., *Israel* I–IV, OUP, London, 1946
13. Perrin, N., *The Kingdom of God in the Teaching of Jesus*, SCM Press, 1963
14. Rad, G. von, *Old Testament Theology*, Oliver & Boyd, Edinburgh, I, 1962; II, 1965
15. Ringgren, H., *Israelite Religion*, SPCK, 1966
16. Rowley, H. H., *Worship in Ancient Israel*, SPCK, 1967
17. Spicq, C., *L'épître aux Hébreux*, II, Gabalda, Paris, 1953

II. DEATH

1. Ariès, P., 'La mort inversée', *Maison-Dieu*, 101, 1970
2. Clerk, N. W., *A Grief Observed*, Faber & Faber, 1961
3. Cope, G., ed., *Death, Dying and Disposal*, SPCK, 1970
4. Feifel, H., ed., *The Meaning of Death*, McGraw-Hill, New York, 1959
5. Gorer, G., *Death, Grief and Mourning in Contemporary Britain*, Cresset Press, 1965
6. Hinton, J., *Dying*, Penguin, Harmondsworth, 1967

7. Lepp, I., *Death and Its Mysteries*, Burns & Oates, 1969
8. Rahner, K., *On the Theology of Death*, Nelson, Edinburgh & London, 1961
9. Scott, N. A., ed., *The Modern Vision of Death*, John Knox, Richmond, 1967
10. Toynbee, A., *et al.*, *Man's Concern with Death*, Hodder & Stoughton, 1968
11. Wilson, M., *The Hospital – A Place of Truth*, University of Birmingham Institute for the Study of Worship and Religious Architecture, 1971

III. ECONOMICS, POLITICS AND WORK

1. Alexander, J., 'Down There', *New Society*, No. 434, 1971
2. Allen F. R., *et al.*, *Technology and Social Change*, Appleton-Century-Crofts, New York, 1957
3. Bennett, J. C., ed., *Christian Social Ethics in a Changing World*, SCM, 1966
4. Blum, F. H., *Work and Community*, Routledge & Kegan Paul, 1968
5. Child, J., *The Business Enterprise in Modern Industrial Society*, Collier-Macmillan, 1969
6. Cox, H., *God's Revolution and Man's Responsibility*, SCM Press, 1969
7. Donald, N. N. & Havighurst, R. J., 'The Meanings of Leisure', *Social Forces*, 37, 1959
8. Dubin, R., *The World of Work*, Prentice-Hall, Englewood Cliffs, 1958
9. Sargant Florence, P., *Labour*, Hutchinson, 1949
10. Glasser, R., *Leisure, Penalty or Prize?*, Macmillan, 1970
11. Illich, I., *The Church, Change and Development*, Urban Training Center Press, Chicago, 1970
12. Jacques, E., 'The Mental Processes in Work', *Glacier Project Papers*, Heinemann, 1965
13. Klein, L., *The Meaning of Work*, Fabian Tract 349, 1963
14. Lupton, T., *On the Shop Floor*, Pergamon, Oxford and London, 1963
15. Matthews, Z. K., ed., *Responsible Government in a Revolutionary Age*, SCM Press, 1966
16. Metz, J. B., 'The Church's "Social Function in the Light of Political Theology"', *Concilium*, 6.4, 1968
17. Miller, D. C. & Form, W. H., *Industrial Sociology*, Harper & Row, New York, 1969
18. Moltmann, J., 'Political Theology', *Theology Today*, XXVIII.1, 1971
19. Munby, D., ed., *Economic Growth in World Perspective*, SCM Press, 1966
20. Parker, S. R., *The Sociology of Industry*, Allen & Unwin, 3rd imp. 1969

21. Richardson, A., *The Biblical Doctrine of Work*, SCM Press, 1958
22. Schuller, S. C., *The New Urban Society*, Concordia, St Louis, 1966
23. Sherif, M., *Science, Conflict and Society*, Freeman, San Francisco, 1969
24. Shimmin, S., 'Concepts of Work', *Occupational Psychology*, 40, 1966
25. Smigel, E. O., ed., *Work and Leisure*, College & University Press, New Haven, 1963
26. *Social Attitudes to Work*, Birmingham University Department of Extra-Mural Studies, 2nd ed. 1966
27. Symanowski, H., *The Christian Witness in an Industrial Society*, Collins, 1964
28. Tawney, R. H., *Religion and the Rise of Capitalism*, Penguin, Harmondsworth, 1940
29. Tax, M., 'The Woman and her Mind: The Story of Everyday Life', *Women's Liberation: Notes from the Second Year*, 1970
30. Thomas, M. M., *The Christian Response to the Asian Revolution*, SCM Press, 1966
31. Walker, C. R., and Guest, R. H., *The Man on the Assembly Line*, Harvard University Press, Cambridge, Mass., 1952.
32. Ward, Barbara, *The Angry Seventies*, Pontifical Commission Justice and Peace, Rome, 1970
33. Weber, Hans-Ruedi, 'Participation in Industry', *Study Encounter*, V.4, 1969
34. Weber, M., *The Protestant and the Spirit of Capitalism*, Allen & Unwin, 1930
35. *Work in Britain Today*, Church Information Office, 1969

IV. HISTORY

1. Bainton, R. H., *Early and Medieval Christianity*, Hodder & Stoughton, 1964
2. Coulton, G. G., *Life in the Middle Ages. I. Religion, Folk-lore and Superstition*, CUP, 1930
3. Davies, G., *The Early Stuarts 1603–1660*, Clarendon Press, Oxford, 1937
4. Dawson, C., *Medieval Religion*, Sheed & Ward, 1935
5. Heer, F., *The Medieval World*, Weidenfeld and Nicolson, 1963
6. More, P. E., & Cross, F. L., edd., *Anglicanism*, SPCK, 1935
7. Poole, R. L., *Illustrations of the History of Medieval Thought*, Williams & Norgate, 1884

V. THE HOLY AND SECULARIZATION

1. Acquaviva, S. S., *L'éclipse du sacré dans la civilisation industrielle*, Mame, Tours, 1967

370   *Bibliography*

2. Altizer, T. J. J., *Mircea Eliade and the Dialectic of the Sacred*, West-minster Press, Philadelphia, 1963
3. Audet, J.-P., 'Le sacré et le profane: leur situation en Christianisme', *Nouvelle Revue Théologique*, LXXIX, 1957
4. Caillois, R., *L'homme et la sacré*, Gallimard, Paris, 3rd ed., 1963
5. Chavchavadze, M., ed., *Man's Concern with Holiness*, Hodder & Stoughton, 1970
6. Cox, H., *The Secular City*, SCM Press, 1965
7. Davidson, R. F., *Rudolf Otto's Interpretation of Religion*, Princeton University Press, 1947
8. Davies, J. G., *The Secular Use of Church Buildings*, SCM Press and Seabury Press, New York, 1968
9. – ed., *Hodge-Hill, St Philip and St James, The Multi-purpose Church*, University of Birmingham Institute for the Study of Worship and Religious Architecture, 1971
10. Eliade, M., *The Sacred and the Profane*, Harper and Row, New York, 1959
11. Grand'maison, J., *Le monde et le sacré*, Editions ouvrières, Paris, I, 1966; II, 1968
12. Håring, B., *Le sacré et le bien*, Editions Fleurus, Paris, 1963
13. Hunt, R. L., ed., *Revolution, Place and Symbol*, International Congress on Religion, Architecture and the Visual Arts, New York, 1969
14. Jenkins, D., *Beyond Religion*, SCM Press, 1962
15. Jones, O. R., *The Concept of Holiness*, Allen & Unwin, 1961
16. Margerie, B. de, 'Le Christ, la sécularisation et la consécration du monde', *Nouvelle Revue Théologique*, XCI, 1969
17. Marinoff, I., 'The Erosion of the Mystery', *New Theology* No. 7, ed. M. E. Marty & D. C. Pearson, Macmillan, New York, 1970
18. Martimort, A.-G., 'Le sens du sacré', *Maison-Dieu*, 25, 1951
19. Martin, D., *The Religious and the Secular*, Routledge & Kegan Paul, 1969
20. Martin, E., & Antoine, P., *La querelle du sacré*, Beauchesne, Paris, 1970
21. Otto, R., *The Idea of the Holy*, OUP, 1939
22. Pelikan, J., *Human Culture and the Holy*, SCM Press, 1959
23. Pratt, V., *Religion and Secularisation*, Macmillan, 1970
24. Rabut, O. A., *Valeur spirituelle du profane*, Editions du Cerf, Paris, 1963
25. Ringgren, H., 'The Prophetical Concept of Holiness', *Uppsala Universitats Arkskrift*, 12, 1948
26. Roguet, A.-M., 'Réflexions sur le sacré à propos de la construction des églises', *Maison-Dieu*, 96, 1968
27. Roqueplo, R., *Expérience du monde. Expérience de dieu?*, Editions du Cerf, Paris, 1968
28. Taylor, M. J., ed., *The Sacred and the Secular*, Prentice-Hall, Englewood Cliffs, 1968
29. Vincent, J. J., *Secular Christ*, Lutterworth Press, 1968

VI. LITERATURE (*Biography, Novels, Plays*)

1. Adamov, A., *L'aveu*, Editions du Saguittaire, Paris, 1946
2. Anderson, D., *The Tragic Protest*, SCM Press, 1969
3. Aulén, G., *Dag Hammarskjöld's White Book*, SPCK, 1970
4. Bayley, J., *Tolstoi and the Novel*, Chatto & Windus, 1966
5. Bellow, S., *Henderson the Rain King*, Weidenfeld & Nicolson, 1959
6. – *Herzog*, Weidenfeld & Nicolson, 1964
7. Bosanquet, M., *The Life and Death of Dietrich Bonhoeffer*, Hodder & Stoughton, 1968
8. Brock, H., *The Sleepwalkers*, Secker, 1932
9. Brod, M., ed., *The Diaries of Franz Kafka, 1914–1923*, Secker, 1947
10. Brook, P., *The Empty Space*, MacGibbon & Kee, 1968
11. Ceccherini, S., *The Transfer*, Eyre & Spottiswoode, 1966
12. Cleaver, E., *Soul on Ice*, Dell, New York, 1968
13. Demetillo, R., *Masks and Signatures*, University of the Philippines, Quezon City, 1968
14. Dumitriu, P., *Incognito*, Collins, 1964
15. Eliot, T. S., *Collected Poems 1909–1935*, Faber & Faber, 1936
16. Esslin, M., *The Theatre of the Absurd*, Eyre & Spottiswoode, 1964
17. Grahame, K., *The Wind in the Willows*, Methuen, 78th imp., 1944
18. Gunn, G. B., ed., *Literature and Religion*, SCM Press, 1971
19. Guzman, G., *Camilo Torres*, Sheed & Ward, New York, 1969
20. Habe, H., *The Poisoned Stream*, Harrap, 1969
21. Hammarskjöld, Dag., *Markings*, trans. by L. Sjöberg & W. H. Auden, Faber & Faber, 1964
22. Jung, C. G., *Memories, Dreams, Reflections*, Collins (Fontana), 1967
23. Kazantzakis, N., *Christ Recrucified*, Cassirer, Oxford, 1960
24. – *The Last Temptation*, Cassirer, Oxford, 1961
25. – *Zorba the Greek*, Cassirer, Oxford, 1959
26. – *The Fratricides*, Cassirer, Oxford, 1967
27. Kessel, J., *Belle de Jour*, Pan Books, 1965
28. Koestler, A., *The Sleepwalkers*, Hutchinson, 1959
29. Lawrence, D. H., *Lady Chatterley's Lover*, Penguin, Harmondsworth, 1960
30. – *The Rainbow*, Heinemann, 1963
31. – *Women in Love*, Penguin, Harmondsworth, 1968
32. McNeish, J., *Fire under the Ashes*, Hodder & Stoughton, 1965
33. Mailer, N., *The Armies of the Night*, Weidenfeld and Nicolson, 1968
34. – *The Prisoner of Sex*, New American Library, New York, 1971
35. Rikhoff, J., *Rites of Passage*, Gollancz, 1967
36. Rolph, C. H., ed., *The Trial of Lady Chatterley*, Penguin, Harmondsworth, 1961
37. Sharp, A., *The Wind Shifts*, Michael Joseph, 1967
38. Sillitoe, A., *Saturday Night and Sunday Morning*, Pan Books, 1960
39. Silone, I., *Bread and Wine*, Methuen, 1936
40. – *Emergency Exit*, Gollancz, 1969
41. Solzhenitsyn, A., *The First Circle*, Collins & Harvill Press, 1968

42. Updike, J., *The Centaur*, André Deutsch, 1963
43. Dusen, H. van, *Dag Hammarskjöld. A Biographical Interpretation of Markings*, Faber & Faber, 1967
44. West, M., *Children of the Sun*, Heinemann, 1957
45. Wilson, C., *The Outsider*, Gollancz, 1956
46. – *Religion and the Rebel*, Gollancz, 1957
47. – *The Strength to Dream*, Gollancz, 1962
48. – *Man without a Shadow*, Barker, 1965
49. – *The Occult*, Hodder & Stoughton, 1971
50. Yeats, W. B., *The Variorum Edition of the Poems of W. B. Yeats*, edd. P.Allt & R. K. Alspach, Macmillan, 1957
51. Zimmermann, W. D., & Smiith, R. G., edd., *I Knew Dietrich Bonhoeffer*, Collins, 1966

VII. PERCEPTION

1. Beloff, J. R., 'Perception and Extrapolation', *Bulletin of the British Psychological Society*, 32, 1957
2. Dretske, F. I., *Seeing and Knowing*, Routledge & Kegan Paul, 1969
3. Dubos, R. J., *Louis Pasteur*, Little, Brown & Co., Boston, 1950
4. Gombrich, E. H., *Art and Illusion*, Phaidon, new ed., 1962
5. Koestler, A., *The Act of Creation*, Hutchinson, 1964
6. Langer, S. K., *Mind: An Essay on Human Feelings*. I, John Hopkins, Baltimore, 1967
7. Malraux, A., *The Metamorphosis of the Gods*, Secker & Warburg, 1960
8. Mucchielli, R., *Introduction à la psychologie structurale*, Dessart, Brussels, 1966
9. Piaget, J., *The Mechanisms of Perception*, Routledge & Kegan Paul, 1969
10. Popper, K. R., *The Logic of Scientific Discovery*, Hutchinson, 1960
11. Tosh, H. and Smith, H. C., edd., *Social Perception*, Van Nostrand, Princeton, 1968

VIII. PHENOMENOLOGY

1. Eliade, M., *Traité de l'histoire de religion*, Payot, Paris, 1929
2. – *Le chamanisme et les techniques archaïques de l'extase*, Payot, Paris, 1957
3. – *Myth and Reality*, Allen & Unwin, 1964
4. – *The Quest, History and Meaning in Religion*, University of Chicago, 1969
5. James, E. O., *The Ancient Gods*, Weidenfeld & Nicolson, 1960
6. Pieper, J., *In Tune with the World. A Theory of Festivity*, Harcourt, Brace & World, New York, 1965
7. van den Leeuw, G., *Religion in Essence and Manifestation*, Allen & Unwin, 1958

IX. PHILOSOPHY (*of Religion*)

1. Baillie, J., *The Interpretation of Religion*, T. & T. Clark, Edinburgh 1929
2. – *Our Knowledge of God*, OUP, 1941
3. – *The Sense of the Presence of God*, OUP, 1962
4. Bloch, E., *Man on His Own*, Herder & Herder, New York, 1970
5. Buber, M., *Between Man and Man*, Kegan Paul, 1947
6. – *Hasidism*, Philosophical Library, New York, 1948
7. – *The Eclipse of God*, Gollancz, 1953
8. – *The Legend of the Baal-Shem*, Harper, New York, 1955
9. – *Tales of the Hasidim, The Early Masters*, Thames & Hudson, 1956
10. – *I and Thou*, 2nd ed., T. & T. Clark, Edinburgh, 1959
11. – *Israel and the World*, Schocken Books, New York, 1963
12. – *The Knowledge of Man*, Allen & Unwin, 1965
13. – *Paths in Utopia*, Beacon Press, Boston, 1966
14. – *Hasidism and Modern Man*, Harper Torchbook, New York, 1966
15. – *Tales of the Hasidim, Later Masters*, Shocken Books, New York, 1966
16. – *For the Sake of Heaven*, Harper Torchbook, New York, 1966
17. Feuerbach, L., *The Essence of Christianity*, Harper Torchbook, New York, 1957
18. Friedman, M., *Martin Buber. The Life of Dialogue*, Routledge & Kegan Paul, 1955
19. – *To Deny our Nothingness*, Gollancz, 1967
20. Hepburn, R. W., *Christianity and Paradox*, Watts, 1958
21. Hick, J. H., *Faith and Knowledge*, Macmillan, 2nd ed., 1967
22. – *Christianity at the Centre*, SCM Press, 1968
23. Mottu, H., 'Feuerbach and Bonhoeffer: Criticism of Religion and the Last Period of Bonhoeffer's Thought', *Union Seminary Quarterly Review*, XXVI, I, 1969
24. Munz, P., *Problems of Religious Knowledge*, SCM Press, 1957
25. Ramsey, I. T., *Religious Language*, SCM Press, 1957
26. – *Models and Mystery*, OUP, 1964
27. Rome, S. & B., edd., *Philosophical Interrogations*, Holt, Rinehart & Winston, New York, 1964
28. Russell, B., *An Outline of Philosophy*, Allen & Unwin, 1927
29. Schlipp, A., & Friedman, M., edd., *The Philosophy of Martin Buber*, Open Court Publishing Co., La Salle and CUP, 1967
30. Smart, Ninian, *Philosophers and Religious Truth*, SCM Press, 1964
31. Smith, J. E., *Experience and God*, OUP, New York, 1968
32. Smith, W. Cantwell, *Questions of Religious Truth*, Gollancz, 1967

X. SOCIAL ANTHROPOLOGY

1. Banton, M., ed., *Anthropological Approaches to the Study of Religion*, Tavistock Publications, 1966

2. Bohannan, P., *Social Anthropology*, Holt, Rinehart & Winston, New York, 1969
3. Chapple E. D., & Coon C. S., *Principles of Anthropology*, Cape, 1943
4. Douglas, M., *Purity and Danger*, Routledge & Kegan Paul, 1966
5. – *Natural Symbols. Explorations in Cosmology*, Barrie & Rockliffe, 1970
6. 'Essays on the Problem of Tribe', *American Ethnological Society*, University of Washington, Seattle and London, 1968
7. Geertz, C., 'Ritual and Social Change, A Javanese Example', *American Anthropologist*, 59, 1957
8. Gluckman, M., ed., *Essays on the Ritual of Social Relations*, Manchester University Press, 1962
9. Goffman, E., *Interaction Rituals*, Doubleday, New York, 1967
10. Goody, J., 'Religion and Ritual: The Definitional Problem', *British Journal of Sociology*, 12, 1961
11. Peacock, J. L., *Rites of Modernization*, University of Chicago, 1968
12. Radcliffe-Brown, A. R., *Structure and Function in Primitive Society*, Cohen & West, 4th imp., 1961
13. Southall, A. P., 'The Illusion of Tribe', *Journal of American and African Studies*, V, 1-2, 1970
14. Turner, V. W., *The Ritual Process*, Routledge & Kegan Paul, 1969
15. van Gennep, A., *The Rites of Passage*, Routledge & Kegan Paul, 1960
16. Wilson, M., 'Nyakyusa Ritual and Symbols', *American Anthropologist*, 56, 1954
17. – *Rituals of Kinship among the Nyakyusa*, OUP, 1957

XI. SOCIOLOGY (*of Religion*)

1. Argyle, M., *Religious Behaviour*, Routledge & Kegan Paul, 1958
2. Berger, P. L., *The Sacred Canopy*, Doubleday Anchor Book, New York, 1969
3. – *A Rumour of Angels*, Doubleday Anchor Book, New York, 1969
4. Berger, P. L., & Luckmann, T., *The Social Construction of Reality*, Allen Lane, Penguin, 1967
5. Bloy, M. B., *The Crisis of Cultural Change*, Seabury Press, New York, 1965
6. Busia, K. A., *Urban Churches in Britain*, Lutterworth, 1966
7. Durkheim, E., *The Elementary Forms of the Religious Life*, Allen & Unwin, 1915 (reprinted 1954)
8. Gardner, J., *Self-Renewal*, Harper, Evanston, 1963
9. Gustafson, J. M., *Treasure in Earthen Vessels*, Harper & Row, New York, 1961
10. Houtart, F., *Sociologie et pastorale*, Fleurus, Paris, 1963
11. Houtart, F., & Rémy, J., *Eglise et société en mutation*, Mame, Paris, 1969
12. – *Milieu urbain et communauté chrétienne*, Mame, Paris, 1969

13. Jennings, H. H., *Leadership and Isolation*, Longman, Green, New York, 2nd ed., 1950
14. Lane, T., & Roberts, K., *Strike at Pilkingtons*, Collins (Fontana), 1971
15. Lee, R., & Martin, M. E., edd., *Religion and Social Conflict* OUP, New York, 1964
16. Malinowski, B., *Magic, Science and Religion and Other Essays*, Free Press, Glencoe, Illinois, 1948
17. McGuyan, G. F., ed., *Student Protest*, Methuen, 1968
18. Mead, G. H., *Mind, Self and Society*, Chicago University Press, 1934
19. Mehl, R., *Traité de sociologie du protestantisme*, Delachaux & Niestlé, Neuchâtel, 1965
20. Nagel, J., ed., *Student Power*, Merlin Press, 1969
21. Rémy, J., 'Communauté et assemblée liturgique dans une vie sociale en voie d'urbanisation', *Maison-Dieu*, 91, 1967
22. Scheller, L. E., *Community Organization. Conflict and Reconciliation*, Abingdon Press, Nashville, 1966
23. Sprott, W. J. H., *Human Groups*, Penguin, Harmondsworth, 1964
24. Toffler, A., *Future Shock*, Random House, New York, 1970
25. Watzke, J., 'Paganization and Dechristianization, or the Crisis in Institutional Symbols. A Problem in Sociological Interpretation', *Social Compass*, XVI/I, 1969
26. Winter, G., *The Suburban Captivity of the Churches*, Doubleday, New York, 1961

XII. THEOLOGY

1. Adolphs, R., *The Grave of God*, Burns & Oates, 1967
2. Altizer, T. J. J., & Hamilton, W., *Radical Theology and the Death of God*, Penguin, Harmondsworth, 1968
3. Berdyaev, N., *The Destiny of Man*, Bles, 1937
4. Bethge, E., *Dietrich Bonhoeffer*, Collins, 1970
5. Bonhoeffer, D., *The Cost of Discipleship*, SCM Press, 1937
6. - *Letters and Papers from Prison*, new enlarged ed., SCM Press, 1971
7. - *Ethics*, 2nd imp., SCM Press, 1971
8. - *No Rusty Swords*, Collins (Fontana), 1970
9. Boros, L., *Meeting God in Man*, Burns & Oates, 1968
10. Butler-Bowdon, W., ed., *The Book of Margery Kempe*, Cape, 1936
11. Chardin, T. de, *Le Milieu Divin*, Collins (Fontana), 1967
12. - *The Future of Man*, Collins (Fontana), 1969
13. Collins, L. J., *Faith under Fire*, Frewin, 1966
14. Cox, H., *On Not Leaving It to the Snake*, SCM Press, 1968
15. Davies, J. G., *The Spirit, the Church and the Sacraments*, Faith Press, 1954
16. - *Dialogue with the World*, SCM Press, 1967
17. Dewart, L., *The Future of Belief*, Burns & Oates, 1967
18. Doms, H., *The Meaning of Marriage*, Sheed & Ward, 1939
19. Ebeling, G., *The Nature of Faith*, Collins (Fontana), 1966

20. Foote, W., ed., *Servants of Peace*, Harper, New York, 1962
21. Garcia, J. A., & Calle, C. R., edd., *Camilo Torres. Priest and Revolutionary*, Sheed & Ward, 1968
22. Gerassi, J., ed., *Revolutionary Priest. The Complete Writings and Messages of Camilo Torres*, Cape, 1971
23. Hamilton, K., *Revolt against Heaven*, Eerdmans, Grand Rapids, 1965
24. – *God is Dead. The Anatomy of a Slogan*, Eerdmans, Grand Rapids, 1966
25. Hamilton, W., *The New Essence of Christianity*, Darton, Longman & Todd, 1966
26. Haughton, R., *The Transformation of Man*, Chapman, 1967
27. Heuvel, A. van den, *Those Rebellious Powers*, SCM Press, 1966
28. – *The Humiliation of the Church*, SCM Press, 1967
29. Howe, R. L., *The Miracle of Dialogue*, Seabury Press, New York, 1963
30. – *Man's Need and God's Action*, Seabury Press, New York, 1966
31. Kee, A., *The Way of Transcendence*, Penguin, Harmondsworth, 1971
32. Keen, S., *Apology for Wonder*, Harper & Row, New York, 1969
33. – *To a Dancing God*, Harper & Row, New York, 1970
34. Kelly, J. N. D., *Early Christian Doctrines*, A. & C. Black, 1958
35. Kierkegaard, S., *Attack upon "Christendom"*, OUP, 1944
36. Lambourne, R. A. L., *Community, Church and Healing*, Darton, Longman & Todd, 1963
37. Lampe, G. W. H., *A Patristic Greek Lexicon*, Clarendon Press, Oxford, 1961
38. Lehmann, P. L., *Ideology and Incarnation*, John Knox Assoc., Geneva, 1962
39. Macmurray, J., *Persons in Relation*, Faber & Faber, 1961
40. Macquarrie, J., *God-Talk*, SCM Press, 1967
41. – *God and Secularity*, Lutterworth, 1968
42. Metz, J. B., *Theology of the World*, Burns & Oates, 1969
43. Moltmann, J., *Theology of Hope*, SCM Press, 1967
44. – *Religion, Revolution and the Future*, Scribner's, New York, 1969
45. – *Hope and Planning*, SCM Press, 1971
46. Nicholls, W., *Systematic and Philosophical Theology* (*The Pelican Guide to Modern Theology*, I), Penguin, Harmondsworth, 1969
47. Niebuhr, H. R., *Christ and Culture*, Faber & Faber, 1952
48. – *Radical Monotheism and Western Culture*, Faber & Faber, 1961
49. Ogden, S., *The Reality of God*, SCM Press, 1967
50. Ogletree, T. W., *The 'Death of God' Controversy*, SCM Press, 1966
51. Oman, J., *The Natural and the Supernatural*, CUP, 1931
52. Pannenberg, W., *What is Man?*, Fortress Press, Philadelphia, 1970
53. – *Basic Questions in Theology*, II, SCM Press, 1971
54. Paton, A., *Instrument of Thy Peace*, Collins (Fontana), 1970
55. Paul, L., *Coming to Terms with Sex*, Collins, 1969
56. Rauschenbusch, W., *A Theology for the Social Gospel*, Macmillan, New York, 1917

57. Reid, G., *The Gagging of God*, Hodder & Stoughton, 1969
58. Robinson, J. A. T., *On Being the Church in the World*, SCM Press, 1960
59. – *Honest to God*, SCM Press, 1963
60. Schillebeeckx, E., *Christ the Sacrament of Encounter with God*, Sheed & Ward, 1963
61. – *God and Man*, Sheed & Ward, 1969
62. – *God the Future of Man*, Sheed & Ward, 1969
63. Slater, G., *Christian Experience Today*, Methodist Church Home Mission Department, 1970
64. Smith, R. Gregor, *The Free Man*, Collins, 1969
65. – ed., *World Come of Age*, Collins, 1967
66. Suenens, L. J., *Corresponsibility in the Church*, Burns & Oates, 1968
67. Tillich, P., *The Protestant Era*, University of Chicago, 3rd imp., 1953
68. – *Systematic Theology*, I, Nisbet, 1953
69. – *Biblical Religion and the Search for Ultimate Reality*, Nisbet, 1955
70. – *Theology of Culture*, OUP, 1964
71. *The Uppsala Report*, WCC, Geneva, 1968
72. Vahanian, G., *The Death of God*, Braziller, New York, 1967
73. Williams, C. W., *The Church*, Lutterworth, 1969
74. Zahrnt, H., *The Question of God*, Collins, 1969

XIII. WORSHIP

1. Allmen, J.-J. von, *Worship. Its Theology and Practice*, Lutterworth, 1965
2. Bloy, M. B. Jr., ed., *Multi-Media Worship*, Seabury Press, New York, 1969
3. Bouyer, L., *Rite and Man*, Burns & Oates, 1963
4. Brightman, F. E., *Liturgies Eastern and Western*, Clarendon Press, Oxford, 1896
5. Cazeneuve, J., *Les Rites et la condition humaine*, Presses universitaires, Paris, 1958
6. Connolly, R. H., *The Liturgical Homilies of Narsai, with an Appendix by Edmund Bishop (Texts and Studies* VIII.1), CUP, 1909
7. Cox, H., *The Feast of Fools. A Theological Essay on Festivity and Fantasy*, Harvard University Press, Cambridge, Mass., 1969
8. Davies, J. G., *Worship and Mission*, SCM Press and Association Press, New York, 1968
9. – 'The Reality of Worship', *The Annual*, No. 38, 1968
10. Davis, C., 'Ghetto or Desert; Liturgy in a Cultural Dilemma', in *Worship and Secularization*, ed. W. Vos (*Studia Liturgica* 7.2/3), 1970
11. Debuyst, F., *Modern Architecture and Christian Celebration*, Lutterworth, 1968

12. – 'Feast Days and Festive Celebrations: Foretastes of Full Communion', *Concilium*, 9.4., 1968
13. Grainger, R., *The Defence of Ritual*, M.A. thesis, University of Birmingham, 1970
14. Greeley, A., 'Religious Symbols. Liturgy and Community', *Concilium*, 2.7, 1971
15. Hovda, R. W., and Huck, G., *There's No Place Like People. Liturgical Celebrations in Home and Small-Group Situations*, Liturgical Conference, Washington, 1969
16. Killinger, J., *Leave it to the Spirit. Commitment and Freedom in the New Liturgy*, SCM Press, 1971
17. 'Living: Liturgical Style', *Risk*, V. 1. 1969
18. Maguire, U., 'The Last Supper: A Study in Group Dynamics', *New Blackfriars*, 49, 1968
19. Pratt, O. and I., *Liturgy is What We Make It*, Sheed & Ward, 1967
20. – edd., *Experience of Liturgy*, Sheed & Ward, 1968
21. *Report of the Theological Commission on Worship*, WCC, Geneva, 1963
22. Schmidt, H., 'Liturgy and Modern Society – Analysis of the Current Situation', *Concilium*, 2.7, 1971
23. Shepherd, M. H., ed., *Worship in Scripture and Tradition*, OUP, New York, 1963
24. Stone, Darwell, *A History of the Doctrine of the Holy Eucharist*, I, Longmans Green, 1909
25. Underhill, E., *Eucharistic Prayers from the Ancient Liturgies*, Longmans Green, 1939
26. West, R. C., *Western Liturgies*, SPCK, 1938
27. White, J. F., *The Worldliness of Worship*, OUP, New York, 1967
28. Wordsworth, J., *Bishop Sarapion's Prayer Book*, SPCK, 1910
29. 'Worship Today', *Study Encounter*, VI, 3, 1970
30. *Worship in the City of Man*, Liturgical Conference, Washington, 1966

Acknowledgments

The passages from T. S. Eliot, *Collected Poems 1909–1962*, C. S. Lewis ('N.W. Clerk'), *A Grief Observed*, and Dag Hammarskjöld, *Markings*, are reprinted by permission of Faber and Faber Ltd. Grateful acknowledgment is also made to the following for permission to quote from the works mentioned: W. H. Allen and Co. Ltd: *Saturday Night and Sunday Morning* by Alan Sillitoe; Bruno Cassirer Ltd: *The Fratricides, Christ Recrucified* and *Zorba the Greek* by Nikos Kazantzakis; Rosica Colin Ltd: *The Transfer* by S. Ceccherini, published by Eyre and Spottiswoode; William Collins and Sons: *Incognito* by P. Dumitriu; Ricaredo Demetillo and the University of the Philippines Press: *Masks and Signatures*; André Deutsch Ltd: *The Centaur* by John Updike; Fontana Books: *Strike at Pilkingtons* by T. Lane and K. Roberts; Victor Gollancz Ltd: *Rites of Passage* by J. Rikhoff; George G. Harrap and Co. Ltd: *The Poisoned Stream* by Hans Habe; A. M. Heath and Co. Ltd: *Hertzog* by Saul Bellow, published by Weidenfeld and Nicolson; William Heinemann Ltd: *Children of the Sun* by Morris West; Methuen and Co. Ltd: *Bread and Wine* by Ignazio Silone; Methuen and Co. Ltd and the Bodleian Library, Oxford: *The Wind in the Willows* by Kenneth Grahame; Laurence Pollinger Ltd and the Estate of the late Mrs Frieda Lawrence: *The Rainbow* by D. H. Lawrence; Sheed and Ward Ltd: *Camillo Torres. Priest and Revolutionary*, by J. A. Garcia and C. R. Calle; George Weidenfeld and Nicolson: *The Medieval World* by Friedrich Heer, and *Man without a Shadow* by Colin Wilson, published by Arthur Barker; M. B. Yeats and the Macmillan Co. of London and Canada: *The Collected Poems of W. B. Yeats*.

Index